Periodization Training for Sports

Third Edition

Library of Congress Cataloging-in-Publication Data

Bompa, Tudor O.
Periodization training for sports / Tudor Bompa, Carlo Buzzichelli. -- Third Edition.
pages cm
Previous edition was authored by Tudor O. Bompa and Michael Carrera.
Includes bibliographical references and index.
1. Periodization training. 2. Weight training. I. Buzzichelli, Carlo, 1973- II. Title.
GV546.B546 2014
613.7'13--dc23

2014014399

ISBN: 978-1-4504-6943-2 (print)

Acquisitions Editor: Justin Klug; **Developmental Editor:** Laura Pulliam; **Managing Editor:** Elizabeth Evans; **Copyeditor:** Tom Tiller; **Indexer:** Dan Connolly; **Permissions Manager:** Martha Gullo; **Graphic Designer:** Julie L. Denzer; **Cover Designer:** Keith Blomberg; **Photograph (cover):** © Yuri Arcurs/age fotostock; **Photographs (interior):** © Human Kinetics, unless otherwise noted; **Photo Asset Manager:** Laura Fitch; **Photo Production Manager:** Jason Allen; **Art Manager:** Kelly Hendren; **Associate Art Manager:** Alan L. Wilborn; **Illustrations:** © Human Kinetics, unless otherwise noted; **Printer:** McNaughton & Gunn

Human Kinetics books are available at special discounts for bulk purchase. Special editions or book excerpts can also be created to specification. For details, contact the Special Sales Manager at Human Kinetics.

Printed in the United States of America   10 9 8 7 6 5 4

The paper in this book is certified under a sustainable forestry program.

Human Kinetics
Website: www.HumanKinetics.com

United States: Human Kinetics
P.O. Box 5076
Champaign, IL 61825-5076
800-747-4457
e-mail: info@hkusa.com

Canada: Human Kinetics
475 Devonshire Road Unit 100
Windsor, ON N8Y 2L5
800-465-7301 (in Canada only)
e-mail: info@hkcanada.com

Europe: Human Kinetics
107 Bradford Road
Stanningley
Leeds LS28 6AT, United Kingdom
+44 (0) 113 255 5665
e-mail: hk@hkeurope.com

Australia: Human Kinetics
57A Price Avenue
Lower Mitcham, South Australia 5062
08 8372 0999
e-mail: info@hkaustralia.com

New Zealand: Human Kinetics
P.O. Box 80
Mitcham Shopping Centre, South Australia 5062
0800 222 062
e-mail: info@hknewzealand.com

E6171

Periodization Training for Sports

Third Edition

Tudor Bompa, PhD
Carlo A. Buzzichelli

**HUMAN
KINETICS**

Contents

Part III Periodization of Strength

Preface

The market is saturated with strength training books, most of which are very traditional and have no distinction from other strength training books. Nearly all discuss some basic physiology, describe various exercises, and suggest a few training methods. Planning is rarely discussed, and periodization (the structuring of training into phases) is seldom mentioned simply because few authors understand its importance.

Strength training is paramount in the development of athletes, but it must consist of more than just lifting weights without a specific purpose or plan. In fact, the purpose of any strength training method should be to prepare athletes for competition—the ideal test of their skills, knowledge, and psychological readiness. To achieve the best results, athletes need to be exposed to a periodization program, or sport- and phase-specific variations in training.

This third edition of *Periodization Training for Sports* shows how to use periodization in structuring a strength training program for athletes in various sports and specifies which training methods are best for each training phase. It also includes an expanded chapter on energy system training and suggests how to optimally integrate strength training and metabolic training for various sports. The phases are planned according to the competition schedule, and each has a specific goal for developing power or muscular endurance. The entire training program is aimed at achieving peak performance for the most important competitions of the year.

This planning strategy, which we call periodization of strength, designates the type of strength to be developed in each training phase to ensure reaching the highest levels of power or muscular endurance. Developing the sport-specific abilities before the competitive phase is essential because they form the physiological foundation on which athletic performance relies. The key element in organizing periodized strength training to develop power or muscular endurance is the sequence in which various types of strength training are planned.

An objective of this book is to demonstrate that strength training is more than just lifting weights for its own sake. You must also be mindful of the goals of specific training phases and consider how to integrate strength training with sport-specific training to develop motor potential and improve performance. This edition of *Periodization Training for Sports* offers a method of reaching training objectives for competition through the use of periodization. This book offers an in-depth look at structuring strength training programs according to the physiological characteristics of the sport and the characteristics of the athlete. The book also challenges many methods of training currently being used in sport training.

Whatever your role in sport—strength coach, sport coach, instructor, personal trainer, athlete, or college student—you will benefit from this book by increasing your knowledge of periodization training and its physiological foundation. Once you apply this concept, you will know that it is the best way to organize a strength training program for improving physiological adaptation, which ultimately produces better performance. Peak performance occurs because you plan for it!

The second edition of Periodization Training for Sports came out in 2005. This third edition represents the evolution derived from research and field work of the training methodology since 2005. You will recognize the superiority of this method over those you have used in the past. You will learn the following:

- The simple physiological concepts that enable the development of sport-specific strength
- The abilities required for achieving performance goals for each sport, such as maximum speed, power, and muscular endurance
- The role of strength training in overall development of the physiological abilities required for reaching the highest possible level in various sports
- The concept of periodization and its specific application to strength training for your sport
- The concept of energy system training and its integration with strength training for your sport
- Actual methods of dividing the annual plan into strength training phases, each with specific objectives
- How to develop several types of strength in a specific sequence to guarantee reaching the highest levels of power or muscular endurance in a particular period of the year
- How to manipulate the loading patterns in each phase to create the specific physiological adaptations for reaching peak performance

Part I (chapters 1 through 7) reviews the main theories influencing strength training and explains that power and muscular endurance are a combined physical quality. It also explains why certain athletic movements require a certain type of strength and why simply lifting weights will not benefit your performance.

A successful strength training program depends on your level of knowledge in physiology of strength. The information in chapter 2, "Neuromuscular Response to Strength Training," is presented simply so that people from all backgrounds can understand it. New to the third edition, a greatly expanded chapter 3, "Energy Systems Training," uses practical examples to illustrate the integration of strength training and metabolic training for various sports. The broader your knowledge in this area, the easier it will be to design programs that result in the transfer of strength training benefits to sport-specific skills. Chapters 4 and 5 underscore the importance of recovery in strength training and contain information on facilitating a faster recovery after workouts and maximization of training adaptations, especially through proper nutrition. Another addition to this book, chapter 7 explains all the methodological concepts pertaining to the periodization of training; this enables you to analyze and design annual plans for various sports. Part I ends with an explanation of training principles and how they apply to strength training.

Part II (chapters 8 through 10) begins with a discussion of the elements in designing a strength training program, namely the manipulation of training variables and how it affects training. Both short- and long-term planning, focusing mainly on weekly programs and the periodization of annual plans, are explained in detail to help you comprehend this concept in training. A brief history of the concept of periodization is also presented.

Part III, chapters 11 through 15, covers all the phases that make up the periodization of strength. For each phase, the best training methods available for taking athletes to the highest level are presented.

In *Periodization Training for Sports*, you will find a more effective, more efficient method of training.

Acknowledgments

We express our sincerest thanks to the entire Human Kinetics team for their hard work and dedication in assembling the third edition of this book. Special thanks to Laura Pulliam, developmental editor, for her patience, advice, and understanding as we worked through implementing her many suggestions that resulted in a more logical and precise book. Finally, this book is dedicated to all the coaches, exercise physiologists, trainers, and health and fitness professionals who strive to bridge the gap between the science and the practice of training.

Part

I

Foundations of Strength Training

1

Strength, Power, and Muscular Endurance in Sports

Almost all physical activities incorporate either force (or strength), speed, or flexibility—or some combination of these elements. Strength exercises involve overcoming resistance; speed exercises maximize quickness and high frequency; endurance exercises involve long distance, long duration, or many repetitions (reps); and flexibility exercises maximize range of motion. Coordination exercises involve complex movements.

Of course, the ability to perform certain exercises varies from athlete to athlete, and an athlete's ability to perform at a high level is influenced by inherited (or genetic) abilities in strength, speed, and endurance. These abilities may be called conditional motor capacities, general physical qualities, or biomotor abilities. *Motor* refers to movement, and the prefix *bio* indicates the biological nature (the body) of these abilities.

However, success in training and competition is not determined solely by an athlete's genetic potential. At times, athletes who strive for perfection in their training—through determination and methodical planning of periodization—reach the podium or help their team win a major tournament. Although talent is extremely important, an athlete's ability to focus on training and to relax in competition can make the difference in his or her ultimate achievement. To move beyond inherited strength or other genetic potential, an athlete must focus on physiological adaptation in training.

Six Strength Training Programs

Athletes and coaches in various sports use six main programs for strength training: bodybuilding, high-intensity training, Olympic weightlifting, power training throughout the year, powerlifting, and periodization of strength. Overall, however, periodization of strength is the most influential training methodology.

Bodybuilding

Bodybuilding is a creative sport in which the bodybuilder and trainer manipulate training variables (such as sets, reps, rest periods, and speed of execution) to produce the highest level of exhaustion, followed by a period of rest and regeneration. Muscle size and strength increase due to adaptations in the form of energy substrate overcompensation and muscle protein accretion.

Bodybuilders are concerned chiefly with increasing their muscle size. To that end, they perform sets of 6 to 12 reps to exhaustion. However, increased muscle size is rarely beneficial to athletic performance (the few exceptions may include younger or lower-level athletes, American football players, and some performers in track-and-field throwing events). More specifically, the slow, repetitive contractions in bodybuilding offer only limited positive transfer to the explosive athletic movements in many other sports. For instance, whereas athletic skills are performed quickly, taking from 100 to 180 milliseconds, leg extensions in bodybuilding take 600 milliseconds (see table 1.1).

There are exceptions. Selected bodybuilding techniques, such as supersets and drop sets, are used during the hypertrophy phase of training for certain sports where the main objective is to increase muscle size. However, because neuromuscular adaptations are not vital to bodybuilding, it does not usually include explosive concentrics or high loads with long rest periods. For this reason, bodybuilding is rarely used in strength training for sports.

Table 1.1 Duration of Contact Phase

Event	Duration (millisec.)
100 m dash (contact phase)	100–200
Long jump (takeoff)	150–180
High jump (takeoff)	150–180
Gymnastics vault (takeoff)	100–120
Leg extension (bodybuilding)	600

Reprinted, by permission, from D. Schmidtbleicher, 1984, Sportliches krafttraining und motorische grundlagenforschung. In *Haltung und bewegung beim menschen: Physiologie, pathophysiologie, gangentwicklung und sporttraining*, edited by W. Berger, V. Dietz, A, Hufschmidt, et al. (Heidelberg: Springer-Verlag Berlin Heidelberg), 155-188.

High-Intensity Training

High-intensity training (HIT) involves using high training loads throughout the year and performing all working sets to at least positive failure. Firm believers in HIT claim that strength development can be achieved in 20 to 30 minutes; they disregard the high-volume strength training for events of long, continuous duration (such as mid- and long-distance swimming, rowing, canoeing, and cross-country skiing).

HIT programs are not organized according to the competition schedule. For sports, strength is periodized according to the physiological needs of the sport in a given phase of training and the date for reaching peak performance. Athletes who use HIT training often gain strength very quickly but tend to lose strength and endurance as their competitive season progresses. Furthermore, the high level of muscle soreness and neural fatigue caused by the intensification methods used in HIT programs (such as forced reps or negative reps) interferes with the more specific physical work, as well as the athlete's technical or tactical work throughout his or her weekly training.

Olympic Weightlifting

Olympic weightlifting exerted important influence in the early days of strength training. Even now, many coaches and trainers use traditional Olympic weightlifting moves (such as the clean and jerk, the snatch, and the power clean) despite the fact that they may or may not work the prime movers—the primary muscles used in specific sport skills. Because exercises that train the prime movers should always be placed at the forefront of any strength training program, coaches should closely analyze the primary movements in their sport to decide whether Olympic weightlifting exercises would be beneficial. For example, American football linemen can benefit from the lifts, but rowers and swimmers, who often use Olympic lifts as part of their strength training regimens, probably do not.

In order to avoid injury, it is also essential to carefully assess the ins and outs of Olympic weightlifting techniques, especially for young athletes and those with no strength training background. Indeed, it is a time-consuming process to master Olympic weightlifting techniques, but one must achieve sufficient technical proficiency to use loads that generate a training effect. In summary, although Olympic weightlifting can be a good way to improve overall body strength and power, strength and conditioning coaches must evaluate both its specificity and its efficiency.

Power Training Throughout the Year

Power training throughout the year is characterized by the use of explosive bounding exercises, medicine ball throws, and weightlifting exercises regardless of the yearly training cycle. Some coaches and trainers, especially in track and field and certain team sports, believe that power training should be performed from the first day of training through the major championship. They theorize that if power is the dominant ability, it must be trained for throughout the year, except during the transition phase (the off-season).

Certainly, power capability does improve by doing power training throughout the year. The key element, however, is not just *whether* the athlete improves but the athlete's *rate* of improvement, both throughout the year and especially from year to year. Strength training has been shown to lead to far better results than power training, especially when the athlete uses periodization of strength. Because power is a function of maximum strength, improving one's power requires improving one's maximum strength. As a result, strength training results in faster power improvement and allows athletes to reach higher levels.

Powerlifting

Powerlifting is the latest trend in strength and conditioning. It is a fascinating sport, growing in popularity, in which participants train to maximize their strength in the squat, bench press, and deadlift. Many powerlifting training methods have emerged in the last two decades, some of which are very specific to geared powerlifting (in which lifters wear knee wraps, a bench shirt, and squat and deadlift suits to increase their lifts). Other methods have been adapted to train athletes in various sports.

The key point, however, is that powerlifters train to maximize one biomotor ability—strength. In contrast, an athlete usually needs to train all biomotor abilities, and more precisely their subqualities, in a sport-specific combination. As a result, a sport coach usually cannot devote the same amount of time to strength training that powerlifters do in terms of both weekly frequency and workout duration. Furthermore, though the squat, bench press, and deadlift are the bread and butter exercises for general strength, an athlete needs to perform exercises that have a higher biomechanical correspondence to the specific motor skill, especially during the specific preparation and competitive phases, as well as convert his or her maximum strength into specific strength—be it power, power endurance, or muscle endurance.

As you can see in table 1.2, powerlifters strength-train much more often during the week throughout the year than do athletes in other individual sports or team sports. This difference is another reason that one cannot simply apply a powerlifting program to other athletes.

Table 1.2   Difference Between Annual Plan for Powerlifting and for Other Sports

	Number of prep phases in annual plan	Duration of prep phases (weeks)	Number of weekly strength training sessions during prep phases	Number of competitive phases in annual plan	Duration of competi- tive phases (weeks)	Number of weekly strength training sessions during competi- tive phases
Powerlifting	1–5	12–24	3–6	1–5	1–5	3–5
Individual sport	1–4	12–20	3–4	1–4	4–20	1–4
Team sport	2	3–8 (or up to 12)	2–4	2	28–36	1–4

Periodization of Strength

Periodization of strength must be based on the specific physiological requirements of a given sport and, again, must result in the highest development of either power, power endurance, or muscular endurance. Furthermore, strength training must revolve around the needs of periodization for the chosen sport and employ training methods specific to a given training phase. The goal is to reach peak performance at the time of major competitions.

All periodization of strength programs begin with a general anatomical adaptation phase that prepares the body for the phases to follow. Depending on the requirements of the sport, it may also be useful to plan one or two hypertrophy or muscle-building phases. One of the goals of periodization of strength is to bring the athlete to the highest possible level of maximum strength within the annual plan so that gains in strength become gains in power, power endurance, or muscular endurance. The planning of phases is unique to each sport and also depends on the individual athlete's physical maturity, competition schedule, and peaking dates.

The concept of periodization of strength for sports has evolved from two basic needs: (1) to integrate strength training into the annual plan and its training phases and (2) to increase the sport-specific strength development from year to year. The first athletic experiment using periodization of strength was conducted with Mihaela Penes, a gold medalist in the javelin throw at the 1964 Tokyo Olympic Games. The results were presented in 1965 in Bucharest and Moscow (Bompa 1965a, 1965b).

The original periodization of strength model was then altered to suit the needs of endurance sports that require muscular endurance (Bompa 1977). This current book discusses periodization of strength models for both power and endurance sports, as well as training methods. The basic periodization of strength model also appears in *Periodization: Theory and Methodology of Training* (Bompa 1999). In 1984, Stone and O'Bryant presented a theoretical model of strength training in which periodization of strength included four phases: hypertrophy, basic strength, strength and power, and peaking and maintenance. A comprehensive book on periodization, *Periodization of Strength: The New Wave in Strength Training* (Bompa 1993a), was followed by *Periodization Breakthrough* (Fleck and Kraemer 1996), which again demonstrated that periodization of strength is the most scientifically justified method for optimizing strength and sport performance.

Sport-Specific Combinations of Strength, Speed, and Endurance

Strength, speed, and endurance are the important abilities for successful athletic performance. The *dominant* ability is the one from which the sport requires a higher contribution; for instance, endurance is the dominant ability in long-distance running. Most sports, however, require peak performance in at least two abilities. In addition, the relationships between strength, speed, and endurance create crucial physical athletic qualities. When athletes and coaches understand these relationships, they can plan effective sport-specific programs for strength training.

Here are a few examples. As illustrated in figure 1.1, the combination of strength and endurance creates muscular endurance—the ability to perform many repetitions against a given resistance for a prolonged period. A different combination, that of maximum strength and maximum speed, results in power—the ability to perform an explosive movement

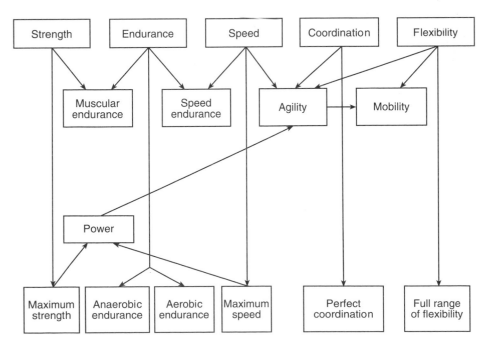

Figure 1.1 Interdependence among the biomotor abilities.

in the shortest possible time. Yet another combination, that of endurance and speed, is called speed endurance—the ability to move at speed for an extended time.

In a more complex example, the combination of speed, coordination, flexibility, and power produces agility, which is demonstrated, for instance, in gymnastics, wrestling, American football, soccer, volleyball, baseball, boxing, diving, and figure skating. It has to be noted that agility is particularly improved through increases in maximum strength (Schmidtbleicher et al. 2014). In turn, flexibility—the range of motion of a joint—is important to training in its own right. Various sports require varying degrees of flexibility to prevent injury and promote optimal performance.

The sport-specific phase of specialized training that occurs following the initial years of training, characterized by multilateral training, is crucial for all national-level and elite athletes who aim for precise training effects. Specific exercises during this period allow athletes to adapt to their specializations. For elite athletes, the relationships between strength, speed, and endurance depend on both the sport and the individual athlete's needs.

Figure 1.2 illustrates three examples in which either strength, speed, or endurance is dominant. In each case, when one biomotor ability dominates, the other two do not participate to a similar extent. The general notion of one ability dominating so totally, however, is pure theory and applies to few sports. In the vast majority of sports, each ability has a given input. Figure 1.3 shows the dominant composition of strength, speed, and endurance in several sports. Coaches and athletes can use the figure to determine the dominant biomotor abilities in their sports.

Each sport has its own specific physiological profile and characteristics. All coaches who design and implement sport-specific training programs must understand the body's energy systems and how they apply to sport training. Although the purpose of this book is to discuss in specific terms the science, methodology, and objectives of strength training for sports, the physiological complexity of each sport also requires strong understanding of the energy systems dominant in that sport and how they relate to training.

The body produces the energy required for neural (strength, power, speed) and metabolic training by breaking down food and converting it into a usable form of fuel known as adenosine triphosphate (ATP). Because ATP has to be constantly replenished and reused, the body relies on three main systems of energy replenishment to facilitate ongoing training: the anaerobic alactic (ATP-CP) system, the anaerobic lactic system, and the aerobic system. The three systems are not independent of each other but collaborate based on the physiological requirements of the sport. Sport-specific program development should always be focused on training the dominant energy system(s) for the chosen sport.

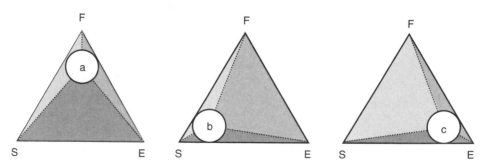

Figure 1.2 Relationships between the main biomotor abilities where (a) strength (F), (b) speed (S), or (c) endurance (E) is dominant.

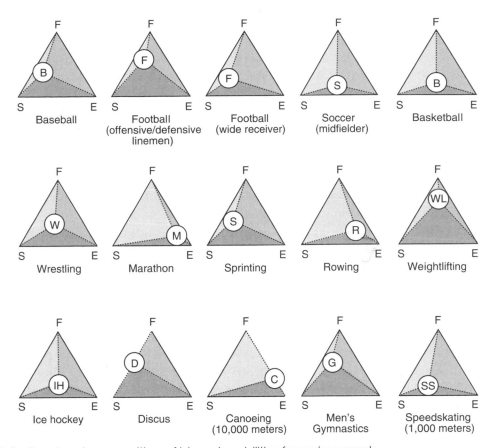

Figure 1.3 Dominant composition of biomotor abilities for various sports.

Specific development of a biomotor ability must be methodical. In addition, a developed dominant ability directly or indirectly affects the other abilities; the extent to which it does so depends strictly on the resemblance between the methods employed and the specifics of the sport. Therefore, development of a dominant biomotor ability may produce either a positive or (rarely) a negative transfer. For example, when an athlete develops strength, he or she may experience a positive transfer to speed and endurance. On the other hand, a strength training program designed only to develop maximum strength may negatively affect the development of aerobic endurance. Similarly, a training program aimed exclusively at developing aerobic endurance may produce a negative transfer to strength and speed. Because strength is a crucial athletic ability, it always has to be trained with the other abilities.

Unfounded and misleading theories have suggested that strength training slows athletes and negatively affects their development of endurance and flexibility. Such theories have been discredited by research (Atha 1984; Dudley and Fleck 1987; Hickson et al. 1988; MacDougall et al. 1987; Micheli 1988; Nelson et al. 1990; Sale et al. 1990). For example, one recent study of cross-country skiers found that maximum strength training alone not only improved the skiers' maximum strength and rate of force development but also produced positive transfer to work economy by increasing the time to exhaustion (Hoff, Gran, and Helgerud 2002). Similarly, another recent study performed on runners and cyclists found improvement in both running and cycling economy and in power output through the combination of endurance training and heavy resistance training (Rønnestad and Mujika 2013).

Combined strength and endurance training with sport-specific loading parameters does not affect improvement of aerobic power or muscular strength; that is, it produces no negative transfer. Similarly, strength programs pose no risk to flexibility, if stretching routines are integrated into the overall training program. Thus, endurance athletes in sports such as cycling, rowing, cross-country skiing, and canoeing can safely use strength and endurance training concurrently with their other training.

For speed sports, in fact, power represents a great source of speed improvement. A fast sprinter is also strong. Muscles that are strong and contract quickly and powerfully enable high acceleration, fast limb movement, and high frequency. In extreme situations, however, maximum loads can affect speed—for example, when speed training is scheduled after an exhausting training session with maximum loads. In this case, fatigue both in the nervous system and at the muscular level impedes neural drive and performance. For this reason, macrocycles aimed at developing maximum strength should include acceleration development and submaximal speed, whereas maximum speed is better developed in conjunction with power. At the training unit level, speed training should always be performed before strength training (see chapter 9).

Most actions and movements are more complex than previously discussed in this chapter. Thus, strength in sports should be viewed as the mechanism required to perform skills and athletic actions. Athletes do not develop strength just for the sake of being strong. The goal of strength development is to meet the specific needs of a given sport—to develop specific strength or combinations of strength in order to increase athletic performance to the highest possible level.

Combining strength (F) and endurance (E) results in muscular endurance (ME). Sports may require muscular endurance of long, medium, or short duration. Before discussing this topic further, we must briefly clarify two terms: *cyclic* and *acyclic*. Cyclic movements are repeated continuously; examples include running, walking, swimming, rowing, skating, cross-country skiing, cycling, and canoeing. For such activities, as soon as one cycle of the motor act is learned, it can be repeated with the same succession, over and over. Acyclic movements, on the other hand, represent a combination of different motor patterns. Examples of acyclic activities include throwing events, gymnastics, wrestling, fencing, and many technical movements in team sports.

With the exception of sprinting, cyclic sports are endurance sports, which means that endurance either is dominant or makes an important contribution to performance in the sport. Acyclic sports, on the other hand, are often power sports. Many sports, however, are more complex and require speed, power, *and* endurance—for example, basketball, soccer, ice hockey, wrestling, and boxing. Therefore, the following analysis may refer to certain skills used in a given sport but not to the sport as a whole.

Figure 1.4 analyzes various combinations of strength, speed, and endurance. The elements are discussed here in a clockwise direction, starting with the F–E (strength–endurance) axis. Each strength combination features an arrow pointing to a certain part of the axis between two biomotor abilities. An arrow placed closer to F indicates that strength plays a dominant role in the sport or skill. An arrow placed closer to the midpoint of the axis indicates an equal (or almost equal) contribution by both biomotor abilities. The farther the arrow is from F, the less important F is, suggesting that the other ability is more dominant; however, strength still plays a role in that sport.

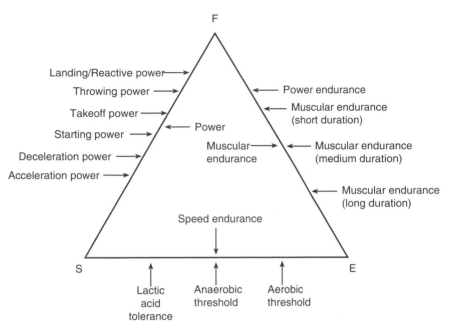

Figure 1.4 Sport-specific combinations among the dominant biomotor abilities.

F–E Axis

The F–E axis applies to sports in which muscular endurance is the dominant strength combination (the inner arrow). Not all sports require equal parts of strength and endurance. For example, swimming events range from 50 to 1,500 meters. The 50-meter event is dominated by speed endurance and power endurance (or, metabolically speaking, lactic power); however, muscular endurance (metabolically speaking, aerobic power and capacity) becomes more important as distance increases.

Power endurance (PE) is on top of the F–E axis because of the importance of strength in activities such as rebounding in basketball, spiking in volleyball, jumping to catch the ball in Australian football and rugby, and jumping to head the ball in soccer. These actions are all power dominant. The same is true for some skills in tennis, boxing, wrestling, and the martial arts. To perform such actions successfully on a consistent basis, athletes must train for endurance as well as for power because the actions are performed 50 to 200 times per contest.

For example, a basketball player must not only jump high to rebound a ball; she must also duplicate such a jump 200 times per game. Consequently, she must train for both power and power endurance; however, the variables of volume and intensity are manipulated to adapt the body for repeated power performance. Nevertheless, we must distinguish between repeated short power actions (as used in team sports) and longer-lasting continuous powerful actions (as used in the 100-meter or 200-meter run and the 50-meter swim). Both of these modalities require power endurance, yet the former's main energy system is the alactic system (used repeatedly) and eventually the lactic system (because of short rest intervals between the powerful actions). In contrast, the latter relies mainly on the power of the lactic system (that is, the lactic system's ability to produce ATP at its maximum rate).

Muscular endurance of short duration (ME short) is the muscular endurance necessary for events ranging from 40 seconds to two minutes, which involves a mix of lactic capacity and aerobic power. In the 100-meter swimming event, for example, the start is a power action, as are the first 20 strokes. From the midpoint of the race to the end, however, muscular endurance becomes at least equally as important as power. In the last 30 to 40 meters, the crucial element is the ability to duplicate the force of the arms' pull to maintain velocity and increase at the finish. Thus muscular endurance contributes strongly to the final result for events such as the 100-meter swim, as well as the 400-meter run; speedskating races of 500 to 1,000 meters; and the 500-meter in canoeing.

Muscular endurance of medium duration (ME medium) is typical of cyclic sports in which activity lasts two to eight minutes and requires aerobic power, such as 200- and 400-meter swimming, 3,000-meter speedskating, mid-distance running, 1,000-meter canoeing, wrestling, martial arts, figure skating, synchronized swimming, and cycling pursuit.

Muscular endurance of long duration (ME long) is the ability to apply force against a standard resistance for a longer period (more than eight minutes; aerobic power to aerobic capacity). Activities that call for ME long include rowing, cross-country skiing, road cycling, and long-distance running, swimming, speedskating, and canoeing.

S–E Axis

The S–E (speed–endurance) axis covers the type of endurance required by most sports. Speed endurance is the ability to maintain speed for 10 to 20 seconds (for example, 50 meters in swimming, 100 or 200 meters in running) or to repeat a high-velocity action several times per game, as in American football, baseball, basketball, rugby, soccer, and power skating in ice hockey. Therefore, athletes in these sports need to train in order to develop their speed endurance. The remaining four types of speed–endurance combination change according to the proportion of speed and endurance as distance increases, as shown in table 1.3.

Table 1.3 Speed–Endurance Combinations

Training	Metabolism	Duration of reps	Lactic acid concentration (mmol)	% of maximum heart rate
Lactic acid tolerance training (LATT)	Lactic capacity	30–60 sec.	12–20	95%–100%
Maximum oxygen consumption training ($\dot{V}O_2$maxT)	Aerobic power	1–6 min.	6–12	95%–100%
Anaerobic threshold training (AnTT)	Both aerobic power and capacity	1–8 min.	4–6	85%–90%
Aerobic threshold training (ATT)	Aerobic capacity	10–120 min.	2–3	70%–75%

F–S Axis

The F–S (strength–speed) axis refers mainly to sports in which power is dominant. For example, landing and reactive power are major components of several sports, such as figure skating, gymnastics, and certain team sports. Proper training for such sports can prevent injury, but many athletes train only for the takeoff part of a jump, with no concern for a controlled and balanced landing. In reality, however, proper landing technique involves an important physical (power) element, particularly for advanced athletes. Athletes must train eccentrically to be able to stick a landing, absorb the shock, and maintain good balance to perform another move immediately.

The power required to control a landing depends on the height of the jump, the athlete's body weight, and whether the landing is performed by absorbing the shock or with the joints flexed but stiff. Testing has revealed that for a shock-absorbing landing, athletes express a force three to four times their body weight, whereas a landing performed with stiff leg joints results in a force of six to eight times body weight. For example, an athlete who weighs 132 pounds (60 kilograms) expresses a force equivalent to 396 to 528 pounds (180 to 240 kilograms) to absorb the shock of landing. The same athlete would express 792 to 1,056 pounds (360 to 480 kilograms) to land with the leg joints stiff. Similarly, when an athlete lands on one leg, as in figure skating, the force at the instant of landing is three to four times body weight for a shock-absorbing landing and five to seven times for landing with stiff leg joints.

Specific power training for landing can be planned so that it enables the athlete to gradually reach much higher tension in the leg muscles than can be achieved through specific skill training. Through periodization of strength, we can train for landing power in a way that is better, faster, and much more consistent. Landing power improves with higher tension. In addition, specific power training for landing, especially eccentric training, allows athletes to build a power reserve—a force greater than the power required for a correct and controlled landing. The higher the power reserve, the easier it is for the athlete to control the landing, and the safer the landing will be.

Reactive power is the ability to generate the force of jumping immediately following a landing (hence the word *reactive*, which, scientifically speaking, refers to reduction of the coupling time—the passage from the eccentric to the concentric action). This kind of power is necessary for martial arts, wrestling, and boxing and for quick changes in direction in other sports, as in American football, soccer, basketball, lacrosse, and tennis. The force needed for a reactive jump depends on the height of the jump and the athlete's body weight. Generally, reactive jumps require a force equal to six to eight times body weight. Reactive jumps from a three-foot (one-meter) platform require a reactive force of 8 to 10 times body weight.

Throwing power refers to force applied against an implement, such as a football, baseball, or javelin. First, athletes have to defeat the inertia of the implement, which is proportional to its mass. Then they must continuously accelerate through the range of motion so that they achieve maximum velocity at the instant of release. The rate of acceleration at release depends directly on the force and speed of contraction applied against the implement.

Takeoff power is crucial in events in which athletes attempt to project the body to the highest point, either to jump over a bar (as in the high jump) or to reach the best height to perform an athletic action (such as catching or spiking a ball). The height of a jump depends directly on the vertical force applied against the ground to defeat the pull of gravity. In most cases, the vertical force performed at takeoff is at least twice the athlete's weight. The higher the jump, the more powerful the legs must be. Leg power is developed through periodized strength training as explained in chapters 13 and 14.

Starting power is necessary in sports that require high acceleration capability to cover the space of one or two steps in the shortest time possible. In order to create high initial acceleration, athletes must be able to generate maximum force at the beginning of a muscular contraction. Physiologically speaking, such ability depends on voluntary motor unit recruitment and rate of force development. The ability to quickly overcome the inertia of the athlete's body weight depends on the athlete's relative strength (maximum strength relative to body weight) and relative power. For such reasons, starting fast, either from a low position in sprinting or from a tackling position in American football, depends on the power that the athlete can exert at that instant and, of course, on his or her reaction time.

Acceleration power refers to the capacity to increase speed rapidly. Like speed, sprinting acceleration depends on the power and quickness of muscle contractions to drive the arms and legs to the highest stride frequency, the shortest contact phase when the foot reaches the ground, and the highest propulsion when the leg pushes against the ground for a powerful forward drive. Recent studies show that this latter characteristic—the ground reaction force during the drive phase—is the most important variable in reaching high speed (Weyand et al. 2000; Kyröläinen et al. 2001; Belli et al. 2002; Kyröläinen et al. 2005; Nummela et al. 2007; Brughelli et al. 2011; Morin 2011; Morin et al. 2012; Kawamori et al. 2013). Thus, an athlete's capacity to accelerate depends on both arm and leg power. Specific strength training for high acceleration benefits most team-sport athletes, ranging from wide receivers in American football to wingers in rugby and strikers in soccer (see table 1.4).

Deceleration power is important in sports in which athletes run fast and often change direction quickly; examples include soccer, basketball, American football, ice hockey, and field hockey. Such athletes are exploders and accelerators, as well as decelerators. The dynamics of these games change abruptly. As a result, players who are moving fast in one direction must often change direction suddenly, with the least possible loss of speed, then accelerate quickly in another direction.

Acceleration and deceleration both require a great deal of leg and shoulder power. The same muscles used for acceleration (quadriceps, hamstrings, and calves) are used for deceleration, except that here they contract eccentrically. To enhance the ability to decelerate and move in another direction quickly, athletes must train specifically for deceleration power.

Soccer players rely on a combination of types of power—reactive, takeoff, starting, acceleration, and deceleration—to master the many techniques needed in game situations.

Table 1.4 Sport-Specific Strength Development

Sport or event	Type(s) of strength required	Sport or event	Type(s) of strength required
Athletics		**Diving**	Takeoff P, reactive P
Short sprint	Reactive P, starting P, acceleration P, PE	**Equestrian**	ME medium
		Fencing	Reactive P, PE
Long sprint	Acceleration P, ME short	**Field hockey**	Acceleration P, deceleration P, ME medium
Middle-distance running	Acceleration P, ME medium		
Distance running	ME long	**Figure skating**	Takeoff P, landing P, PE
Long jump	Acceleration P, takeoff P, reactive P	**Football (American)**	
		Linemen	Starting P, reactive P
Triple jump	Acceleration P, reactive P, takeoff P	Linebackers, quarterbacks, running backs, inside receivers	Starting P, acceleration P, reactive P
High jump	Takeoff P, reactive P		
Throws	Throwing P, reactive P	Wide receivers, defensive backs, tailbacks	Acceleration P, reactive P, starting P
Baseball	Throwing P, acceleration P		
Basketball	Takeoff P, PE, acceleration P, deceleration P	Football (Australian)	Acceleration P, takeoff P, landing P, ME short and medium
Biathlon	ME long	**Gymnastics**	Reactive P, takeoff P, landing P
Boxing	PE, reactive P, ME medium and long	**Handball (European)**	Throwing P, acceleration P, deceleration P
Canoeing and kayaking			
500 m	ME short, acceleration P, starting P	**Ice hockey**	Acceleration P, deceleration P, PE
1,000 m	ME medium, acceleration P, starting P	**Martial arts**	Starting P, reactive P, PE
		Rhythmic sportive gymnastics	Reactive P, takeoff P, ME short
10,000 m	ME long	**Rowing**	ME medium and long, starting P
Cricket	Throwing P, acceleration P		
Cycling		**Rugby**	Acceleration P, starting P, ME medium
Track, 200 m	Acceleration P, reactive P	**Sailing**	ME long, PE
		Shooting	ME long, PE
4,000 m pursuit	ME medium, acceleration P	**Skiing**	
		Alpine	Reactive P, ME short
Road racing	ME long	Nordic	ME long, PE

(continued)

Table 1.4 *(continued)*

Sport or event	Type(s) of strength required	Sport or event	Type(s) of strength required
Soccer		**Swimming**	
Sweepers, fullbacks	Reactive P, acceleration P, deceleration P	Sprinting	Starting P, acceleration P, ME short
Midfielders	Acceleration P, deceleration P, ME medium	Mid-distance	ME medium, PE
		Long-distance	ME long
Forwards	Acceleration P, deceleration P, reactive P	**Synchronized swimming**	ME medium, PE
		Tennis	PE, reactive P, acceleration P, deceleration P
Speedskating			
Sprinting	Starting P, acceleration P, ME short	**Volleyball**	Reactive P, PE, throwing P
Mid-distance	ME medium, PE	**Water polo**	ME medium, acceleration P, throwing P
Long-distance	ME long		
Squash and handball	Reactive P, PE	**Wrestling**	PE, reactive P, ME medium

Key: ME = muscular endurance, P = power, PE = power endurance.

Role of Strength in Water Sports

For sports performed in or on water—such as swimming, synchronized swimming, water polo, rowing, kayaking, and canoeing—the body or boat moves forward as a result of force. As force is exerted against the water, the water exerts an equal and opposite force, known as drag, on the body or boat. As the boat or the swimmer moves through the water, the drag slows the forward motion or glide. To overcome drag, athletes must produce equal force to maintain speed and superior force to increase speed.

The magnitude of the drag acting on a body moving through the water can be computed using the following equation (Hay 1993):

$$Fd = CdPAV^2/2$$

In this equation, Fd = drag force, Cd = coefficient of drag, P = fluid density, A = frontal area exposed to the flow, and V^2 = body velocity relative to the water. The coefficients of drag refer to the nature and shape of the body, including its orientation relative to the water flow. Long and slender vessels (such as canoes, kayaks, and racing shells) have a smaller CD if the long axis of the boat is exactly parallel to the water flow.

A simplified version of the equation is as follows.

$$D \sim V^2$$

It means that drag is proportional to the square of velocity. This equation is not only easier to understand but also easier to apply.

In water sports, velocity increases when athletes apply force against the water. As force increases, the body moves faster. However, as velocity increases, drag increases proportionally to the square of velocity. Here is an example to demonstrate. Assume that an athlete swims or rows at 2 meters (about 6.5 feet) per second:

$$D \sim V^2 = 2^2 = 4 \text{ kilograms (8.8 pounds)}$$

In other words, the athlete pulls with a force of 4 kilograms (8.8 pounds) per stroke. To be more competitive, the athlete has to swim or row faster—say, at 3 meters (9.8 feet) per second:

$$D \sim V^2 = 3^2 = 9 \text{ kilograms (19.8 pounds)}$$

For an even higher velocity of 4 meters (13 feet) per second, drag is 16 kilograms (35 pounds).

In order to pull with increased force, of course, one must increase maximum strength, because a body cannot generate increased velocity without increasing the force per stroke unit. The training implications are obvious: Not only must the athlete increase maximum strength, but also the coach must ensure that the athlete exerts almost the same force on all strokes for the duration of the race, because all water sports have a strong endurance component. This reality means that, as suggested in chapter 14, training must include both a phase addressing maximum strength and a phase addressing adequate muscular endurance.

2

Neuromuscular Response to Strength Training

To enhance strength performance, one must understand the science behind strength training and learn how anatomy and physiology apply to human movement. More specifically, coaches and athletes who understand muscle contraction and the sliding filament theory (discussed in this chapter) know why the speed of contraction relates to load and why more force is exerted at the beginning of a contraction than at the end. Similarly, coaches who understand muscle fiber types and recognize the role played by genetic inheritance know why some athletes are better than others at certain types of sporting activity (for example, speed, power, or endurance). Unfortunately, despite the value of such knowledge for effective training, many athletes and coaches avoid reading academic physiology texts or other books filled with scientific terminology. This book, however, explains the scientific basis of strength training clearly and simply.

Understanding muscle adaptation and its dependence on load and training method makes it easier to grasp why certain types of load, exercise, or training method are preferred for some sports and not for others. Success in strength training depends on knowing the types of strength and how to develop them, as well as the types of contraction and which are best for a given sport. This knowledge helps both coaches and athletes understand the concept of periodization of strength faster and more easily, and improvement soon follows.

Body Structure

The human body is constructed around a skeleton. The junction of two or more bones forms a joint held together by tough bands of connective tissue called ligaments. This skeletal frame is covered with 656 muscles, which account for approximately 40 percent of total body weight. Both ends of the muscle are attached to the bone by dense connective tissues called tendons. Tendons direct the tension in muscles to bones—the greater the tension, the stronger the pull on the tendons and bone, and, consequently, the more powerful the limb movement.

The periodized training proposed in this book consistently challenges the neuromuscular system as the load and type of training elicits physiological adaptations that generate more strength and power for sport performance. Our bodies are very plastic and adapt to the stimuli to which they are exposed. If the proper stimulation is applied, the result is optimal physiological performance.

Muscle Structure

A muscle is a complex structure that allows movements to occur. Muscles are composed of sarcomeres, which contain a specific arrangement of contractile proteins—myosin (thick filaments) and actin (thin filaments)—whose actions are important in muscle contraction. Thus a sarcomere is a unit of contraction in muscle fiber and is composed of the myosin and actin protein filaments.

Beyond these basics, a muscle's ability to contract and exert force depends specifically on its design, the cross-sectional area, and the length and number of fibers within the muscle. The number of fibers is genetically determined and is not affected by training; the other variables, however, can be. For example, the number and thickness of myosin filaments is increased by dedicated training with maximum strength loads. Increasing the thickness of muscle filaments increases both the muscle's size and the force of contraction.

Our bodies include different types of muscle fibers, which are grouped, and in essence each group reports to a single motor unit. Altogether, we have thousands of motor units, which house tens of thousands of muscle fibers. Each motor unit contains hundreds or thousands of muscle fibers that sit dormant until they are called into action. The motor unit rules over its family of fibers and directs their action by implementing the all-or-none law. This law means that when the motor unit is stimulated, the impulse sent to its muscle fibers either spreads completely—thus eliciting action by all fibers in the family—or does not spread at all.

Different motor units respond to different loads in training. For instance, performing a bench press with 60 percent of 1-repetition maximum (1RM) calls up a certain family of motor units, whereas larger motor units wait until a higher load is used. Because motor unit recruitment depends on load, programs should be designed specifically to achieve activation and adaptation of the primary motor units and muscle fibers that dominate the chosen sport. For instance, training for short sprints and field events (such as the shot put) should use heavy loads to facilitate the force development required to optimize speed and explosive performance.

Muscle fibers have different biochemical (metabolic) functions; specifically, some are physiologically better suited to work under anaerobic conditions, whereas others work better under aerobic conditions. The fibers that rely on and use oxygen to produce energy are called aerobic, Type I, red, or slow-twitch fibers. The fibers that do not require oxygen are called anaerobic, Type II, white, or fast-twitch fibers. Fast-twitch muscle fibers are further divided into IIA and IIX (sometimes referred to as IIB, though the IIB phenotype is practically nonexistent in humans [Harrison et al. 2011]).

Slow-twitch and fast-twitch fibers exist in relatively equal proportion. However, depending on their function, certain muscle groups (e.g., hamstrings, biceps) seem to have a higher proportion of fast-twitch fibers, whereas others (e.g., the soleus) have a higher proportion of slow-twitch fibers. The characteristics of slow-twitch and fast-twitch fibers are compared in table 2.1.

Table 2.1 Comparison of Fast-Twitch and Slow-Twitch Fibers

SLOW-TWITCH	FAST-TWITCH
Red, Type I, aerobic	White, Type II, anaerobic
• Slow to fatigue • Smaller nerve cell—innervates 10 to 180 muscle fibers • Develops long, continuous contractions • Used for endurance • Recruited during low- and high-intensity work	• Fast to fatigue • Large nerve cell—innervates 300 to 500 (or more) muscle fibers • Develops short, forceful contractions • Used for speed and power • Recruited only during high-intensity work

These characteristics can be affected by training. Studies by the Danish researchers Andersen and Aagaard (1994, 2008, 2010, 2011) show that IIX fibers develop the characteristics of IIA fibers when subjected to voluminous training or training that is lactic in nature. That is, the myosin heavy chain of these fibers gets slower and more efficient at dealing with the lactic work. The change can be reversed by reducing training volume (tapering), whereupon the IIX fibers revert to their original character as the fastest-contracting fibers (Andersen and Aagaard 2000). Strength training also increases fiber size, which generates greater force production.

A fast-twitch motor unit's contraction is faster and more powerful than that of a slow-twitch motor unit. As a result, a higher proportion of fast-twitch fibers is usually found in successful athletes in speed and power sports, but they also fatigue faster. In contrast, athletes with more slow-twitch fibers are more successful in endurance sports because they are able to perform work of lower intensity for a longer time.

Recruitment of muscle fibers follows the size principle, also known as the Hennemann (1965) principle, which states that motor units and muscle fibers are recruited in order from smallest to largest, beginning always with slow-twitch muscle fibers. If the load is of low or moderate intensity, slow-twitch muscle fibers are recruited and exercised as workhorses. If a heavy load is used, slow-twitch fibers start the contraction, but it is quickly taken over by fast-twitch fibers. When a set of repetitions with a moderate load is taken to failure, the motor units composed of faster-twitch fibers are gradually recruited to maintain the force output while previously recruited motor units fatigue (see figure 2.1).

Differences can be observed in the distribution of muscle fiber types in athletes involved in different sports. To illustrate the point, figures 2.2 and 2.3 provide a general profile of fast- and slow-twitch fiber percentages for athletes in selected sports. For example, the drastic differences between sprinters and marathon runners clearly suggest that success in some sports is determined at least partly by an athlete's genetically established makeup of muscle fiber.

Thus the peak power generated by athletes is also related to fiber type distribution—the higher the percentage of fast-twitch fibers, the greater the power generated by the athlete. The percentage of fast-twitch fibers also relates to speed—the greater the speed displayed by an athlete, the higher his or her percentage of fast-twitch fibers. Such individuals make great sprinters and jumpers, and with this natural talent they should be channeled into speed- and power-dominant sports. Attempting to make them, say, distance runners would be a waste of talent; in such events, they would be only moderately successful, whereas they could excel as sprinters or baseball or football players (to mention just a few speed- and power-related sports).

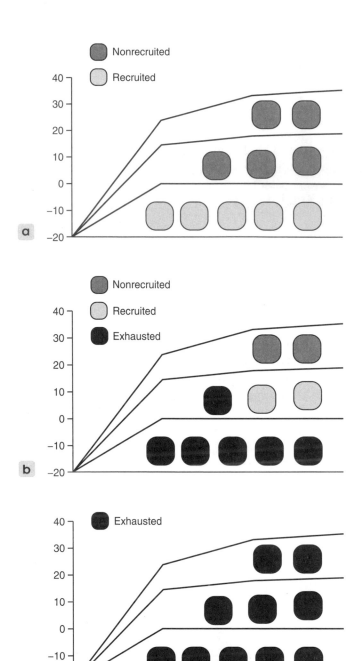

Figure 2.1 Sequential motor unit recruitment in a set taken to concentric failure.

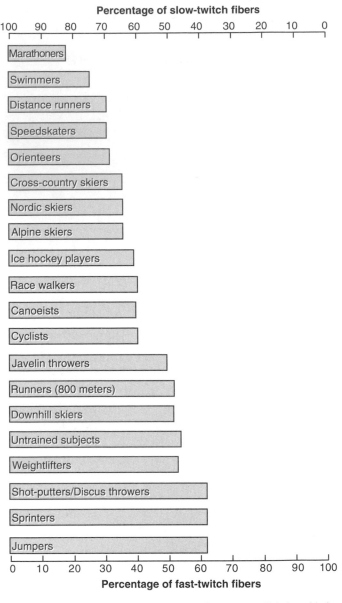

Figure 2.2 Fiber type distribution for male athletes. Note the dominance in slow-twitch fibers for athletes from aerobic-dominant sports and in fast-twitch fibers for athletes from speed- and power-dominant sports.

Data from D.L. Costill, J. Daniels, W. Evans, W. Fink, G. Krahenbuhl, and B. Saltin, 1976, "Skeletal muscle enzymes and fiber composition in male and female track athletes," *Journal of Applied Physiology* 40(2): 149-154, and P.D. Gollnick, R.B. Armstrong, C.W. Saubert, K. Piehl, and B. Saltin, 1972, "Enzyme activity and fiber composition in skeletal muscle of untrained and trained men," *Journal of Applied Physiology* 33(3): 312-319.

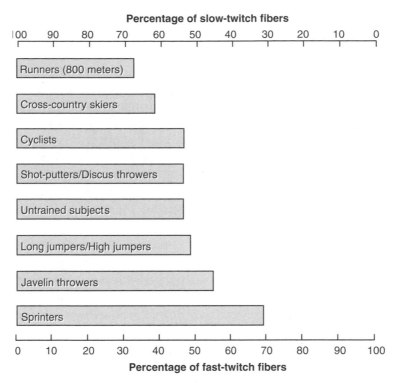

Figure 2.3 Fiber type distribution for female athletes.

Data from D.L. Costill, J. Daniels, W. Evans, W. Fink, G. Krahenbuhl, and B. Saltin, 1976, "Skeletal muscle enzymes and fiber composition in male and female track athletes," *Journal of Applied Physiology* 40(2): 149-154, and P.D. Gollnick, R.B. Armstrong, C.W. Saubert, K. Piehl, and B. Saltin, 1972, "Enzyme activity and fiber composition in skeletal muscle of untrained and trained men," *Journal of Applied Physiology* 33(3): 312-319.

Mechanism of Muscular Contraction

As described earlier, muscular contraction results from a series of events involving the protein filaments known as myosin and actin. Myosin filaments contain cross-bridges—tiny extensions that reach toward actin filaments. Activation to contract stimulates the entire fiber, creating chemical changes that allow the actin filaments to join with the myosin cross-bridges. Binding myosin to actin by way of cross-bridges releases energy, causing the cross-bridges to swivel, thus pulling or sliding the myosin filament over the actin filament. This sliding motion causes the muscle to shorten (contract), which produces force.

To visualize it in another way, imagine a rowboat. The boat's oars represent the myosin filaments, and the water represents the actin filaments. As the oars hit the water, the boat is forcefully pulled forward—and the more oars in the water, and the greater the rowers' strength, the greater the force production. In similar fashion, increasing the number and thickness of myosin filaments increases force production.

The sliding filament theory described earlier provides an overview of how muscles work to produce force. The theory involves a number of mechanisms that promote effective muscle contraction. For instance, the release of stored elastic energy and reflex adaptation are vital to optimizing athletic performance, but these adaptations occur only when the proper stimulus is applied in training. For instance, an athlete's ability to use stored elastic energy to jump higher or propel the shot put farther is optimized through explosive movements, such as those used in plyometric training. However, the muscle components—such as the series elastic components (which include tendons, muscle fibers,

23

and cross-bridges)—are unable to effectively transfer energy to the movement unless the athlete strengthens the parallel elastic components (i.e., ligaments) and collagen structures (which provide stability and protection from injury). If the body is to withstand the forces and impacts that the athlete must go through in order to optimize the muscles' elastic properties, anatomical adaptation must precede power training.

A reflex is an involuntary muscle contraction brought about by an external stimulus (Latash 1998). Two main components of reflex control are the muscle spindles and the Golgi tendon organ. Muscle spindles respond to the magnitude and rapidity of a muscle stretch (Brooks, Fahey, and White 1996), whereas the Golgi tendon organ (found within the muscle–tendon junction [Latash 1998]) responds to muscle tension. When a high degree of tension or stretch develops in the muscles, the muscle spindles and the Golgi tendon organ involuntarily relax the muscle to protect it from harm and injury.

When these inhibitory responses are curtailed, athletic performance is increased. The only way to do so is to adapt the body to withstand greater degrees of tension, which increases the threshold for the activation of the reflexes. This adaptation can be achieved through maximum strength training that uses progressively heavier loads (up to 90 percent of 1RM or even more), thus causing the neuromuscular system to withstand higher tensions by consistently recruiting a greater number of fast-twitch muscle fibers. The fast-twitch muscle fibers become equipped with more protein, which aids in cross-bridge cycling and force production.

All sporting movements follow a motor pattern known as the stretch–shortening cycle, which is characterized by three main types of contraction: eccentric (lengthening), isometric (static), and concentric (shortening). For example, a volleyball player who quickly squats only to jump and block a spike has completed a stretch–shortening cycle. The same is true for an athlete who lowers the barbell to the chest and rapidly explodes by extending the arms. To fully use the physiological assets of a stretch–shortening cycle, the muscle must change quickly from a lengthening to a shortening contraction (Schmidtbleicher 1992).

Muscular potential is optimized when all the intricate factors that affect the stretch–shortening cycle are called into action. Their influence can be used to enhance performance only when the neuromuscular system is strategically stimulated in the appropriate sequence. Toward this end, periodization of strength builds the planning of phases on the physiological makeup of the chosen sport. Once the ergogenesis, or energy systems' contribution, profile of the sport is outlined, the phases of training are planned in a sequential, stepwise approach to transfer positive neuromuscular adaptations to practical hands-on human performance. Therefore, understanding applied human physiology, and a snapshot goal for each phase, helps coaches and athletes integrate physiological principles into sport-specific training.

To reiterate, the musculoskeletal frame of the body is an arrangement of bones attached to one another by ligaments at the joints. The muscles crossing these joints provide the force for body movements. Skeletal muscles do not, however, contract independently of one another. Rather, the movements performed around a joint are produced by several muscles, each of which plays a different role, as discussed in the following paragraphs.

Agonists, or synergists, are muscles that cooperate to perform a movement. During movement, antagonists act in opposition to agonists. In most cases, especially in skilled and experienced athletes, antagonists relax, allowing easy motion. Because athletic movements are directly influenced by the interaction between agonist and antagonist muscle groups, improper interaction between the two groups may result in a motion that is jerky or performed rigidly. Therefore, the smoothness of a muscular contraction can be improved by focusing on relaxing the antagonists.

For this reason, co-contraction (the simultaneous activation of agonist and antagonist muscle to stabilize a joint) is advisable only during the early phases of rehabilitation from an injury. A healthy athlete, on the other hand, especially one in a power sport, should not perform exercises (such as those on unstable surfaces) to elicit co-contractions. For instance, one distinct characteristic of elite sprinters is very low myoelectrical activity of the antagonist muscles in each phase of the stride cycle (Wysotchin 1976; Wiemann and Tidow 1995).

Prime movers are muscles primarily responsible for producing a joint action that is part of a comprehensive strength movement or a technical skill. For example, during an elbow flexion (biceps curl), the prime mover is the biceps muscle, whereas the triceps acts as an antagonist and should be relaxed to facilitate smoother action. In addition, stabilizers, or fixators, which are usually smaller muscles, contract isometrically to anchor a bone so that the prime movers have a firm base from which to pull. The muscles of other limbs may come into play as well, acting as stabilizers so that the prime movers can perform their motion. For instance, when a judoka pulls the opponent toward himself holding his judogi, muscles in his back, legs, and abdomen contract isometrically to provide a stable base for the action of the elbow flexors (biceps), shoulder extensors (rear delts), and scapular adductors and depressors (traps and lats).

Types of Strength and Their Training Significance

Training can involve various types of strength, each of which is significant for certain sports and athletes. We can distinguish types of strength in terms of the qualities of strength, the force–time curve, the type of muscle action, the athlete's body weight, and the degree of specificity.

Strength: Its Qualities

The desired effect of a strength training method always falls into one of the following three categories or qualities: maximum strength, power, and muscular endurance.

Maximum Strength

Maximum strength is the highest force that can be exerted by the neuromuscular system during a contraction. This quality is increased through a combination of structural adaptation (hypertrophy) and, mostly, neural adaptation (mainly in the form of improved intermuscular and intramuscular coordination). Maximum strength refers to the heaviest load that an athlete can lift in one attempt and is expressed as 100 percent of maximum or 1RM. For training purposes, athletes must know their maximum strength for the most important (fundamental) exercises because it provides the basis for calculating loads for almost every strength phase.

Power

Power is the product of two abilities—strength and speed—and is itself the ability to apply the highest force in the shortest time. Unlike powerlifting, in which the athlete expresses (maximum) strength without time limitation, athletes in all other sports face time constraints in applying as much force as possible. Examples include footstrikes by running athletes in individual and team sports, punches and kicks in combat sports, and bat swings and ball throws in baseball. Power is trained by using methods that enhance quick expression of force, thus improving the firing rate of the active motor units. Power can be maximized only by using its specific methods after a maximum strength phase of training.

Muscular Endurance

Muscular endurance is a muscle's ability to sustain work for a prolonged period. Most sports involve an endurance component, and muscular endurance methods train both the neural and metabolic aspects specific to a sport. We distinguish four types of sport-specific muscle endurance method: power endurance (10 to 30 seconds, or less than 15 seconds with incomplete rest; lactic power), muscle endurance short (30 seconds to 2 minutes; lactic capacity), muscle endurance medium (2 to 8 minutes; aerobic power), and muscle endurance long (more than 8 minutes; aerobic capacity).

Strength: Force–Time Curve

If we analyze a force–time curve (see figure 2.4), we can distinguish the following types of strength: starting strength, explosive strength (rate of force development), power (starting strength plus explosive strength), and maximum strength.

Starting Strength

Starting strength is expressed at the start of a concentric action and is usually measured at 50 milliseconds. Its level depends on the ability to voluntarily recruit as many motor units as possible (i.e., intramuscular coordination) at the beginning of the movement.

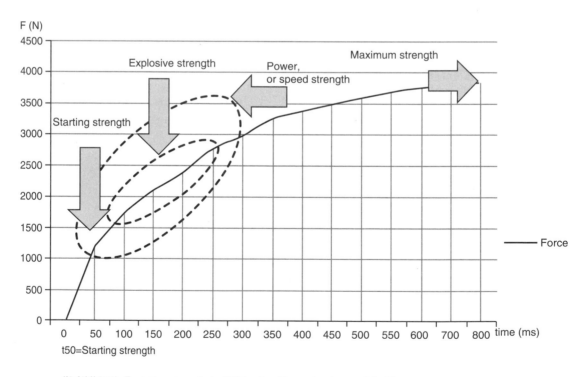

$(f2-f1)/(t2-t1)$=Explosive strength (or RFD, rate of force development) in N/ms

Figure 2.4 Force–time curve.

Explosive Strength or Rate of Force Development

Explosive strength is the rate at which force increases at the beginning of the concentric action. Its level depends on the ability to either recruit more motor units or increase the firing rate of the active units in order to increase force output.

Power

Taken together, starting strength and explosive strength represent what we call power, or, according to other authors, "speed-strength." A high level of power is usually needed in order to excel in sports due to the limited time available for force application in sport actions.

Maximum Strength

Maximum strength is the maximum amount of force that an athlete can achieve in a movement.

Strength: Muscle Action

We can distinguish three types of strength according to muscle action: concentric, isometric, and eccentric.

Concentric Strength

In a concentric action, the muscle creates tension and shortens, thus moving a joint. Maximum strength is normally measured as the highest load that can be lifted concentrically, either preceded or followed by an eccentric action.

Isometric Strength

In an isometric action, a muscle creates tension without shortening or lengthening; this result happens when the force generated equals the external resistance or when the external resistance is immovable. A high incidence of isometric actions by the prime movers is required in many motor sports, as well as in BMX, sailing, and combat sports. The need for such actions must be reflected in the athlete's strength training program. Isometric strength can be up to 20 percent higher than concentric strength.

Eccentric Strength

In an eccentric action, a muscle create less tension than the external resistance, thus the muscle lengthens. A high level of eccentric strength is advisable for sports that require jumping, sprinting, and changing direction. Eccentric strength can be up to 40 percent higher than concentric strength.

Strength: Relation to Body Weight

Maximum strength training methods elicit both neural and muscular adaptations. As described in the following chapters, the loading parameters can be manipulated in such a way as to increase either the athlete's body weight and strength or only strength, but maintain body weight. For this reason, we distinguish two types of strength: absolute and relative.

Absolute Strength

Absolute strength is an athlete's capacity to exert maximum force regardless of body weight. A high level of absolute strength is required in order to excel in some sports (for example, the shot put and the heaviest weight categories in weightlifting and wrestling). Increases in strength parallel gains in body weight for those athletes who follow a training program aimed at increasing absolute strength.

Relative Strength

Relative strength is the ratio between maximum strength and body weight. A high level of relative strength is important in gymnastics, sports in which athletes are divided into weight categories (such as wrestling, boxing, judo, Brazilian jiu-jitsu, and mixed martial arts), team sports that require frequent changes of direction, and track-and-field sprints and jumps. For instance, a gymnast may be unable to perform the iron cross on the rings unless the relative strength of the muscles involved is at least one to one; in other words, the absolute strength must be at least sufficient to offset the athlete's body weight. Of course, the ratio is changed by a gain in body weight—as body weight increases, relative strength decreases, unless strength increases accordingly. For this reason, the training programs aimed at increasing relative strength do so by eliciting the neural adaptations to strength training, rather than increasing muscle size and overall body weight.

Strength: Degree of Specificity

We distinguish two types of strength according to the degree of sport-specific biomechanical and physiological similarity of the training means and methods employed in a program: general strength and specific strength.

General Strength

General strength is the foundation of the entire strength training program and should be the main focus in the first years of sport training. Low general strength may limit the athlete's overall progress. It leaves the body susceptible to injury and potentially even asymmetrical shape or decreased ability to build muscle strength, as well as lower capacity for developing sport-specific skills.

Contributors to the development of an athlete's general strength include anatomical adaptation, hypertrophy, and maximum strength macrocycles. Anatomical adaptation is devoted to development of overall core strength, along with muscle balance and injury prevention through tendon reinforcement. As the name implies, anatomical adaptation prepares the body for the more difficult phases that follow. General strength is further increased through the structural changes elicited by hypertrophy macrocycles and the neural adaptations that result from maximum strength macrocycles.

Specific Strength

Specific strength training takes into account the characteristics of the sport, such as the ergogenesis (energy systems contributions), the planes of movement, the prime movers, the joints' range of motion, and the muscles' actions. As the term suggests, this type of strength is specific to each sport and requires a good deal of analysis. Therefore, it is invalid to compare the strength levels of athletes involved in different sports. Specific strength training should be incorporated progressively toward the end of the preparatory phase for all advanced athletes.

Strength Reserve

Strength reserve is the difference between maximum strength and the strength required to perform a skill under competitive conditions. For example, one study using strength-gauged techniques measured rowers' mean force per stroke during a race, which was 123 pounds (56 kilograms) (Bompa, Hebbelinck, and Van Gheluwe 1978). The same subjects were found to have absolute strength in power-clean lifts of 198 pounds (90 kilograms). Subtracting the mean strength per race (123 pounds or 56 kilograms) from absolute strength (198 pounds or 90 kilograms) indicates a strength reserve of 75 pounds (34 kilograms). In other words, the ratio of mean strength to absolute strength is about 1 to 1.6.

Other subjects in the same study were found to have a higher strength reserve and a ratio of 1 to 1.85. Needless to say, these subjects performed better in rowing races, which supports the conclusion that an athlete with a higher strength reserve is capable of performing at a higher level. Therefore, a strength and conditioning coach should aim to help athletes reach the highest possible level of maximum strength during the weekly time devoted to strength training in a rational ratio with more sport-specific sessions, in order to prevent a negative transfer.

Strength Training and Neuromuscular Adaptations

Systematic strength training produces structural and functional changes, or adaptations, in the body. The level of adaptation is evidenced by the size and strength of the muscles. The magnitude of these adaptations is directly proportional to the demands placed on the body by the volume (quantity), frequency, and intensity (load) of training, as well as the body's capability to adapt to such demands. Training rationally adapts to the stress of increasing physical work. In other words, if the body is presented with a demand rationally greater than it is accustomed to and enough recovery time is given to trained physiological systems, it adapts to the stressor by becoming stronger.

Until a few years ago, we believed that strength was determined mainly by the muscles' cross-sectional area (CSA). As a result, weight training was used to increase "engine size"—that is, to produce muscular hypertrophy. However, though CSA is the single best predictor of an individual's strength (Lamb 1984), strength training research since the 1980s (and authors such as Zatsiorsky and Bompa) have shifted the focus to the neural component of strength expression. In fact, the primary role of the nervous system in strength expression was well documented by a 2001 review (Broughton).

Neural adaptations to strength training involve disinhibition of inhibitory mechanisms, as well as intra- and intermuscular coordination improvements. Disinhibition affects the following mechanisms:

- Golgi tendon organs—sensory receptors, located near the myotendinous junction, that elicit a reflex inhibition of the muscle they supply when it undergoes excessive tension, either by shortening or passive stretching

- Renshaw cells—inhibitory connecting neurons (interneurons) found in the spinal cord, whose role is to dampen the rate of discharge of alpha motor neurons, thus preventing the muscular damage derived from tetanic contraction

- Supraspinal inhibitory signals—conscious or unconscious inhibitory signals that come from the brain

The components of intramuscular coordination are as follows:

- Synchronization—the capacity to contract motor units simultaneously or with a minimum latency (that is, with a delay less than five milliseconds)
- Recruitment—the capacity to recruit motor units simultaneously
- Rate coding—the capacity to increase firing rate (motor unit discharge rate) in order to express more strength

Adaptations in intramuscular coordination transfer well from one exercise to another, as long as the specific motor pattern is established (intermuscular coordination). For instance, the maximum voluntary recruitment of motor units developed through maximum strength training can be transferred to a sport-specific exercise skill as long as its technique is known by the athlete. The objective of maximum strength macrocycles is to improve motor unit recruitment of the prime movers, whereas power macrocycles work mainly on rate coding. Contrary to popular belief, these two aspects of intramuscular coordination—recruitment and rate coding—play greater determinant roles than synchronization does in muscular force production.

Intermuscular coordination, on the other hand, is the capacity of the nervous system to coordinate the "rings" of the kinetic chain, thus making the gesture more efficient. With time, as the nervous system learns the gesture, fewer motor units get activated by the same weight, which leaves more motor units available for activation by higher weights (see figure 2.5, *a* and *b*). Therefore, to increase the weight lifted in a given exercise over the long term, intermuscular coordination training (technique training) is the key.

Despite the fact that the hypertrophic response to training is immediate (Ploutz, et al. 1994), the accretion of muscular protein becomes evident only after six weeks or more (Moritani and deVries 1979; Rasmussen and Phillips 2003). These proteins, which represent the specific adaptive response to the imposed training, stabilize the achieved neural adaptations. This is the way to read the famous study by Moritani and deVries (see figure 2.6) because the neural adaptations, once they take place, are neither at their full potential nor absolutely stable. Therefore, to increase strength over time, one must keep training the factors discussed here. This is particularly true of intermuscular coordination, which allows load increase in the midterm and the long term on the basis of ever-increasing system efficiency, as well as specific hypertrophy.

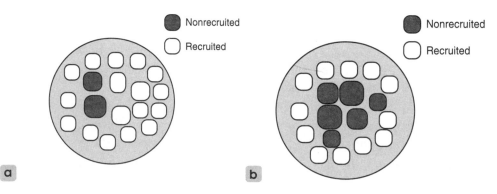

Figure 2.5 Over time, strength training for intermuscular coordination reduces the motor unit activation necessary to lift the same load, thus leaving more motor units available for higher loads.

For years, Eastern European training methodologists and coaches have been using training intensity zones as brackets of 1RM to design and analyze strength training programs. According to most of the strength training methodology literature, the best training zones to elicit maximum strength gains were zones 2 and 1 (loads from 85 percent and up). In more recent years, the focus has shifted from zone 1 loads (those over 90 percent) to zone 3 loads (those from 70 percent to 80 percent). This shift has occurred on the basis of field experience of weightlifters (except for the Bulgarian and Greek schools and their North American clones, who have used very high intensities very frequently and, not coincidentally, have had a sad story of positive doping tests), as well as Russian and Italian powerlifters.

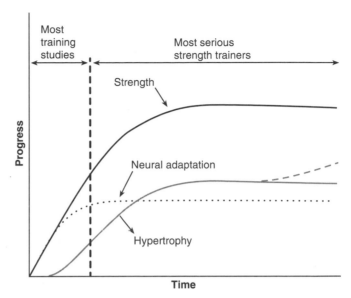

Figure 2.6 Neural and muscular adaptations to strength training over time, according to Moritani and deVries (1979).

Adapted, by permission, from T. Moritani and H.A. deVries, 1979, "Neural factors versus hypertrophy in the time course of muscle strength gain," *American Journal of Physical Medicine* 58(3):115-130.

That is, analysis of the best weightlifters' programs (Roman 1986) and powerlifters has shown a concentration of training loads in zone 3. Again, identifying zone 3 as the most important zone for maximum strength development is a fundamental change because almost all classic literature about strength training has indicated that training loads for maximum strength development should be 85 percent of 1RM or higher.

The field has shown us that

a. the majority of adaptations of the neuromuscular system necessary to increase maximum strength involve loads lower than 90 percent of 1RM and

b. the time of exposure to loads of 90 percent or higher (necessary in order to elicit adaptations specific to that intensity range) should be very short.

Table 2.2 summarizes the neuromuscular adaptations for each intensity range. From this table, we learn that

• the majority of intramuscular coordination gains involve loads over 80 percent;

• the majority of intermuscular coordination gains involve loads under 80 percent; and

• we need to use the full spectrum of intensities to maximize neuromuscular adaptations and, consequently, maximum strength.

From this table, taking into consideration the training methodology, we can infer the following points.

• In a preparation phase with limited time for development of maximum strength—or when the coaching of the same group of athletes will probably last only one season—the average intensities used in the maximum strength macrocycles will be higher (80 percent to 85 percent of 1RM). This approach is usually taken in team sports.

Table 2.2 Neural Adaptations According to Strength Training Zones

Adaptations	INTENSITY ZONES (% OF 1RM)					
	6	5	4	3	2	1
	40–60	60–70	70–80	80–85	85–90	90–100
Intramuscular coordination:						
• Synchronization	****	****	****	****	****	****
• Recruitment	**	***	****	****	****	****
• Rate coding	****	***	***	***	****	****
Intermuscular coordination	****	****	***	***	**	*
Disinhibition of inhibitory mechanisms	*	***	***	***	****	****
Specific hypertrophy	**	****	****	***	**	**

Adaptation stimulus: **** = very high; *** = high; ** = medium; * = low

All loads are supposed to be moved with the most explosive (and technically correct) concentric action that the load allows.

- In the preparation phase for an individual sport with ample time for development of maximum strength—and especially when a multiyear perspective projects continuous progression in the midterm and long term—the periodized strength plan will focus mostly on intermuscular coordination. Thus the average, not the peak, intensities used in maximum strength macrocycles will be lower (70 percent to 80 percent of 1RM).

- Nevertheless, for the development of maximum strength, every periodized plan starts with lower intensities, higher times under tension per set (which favor the anatomical adaptations), and a focus on technique so that higher intensities will elicit high muscular tension later on.

Because different types of adaptation can occur, periodization of strength offers a seven-phase approach that follows the physiological rhythm of the neuromuscular system's response to strength training. The seven phases are anatomical adaptation, hypertrophy, maximum strength, conversion, maintenance, cessation, and compensation. Depending on the physiological demands of the sport, the periodization of strength involves combining, in sequence, at least four of the phases: anatomical adaptation, maximum strength, conversion to specific strength, and maintenance. All models for periodization of strength begin with an anatomical adaptation phase. Five of the seven possible phases are discussed briefly in the following paragraphs. The remaining two phases—to be used during the taper and transition periods—are discussed in later chapters.

Phase 1: Anatomical Adaptation

The anatomical adaptation phase lays the foundation for the other phases of training. The name of this phase reflects the fact that the main objective of strength training is not to achieve an immediate overload but rather to elicit a progressive adaptation of the athlete's anatomy. The anatomical adaptation phase emphasizes "prehabilitation" in the hope of preventing the need for rehabilitation. The main physiological objectives of this phase are to (1) strengthen the tendons, ligaments, and joints, which is doable through a higher volume of training than in the remainder of the year, and (2) increase bone mineral content and proliferation of the connective tissue. In addition, regardless of the sport, this phase improves cardiovascular fitness, adequately challenges muscular strength, and tests and prompts the athlete to practice neuromuscular coordination for strength movement patterns. This phase does not focus on increasing the cross-sectional area of muscle, but that result may occur even so.

Tendons are strengthened by implementing a time under tension per set that falls between 30 and 70 seconds (the time under tension that sees the anaerobic lactic system as the main energy system). The hydrogen ions released by lactic acid have been proven to stimulate the release of growth hormone and therefore collagen synthesis, which is also stimulated by eccentric load (Crameri et al. 2004; Miller et al. 2005; Babraj et al. 2005; Kjaer et al. 2005; Doessing and Kjaer 2005; Langberg et al. 2007; Kjaer et al. 2006). For this reason, the majority of the time under tension is spent in the eccentric phase of the exercise (3 to 5 seconds per repetition). Muscular balance is achieved both by using an equal training volume between agonist and antagonist muscles around a joint and by making greater use of unilateral exercises than bilateral ones.

Phase 2: Hypertrophy

Hypertrophy—the enlargement of muscle size—is one of the most visible signs of adaptation to strength training. The two main physiological objectives of this phase are (1) to increase muscle cross-sectional area by increasing muscle protein content and (2) to increase storage capacity for high-energy substrates and enzymes. Many principles used in hypertrophy training are similar to those used in bodybuilding, but there are also differences. Specifically, athletic hypertrophy programs use a lower average number of reps per set, a higher average load, and a longer average rest interval between sets.

In addition, athletes should always try to move the weight as fast as possible during the concentric phase of the lift. Bodybuilders train to exhaustion using relatively light to moderate loads, whereas athletes rely on heavier loads and focus on movement speed and rest between sets. Although hypertrophic changes occur in both fast-twitch and slow-twitch muscle fibers, this way, with athletic hypertrophy training, more changes take place in the fast-twitch fibers (Tesch, Thorsson, and Kaiser 1984; Tesch and Larsson 1982). When hypertrophy training produces chronic changes, it provides a strong physiological basis for nervous system training.

When a muscle is forced to contract against a resistance, as happens in strength training, blood flow to the working muscle suddenly increases. This transient increase, known as short-term hypertrophy or "pump," temporarily increases the size of the muscle. Short-term hypertrophy is experienced during every strength training bout and usually lasts one to two hours after the training session. Although the benefits of a single bout of strength training are quickly lost, the additive benefits of multiple training sessions lead to a state of athletic hypertrophy, which results from structural changes at the muscle fiber level. Because it is caused by an increase in the size of muscle filaments, its effects endure. This form of hypertrophy is desired for athletes who use strength training to improve their athletic performance. In this manner, muscular adaptations result in a stronger muscular engine that is prepared to receive and apply nervous system signals.

Phase 3: Maximum Strength

In most sports, the development of maximum strength is probably the single most important variable. Maximum strength depends on the diameter of the cross-sectional area of the muscles, the capacity to recruit fast-twitch muscle fibers, their frequency of activation, and the ability to simultaneously call into action all the primary muscles involved in a given movement (Howard et al. 1985). These factors involve both structural and neural flow changes that occur as a function of training with moderate weights lifted explosively, as well as heavy loads (up to 90 percent of 1RM, or even more). These adaptive responses can also be elicited by eccentric training with loads greater than 100 percent of 1RM, although its practical application is limited to very few situations.

The popularity of maximum strength training is rooted in the positive increase in relative strength. Many sports—such as volleyball,

Football players rely on athletic hypertrophy to improve speed, agility, and power.

gymnastics, and boxing—require greater force generation without a concomitant increase in body weight. In fact, an increase in maximum strength without an associated increase in body weight characterizes the maximum strength phase as central nervous system training (Schmidtbleicher 1984).

An athlete could benefit from traditional maximum strength training methods, such as performing high loads with maximal rest (three to five minutes) between sets. However, to increase the weight lifted in an exercise over the long term, the key is intermuscular coordination training (technique training). With time, as the nervous system learns the gesture, fewer motor units get activated by the same weight, thus leaving more motor units available for activation by higher weights. In addition, the concentric action should be explosive in order to activate the fast-twitch muscle fibers (responsible for the highest and fastest force generation) and to achieve the highest specific hypertrophy.

Thus, intermuscular coordination training is the preferred method for general strength. That is, it provides the base for later macrocycles in which intramuscular coordination is trained by using higher loads and longer rest intervals. Furthermore, periodization of strength continually stresses and engages the nervous system by altering loads, sets, and training methods.

The physiological benefits for sport performance lie in an athlete's ability to convert gains in strength, and possibly muscle size, to the specific strength demanded by his or her particular sport. Building the foundation sets the stage, adding muscle generates force, and adapting the body to use heavy loads improves the capability to voluntarily involve its largest engines (the fast-twitch motor units). Once the mind–muscle connection is made, the physical requirements of the sport determine the next phase.

Phase 4: Conversion to Specific Strength

Depending on the sport, a maximum strength phase of training can be followed by one of three fundamental options: conversion to power, power endurance, or muscular endurance. Conversion to power or power endurance is accomplished by using relatively moderate to heavy loads (40 percent to 80 percent of 1RM) with the intention of moving the weight as quickly as possible, the difference being the duration of the sets. Engaging the nervous system, such methods as ballistic training and upper- or lower-body plyometric training improve an athlete's high-velocity strength or ability to recruit and engage the high-powered fast-twitch motor units. A strong foundation of maximum strength is a must for maximizing the rate of force production. In fact, even maximum strength training with high loads moved at low velocity has been shown to transfer to gains in power if the athlete attempts to move the weight as quickly as possible (Behm and Sale 1993).

Depending on the demands of the sport, muscular endurance can be trained for short, medium, or long duration. Short muscle endurance as the main energy system is the anaerobic lactic, whereas medium and long muscle endurance are predominately aerobic. Conversion to muscular endurance requires more than performing 15 to 20 reps per set; indeed, it can require as many as 400 reps per set, implemented concomitantly with metabolic training. In fact, metabolic training and muscular endurance training pursue similar physiological training objectives.

Recall that the body replenishes energy for muscular contractions through the combined efforts of three energy systems: the anaerobic alactic, the anaerobic lactic, and the aerobic. Training for conversion to muscular endurance requires heightened adaptation of the aerobic and the anaerobic lactic systems. The main objectives of aerobic training include improvement in physiological parameters, such as heart efficiency; biochemical parameters, such as increased mitochondria and capillary density, which result in greater diffusion and use of oxygen; and metabolic parameters, which result in greater use of fat as energy and an increased rate of removal and reuse of lactic acid. Adapting the neuromuscular and cardiovascular systems physiologically, biochemically, and metabolically provides invaluable benefit to athletes in many endurance sports. To maximize performance in muscular endurance sports, maximum strength training must be followed by a combination of specific metabolic training and specific strength training to prepare the body for the demands of the sport.

Phase 5: Maintenance

Once the neuromuscular system has been adapted for maximum performance, it is time to put the gains to the test. Unfortunately, most athletes and coaches work hard and strategically as the competitive season approaches but cease to train strength once the season begins. In reality, maintaining the strong and stable base formed during precompetitive phases requires the athlete to continue training during the competitive season. Failure to plan at least one weekly session dedicated to strength training results in decreased performance or early onset of fatigue as the season wears on.

Staying up is always easier than falling down and then attempting to get on one's feet again. Periodization of strength involves planning phases to optimize physiological adaptation and planning to maintain the benefits for as long as the season lasts. When the season is over, serious athletes can take two to four weeks off to regenerate their minds and bodies.

Stimulating the body for optimal performance takes time, planning, and persistence. Physiology is helpful in planning the program, but performance improvement is achieved through practical application of the many principles and methods of training inherent in the periodization of strength.

3

Energy Systems Training

This book focuses on discussing, in specific terms, the science, methodology, and objectives of strength training for sports. However, each sport has its own physiological profile, and all trainers who design and implement sport-specific programs must understand the human body's energy systems and how they apply to sport training. More specifically, the physiological complexity of each sport requires trainers to understand the energy systems dominant in a given sport and how they relate to strength training. Trainers who separate strength training and its programming requirements from other physiological characteristics of their sport make a mistake that, over time, may affect their rate of success. This chapter illustrates how to integrate strength training and the specific energy systems training needed by different sports.

Energy Systems

Energy is the capacity to perform work, which, in turn, is the application of force, or the contracting of muscles to apply force against a resistance. Therefore, of course, energy is required in order to perform physical work during a sport activity. The body derives energy from muscle cells' conversion of the components of foods' macronutrients into a high-energy compound called adenosine triphosphate (ATP), which is stored in muscle cells. As its name suggests, ATP consists of one molecule of adenosine and three molecules of phosphate. Adenosine diphosphate (ADP), on the other hand, consists of one molecule of adenosine and two molecules of phosphate. In the process of creating energy, ATP is broken down into ADP + P (phosphate). To ensure a steady supply of ATP for a continuous supply of energy, ADP attaches itself to another phosphate molecule to reproduce ATP. This extra phosphate is donated by creatine phosphate, which is also stocked in the muscle cell.

When an athlete trains with weights or performs metabolic exercise, the energy required for muscular contraction is released by converting high-energy ATP into ADP + P. When this energy is released, movement is performed. In order to continue training, the body must continually replenish its cells' ATP supply, because it can store only a limited amount of ATP in muscle cells (5 to 6 millimoles per kilogram of wet muscle) and because a cell cannot fully use its own ATP (which is used up to 60 percent to 70 percent at the most).

The Three Energy Systems

The body can replenish its ATP supply by using any one of three energy systems, depending on the type of training: the anaerobic alactic (or ATP-CP) system, the anaerobic lactic system, or the aerobic system.

Anaerobic Alactic (ATP-CP) System

Muscles can store only a small amount of adenosine triphosphate (ATP). For this reason, energy is depleted rapidly by strenuous training. For example, the ATP stored in muscle may fuel only the first two seconds of an all-out sprint or the first 2 to 5 reps of an exhausting 12- to 15-rep set. If the athlete feels a burning sensation in the exercising muscles by the end of the 15th rep, this is an indication that both the ATP-CP and the lactic acid systems were involved in releasing energy during the set.

In response to the depletion of ATP in the muscle, creatine phosphate (CP), also called phosphocreatine, breaks down into creatine (C) and phosphate (P). Like ATP, creatine phosphate is stored in muscle cells. The transformation of CP into C and P does not release energy immediately usable for muscular contraction. Rather, the body uses this energy to resynthesize ADP + P into ATP, which, as we have seen, is usable energy for muscle contraction.

Because CP is stored in limited amounts, the ATP-CP system can supply energy for only a very brief time—up to 8 to 10 seconds of maximum effort (energy for submaximal effort can be provided for slightly longer). This system is the body's chief source of energy for extremely quick and explosive activities, such as the 60-meter dash, diving, weightlifting, and jumping and throwing events in track and field. Because dietary creatine can increase cells' volume by increasing their water content and can sustain protein synthesis, as well as increase the energy capacity of the anaerobic alactic system, creatine supplements have become popular among athletes who value strength, size, and power for such activities as sprinting, throwing, playing hockey or soccer, and bodybuilding since the late 90s.

Anaerobic Lactic System

The body reacts differently to longer bouts of intense exercise (lasting between 10 and 60 seconds), such as the 200-meter and 400-meter dashes and weight training sets of up to 50 quick reps, those found in the conversion to short muscular endurance training phase. For the first 8 to 10 seconds, the anaerobic *alactic* system provides energy. Despite reaching its peak power of ATP production after only five to six seconds, it is after about 10 seconds that the anaerobic *lactic* system becomes the main provider of energy (Hultman and Sjoholm 1983).

The anaerobic lactic system provides energy by breaking down a substance called glycogen (the storage form of glucose or sugar in the body) that is stored in muscle cells and in the liver, which releases energy to resynthesize ATP from ADP + P. The absence of oxygen during the breakdown of glycogen creates a by-product called lactic acid. When high-intensity training continues for a prolonged time, large quantities of lactic acid accumulate in the muscle, causing fatigue and gradually preventing the body from maintaining the same level of power output.

Continuous use of glycogen during exercise eventually causes glycogen to be depleted. Glycogen can be easily restored by eating simple carbohydrate right after training (especially in the form of carbohydrate powders, such as maltodextrines and amylopectin) and then eating complex carbohydrate (starches), fruits, and vegetables, as well as getting plenty of rest.

Aerobic System

The aerobic system requires 60 to 80 seconds to start producing energy for the resynthesis of ATP. Unlike the other systems, this one allows the resynthesis of ATP in the presence of oxygen, meaning that it can resynthesize energy through the breakdown of glycogen, fat, and protein. For this process to happen, the required amount of oxygen must be transported to the muscle cells, which requires an increase in heart rate and in the rate of breathing. Both the anaerobic lactic (anaerobic glycolysis) and aerobic (aerobic glycolysis) systems use glycogen as the source of energy for resynthesizing ATP. However, unlike the anaerobic lactic system, the aerobic system produces little or no lactic acid, thus enabling the body to continue to exercise.

As a result, the aerobic system is the primary energy source for events lasting from just over one minute to three hours. Prolonged work beyond two hours may result in the

Track athletes in events longer than 800 meters primarily use the aerobic energy system to break down glycogen, fat, and protein to fuel the body.

breakdown of fat and protein, substances that are needed to replenish ATP as the body's glycogen supply is depleted. In all cases, the breakdown of glycogen, fat, or protein produces by-products in the form of carbon dioxide and water, both of which are eliminated from the body through breathing and sweating. As a person's aerobic capacity improves, her or his ability to use fat for fuel also improves.

Bridging the Theory–Practice Gap in Energy Systems Training

Coaches without real knowledge of energy systems often intuitively develop programs that train the dominant energy system for their sport. For instance, sprint coaches intuitively train their athletes with sprint distances even though they are unfamiliar with the benefits of such training on the nervous system and the anaerobic energy systems. However, energy systems training should also take into consideration the recruitment of muscle fiber types. Improvement in energy system efficiency depends on the neuromuscular system's ability to withstand the development of tension and fatigue resulting from chronic training. For instance, continual training of the anaerobic lactic system makes the fast-twitch muscle fibers able to generate force in the presence of lactic acid accumulation. This result is accomplished through an increase in motor unit recruitment and the reuse of lactic acid by the slow-twitch muscle fibers. Anaerobic metabolism can be maximized by designing a program that combines maximum strength and power endurance training with 150- to 400-meter sprinting.

The energy system tapped to produce energy during an athletic activity depends directly on the intensity and duration of the activity. The anaerobic alactic system primarily produces energy for all sports of short duration (up to 8 to 10 seconds), in which speed and power are the dominant abilities. Alactic system-dominant sports include short sprinting, throwing and jumping events in track and field, ski jumping, diving, vaulting in gymnastics, and Olympic weightlifting. The movements in these sports are explosive and of short duration and use high loads; in other words, they require maximum strength and power. Therefore, the anaerobic alactic energy system is used in conjunction with the recruitment of a high number of fast-twitch muscle fibers (for maximum strength) and an increase in the discharge rate of those fibers (for maximum power).

The anaerobic lactic system, on the other hand, is the main energy provider for high-intensity sporting activities of prolonged duration (15 to 60 seconds). A partial list of anaerobic lactic system-dominant sports includes the 200- and 400-meter running events in track and field, 50-meter swimming, track cycling, and 500-meter speedskating. Performance in these sports requires maximum power of both the anaerobic alactic system and the anaerobic lactic system. The maximum capacity of the anaerobic metabolism is required for sports of slightly longer duration, such as mid-distance events in track and field, 100- and 200-meter swimming, 500-meter canoeing and kayaking, 1,000-meter speedskating, most events in gymnastics, alpine skiing, rhythmic gymnastics, and pursuit in track cycling.

The purpose of strength training for these sports is to develop either power endurance or muscle endurance of short duration. The athlete must be able not only to increase the discharge rate of the fast-twitch muscle fibers but also to maintain the level of discharge for a longer time (from 10 to 120 seconds). Recall that gains in power endurance and muscular endurance of short duration are possible only as a result of increasing maximum strength. Therefore, athletes in these sports should develop a strong foundation of maximum strength.

As previously mentioned, the aerobic energy system is used to produce the energy for sports ranging from one minute to more than three hours. Many coaches have difficulty understanding how to train for events with such a wide range of duration. As a rule of thumb, the closer the event's duration is to one minute, the lower the aerobic contribution to overall performance will be. The opposite is also true: The longer the duration is, the more dominant the aerobic system will be.

The same reasoning applies if we want to differentiate between power and capacity of the aerobic energy system. The power output reached at maximum aerobic power can usually be sustained for 6 minutes (Billat et al. 2013), whereas maximum aerobic power can be maintained up to 15 minutes if the power output is adjusted (Billat et al. 1999). Therefore, any event lasting 1 to 15 minutes requires a high level of aerobic power; in addition, for events longer than 15 minutes, the closer to the 15-minute limit the event is, the higher the required aerobic power level is, as compared with the higher aerobic capacity requirements for longer events. Many sports belong in the aerobic-dominant category: long- (and to some degree mid-) distance events in track and field; swimming; speedskating, 1,000-meter kayaking and canoeing; wrestling; figure skating; synchronized swimming; rowing; cross-country skiing; cycling (road races); and triathlon. Athletes in all of these sports benefit physiologically from training muscular endurance of medium or long duration.

Although most sports fall somewhere along a clear continuum of varying energy system contributions, special consideration must be applied to team sports, boxing, the martial arts, and racket sports—that is, to sports characterized by intermittent activity. In these sports, all three energy systems are used according to the intensity, rhythm, and duration of the competition. Most of these sports use the anaerobic energy pathway during the active part of competition and rely on strong aerobic power for quick recovery and regeneration between actions (Bogdanis et al. 1996) (creatine phosphate resynthesis through the aerobic phosphorylation). As a result, this sport category requires a high proportion of training dedicated to the improvement of maximum strength, power, and power endurance.

Table 3.1 illustrates the relationships between the energy systems and the type of strength training suggested for the sports falling into each category. This table clearly shows the need for maximum strength training throughout the energy system continuum. Regardless of whether the sport is primarily anaerobic, aerobic, or characterized by equal contributions from both systems, the development of maximum strength provides the foundation on which other dominant abilities are maximized. More specifically, increased

Table 3.1 Relationships Between Energy Systems and Strength Training Methods

ENERGY SYSTEM	ANAEROBIC (OXYGEN INDEPENDENT)				AEROBIC (OXYGEN DEPENDENT)		
	Alactic		Lactic acid				
Modality	Power	Capacity	Power	Capacity	Power		Capacity
Duration	1–6 seconds	7–8 seconds	8–20 seconds	20–60 seconds	1–2 minutes	2–8 minutes	8–>120 minutes
Type of strength training needed	MxS, P		MxS, P, PE	MxS, P, PE, MES	MxS, P, PE, MEM	MxS, PE, MEM	MxS (<80% of 1RM), PE, MEL

Key: MEL= muscle endurance long, MEM = muscle endurance medium, MES = muscle endurance short, MxS = maximum strength, P = power, and PE = power endurance.

muscle fiber density (the laying down of protein filaments in muscle) and improved motor unit recruitment patterns result in more muscle being available for use in sports that require a high power output (anaerobic-dominant sports) and in endurance-based sports, as the slow-twitch muscle fibers increase in size and provide greater surface area for capillarization and mitochondrial density.

Again, every sport has its own physiological profile and its own distinctive combination of required biomotor abilities. Consequently, effective training specialists understand intimately what separates one sport from another and successfully apply these physiological principles in the day-to-day training process. To help you apply sport-specific characteristics in training, the following passages discuss how energy systems relate to metabolic training and how the six intensity zones can be used in most sport training along with strength training.

To better understand the relationship between the duration of effort and the contribution of energy systems to energy production, please refer to table 3.2. As you can infer from table 3.2, the transition from anaerobic to aerobic dominance in energy contribution happens once the effort lasts more than one minute (see figure 3.1).

Table 3.2 demonstrates that a number of sports demand the energy produced by all three energy systems. When a sport combines energy systems, the training and physiology associated with that sport are more complex. The spectrum of energy systems training—and their individual zones' physiological and training characteristics—are reflected in the six intensity zones presented in table 3.3. The table indicates the type of training for each intensity zone, the suggested duration of reps or drills, the suggested number of reps, the necessary rest interval to achieve the training goal, the lactic acid concentration following a rep, and the percentage of maximum intensity necessary to stimulate a given energy system.

However, practical application of the six intensity zones must be planned according to an athlete's potential, his or her work tolerance, and the specifics of a given training phase. The following brief analysis of the intensity zones addresses certain details of each type of energy systems training. The application of intensity zones to an athlete's training is usually more familiar to coaches of individual sports than to coaches of team sports. The methodology used to apply the intensity zones to the training of any sport determines the training efficiency and performance outcome.

Table 3.2 Energy System Contributions in Track-and-Field Performance

Event	Duration	ATP-CP	GLYCOGEN Lactic	GLYCOGEN Aerobic	Triglyceride (fatty acid)
100 m	10 sec.	53%	44%	3%	—
200 m	20 sec.	26%	45%	29%	—
400 m	45 sec.	12%	50%	38%	—
800 m	1 min. 45 sec.	6%	33%	61%	—
1,500 m	3 min. 40 sec.	—	20%	80%	—
5,000 m	13 min.	—	12.5%	87.5%	—
10,000 m	27 min.	—	3%	97%	—
Marathon	2 hr. 10 min.	—	—	80%	20%

Sources: K.A. van Someren, 2006, The physiology of anaerobic endurance training. In *The physiology of training*, edited by G. Whyte (Oxford, UK: Elsevier), 88; E. Newsholme, A. Leech, and G. Duester, 1994, *Keep on running: The science of training and performance* (West Sussex, UK: Wiley).

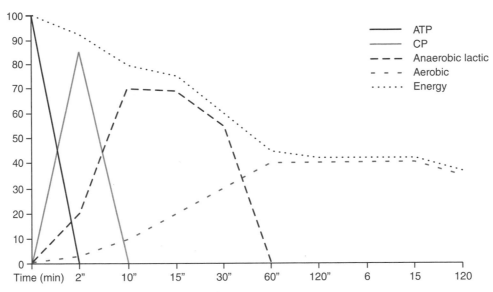

Figure 3.1 Energy provision of the energy systems.

Table 3.3 Physiological Characteristics of Energy Systems Training and Its Six Intensity Zones

Intensity zone	Type of training	Duration of rep	Number of reps	Rest interval (work-to-rest ratio)	TRAINING MODALITY		% of max intensity
					Sets	Series of sets	
1	Alactic system	1–8 sec.	6–12	1:50–1:100	✓	✓	95–100
2	Lactic system (power—short)	3–10 sec.	10–20	1:5–1:20	✓	✓	95–100
	Lactic system (power—long)	10–20 sec.	1–3	1:40–1:130	✓	—	95–100
	Lactic system (capacity)	20–60 sec.	2–10	1:4–1:24	✓	✓	80–95

Intensity zone	Type of training	Duration of rep	Number of reps	Rest interval (work-to-rest ratio)	Lactic acid concentration (mmol)	% of max heart rate	% of $\dot{V}O_2max$
3	Max oxygen consumption	1–6 min.	8–25	1:1–1:4	6–12	98–100	95–100
4	Anaerobic threshold training	1–10 min.	3–40	1:0.3–1:1	4–6	85–95	80–90
5	Aerobic threshold training	10–120 min.	— (continuous steady state)		2–3	75–80	60–70
6	Aerobic compensation	5–30 min.	— (continuous steady state)		2–3	55–75	45–60

Intensity Zone 1

Anaerobic alactic system training is the sport-specific energy system for all sports in which the anaerobic alactic energy system is dominant and in which the scope is to train speed and explosiveness. To benefit from training in intensity zone 1, athletes must use very short (no longer than eight-second), fast, or explosive reps or technical and tactical drills. To do so, they must plan intensities of sport-specific exercises at over 95 percent of their maximum performance, with a rest interval long enough for complete fuel restoration (creatine phosphate).

The main scope of this training is to increase acceleration, maximum speed, fast first steps, quick reaction, and fast but short performance of technical and tactical drills using ATP and creatine phosphate (CP) in the muscle as fuel. To fully replenish the muscles' CP supply, the athlete requires long recovery intervals between reps. If the rest interval is disregarded, as often happens in some team sports and martial arts, the restoration of CP is incomplete. As a result, anaerobic glycolysis gradually becomes a major source of energy (from alactic capacity to lactic power with short distances). This condition produces high amounts of lactic acid that force the athlete to either stop or slow down the action (and, in the worst case scenario, risk injury).

In novice athletes, an aggressive increase in lactic acid buildup is often followed by muscle stiffness and discomfort, as well as a decrease in performance intensity. This result can be avoided by allowing full recovery, which usually requires a rest interval of one minute for every second of maximal effort between acceleration or speed reps and an interval of three to eight minutes between maximum-strength sets (depending on the percentage of 1RM, as well as the athlete's body weight, strength level, and neuromuscular efficiency). Recovery can also be aided by light stretching of the antagonist muscles and by massage of the agonist muscles between sets.

Intensity Zone 2

Lactic acid training increases an athlete's ability to perform during lactic efforts and tolerate lactic acid buildup; it is useful for fast reps of 15 to 90 seconds. Very high levels of lactic acid buildup can result from high-intensity reps of 40 to 50 seconds, although the fastest rate of lactic acid accumulation happens with maximum effort between 12 and 16 seconds. Power output during lactic efforts is improved via the increase of the lactic energy system's metabolic enzymes, as well as adaptations of the nervous system. In fact, performance in lactic power events (10 to 20 seconds in duration) seems to be subject to a major limitation involving the nervous system's ability to maintain the frequency of discharge to the muscles rather than any metabolic reasons (Vittori 1991).

On the other hand, lactic acid tolerance increases as a result of skeletal muscles' repeated removal of lactic acid from the bloodstream. Recent studies have demonstrated that lactate transporters increase in number as a function of high-intensity training (Bonen 2001). The ability to clear lactic acid from the bloodstream and transport it to slow-twitch muscle fibers for energy usage is an adaptive response that delays fatigue and inevitably improves performance in sports that require lactic acid tolerance.

An athlete can perform better for longer if his or her nervous system is trained to maintain the frequency of discharge for the duration of a lactic effort or if he or she can tolerate the pain of acidosis (high lactic acid concentrations in the blood). Therefore, the purposes of training in intensity zone 2 are to adapt to the nervous strain of longer maximum-intensity efforts, to resist the acidic effect of lactic acid buildup, to buffer the effects of lactic acid, to increase lactic acid removal from the working muscles, and to increase the athlete's physiological and psychological tolerance of the pain of training and of challenging competitions.

Training for intensity zone 2 comes in the following three variations.

1. **Lactic power short:** Organize a series of shorter near-maximum and maximum-intensity reps or drills (3 to 10 seconds) with shorter rest intervals (15 seconds to 4 minutes, depending on duration of effort, number of reps, and relative intensity) that result in only partial removal of lactic acid from the system. The physiological consequence of this type of training is that the athlete tolerates increased amounts of lactic acid while producing high levels of anaerobic power under the condition of extreme acidosis. This method is often used as the competitive season approaches and the athlete's system is challenged to the maximum capacity.

2. **Lactic power long:** Organize near-maximum and maximum-intensity reps of longer duration (10 to 20 seconds) that make the lactic acid energy system work at its maximum rate of energy production. This method is one of the highest possible stressors for the neuromuscular system. Therefore, to repeat the same quality of work, the athlete needs very long rest intervals (12 to 30 minutes, depending on the athlete's performance level and the number of reps) to facilitate complete removal of lactic acid and recovery of the central nervous system. If the rest interval is not long enough, recovery is incomplete, and injury risk is high.

3. **Lactic capacity:** Organize high-intensity reps of longer duration (20 to 60 seconds) that result in increased amounts (well over 12 millimoles) of lactic acid. To repeat the same quality of work, the athlete needs moderate rest intervals (four to eight minutes, depending on duration of effort, number of reps, and relative intensity) to facilitate near-complete removal of lactic acid. If the rest interval is not long enough, removal is incomplete, and acidosis is severe. Under these conditions, the athlete is forced to slow the speed of a rep or drill below the intended level. Consequently, the athlete does not achieve the planned training effect, which is to increase his or her ability to tolerate lactic acid buildup. Rather, the athlete will end up training the aerobic system.

Psychologically, the purpose of lactic tolerance training is to push the athlete beyond the pain threshold. However, this type of training should not be used more than two times per week, because it exposes the athlete to critical levels of fatigue. Overdoing it may bring the athlete closer to the undesirable effects of injury, overreaching, and overtraining.

Intensity Zone 3

Maximum oxygen consumption training elicits physiological adaptations such as increases in plasma volume, stroke volume and cardiac output, capillarization, and, ultimately, maximal oxygen consumption. In other words, these adaptations result in increased efficiency in oxygen transportation and usage. This increase is important because training and competition heavily tax both the central system (including the heart and lungs) and the peripheral system (including the muscles, capillaries, and mitochondria). Therefore, improved oxygen transportation to the muscle cell (and, especially, increased efficiency in oxygen use) improves performance in sports in which the aerobic system is dominant or very important.

Achieving these effects requires training periods of one to six minutes at 90 percent to 100 percent of maximum oxygen consumption (higher intensity for shorter reps and slightly lower intensity for longer reps). The number of reps performed in a training session depends on the specific duration of the sporting event—the longer the duration, the lower the number of (longer) reps. Therefore, in a given training session, an athlete might derive similar benefits from performing, say, six reps of three minutes each at 100 percent of $\dot{V}O_2$max or eight reps of five minutes each at 95 percent of $\dot{V}O_2$max. This zone of training is very popular in sports (such as hockey) that alternate high-intensity movement with rest between shifts.

Intensity Zone 4

Anaerobic threshold training refers to an intensity of work in which the rate of lactic acid diffusion in the blood equals the rate of removal (4 to 6 millimoles). The objective of training in this zone is to increase the intensity at which the 4-millimole rate is reached (that is, to raise the anaerobic threshold) so that the athlete can maintain intensive work without accumulating excessive lactic acid.

This training can use shorter reps of one to six minutes with an intensity between 85 percent and 90 percent of $\dot{V}O_2$max or 92 percent to 96 percent of maximum heart rate but with slightly longer rests between bouts (work-to-rest ratio between 1:0.5 and 1:1). Such training can stimulate the anaerobic metabolism without a significant rise in lactic acid production. This effect can also be achieved through longer reps: five to seven 8- to 15-minute reps at 80 percent to 85 percent of $\dot{V}O_2$max or 87 percent to 92 percent of maximum heart rate with a work-to-rest ratio between 1:0.3 and 1:0.5.

Intensity zone 4 is often used in combination with intensity zone 2 (within the microcycle) as the athlete pushes the body to tolerate lactic acid buildup by training at the threshold of lactate accumulation. Remember that without imposing a new physiological challenge, the athlete cannot experience overcompensation or an increase in physical performance beyond the previous level of adaptation.

Intensity Zone 5

Aerobic threshold training is intended to increase an athlete's aerobic capacity, which is vital in many sports, especially those in which the oxygen supply functions as a limiting factor for performance. Examples include medium- and long-duration running, swimming, and rowing. This type of training develops the functional efficiency of the cardiorespiratory system and the economical functioning of the metabolic system and increases the athlete's capacity to tolerate stress for long periods of time.

As with any other intensity zone, when training in this intensity zone, sufficient hydration is very important. Insufficient hydration can reduce skin blood flow and the rate of sweating, which reduces heat dissipation and therefore can lead to hyperthermia (Coyle 1999). This effect, of course, can tremendously hinder performance by impairing cardiac output, stroke volume, and blood flow to the working muscles.

The purpose of aerobic threshold training is to increase aerobic capacity through the use of a high volume of work, either without interruption at a uniform pace or through interval training with long reps (over 10 minutes) at intensities of moderate to medium-fast speed (with a lactic acid concentration of 2 to 3 millimoles and a heart rate of about 130 to 150 beats per minute). The ideal time to improve the aerobic capacity of athletes is during the preparatory phase.

Athletes in team sports, combative sports, and racket sports respond best when aerobic training is not planned in the traditional form of long, easy, distance runs. These sports require interval training repetitions in general preparation and specific high-intensity tactical drills in the second part of the preparatory phase. Athletes involved in long-distance events, on the other hand, must use aerobic threshold training even during the competitive phase so that they continue to support the physiological environment that uses free fatty acid as a primary source of fuel.

Intensity Zone 6

Aerobic compensation training facilitates athletes' recovery following competitions and the high-intensity training sessions characteristic of intensity zones 2 and 3. Specifically, to eliminate metabolites from the system and speed recovery and regeneration, workouts must be planned using very light intensity (45 to 60 percent of $\dot{V}O_2max$).

High-intensity endurance training is a necessary component of adaptation and performance enhancement. However, strenuous exercise often negatively affects the body before it can recover and become stronger. Recovery and regeneration can be aided by active recovery methods such as cycling or running for 5 to 20 minutes at about 50 percent of maximum capacity.

In contrast, following strenuous endurance-type training with static rest (such as lying or sitting down) can delay regeneration of the body's systems and removal of the by-products of training. Recovery and regeneration are slowed by elevated levels of plasma cortisol and adrenaline and by decreased levels of white blood cells and low levels of immune system catalysts such as neutrophils and monocytes (Hagberg et al. 1979; Jezova et al. 1985; Wigernaes et al. 2001).

On the other hand, active recovery (along with proper postworkout nutrition) has been shown to counteract the increase in cortisol and adrenaline; override the drop in white blood cell count; and eliminate the drop in neutrophil and monocyte count (Hagberg et al. 1979; Jezova et al. 1985; Wigernaes et al. 2001). In other words, active recovery reignites immune system function following strenuous training, which in turn allows the body to regenerate faster.

Therefore, by the end of the training session, the difficult part of the workout is complete, but athletes who are willing to live with the sacrifice needed for improvement and adaptation should devote another 15 to 20 minutes to foster healing and regeneration. Choosing not to do so slows the recovery process and may negatively affect the next training session; it also leads to overtraining and injury. During very demanding weeks of training, intensity zone 6 may be used one to three times, sometimes in combination with other intensities (in that case at the end of a workout).

The six intensity zones for training the energy systems apply not only to athletes in endurance-dominant sports but also to those in team, contact, and racket sports, who can also benefit greatly from developing sport-specific physical abilities through this training methodology. These sports use the three energy systems in specific proportions. Therefore, the sport-specific proportion must be properly trained by using specific technical and tactical drills designed with knowledge of the intensity and duration of the six intensity zones.

For instance, to train the anaerobic alactic system, athletes do not have to plan only short, maximum-velocity sprints. They can realize the same, yet more specific, benefits by using specific and short but very fast technical or tactical drills. The closer the technical and tactical skills are to those used in the sport, the greater the specific adaptations will be.

Special consideration should be given to training in intensity zone 5, which traditionally involves long-distance, slow-pace jogging. Athletes are more successful and react more positively if they use technical or tactical drills with lower intensity but with the duration, number of reps, and rest intervals suggested in table 3.3.

In intensity zone 6 (aerobic compensation training), training is usually organized following a game or tournament or a very demanding workout session. The desired compensation benefits can be achieved through low-intensity, longer-duration technical drills, especially if the session is fun and incorporates psychological relaxation and physiotherapeutic techniques, such as massage and stretching.

How to Integrate Strength and Energy Systems Training

Now that we have addressed the six zones for training the energy systems, the question is how to integrate them with sport-specific strength training programs. The following sections provide examples focused mostly on two types of plan—the annual plan and the microcycle—because these two are the most important and practical of all the plans in the methodology of training. More information on microcycles and annual plans is presented in chapters 9 and 10, respectively.

Annual Plan

Sport training is complex because every sport requires time for the athlete to develop in a variety of areas: technical and tactical skills; sport-specific speed, endurance, strength, power, agility, and quickness; and social and psychological relationships. The question is how to integrate these complex training elements to ensure peak performance and facilitate recovery and regeneration after competition and between training sessions. To help answer this question, figures 3.2-3.9 illustrate the application of strength and energy systems training in various annual plans and microcycles. Generally, energy systems training progresses from the preparatory phase to the competitive phase so that best adaptation is reached at the right time for major competitions. Improvements are possible only if adaptation increases from year to year.

Figure 3.2 presents an annual plan used by a college basketball team, but you can use this model to design annual training plans for other team sports as well. The first two rows indicate the months of the year and the specific training phases for a college basketball team. The next two rows present periodization of strength, endurance, and speed. The figure suggests the following phases for the periodization of strength: anatomical adaptation; maximum strength; and the conversion of maximum strength to sport-specific power and power endurance, which, in turn, improve agility and quickness.

The order in which the energy system zones are listed for each training phase indicates the emphasis placed on each energy system. For instance, in the first two microcycles, a higher volume of training for intensity zone 4 (anaerobic threshold training) than for intensity zone 3 is suggested.

The progression from aerobic-dominant types of training (intensity zones 4 and 3) to lactic acid tolerance and anaerobic alactic system training (zone 1, acceleration, quickness, and agility) should follow the natural progression of the annual plan, beginning with the preparatory phase and moving into the competitive phase. In each training phase, the intensity zones are prioritized—the first intensity is always the main training objective.

During the early preparatory phase (July and early August), nonspecific training methods can be used; from the second part of August onward, however, sport-specific drills must be prioritized. The coach must design specific drills that train sport-specific intensities in preparation for the competitive phase (intensity zones 1, 2, and 3).

Periodization month	July	Aug.	Sept.	Oct.	Nov.	Dec.	Jan.	Feb.	Mar.	Apr.	May	June
Training phase	Preparatory				Competitive						Transition	
Periodization of strength	AA	MxS	P, PE		Maintenance: MxS, P, PE						Compensation	
Periodization of endurance and speed (energy systems training zones)	Weeks 1 and 2: 4, 3 Weeks 3 and 4: 3 Weeks 5 and 6: 3, 2	3, 2, 1, 6	2, 1, 3, 6		2, 1, 3, 6						5	

Key: AA = anatomical adaptation and MxS = maximum strength, P = power, and PE = power endurance.

Figure 3.2 Suggested Guidelines for Integrating Strength and Energy Systems Training in a College Basketball Team's Annual Plan

Unlike team sports, many endurance-dominant individual sports involve an annual plan with one or two major peaks:

1. Annual plan with one peak (see figure 3.3): Sports with this type of plan include distance running, rowing, cross-country skiing, triathlon, road cycling, marathon canoeing, and speedskating. In this plan, the integration of energy systems and strength training is periodized to facilitate best performance during the competitive phase (months 8 to 11, or May to August for those in the Northern hemisphere). The first transition phase (T) is one week long, whereas the second transition phase is four weeks long.

2. Annual plan with two major peaks (see figure 3.4): Sports with this type of plan include those with indoor and outdoor championships (such as track and field) or winter and summer championships (such as swimming). Therefore, the energy systems and strength training are periodized to peak for the two competitive phases.

Macrocycle	1	2	3	4	5	6	7	8	9	10	11	12
Training phase	Prep.		T	Prep.				Comp.				T
Periodization of strength	AA	MxS (60–70% of 1RM)		MxS (70%–80% of 1RM), MEL		Maint.: MxS (70–80% of 1RM), MEL		Maint.: MxS (70%–80% of 1 RM), MEL				AA
Periodization of endurance (energy systems training zones)	5, 4		5	4, 5, 3		3, 4, 2, 5, 6		3, 4, 2, 6				5

Key: AA = anatomical adaptation, comp. = competitive, maint. = maintenance, MEL = muscle endurance long, MxS = maximum strength, prep. = preparatory, and T = transition.

Figure 3.3 Suggested Annual Plan for Endurance-Dominant Sports With One Peak (One Major Competitive Phase)

Periodization month	Oct.	Nov.	Dec.	Jan.	Feb.	Mar.	Apr.	May	June	July	Aug.	Sept.
Training phase	Prep. 1			Comp. 1			T	Prep. 2	Comp. 2			T
Periodization of strength	AA	MxS (70%–80% of 1RM)	ME	Maint.: MxS (70%–80% of 1RM), ME			AA	MxS (70%–80% of 1RM)	Maint.: MxS (70%–80% of 1RM), MEL			AA
Periodization of endurance (energy systems training zones)	5, 4		3, 2, 5, 4, 6	2, 3, 5, 4, 6			5	3, 2, 5, 4, 6	2, 3, 5, 4, 6			5

Key: AA = anatomical adaptation, ME = muscular endurance (either M-EM or ME-EL, depending on the event), MxS = maximum strength, and T = transition.

Figure 3.4 Suggested Annual Plan for Individual Endurance Sports With Two Peaks

The duration of the first transition phase (T) is two weeks. A one-week transition may also be planned after maximum strength training in each of the two preparatory phases. The second preparatory phase (prep. 2) is shorter in some sports, such as mid- and long-distance track-and-field events. In these cases, athletes must train the foundation of aerobic endurance during preparatory phase 1 and maintain it during the first phase of competition (comp. 1). Doing it differently would result in lower performance at the end of competitive phase 2, which is when major championships are scheduled.

You may have noticed that the suggested training intensities for aerobic-dominant sports shown in figures 3.3 and 3.4 do not include intensity zone 1 (anaerobic alactic system training). North American training specialists may find this absence surprising because they consider speed training (that is, anaerobic alactic system training) essential for good performance in these aerobic-dominant sports. However, for aerobic-dominant sports—road cycling, triathlon, distance running, cross-country skiing, marathons, and half marathons—speed trained for 1 to 10 seconds is immaterial to final performance.

Therefore, the key element to success in aerobic-dominant sports is not the high-velocity training typical of intensity zone 1 but the *mean* velocity per race, which is trained in intensity zones 3 through 5. In addition, training for intensity zone 1, which is often planned prior to major competitions, is far too stressful, both physiologically and psychologically. As a result, the athlete enters the race with undesirable residual fatigue in the muscles and nervous system. Thus, rather than stressing intensity zone 1, an athlete is better off using sensible strength training to achieve increases in speed and running economy.

For mid-distance events, on the other hand, intensity zone 1 is essential, along with strength training, for increasing maximum velocity. Even so, intensity zones 2, 3, and 4 must be stressed more than zone 1, in obvious proportions, because lactic acid tolerance, aerobic power, and anaerobic threshold level are key factors in these events.

Figure 3.5 presents an annual plan for contact sports, such as martial arts, boxing, and wrestling. Because competition dates can differ between sports, the months of the year are numbered rather than named. This is a tri-cyclic annual plan because it gears training to three major competitions. Such a plan is very condensed, and relatively complicated, because of the limited time available to establish the foundations of training. This is why, if possible, we make the first cycle longer, to spare more time for training fundamentals, including the improvement of technical skills.

Periodization month	1	2	3	4	5	6	7	8	9	10	11	12
Training phase	Prep. 1			Comp. 1	T	Prep. 2		Comp. 2	T	Prep. 3	Comp. 3	T
Periodization of strength	AA	MxS	P, PE	Maint.: P, PE	AA	MxS	P, PE	Maint.: P, PE	AA	MxS	P, PE	Maint.: P, PE	AA
Periodization of endurance and speed (energy systems training zones)	4, 5	3, 2, 1, 6		3, 2, 5, 1	5	3, 2, 1, 6		3, 2, 5, 1	5	3, 2, 1, 6	3, 2, 5, 1	5

Key: AA = anatomical adaptation, comp. = competitive, maint. = maintenance, MxS = maximum strength, P = power, PE = power endurance, prep. = preparation, and T = transition.

Figure 3.5 Suggested Annual Plan for Integrating Strength and Energy Systems Training for Contact Sports

Microcycle

Integrating strength and energy systems is a training necessity not only for annual plans but also for microcycles. Application is illustrated in the following two examples. The first example, shown in figure 3.6, illustrates a weekly microcycle for racket sports. This microcycle is also applicable to contact sports and martial arts.

Each training day shown in figure 3.6 addresses several training objectives, which may include technical or tactical objectives, as well as the types of strength training needed for this type of sport. All technical and tactical sessions should use mostly sport-specific drills according to the physiology of each intensity zone. In other words, strength and conditioning coaches would do well to elicit sport-specific adaptations by designing sport-specific drills for each intensity.

As an example, consider intensity zone 3. Designing sport-specific drills for one to six minutes is more beneficial for an athlete's sport-specific adaptation than asking him or her to run for one to six minutes at the required intensity. If duration and specific intensity are tailored for the technical and tactical drills—especially from the second part of the preparatory phase onward—the sport-specific adaptation is far superior to that realized from nonspecific types of training. Nonspecific training must be planned mostly during the early part of the preparatory phase. As competition approaches, sport-specific drills

	Monday	Tuesday	Wednesday	Thursday	Friday	Saturday	Sunday
Type of training session	Technical and tactical	Technical and tactical	Tactical	Technical and tactical	Tactical	Off	Off
Periodization of strength	MxS, P	PE	—	MxS, P	PE		
Periodization of endurance and speed (energy systems training zones)	1	2, 3, 6	4	1, 2, 6	3, 5		

Key: MxS = maximum strength, P = power, and PE = power endurance.

Figure 3.6 Suggested Integration and Alternation of Energy Systems and Strength Training in the Microcycle for Racket Sports

must be dominant. Consequently, for a combat sport, consider the duration and number (both in a fight and in a tourney) of rounds and use both shorter with higher mean intensity and longer rounds in training to better prepare your fighters.

Monday's training session involves technical and tactical training and intensity zone 1 (alactic system training). Because this workout taxes the anaerobic alactic system, the suggested strength training addresses power and maximum strength. Tuesday's training involves sport-specific lactic acid power or capacity matched with power endurance in the gym. The main benefit of this strategy is that the lactic acid system is also taxed for power endurance training, and, as a result, the rate of post-training recovery is the same. It would be a physiological design error to match intensity zones 2 and 3 with, say, maximum strength, because the rate of recovery and regeneration of each system is different. For faster regeneration between workouts, intensity zone 6 training (aerobic compensation) is planned at the end of the workout.

To alternate energy systems and therefore facilitate recovery and regeneration between training days for each system, the program for Wednesday is directed toward a different energy system: the aerobic system. Thursday's training focuses on anaerobic systems, whereas the Friday program starts with sport-specific tactical drills and then moves to aerobic power and finally to low-intensity aerobic threshold work. At the end of Friday's training session, we suggest power endurance training, but with a higher number of reps (30 reps for two or three sets).

The second example, shown in figure 3.7, is created for aerobic-dominant sports, such as long-distance events in running, swimming, road cycling, and cross-country skiing.

Each of the six training days shown in figure 3.7 addresses specific training objectives. On Monday, for instance, the major training goal is aerobic endurance to stimulate central and peripheral adaptations. This must be a major concern for any athlete in this type of sport because of the need to transport and use oxygen and to use free fatty acid as fuel during races. These needs are addressed by planning long reps (such as six reps of 10 minutes each or four reps of 20 minutes each) or nonstop aerobic training of long duration. Strength training planned at the end of the workout must address the same energy system—for example, through muscular endurance work of long duration (addressed in chapter 14).

On Tuesday, the major objective is to improve maximum oxygen consumption via reps of one to six minutes followed by compensation training (intensity zone 6). Although the type of strength training suggested for Tuesday (maximum strength below 80 percent of

	Monday	Tuesday	Wednesday	Thursday	Friday	Saturday	Sunday
Type of training session	Aerobic	Aerobic	Lactic acid and aerobic	Aerobic	Aerobic/ lactic acid	Aerobic	Off
Periodization of strength	MEL	MxS (<80% of 1RM)	—	MEL	—	P	
Periodization of endurance and speed (energy systems training zones)	4, 5	3, 6	2, 6, 5	4, 5	4, 2, 6	5	

Key: MEL = muscle endurance long, MxS = maximum strength, and P = power.

Figure 3.7 Suggested Integration of Strength and Metabolic Training in the Microcycle for Aerobic-Dominant Sports (Late Preparatory or Competitive Phase)

1RM) does not match the dominant energy system taxed in that day, it is needed in order to maintain the neuromuscular system's efficiency, in order to maintain, for instance, running economy. If this type of strength training is neglected (that is, if maximum strength is not maintained), the athlete will not maintain the force output necessary to reach performance objectives at the end of the competitive phase.

The program suggested for Wednesday is a difficult one. It starts with intensity zone 2 to train the body and mind to adapt—and therefore to tolerate the pain and stress of lactic acid buildup—using interval training that alternates between high and low intensity for 10 to 20 reps of 60 seconds each. The benefit of this type of training is felt in the early part of a race when the runner is able to tolerate lactic acid buildup. The zone 2 work is followed immediately by work in zone 6 so that the body can compensate after such physiological and psychological stress. After completing one 10-minute bout in zone 6, the athlete can perform two 10-minute bouts in zone 5, once again followed by 15 minutes of compensation training (zone 6). Sometimes the recovery following a set is more important to adaptation than the set itself.

On Thursday, we suggest once again stressing intensity zones 4 and 5 to improve the efficiency of the metabolic system, using free fatty acid as a fuel. At the end, plan a strength training program for muscular endurance of long duration. For Friday, the plan is more complex. The main objective of this session is to adapt the athlete to perform lactic acid system training (zone 2) based on the residual fatigue that resulted from first performing anaerobic threshold training (zone 4). Such a combination of training duplicates the physiological state that the athlete experiences at the end of a race, when he or she must produce energy via the anaerobic system. Once again, the session ends with 20 minutes of compensation training (zone 6). The microcycle ends on Saturday with an easier aerobic training session (aerobic threshold training, or zone 5), followed by 20 minutes of power training.

The number of strength training sessions suggested here might seem high. In actuality, the exercises have to be very specific and therefore as few as possible (i.e., between two and four exercises). Athletes might finish such a strength training session in 15 to 20 minutes, which is not a long time considering the potential gains in specific adaptations.

Importance of Strength Training for Endurance Sports

Many athletes and strength and conditioning coaches labor under misconceptions about the use of strength or metabolic training, regardless of whether the sport is speed or power dominant or aerobic endurance dominant. Some of these misconceptions are addressed in the following discussion.

Misconception: Sports that are aerobic endurance dominant don't need strength training.

In many of these sports, such as running and cross-country skiing, the force of the propulsion phase (pushing off against the ground to project the body forward) is the essential element for improved performance. The same is true for the arms' drive through the water in swimming; the force applied against the pedal in road cycling; and the force of the blade drive through the water in rowing, canoeing, and kayaking. Therefore, relying solely on specific training is far from sufficient to improve performance from year to year. Higher velocity is possible only as a result of superior force application against resistance (i.e., gravity, snow, terrain profile, or water).

To demonstrate the importance of strength training, let's consider a brief example from running. Figure 3.3 shows the periodized strength training necessary to improve the propulsion phase and, as a result, the mean velocity in a race. To improve propulsion, an athlete must increase the force applied against the ground. This increase is possible only if the athlete uses maximum strength, as indicated in figure 3.3.

An athlete can address this need through four simple exercises: half squat, reverse hyperextension, knee lift, and calf raise. These exercises strengthen the major muscle groups (including the quadriceps and adductors mostly activated at ground contact and the glutei, hamstrings, gastrocnemius, and soleus mostly activated during the propulsion phase) and adapt the iliopsoas muscle group to lift the knee repeatedly and higher during running. The results—"delayed activation of less efficient Type II fibers, improved neuromuscular efficiency, conversion of fast-twitch Type IIx fibers into more fatigue-resistant Type IIa fibers, or improved musculo-tendinous stiffness" (Rønnestad and Mujika 2013)—enable faster running.

A long-distance event requires much more than the improvement of force per stride using elements of maximum strength. Athletes must convert this gain into muscular endurance of long duration so that the same force is applied for the duration of the race. Thus the desired benefit is not velocity just for the start but increased *mean* velocity in a race. Let us suppose that recruitment of more muscle fibers during the propulsion phase increases stride length by 1 centimeter (about 3/8 of an inch). Given that a runner performs 50,000 strides during a marathon, the cumulative gain per race is 500 meters (about 550 yards). Depending on the runner's performance time, this difference could mean running the race at a pace that is faster by one and a half or two minutes!

Misconception: Uphill running develops enough leg strength for endurance athletes.

Endurance athletes who are asked why they do uphill running generally answer, "To improve leg strength." However, for an activity to qualify as a strengthening exercise, it must considerably increase the strength reserve in relation to the sport-specific action. This has not been proven to be the case for uphill running.

Uphill sprinting intended to increase acceleration power (and improve acceleration technique) for power athletes is performed in repetition training mode, meaning that the athlete runs uphill for about 10 to 50 yards or meters (in the alactic system time zone) within a set time, then jogs or walks back to the starting point. Between reps, the athlete takes a rest interval of one to six minutes, depending on the distance. Training demand depends on the distance of a rep, the time used to perform it, and the degree of the slope's inclination (a slope of more than 10 degrees is regarded as very challenging).

Uphill running in interval training mode, on the other hand, can provide a major benefit for the cardiorespiratory system. For this purpose, the training uses longer reps of 25 to 50 yards or meters, lower intensities, and shorter rest intervals: 4 sets × 5 reps of 50 yards (or meters), at 60 percent to 70 percent of the best flat time, with a 30-second rest interval between reps and a three-minute rest interval between sets.

When an athlete runs uphill, her or his heart rate ranges from 160 to more than 170 beats per minute. Such a rate demonstrates that the heart is highly stimulated and that uphill running strengthens the heart by increasing the heart's stroke volume, or force, for pumping more blood to the working muscles. As a result, the muscles are supplied with more nutrients and with the oxygen needed to produce energy. Therefore, an uphill workout can follow the specifics of energy systems training. The best time to use uphill running as a training method to develop the cardiorespiratory system is from the second part of the preparatory phase onward, following the development of the aerobic foundation.

Misconception: Long-distance aerobic training is necessary in order to develop endurance for team, racket, and contact sports and the martial arts.

Although the methodology for developing motor abilities for sport has been improving constantly, some antiquated methods are still in use, especially in the area of developing endurance. In these speed- and power-dominant sports, however, the role of aerobic endurance is less important (except for some team sports, such as soccer, lacrosse, and water polo). And yet, in sports such as American football, cricket, baseball, hockey, and basketball, long-distance jogging is still prescribed to develop aerobic endurance even though this work does not correspond to sport-specific performance demands. During a game, for instance, an American football linebacker performs 40 to 60 short accelerations of three to six seconds each with rest intervals of one to three minutes. This performance will not be improved by running five miles.

Instead, athletes in these sports should be trained by using interval training methodology and specific speed endurance and power endurance training. For example, the athlete could perform jump squats followed by 10- to 15-yard (meter) acceleration sprints—two or three series of two sets of four to six reps, with rest intervals of one minute between reps and three minutes between sets, as well as five or more minutes of active recovery between series. To reach the required training level, athletes need four to six weeks of training, starting with sixteen total 15-yard (meter) sprints: 2 series × 2 sets × 4 reps of 15 yards (meters), with a rest interval of one minute between reps, three minutes between sets, and five minutes between series. Figure 3.8 illustrates a periodized program for specific endurance in the preparatory phase for athletes competing in this group of sports.

	General preparation	Early specific preparation	Late specific preparation
Periodization of endurance	Aerobic endurance	Aerobic and anaerobic endurance	Specific endurance
Type of repetition	Longer (600–400 m) in sets of reps of the same distance or descending ladders (varying intensity according to the distance of each repetition). In both cases there is a weekly variation of distances and intensities, from general to more specific training parameters. Distances can be broken down to perform more sport-specific shuttle runs, too.	Shorter (50–200 m)	Position specific
Intensity zones	4, 3	3, 2	2, 3
Type of training	Nonspecific training	Specific technical and tactical drills	Position-specific speed endurance; technical and tactical drills; aerobic power maintenance

Total volume of training (total distance) and repetition distances are based on the physiological requirements of the sport and on the specifics of the position: distance, type of speed required (e.g., direction changes, stop-and-go), and mean number of repetitions per game. Intensity of repetitions is based on individual characteristics as they have emerged from previous testing (for instance, 600 meters or yards at 80 percent of maximum aerobic velocity).

Figure 3.8 Suggested Preparatory Phase for Speed- and Power-Dominant Sports

Long reps performed during general preparation are nonspecific. From the early specific preparation stage onward, however, training must be more specific. Specific anaerobic alactic and lactic acid endurance will be better improved through specific technical and tactical drills. Coaches should design specific drills for each intensity zone so that their athletes are trained according to the physiological needs of their sport and position.

Misconception: Speed training must be accomplished by means of a game or other sport-specific method.

To the contrary, speed can also be developed using nonspecific training methods and techniques. Speed represents the ability to cover a given distance as fast as possible. In fact, depending on the distances covered in a given team or racket sport, we should distinguish between acceleration training and maximum speed training. Acceleration training addresses the distance covered in a time period between one and four seconds with closer angles at the hip and knee, forward lean, and higher activation of the quadriceps (knee extensors). Maximum speed training, in contrast, addresses the distance covered in a time period between four and six seconds with more open angles at the hip and knee, upright posture, and higher activation of the glutes and hamstrings (hip extensors).

Thus, for team and racket sports, where most sprints last less than five seconds, we should speak of acceleration (rather than speed) training. In some other sports, such as the martial arts and boxing, speed represents the ability to quickly deliver an offensive action (such as a punch) or to quickly react to such an action delivered by the opponent. In both cases, speed involves both a strength component and a power component. Equally true, in both cases, an athlete will never be fast before being strong! Therefore, strength and power training can improve speed.

The fact that general training means and methods addressing strength and power will improve speed is linked to the trainability of speed versus endurance. In fact, endurance is much more trainable than speed, which is more genetically set. For this reason, long-endurance athletes train specifically for up to 90 percent of their total yearly training time, which means they run, row, swim, or cycle during most of their training. Speed athletes, on the other hand, perform a high percentage of general work in order to improve their strength and power, which in turn improve their speed.

The development of sport-specific speed is achieved through two major training phases (see figure 3.9). Develop specific speed (different direction, changes of direction, and so on) with long rest intervals between reps (one minute for every 10 yards [meters] the athlete is covering in the repetitions). Start with acceleration over a short distance (10 to 20 yards or meters) and progressively increase the distance to 30, 40, and eventually 50 yards or meters. In establishing the maximum distance to be covered for each sport or player position, the first element to consider is the range of sport-specific distances covered in competition. Most team sports require numerous accelerations of one to four seconds or 5 to 30 yards or meters, but if you want or need to train maximum speed, then the repetitions must be maximal for four to six seconds or 30 to 50 yards or meters).

The other critical element is the athlete's form during the repetition. If the form (running technique) deteriorates toward the end of a repetition, the athlete lacks the necessary power to continue high-quality speed training. Another sign that the distance is longer than the athlete can perform with good form and adequate power is rigidity during running (contracted facial muscles, grimaces, or rigid and lifted shoulders).

For the martial arts and contact sports, speed in delivering a strike can be developed by using training equipment such as medicine balls and power balls. Such a program can also be periodized by starting with heavier weights and decreasing them as the competition phase approaches. This method maximizes the athlete's maximum speed in delivering an

		General preparation		Specific preparation	
Periodization of strength		AA	MxS	MxS	MxS (maint.), P	MxS (maint.), PE
Periodization of speed	Nonspecific	—	—	Acceleration (uphill and flat)	Acceleration (flat), maximum speed quickness, agility	—
	Specific	—	—	—	—	Action–reaction, quick direction changes, stop-and-go agility, max velocity in different directions

Key: Maint. = maintenance, MxS = maximum strength, P = power, and PE = power endurance.

Figure 3.9 Integration of strength and speed training.

offensive action. Avoid ankle and wrist weights because they disrupt the motor pattern because their force vector (gravity) is perpendicular to the resulting force vector of the offensive action which has a forward, not downward, direction.

When integrated, strength training and energy systems training can greatly affect an athlete's physiological adaptation to his or her sport. To design and implement effective sport-specific programs, strength and conditioning coaches need a subtle understanding of the major energy systems, the phases of training, and of course the practical application of intensity zones. As a rule of thumb, each training session should be designed to include activities that stress the same energy system. This approach forces the body to train one system at a time and leaves the other systems fresh for other training days.

In addition, intensity zone training is best used in combination with sport-specific technical and tactical drills. In the early to middle preparatory phase, it is fine to use traditional methods of metabolic training to improve the anaerobic threshold, or maximum oxygen consumption. As the competitive phase approaches, however, athletes must integrate energy system training using sport-specific drills and the type of strength (e.g., power endurance or muscular endurance) that is specific to their sport.

4

Fatigue and Recovery

The training process is a "set of artificial stimuli set upon the body to elicit morpho-functional adaptations" (Verkhoshansky). However, the structural and functional adaptations cannot fully take place when most of the body's energy is directed toward training. For adaptation to occur, training programs must intersperse work periods with rest (for instance, planning an unloading week at the end of a macrocycle) and alternate various levels of intensity throughout the microcycle while avoiding large increments in training load. This practice creates a good work-to-rest balance and prevents the accumulation of residual fatigue or "internal load."

To improve performance, training loads must be high enough to stimulate adaptation, but exposing an athlete to loads beyond his or her capacity—or underestimating the necessary rest—decreases the athlete's ability to adapt to training and make progress. Failure to adapt triggers biochemical and neural reactions that take the athlete from fatigue to chronic fatigue and ultimately to the undesirable state of overtraining. Fortunately, recovery techniques can be implemented to allow the body to adapt more quickly to voluminous or intensive microcycles. Some of these techniques, such as massage and contrast showers, can be used year-round (and more frequently during the late preparatory phase and competitive phase). Others can be limited to just the competitive phase, when the athlete most needs full functional restoration and a low level of internal load.

Fatigue

Athletes are constantly exposed to various types of training load, some of which exceed their tolerance thresholds. As a result, adaptation decreases, and overall performance is affected. When athletes drive themselves beyond their physiological limits, they risk an accumulation of fatigue—the greater the fatigue, the greater the negative training effects, such as low rate of recovery, decreased coordination, and diminished power output. Fatigue from training can also increase if an athlete experiences personal stresses outside of the training environment.

The phenomena commonly associated with exercise-induced fatigue—overreaching and overtraining—are physiologically and psychologically complex. Fatigue can affect an athlete's force-generating capacity or cause inability to maintain a required force. Although much research has been devoted to fatigue, neither the exact sites nor the exact causes are well known. Still, coaches and instructors should become as informed as possible in this area so that they can create better plans to avoid fatigue, overreaching, and overtraining in their athletes.

Although fatigue is assumed to originate in the muscles, the central nervous system (CNS) plays a fundamental role because neurotransmitter levels—and the consequent psychological states—greatly affect neural transmission, hormone levels, and, ultimately, general fatigue. In fact, it is now well established that the CNS limits performance to a greater extent than once thought (Enoka and Stuart 1992; Schillings et al. 2000; Noakes et al. 2005; Weir at al. 2006).

The CNS involves two basic processes: excitation and inhibition. Excitation is a stimulating process for physical activity, whereas inhibition is a restraining process. Throughout training, these two processes alternate. As a result of any stimulation, the CNS sends a nerve impulse to the working muscle, causing it to contract. The impulse's speed, power, and frequency depend directly on the state of the CNS. Nerve impulses are most effective when (controlled) excitation prevails, resulting in a good performance. When fatigue inhibits the nerve cell, the muscle contraction is slower and weaker. Thus, the electrical activation of the CNS is responsible for the number of motor units recruited and the frequency of discharge, which ultimately affect contraction force.

Nerve cell working capacity cannot be maintained for very long, and it decreases under the strain of training or competition. If high intensity is maintained, the nerve cell assumes a state of inhibition to protect itself from external stimuli. Consequently, fatigue should be viewed as a self-protecting mechanism intended to prevent damage to the contractile mechanism of the muscle.

Furthermore, intense exercise leads to the development of acidosis, which is caused primarily by the buildup of lactic acid in the muscle cell. A high level of acidosis can affect the release of the calcium required for muscular contraction. In essence, then, an excitatory nerve impulse may reach the muscle membrane but be blocked by an inhibited calcium-release membrane (Enoka and Stuart 1992).

Coaches should watch for symptoms of fatigue. In speed and power sports, fatigue is visible to the experienced eye. Athletes react more slowly to explosive activities and show a slight impairment in coordination and an increase in the duration of the contact phase in sprinting, bounding, rebounding, jumping, and plyometrics. These activities rely on activation of fast-twitch muscle fibers, which are more easily affected by fatigue than are slow-twitch fibers. Therefore, even slight inhibition of the CNS affects their recruitment. In endurance events, fatigue is generally expressed through the breakdown of technique and, of course, a gradual decrease in the average speed of movement.

Skeletal muscle produces force through the activation of its motor units and the regulation of their firing frequency, which increases progressively to enhance force output. Fatigue that inhibits muscular activity can be neutralized to some extent by a modulating strategy of altering firing frequency. As a result, the muscle can maintain force more effectively under a certain state of fatigue. However, if the duration of sustained maximum contraction increases, the frequency of the motor units' firing decreases, signaling that inhibition will become more prominent (Bigland-Ritchie et al. 1983; Hennig and Lomo 1987).

As Marsden, Meadows, and Merton (1971) demonstrated, firing frequency at the end of a 30-second maximum voluntary contraction decreased by 80 percent as compared with the frequency at the start of the contraction. Both De Luca and Erim (1994) and Conwit, et al. (2000) reported similar findings: As contraction duration increased, the activation of large motor units increased, yet the firing rate was below their usual activation frequency threshold level.

These findings should alarm those who promote the theory (especially in American football) that strength can be improved only by performing each set to exhaustion. The fact that the firing frequency decreases as more reps are performed to failure discredits this highly acclaimed method.

As contractions progress, fuel reserves become depleted, resulting in longer motor unit relaxation time and a lower frequency of muscle contraction, which, in turn, results in a lower power output. Fatigue is the suspected cause of such neuromuscular behavior. This reality should warn practitioners that short rest intervals (the standard one to two minutes) between two sets of maximum neural load are insufficient to relax and regenerate the neuromuscular system to produce high activation in subsequent sets.

When analyzing the functional capacity of the CNS during fatigue, coaches should consider the athlete's perceived fatigue and his or her past physical capacity achieved in training. When physical capacity is above the level of fatigue experienced in testing or competition, it enhances motivation and, as a result, the ability to overcome fatigue. Thus, this ability to overcome fatigue during competition has to be trained, especially for those sports in which mental resiliency to fatigue is paramount, such as team sports, racket sport, and contact sports.

Adenosine Triphosphate, Creatine Phosphate, and Glycogen Depletion

Depending on the nature of the activity, muscular fatigue occurs when creatine phosphate (CP) in the working muscle is depleted or when muscle glycogen is exhausted (Sahlin 1986). The end result is obvious: The work performed by the muscle decreases.

For high-intensity activities of short duration, such as low-rep sets or short sprints, the immediate sources of energy for muscular contraction are adenosine triphosphate (ATP) and CP. Depletion of these stores in a muscle limits its ability to contract (Karlsson and Saltin 1971). During rest intervals, however, the aerobic system works powerfully to restore phosphates through a process referred to as aerobic phosphorylation. As a result, decent aerobic conditioning is needed even in speed and power sports (Bogdanis 1996).

In a muscle that is depleted of glycogen—due, for instance, to the long intermittent activity typical of team sports—ATP is produced at a lower rate than it is consumed. Studies show that glycogen is essential to a muscle's ability to maintain high force (Conlee 1987) and that endurance capability during prolonged moderate to heavy physical activity relates directly to the amount of glycogen in the muscle prior to exercise (Saltin 1973; Balsom et al. 1999). Thus fatigue can also occur as a result of muscle glycogen depletion (Bergstrom et al. 1967).

In prolonged submaximal work, such as muscular endurance of medium or long duration, glucose and fatty acid are used to produce energy. This process requires oxygen. When the oxygen supply is limited, carbohydrate is oxidized instead of free fatty acid. Maximum free fatty acid oxidation is determined by the inflow of fatty acid to the working muscle and by the athlete's aerobic training status because aerobic training increases both the availability of oxygen and the capability of free fatty acid oxidation (Sahlin 1986). Therefore, contributors to muscular fatigue include lack of oxygen, lack of oxygen-carrying capacity, and inadequate blood flow (Bergstrom et al. 1967).

Lactic Acid Accumulation

After a few seconds of maximal contractions, the anaerobic lactic system begins to use muscle glycogen to produce ATP, and lactate begins to accumulate. Taken together, the simultaneous decrease of creatine phosphate and buildup of lactic acid decrease the muscle's ability to contract maximally (Fox, Bowes, and Foss 1989). This matters for athletic movements requiring quickness or force of contraction because they rely on the contraction of the powerful fast-twitch fibers. Such actions are anaerobic, which means that they rely on anaerobic types of fuel, thus resulting in increased production—and the accumulation of—lactic acid. During performance of high-intensity (heavy-load) sets to failure, unless the set's total time under tension is less than eight seconds, fast-twitch fibers produce high levels of lactate, thus blocking any immediate excitation stimulation from the CNS. Therefore, the next high-intensity set can be performed only after a longer rest period (see the section titled Rest Interval in chapter 7).

The biochemical exchanges during muscle contraction result in the liberation of hydrogen ions that in turn produce acidosis or the not-yet-clearly-understood "lactate fatigue," which seems to determine the point of exhaustion (Sahlin 1986). The more active a muscle is, the greater its hydrogen ion concentration is, and thus the higher its level of blood acidosis. Hydrogen ions also stimulate the release of growth hormone from the anterior pituitary (Roemmich and Rogol 1997; Takarada et al. 2000; Godfrey et al. 2003; Kraemer and Ratamess 2005). Despite its name, the main effect of the growth hormone spike elicited by metabolically intensive training is the increase of lypolysis (fat burning) (Wee et al. 2005; Yarasheski et al. 1992; Goto et al. 2007; Jorgensen et al. 2003), which is one reason that lactic workouts are so effective for fat loss. Other reasons include the high caloric expenditure per minute and the excess post-exercise oxygen consumption, which causes an increase in metabolism that lasts up to 24 hours. Despite popular belief, then, spikes in exercise-induced growth hormone—or testosterone, for that matter (White et al. 2013)—do not affect muscle growth (Helms 2010).

Increased acidosis also inhibits the binding capacity of calcium through inactivation of troponin, a protein compound. Because troponin is an important contributor to muscle cell contraction, its inactivation may foster the onset of fatigue (Fabiato and Fabiato 1978). The discomfort produced by acidosis can also be a contributing factor in psychological fatigue (Brooks and Fahey 1985). Muscle acidosis is not, however, the cause of the muscle soreness experienced after a training session. In fact, as shown in table 4.1, lactate removal is fairly fast, because it is oxidized by muscle fibers and also converted by the liver back to glucose (via the Cori cycle).

Table 4.1 Time Needed for Blood and Muscle Lactate Removal

Percentage	Time (min.)
25–30	10
50–60	25
90–100	75

Reprinted, by permission, from T.O. Bompa and F. Claro, 2009, *Periodization in rugby* (Aachen, Germany: Meyer & Meyer Sport), 33.

Muscle Soreness

Muscle soreness can occur after training when athletes first start a strength training program, when they perform unfamiliar exercises that work muscles other than those they normally use, when they use heavier loads than they are used to, or when the eccentric phase of an exercise is emphasized. Soreness is also experienced by beginners who are exposed to heavy loads without adequate adaptation.

The fact that exercise initiates damage is explained by two basic mechanisms: the disturbance of metabolic function and the mechanical disruption of the muscle cell. The metabolic mechanism of muscle damage is at work during prolonged submaximal work to exhaustion, which is typical of some bodybuilding methods. Direct loading of the muscle, especially during the eccentric contraction phase, may cause muscle damage, which may then be aggravated by metabolic changes. One of the most noticeable types of damage is disruption of the muscle cell membrane (e.g., swollen mitochondria, lesion of the plasma membrane, distortion of myofibrillar components, sarcolemmal disruption) (Friden and Lieber 1992).

As compared with concentric contraction, eccentric contraction produces greater muscle tension, selective deactivation of slow-twitch muscle fibers, and greater activation of fast-twitch motor units (Nardone et al. 1989). Athletes who use the eccentric method without enough strength training background to tolerate it, or without achieving connective tissue adaptation, suffer discomfort and muscle damage. Eccentric contraction produces more heat than concentric contraction does at the same workload. The increased temperature can damage structural and functional components in the muscle cell (Armstrong 1986; Ebbing and Clarkson 1989).

Both mechanisms of muscle damage are related to muscle fibers that have been slightly stressed, which is reflected in a high level of the enzyme creatine kinase—a marker of muscle damage—for up to 48 hours after the training session. Discomfort sets in during the first 24 to 48 hours following the exercise and is thus called delayed-onset muscle soreness. Nevertheless, muscle fibers usually return quickly to their normal pre-injury status. If the stress is severe, however, the muscle becomes traumatized. Therefore, a training session that is too intensive or voluminous can cause a sensation of dull, aching pain combined with tenderness and stiffness that can take up to seven days to disappear.

The prevention of muscle soreness takes several forms, from training to nutrition. The most important preventive technique for a coach to consider is that of progressive load increase in training. Periodization of strength also helps athletes avoid discomfort, muscle soreness, and other negative training outcomes. In addition, the body is better prepared for work if the athlete performs an extensive overall warm-up. Superficial warm-ups, on the other hand, can easily result in strain and pain. Stretching is also strongly recommended at the end of a training session. After the extensive muscle

Closely monitoring training helps prevent overtraining, fatigue, and injury.

contraction that is typical of strength training, muscles are slightly shorter, and it takes several hours for them to return to resting length. One to three minutes of stretching helps the muscles reach their resting length faster, which is optimal for biochemical exchanges at the level of muscle fiber. Stretching also seems to ease muscle spasms.

Muscle soreness prevention and recovery also benefit from proper postworkout nutrition (addressed in chapter 5) and overall diet. Athletes exposed to heavy loads in strength training require more protein and carbohydrate and might benefit from supplements, such as specific amino acids. Inadequate postworkout nutrition may delay muscle recovery from the strain of a workout. Conventionally, massage has also been believed to relieve muscle soreness, and certainly it reduces muscle tone (myoelectric activity at rest) and favors blood flow and recovery.

Coaches and athletes should keep in mind, however, that the best plan is to prevent muscle soreness in the first place. And the best prevention strategy is a progression in the use of eccentric contraction. Remember that slowing down the eccentric phase increases muscle fiber damage, as does increasing the load, so plan accordingly.

Overtraining

Signs of overtraining are signals that an athlete is adapting poorly, or not at all, to the training regimen. Overtraining doesn't usually settle in overnight; rather, it is a slow process resulting from a prolonged training program that lacks sessions for recovery and periods of regeneration. Without proper rest, relaxation, and recovery, the athlete coasts into a state of chronic fatigue and poor motivation.

Classic signs of overtraining include a heart rate that is higher than usual; irritability; trouble sleeping; loss of appetite; and, of course, muscles that are fatigued, sore, and tight. At times, signs of overtraining appear during recovery from intense training programs. If these signs persist for a few days after one or two intense bouts, they may indicate overreaching rather than overtraining. In other words, the athlete may be working at a level above his or her physiological comfort zone. With proper rest and recovery, the athlete will successfully overcome the fatigue and be ready for the next challenge. Lack of proper recovery, however, can quickly draw the athlete from a state of overreaching to a state of overtraining.

Recognizing Overtraining

Here are a few strategies to help you determine whether an athlete is entering a state of overtraining.

Record the heart rate.

An athlete or coach can record a daily morning heart rate to determine whether the athlete is working at the appropriate training level. A morning heart rate recording is best because the athlete is rested and not yet influenced by the stresses of the day. An increased resting heart rate over a two- or three-day period may be a sign of overreaching. In this case, the coach should reduce the training program's intensity level (possibly planning "aerobic compensation" sessions) and keep a close eye on the heart rate over the next 24 to 48 hours.

Keep a training log.

This simple concept often causes a lot of complaining among athletes. They generally don't have a problem with recording their loads or times in training, but they shy away from recording the intensity level of a session or the level of fatigue. Athletes train and sacrifice to be the best, and admitting that a training session was too intense is not part of their nature. Thus the coach should keep a close eye on the athlete and take the time to communicate the importance of not exceeding one's physical tolerance. The coach may need to keep a specific log book describing the physiological impact of training on the athlete. The log should include how the athlete felt immediately after a workout, after a few hours, and the next morning.

Use a handgrip dynamometer.

A handgrip dynamometer (a squeezing device held in the hand that records pressure) offers a quick and effective way to objectively measure overtraining or daily fatigue. It can also serve as a good indicator of CNS fatigue. Before every workout, the athlete squeezes the dynamometer one hand at a time and records the score. If the score constantly decreases or is lower on a particular day, the athlete may be experiencing CNS fatigue and need to recover.

Coaches should remember that psychological stress can also affect an athlete's response to training, even though it may not produce visible signs. The mere fact that the planned program calls for a high-intensity training day does not mean that the coach or athlete cannot adjust the program to the athlete's current physical or emotional state. Sometimes less is more, and sometimes rest has a stronger effect on adaptation than training does.

Use a heart rate variability monitor.

Heart rate variability (HRV) is a physiological phenomenon involving variation in the time interval between heartbeats (referred to as the R-R interval). The interval varies in response to factors such as fatigue, relaxation, emotional states, thoughts, and, of course, training stress. Heart rate responds quickly to all of these factors in order to better adapt the functions of the organism to the environmental situation.

Such changes are independent of our central nervous system control. In fact, they are related to the autonomic nervous system and, more specifically, to interaction between the sympathetic and parasympathetic systems. The sympathetic system is the activation system and produces a series of effects, such as increased heart rate, increased blood pressure, peripheral vasoconstriction, dilatation of the bronchi, pupillary dilation, increased sweating, release of energy substrates in the bloodstream, reduced digestion and inhibition of appetite—that is, the fight-or-flight stress response. The chemical mediators of this set of responses are noradrenaline, adrenaline, corticotropin, and several corticosteroids.

In contrast, when the parasympathetic system is dominant, it produces a slower heart rate, a decrease in blood pressure, slow and deep breathing, muscle relaxation, pupillary constriction, and increased appetite and digestion. This system acts through the chemical messenger acetylcholine. Its dominance is the body's response to a situation of calm, rest, tranquility, and the absence of danger and stress.

The state of one's body at any given time is determined by the balance between the sympathetic and parasympathetic systems (neurovegetative balance). A critical factor is the human body's ability to change its balance toward one system or the other. Practically speaking, after a night's rest, if a high-load training session is planned for that day, we want the body to be in a recovered state (parasympathetic dominance). A high sympathetic tone at rest, on the other hand, indicates a high oxygen demand for the ATP generation that is needed for recovery, and it correlates with low levels of the neurosteroid DHEAS (Chen et al. 2011). In this case, a lower load session should be planned instead.

Aerobic compensation sessions have been proven to speed up recovery by lowering the sympathetic system's tone. Several consecutive days of sympathetic hypertone are a sign of overreaching that might lead to overtraining unless appropriate load-reducing measures are taken.

We are fortunate these days to have affordable HRV monitoring devices (e.g., BioForce, Omegawave) to assess the body's response to training and prevent overtraining. Such devices can help in the following ways: confirming the internal load (residual fatigue) dynamics planned throughout a microcycle or macrocycle; enhancing our knowledge of the body's response to our training methods; helping individualize volume, intensity, and frequency, thus optimizing the training program for each athlete; and helping us spot and quantify the effect of stressors outside of the training environment (such as work, school, family, and lifestyle).

Implementing Recovery Techniques

Chronic muscle soreness and joint inflammation may be signals to decrease training volume and intensity. If the response to training seems intolerable hours and days after training, the coach can try implementing a few recovery techniques following the workout. For example, stretching provides a good way to restore mobility and decrease susceptibility to injury and to relax the body at the end of a workout. Passive, partner-assisted stretches offer an ideal way to fully stretch the muscles and relax while the workout partner or coach does the work. Along with implementing recovery techniques to reduce or elimi- nate the signs of overtraining, however, the coach should also alter the training program to facilitate regeneration.

Another way to regenerate the body after a workout is to perform 5 to 10 minutes of light aerobic activity, such as jogging or cycling. It also provides an active way to remove some of the substances, such as lactic acid and muscle debris, that accumulate during training and can impede recovery. An athlete can also promote muscle and tendon recov- ery by doing contrast showers, cycling between hot and cold water, which is a great way to increase blood flow from the skin to the organs and eliminate waste products from the muscles, as well as reduce inflammation. Athletes should alternate 30 to 60 seconds of hot water with 30 to 60 seconds of cold water for two or three sets. Of course, this technique takes a little getting used to, but it is extremely effective.

Recovery from short-term overtraining should start with the interruption of training for three to five days. Following this rest period, the athlete should resume training by alternating each training session with a day off. If overtraining is severe and the athlete needs more recovery time, every week of training missed will require roughly two weeks of work to reattain the previous level of conditioning (Terjung and Hood 1986).

Recovery

Various techniques are available for recovery from fatigue. Understanding how to use these techniques during training is just as important as knowing how to train effectively. Training programs constantly implement new loads and intensity levels, but the recovery methods used often do not keep pace. This gap can produce setbacks for athletes in peaking and regeneration after training. About 50 percent of an athlete's final performance depends on the ability to recover; if recovery is inadequate, adaptation may not be achieved.

No single factor controls recovery; rather, various factors contribute to varying degrees. The main factors include age, training experience, sex, environment, availability of energy substrates, and emotional state. Older athletes generally take longer to recover than younger athletes do. On the other hand, athletes who are better trained and more experienced generally require less time to recuperate than less experienced athletes do because of their ability to adapt more quickly to a given training stimulus. Sex can also affect the rate of recovery due to differences in the endocrine system; specifically, female athletes tend to recover more slowly than male athletes do. Environmental factors affecting recovery include time differences, altitude, and climate. Recovery is also affected by the replenishment of nutrients at the cellular level. Specifically, the restoration of protein, fat, carbohydrate, and ATP-CP in working muscle cells is required for cellular metabolism and for the production of energy (Fox, et al. 1989; Jacobs et al. 1987). Finally, recovery can be impeded by fear, indecisiveness, or lack of willpower.

The neuroendocrine response to training is an important component in recovery from strength training. As mentioned in chapter 5, immediately after a strength training session the body is in a negative balance because protein breakdown is greater than protein synthesis. Furthermore, the testosterone-to-cortisol ratio is lower, which places the body in a state of catabolism. The body's imbalance can be addressed by ingesting a protein and carbohydrate mixture in the form of a shake immediately after high-intensity training. Doing so can return the body to a state of positive balance by lowering the cortisol level, speeding up the refilling of muscle glycogen, and supporting the synthesis of muscle protein, thus kickstarting the recovery and regeneration process.

Recovery is a slow process that corresponds directly to the training load employed. Similarly, the curve of recovery—which represents the body's ability to reach homeostasis (its normal biological state)—is not linear (see figure 4.1). In the first third of the recovery process, 70 percent of recovery occurs; in the next two thirds, respectively, 20 percent and 10 percent of recovery occurs. The time interval for recovery depends on the energy system being taxed. Table 4.2 lists recommended recovery times for different physiological systems.

For greatest effectiveness, athletes should use recovery techniques after each training session, and more so during specific preparation and competitive phases (Fry, Morton,

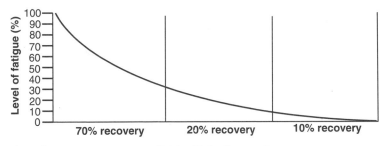

Figure 4.1 Dynamics of a recovery curve divided into three phases.

Table 4.2 Recovery Times After Exhaustive Training

Recovery process	Recovery time
Restoration of ATP-CP	2–8 min.
Restoration of muscle glycogen: After prolonged exercise After intermittent exercise	10–48 hours 5–24 hours
Removal of lactic acid from muscle and blood: With active recovery With passive rest	30 min.–1 hour 1–2 hours

Adapted from M.L. Foss and S.J. Keteyian, 1998, *Fox's physiological basis for exercise and sport*, 6th ed. (New York: McGraw Hill), 67.

and Keast 1991; Kuipers and Keizer 1988). The following subsections address modalities that can be used in a microcycle to favor training adaptations and recovery.

Active Recovery

Active recovery involves the rapid elimination of waste products (i.e., lactic acid) during moderate aerobic recovery exercise. For example, 62 percent of lactic acid is removed during the first 10 minutes of continuous light jogging, and an additional 26 percent is removed in the next 10 minutes. Thus, it is advantageous to implement an active recovery period of 10 to 20 minutes after lactic training sessions (Bonen and Belcastro 1977; Fox et al. 1989).

Complete or Passive Rest

Complete rest, or passive rest, is perhaps the one necessity that all athletes have in common. To function at full capacity, most athletes require about 10 hours of sleep per day, a portion of which usually takes the form of naps. Athletes should also have regular sleeping habits and be in bed no later than 11:00 p.m. In addition, practicing relaxation techniques prior to bedtime can put the athlete's mind in a more restful state (Gauron 1984). Recently, cell phone application, such as SleepAsAndroid, are being used by athletes to effectively self-monitor their sleeping patterns and adjust them to have a more healthy and performance-supporting lifestyle.

Massage

Massage is the systematic manipulation of soft body tissues for therapeutic purposes, and it is the treatment of choice for most athletes (Cinique 1989; Yessis 1990). To achieve the best results from massage therapy, athletes are urged to use a certified specialist. The physiological effects of massage result from mechanical intrusion, sensory stimulation, or both.

The mechanical effects of massage include relief of muscle fatigue and reduction of excessive swelling. In fact, massage can be especially beneficial when treating certain types of inflammation. It also stretches myofascial adhesions. The mechanical pressure and stretching of tissue help mobilize myofascial adhesions for removal by the circulatory system. In addition, massage increases blood circulation. Squeezing relaxed muscles empties veins in the direction of the applied pressure, which stimulates small capillaries to open and increases blood flow in the massaged area. At rest, about 4 percent of capillaries are open, and this number can be increased to 35 percent through massage (Bergeron 1982). The result is increased availability of fresh blood to the massaged area, which allows greater interchange of substances between capillaries and tissue cells.

Massage also increases lymphatic circulation. It assists circulation in the veins and the return of fluid (lymph) from the tissues. Unlike veins, which have one-way valves, lymphatic vessels have no valves; thus lymph can move in any direction, depending on external pressure. The primary movers of lymph are gravity and muscle pumping (including breathing activities). Massage is the most effective external means of moving extravascular fluid into the lymph vessels and through these vessels into the circulatory system. This process might be described as a cleaning-out action.

The sensory effects of massage are primarily reflexive and are not fully understood. Massage may relieve pain and tenderness by slowly increasing sensory input to the CNS. This effect necessitates massaging gradually into the painful area. Light stroking of the skin results in temporary dilation of capillaries. The stronger the stroking is, the greater and more prolonged the dilation will be. Massage has only a local effect on metabolism, which is due primarily to increased circulation throughout the massaged area. The breakdown of waste products and their absorption into the circulatory system may be increased up to two and a half times above the resting level.

Massage also relieves muscle spasm. Light stroking of an involuntary muscle contraction, such as a muscle spasm, may bring about relaxation through reflex mechanisms. Muscle spasms should first be stroked lightly in a direction parallel to the muscle fibers. If this approach fails, firm pressure should be applied to the muscle belly with both hands. If this tactic also fails, deep thumb pressure into the muscle belly may help. In all cases, only gentle stretching is recommended for the muscle in spasm. The severity of the spasm may be increased by firm or deep pressure or sudden, violent stretching.

Deep tissue massage should be planned for the day before an intensive session or for two or three days before competition. Myofascial release techniques—very important for peak performance in speed and power sports—can complement massage and be used on the day before competition or even on the very day of competition.

Hot and Cold Therapy

Relaxation and regeneration can also be achieved through heat therapy in the form of steam baths, saunas, and heat packs. Although heat packs primarily heat the skin and not the underlying tissues, this modality is still useful. If applied long enough (for at least 20 minutes), heat can increase the circulation around a muscle. The only drawback is that the skin may become too hot before any muscle tissue has been heated. The best uses of heat may be to help athletes relax and to heat surface rather than deep muscle tissue.

Cold therapy can provide important physiological benefits for recovery. Treatments include 5 to 10 minutes of ice baths, ice whirlpools, or cold packs for 10 to 15 minutes. Rubbing ice immediately after a muscle strain may reduce swelling. Perhaps the best time to use ice is immediately following an intense training session in which microtearing of the muscle tissue is likely.

Diet and Dietary Supplementation

Ideally, athletes should maintain an energy balance each day; that is, their daily energy expenditure should roughly match their energy intake. Athletes can judge rather easily whether their diet is adequate in calories. If they are losing weight while on a rigorous workout schedule, they probably are not consuming enough calories.

According to Fahey (1991), diet may also play a part in muscle tissue recovery. Aside from the obvious need for protein (in particular, animal protein), carbohydrate is also required. Recovery from muscle injury has been shown to be delayed when muscle carbohydrate stores are inadequate. Thus, from the standpoints of both energy expenditure and recovery, athletes must pay strict attention to diet.

However, even if they consume a sufficient and well-balanced diet, athletes should not shy away from taking vitamin and mineral supplements. No matter how well balanced a diet may be, it usually cannot replenish all the vitamins and minerals used during a training session or competition. In fact, athletes typically experience a deficiency in all vitamins except vitamin A (Yessis 1990). During periods of heavy training, supplements should be as much a part of the training table as any other nutrient.

In planning a supplement program, coaches and athletes should consider each period of training throughout the annual plan and adjust supplements accordingly. For example, during the transition phase, the need for large doses of vitamins (particularly vitamins B$_6$, B$_{12}$, and C and certain minerals) is much lower because of the decreased intensity and volume of training. Planning for vitamin and mineral supplements can be made relatively easy by putting them in chart form with columns representing specific phases during the yearly training plan.

According to Clark (1985) and Yessis (1990), the choice of mealtime can also affect the rate of recovery. These authors believe that athletes should develop an eating pattern in which their daily intake is divided into at least four small meals rather than three large ones. The authors reason that such a pattern enables the body to better assimilate and digest food. They recommend that about 20 to 25 percent of daily intake be consumed in the early morning meal, 15 to 20 percent in a second breakfast, 30 to 35 percent in the midday meal, and 20 to 25 percent in the evening meal. Athletes should allow no more than four hours to pass between meals and no more than 12 hours between the evening meal and breakfast.

Clark (1985) and Yessis (1990) also believe that athletes should not eat immediately before a training session, because a full stomach raises the diaphragm, forcing the cardiovascular and respiratory systems to work harder. Athletes should also avoid eating a solid meal right after training because few gastric juices are secreted during that time. Instead, athletes should consume only fluids that contain carbohydrate, protein, and amino acid supplements directly after training. The post-training solid meal can follow 30 to 60 minutes later.

Psychological Recovery

Psychological recovery involves factors such as motivation and willpower, which can be affected by stress from both physical and psychological stimuli. The speed of the body's reaction to various external and internal stimuli greatly affects athletic performance. The more focused athletes are, the better they react to various training stimuli and the greater their working capacity. It is not surprising, then, that lifestyle almost always affects an athlete's rate of recovery. The recovery process can be negatively affected, for example, by a poor relationship with a significant other, a sibling, a parent, a teammate, or a coach. An athlete who experiences deep emotional problems that affect his or her motivation and willpower may benefit from seeing a sport psychologist.

In addition, relaxation techniques can greatly improve an athlete's ability to focus. If the brain is relaxed, all other parts of the body assume the same state (Gauron 1984). Perhaps the best time to employ such methods is just before retiring for the evening. For example, a warm bath or shower before bed may induce a more relaxed state.

MUSCLE DAMAGE RECOVERY

During the early aftermath of an injury (about two to four hours afterward)—in other words, during the acute phase—the injury is best treated with compression, ice, elevation, and (depending on the extent of damage) either active or complete rest. For first-degree muscle strain, gentle movement under the pain threshold can be performed two hours after the injury and every few hours in order to reduce neural inhibition and speed the recovery of strength in the following days.

The first hour after an injury is also very important for recovery; indeed, it is fundamental to compress the damaged area and ice it as soon as possible in order to reduce swelling. Delaying such actions can retard full recovery by days. Ice should be applied for 15 to 20 minutes every 2 or 3 hours, and compression should be maintained as long as possible for the first 36 hours. Like nonsteroidal anti-inflammatories, however, ice should be limited to only the first 48 hours in order to counteract the body's initial, excessive inflammatory response but not to hinder tissue repair (Hubbard et al. 2004; Takagi et al. 2011; Haiyan et al. 2011).

In the last few years, the R in the traditional RICE acronym (rest, ice, compression, elevation) has been changed from rest to restricted activity due to recognition of the importance of movement in accelerating recovery from injury. In addition, light resistive exercise can be used after the initial 72 hours and can be progressed to actual strengthening in the following days. Specifically, eccentric–concentric actions below and above the painful range of motion, as well as isometrics, can be used to strengthen the damaged muscle and speed up functional recovery. In the case of an injured limb, the athlete should not neglect training the opposite (uninjured) limb; in fact, doing training the other limb may allow the injured limb to benefit from the "cross-training effect" and functionally recover in a shorter time (Hellebrandt et al. 1947; Gregg and Mastellone 1957; Devine et al. 1981; Kannus et al. 1992; Zhou 2003; Lee 2007; Sariyildiz et al. 2011).

Absolute rest is contraindicated for injury recovery, especially for athletes, because fundamental factors for tissue repair include blood circulation and its tissue-nourishing effect, as well as the endocrine, autocrine, and paracrine anabolic hormones stimulated by exercise. Some illuminated physiotherapists have borrowed the Chinese medicine concept of "surrounding the dragon," indicating a rehabilitation approach in which only the injured muscle group is trained in a special way, whereas the rest of the body is trained both neuromuscularly and metabolically to retain preinjury biomotor abilities as much as possible. For instance, for athletes who cannot run due to injury, the World Athletics Center's education director Dan Pfaff (coach of several Olympic medalists in track and field), implements bike workouts (alactic, short lactic, and long lactic) to retain their metabolic level of conditioning. Finally, recognizing the special physiological status of an athlete, his or her rehabilitation should, as much as possible, follow an active approach that is performance milestone-based rather than the inactive, timeline-based approach commonly used for rehab patients.

5

Sport Nutrition

Nutrition is often discussed in locker rooms and gyms across North America and beyond. For example, common subjects of discussion during training include how much protein to consume and what supplements to take. Though this chapter does not provide detailed coverage of athletic nutritional requirements, it does address guidelines for pregame, in-game, and postgame (or exercise-session) nutrition.

An athlete's default diet determines what other nutrition he or she needs in order to meet the specific nutritional demands of his or her individual training program. Most athletes consume a considerable number of calories in order to satisfy their energy requirements and promote recovery following a training session. However, training of all types depletes glycogen stores and causes some degree of muscle breakdown. Therefore, what and when an athlete eats following a training session or game is vital to recovery, regeneration, and physiological improvement—just as vital, in fact, as rest and the use of active recovery techniques (see chapter 4).

What Is Correct Nutrition?

In 2003, the International Olympic Committee released the following position statement: "The amount, composition, and timing of food intake can profoundly affect sports performance. Good nutritional practice will help athletes train hard, recover quickly, and adapt more effectively with less risk of illness and injury" (International Olympic Committee 2010).

In fact, as stated by John Berardi (nutritionist for several Canadian and American Olympic teams and professional athletes in various sports), the high volume and frequency of a competitive athlete's training regimen mean that he or she must consume both a large number of calories and precise amounts of macro- and micronutrients (Berardi and Andrews 2009). These nutrients quickly refill the athlete's energy substrates, sustain the morpho-functional adaptations stimulated by training, and support the athlete's immune system—all while helping the athlete maintain his or her desired body weight and percentage of body fat. Correct nutrition should be based on the following five principles (Berardi and Andrews 2009).

Habit 1: Eat every two to four hours.

Contemporary research shows that eating at regular "feeding intervals" stimulates metabolism, balances blood sugar, helps prevent overeating driven by hunger, and helps the body burn extra fat mass while maintaining lean mass. This habit also ensures that active people, who have greater caloric demands, can meet their caloric needs without eating calorically dense foods that promote fat storage.

Habit 2: Eat complete, lean protein at each feeding opportunity.

Good sources of protein include lean red meat, salmon, eggs, low-fat plain yogurt, and supplemental proteins such as milk protein isolates and whey protein isolates. Some experts claim that additional protein is harmful or unnecessary. However, contemporary research is fairly clear: A high-protein diet is safe and may be important for achieving the best health, body composition, and athletic performance. By following this habit, athletes ensure adequate protein consumption, stimulation of metabolism, improved muscle mass and recovery, and reduction of body fat.

Habit 3: Eat vegetables at each feeding opportunity.

Science has shown that vegetables contain numerous micronutrients (vitamins and minerals). Vegetables also contain important phytochemicals (plant chemicals) that are essential for optimal physiological functioning. In addition, both vegetables and fruits provide the blood with an alkaline load, which balances the acid load presented to the blood by protein and grain. Too little alkalinity and too much acid lead to the loss of bone strength and muscle mass. A good balance can be ensured by eating two servings of fruits or vegetables at every meal.

Habit 4: For fat loss, eat carbohydrates other than fruits and vegetables only after exercise.

This timing strategy works well in people with stubborn and hard-to-remove body fat stores. It also works well for minimizing fat gain in people who are interested in gaining muscle.

Habit 5. Eat healthy fats daily.

Healthy fats include monounsaturated fat (found in extra-virgin olive oil, some nuts, and avocado) and polyunsaturated fat (found in some nuts, some vegetable oils, and fish oil supplements).

Of course, these recommendations must be modified according to the athlete's body type (ectomorph, mesomorph, or endomorph), his or her body composition goals, the sport's ergogenesis, and the current phase of the annual plan (nutrition periodization is addressed a bit later in this chapter).

An ectomorph, or an athlete who needs to build body mass, can eat simple carbohydrate and fast-digesting protein before, during, and after a training session. He or she can also eat carbohydrate-dense food, such as pasta and whole-grain cereal, at every meal. A mesomorph can use simple carbohydrate and fast-digesting protein during and after a training session and eat carbohydrate-dense food (again, pasta or whole-grain cereal) at the main meal after the workout. An endomorph, or an athlete who needs to reduce body fat, can consume an intra-workout drink containing glucogenic amino acids (BCAA, glutamine, glycine, and alanine) and postpone the main meal after the workout by one hour in order to maximize the lipolytic effect of the growth hormone released during the workout.

IMPROVING THE ATHLETE'S BODY COMPOSITION

Change in body composition is defined as positive when lean body mass increases and fat mass decreases. We must keep in mind the following basic principles:

- Diet is the single factor that most determines variations in body composition.
- Weight loss and weight gain are functions of energy balance—the difference between calories taken in and calories burned. Mere weight loss alone does not ensure that body *composition* has improved.
- The ratio between the macronutrients' intake determines the quality (defined as the difference between lean body mass and fat-free mass) of weight gain or weight loss. Eventual changes in carbohydrate and fat intake should be inversely proportional to each other.
- Given the same diet, the combination of dieting and weight training always leads to a higher percentage of lean body mass (with all of the implied benefits) than does dieting alone.
- It is possible to simultaneously increase lean body mass and decrease fat mass. In fact, this pair of changes always happens to well-trained subjects—those whose trainers use methodological concepts, such as the alternation of energy systems and the periodization of strength—who follow a proper diet in order to improve body composition.

Guidelines for Carbohydrate, Protein, and Hydration

The famous food pyramid, created in 1992 by the U.S. Department of Agriculture, mirrored the underlying philosophy of the "old" dietetics. This approach viewed the improvement of body composition as depending on restricted calorie intake and reduced fat intake. Thus the pyramid implied that carbohydrate (in the form of pasta, rice, bread, or processed cereals in general) was good, whereas every form of fat (be it animal or vegetable, saturated or unsaturated) was evil.

In 2005, the pyramid was changed and renamed MyPyramid. MyPyramid was criticized as being too influenced by industry interests and prompted Walter Willet and Patrick Skerrett of the Harvard School of Public Health to release an adjusted version called the Harvard Healthy Eating Pyramid in the same year. The improved pyramid version included the following modifications: lower intake of processed cereals, higher intake of whole-grain cereals, higher intake of fruits and vegetables, higher intake of meat and beans, and a distinction between unsaturated fat (mostly from vegetable sources; suggested) and saturated fat (to be limited). The pyramid, though, failed to distinguish between lean and fat meat, and between oil rich in omega-3 and oil rich in omega-6 and had no reference to meal timing (Berardi and Andrews 2009).

The following paragraphs cover our suggested intake guidelines for carbohydrate, protein, and hydration.

Carbohydrate

During digestion, carbohydrate is broken down and absorbed as monosaccharides and disaccharides, most of which is glucose, the primary energy source for most human cells.

It is advisable to concentrate the highest percentage of daily carbohydrate intake around the training session and to maintain the macronutrient proportions at 55 percent carbohydrate, 30 percent protein, and 15 percent fat. There can be periods in the annual plan when the ratio can be changed to favor the adaptations of training. We will discuss this topic in the section on nutrition periodization. This macronutrient ratio should be used by power athletes as well as endurance athletes who traditionally employ a much higher ratio of 70 percent carbohydrate and 15 percent fat. The ratio suggested here elicits greater sensitivity to insulin than is the case with chronically high carbohydrate intake. A greater insulin sensitivity, other than having beneficial effects on the health of an athlete as well as his or her body composition, actually amplifies the effect of carbohydrate loading that occurs by changing the ratio to 70 percent carbohydrate, 15 percent protein, 15 percent fat for the three or four days immediately preceding a competition day. This strategy is recommended to increase the amount of glycogen stored in the muscles for most glycolytic and aerobic sports but not for anaerobic alactic speed and power sports, because they do not rely on glycogen as their primary energy substrate, and this approach might lead to unfavorable changes in body composition.

Bear in mind that not all carbohydrate sources are the same. Simpler carbohydrate, often referred to as "sugar," is digested faster and reaches the bloodstream in the form of glucose at a higher rate than "complex" carbohydrate, which is made of longer-chains of saccharides that are digested more slowly. The degree of carbohydrate complexity in a food source determines its glycemic index—that is, its capacity to raise the level of blood glucose. A more accurate indicator of this capacity is glycemic *load*, which is the glycemic index multiplied by the fraction of the carbohydrate present in a serving of a given food.

Tables 5.1 and 5.2, depict the difference between glycemic index and glycemic load for various foods. Table 5.3 provides the recommended time of consumption during the day, which can make a big difference in proper nutrition. In fact, the sharp rise in blood glucose elicited by the intake of simple carbohydrate causes the pancreas to release more insulin, which can be defined as a storage hormone. Its release right after a training session provides a host of positive effects on training adaptation, whereas a series of insulin spikes during the day would negatively affect the athlete's body composition and health. Thus, an athlete should mostly consume complex carbohydrate.

Table 5.1 Glycemic Index and Glycemic Load of Common Foods

Food	Glycemic index	Serving size (g)	Glycemic load
Fruits			
Apple, fresh	34	120	5
Apple juice, unsweetened	41	250	11
Apricot, dried	32	60	8
Apricot, fresh	57	120	5
Banana, ripe	51	120	13
Cantaloupe	65	120	4
Cherries	22	120	3
Cranberry juice	68	250	24
Grapefruit	25	120	3

Food	Glycemic index	Serving size (g)	Glycemic load
Grapes	46	120	8
Kiwi	53	120	6
Mango	51	120	8
Orange	42	120	5
Orange juice	52	250	12
Peach	42	120	5
Pear	38	120	4
Pineapple	59	120	7
Plum	39	120	5
Prunes, pitted	29	60	10
Raisins	64	60	28
Strawberries, fresh	40	120	1
Strawberry jam	51	30	10
Tomato juice, no sugar added	38	250	4
Watermelon	72	120	4
Other foods			
Bagel, white, frozen	72	70	25
Baguette, white, plain	95	30	15
Corn flakes (Kellogg's)	92	30	24
Corn Pops (Kellogg's)	80	30	21
Potato, baked	85	150	26
Potato, French fries, frozen	75	150	22
Potato, instant mashed	85	150	17
Potato, sweet	61	150	17
Potato, white, cooked	50	150	14
Rice noodles, dried, boiled	61	180	23
Rice pasta, brown, boiled	92	180	35
Soft wheat spaghetti, boiled	46	180	22
Hard wheat spaghetti, al dente	37	180	16
Whole-wheat spaghetti, boiled	34	100	11

Table 5.2 Glycemic Index and Glycemic Load Ratings

		Low	Medium	High
Glycemic index	How fast a carbohydrate can enter the bloodstream and raise blood glucose level (glycemia)	<55	55–70	>70
Glycemic load	How much a serving of a certain food raises blood glucose level	<10	10–20	>20

Table 5.3   Suggested Timing of Carbohydrate Ingestion According to Glycemic Load

Carbohydrate type (across) and timing (below)	Low glycemic load	Medium glycemic load	High glycemic load
Presession meal (3–4 hrs. before)	****	**	—
Presession snack (1–2 hrs. before)	***	***	—
Intra-session drink	*	*	****
Postsession drink (within 45 min.)	—	—	****
Postsession meal (2 and 4 hrs. after)	**	**	—

Key: * = recommended in very low dosage (50 milligrams per kilogram (2.2 pounds) of lean body mass (LBM)), ** = recommended in low dosage (250 milligrams per kilogram of LBM), *** = recommended in moderate dosage (400 milligrams per kilogram of LBM), and **** = recommended in high dosage (800 milligrams per kilogram of LBM).

Protein

Protein, which consists of amino acids, is extremely important for building muscle tissue and sustaining a host of physiological functions. Optimal protein intake varies from athlete to athlete and depends in part on the volume of weight training performed and the objectives of the current training phase. Generally, however, most athletes should consume 1.2 to 2 grams of protein daily per kilogram (2.2 pounds) of lean body mass during the anatomical adaptation, conversion, and maintenance phases. More specifically, a long-endurance athlete should usually consume a protein amount in the lower part of the range, whereas a power athlete should consume an amount in the higher part of the range.

During the hypertrophy and maximum strength phases, athletes should consider eating between 2 and 3 grams of protein per kilogram of lean body mass, because these phases involve very high intensity strength training (Tipton and Wolfe, 2004). As discussed earlier in the chapter, protein intake should involve a variety of sources, including lean red meat, eggs, low-fat plain yogurt or cheese, poultry, fish, protein shakes, and an occasional protein bar.

Hydration

Water represents about 60 percent of human body weight. Upon losing 1 percent to 2 percent of body weight due to liquid loss, a person feels thirst, which in itself implies a decrease in endurance performance. Dehydration by 4 percent results in cramps, which are preceded by a reduction in strength and coordination skills. Thus the sensation of thirst is not a good indicator of the athlete's state of hydration; therefore, it is advisable not merely to respond to it but to prevent it.

To do so, athletes must drink plenty of water—before, during, and after training or competition. A well-hydrated body is better able to fight both muscular and cardiovascular fatigue. Generally speaking, we need about three quarts (liters) of water per day, one of which is usually taken in with food. An additional half liter is necessary in a warm climate, and in the case of training in such a climate the daily requirement can double. The hydration strategy to adopt is as follows: 17 ounces (500 milliliters) of fluid taken 30 minutes before training plus 8.5 ounces (250 milliliters) every 15 minutes.

If you want to add carbohydrate, the solution must not exceed a concentration of 10 percent in order to avoid delaying absorption and to prevent gastrointestinal problems

Figure 5.1 shows a possible periodization of nutrition for a power-and-speed sport. During the maximum strength phase, protein and calories are increased to promote an anabolic effect, whereas carbohydrate is increased during the more specific training phases that heavily tax the anaerobic lactic system. During the competitive phase, caloric intake is reduced because the reduction in overall training load decreases the athlete's energy expenditure.

Figure 5.1   Sample Diet Periodization for a Power-and-Speed Sport

Training phase	Preparatory				Competitive	
Subphase	General		Specific		Precompetitive	Competitive
Macrocycle	1 … 2		3 … 4 … 5		6	7 … 8 … 9
Microcycle	1 2 3 4 5	6 7 8	9 10 11 12	13 14 15 16	17 18 19	20 21 22 23 24 25
Strength periodization	Anatomical adaptation	Maximum strength		Power	Power endurance	Maintenance
Speed periodization	—	Introduction of technical elements—general speed	Alactic speed (acceleration)	Alactic speed (maximum speed)	Alactic speed (maximum speed) and lactic speed (speed endurance)	Maintenance
Endurance periodization	Aerobic endurance (specific modality)		Aerobic and specific endurance		Specific endurance	Maintenance
Nutrition	Balanced —3:2:1*	Hypercaloric** —3:2:1		Balanced —3:2:1	Hyperglucidic*** —4:2:0.5	

*Total daily protein intake at 2 grams per kilogram (2.2 pounds) of lean body mass (LBM). Intake proportions of macronutrients: 3 carbohydrate, 2 protein, and 1 fat. For example, for a power athlete with 80 kilograms (177 pounds) of LBM: 2,320 calories from 240 grams of carbohydrate, 160 grams of protein, and 80 grams of fat.

**Protein at 2.5 grams per kilogram of LBM. Intake proportions: 3 carbohydrate, 2 protein, and 1 fat. For example, for an athlete with 80 kilograms (177 pounds) of LBM, 2,900 calories sourced as follows: 2.5 grams of protein × 80 kilograms of LBM = 200 grams of protein × 4 calories per gram of protein = 800 calories from protein; 200 grams of protein × 1.5 (per the 3:2:1 ratio) = 300 grams of carbohydrate × 4 calories per gram of carbohydrate = 1,200 calories from carbohydrate; and 200 grams of protein ÷ 2 (per the 3:2:1 ratio) = 100 grams of fat × 9 calories per gram of fat = 900 calories from fat; thus a total of 800 (protein) + 1,200 (carbohydrate) + 900 (fat) = 2,900 calories.

***Protein at 2 grams per kilogram of LBM. Intake proportions: 4 carbohydrate, 2 protein, and 0.5 fat. For example, for an athlete with 80 kilograms (177 pounds) of LBM, 2,280 kilocalories sourced from 320 grams of carbohydrate, 160 grams of protein, and 40 grams of fat. Calories reduced during taper phase, mainly through reduction of fat, to match lower energy expenditure and thereby maintain optimal body composition and specific performance.

© Adam Davy/Press Association

To fight fatigue, an athlete should drink water before, during, and after competition.

(the percentage should be lowered to 4 percent in a very hot climate). Electrolytes can be added in 2:1:1 proportions of sodium, potassium, and magnesium and for no more than 500 milligrams total—250 milligrams, 125 milligrams, and 125 milligrams, respectively. Athletes who compete in events or competitions lasting longer than 45 minutes can benefit from sport drinks that help replace lost electrolytes. Studies show that sipping about 5 ounces (150 milliliters) of a sport drink at 20-minute intervals can help decrease the reliance on muscle glycogen stores and thus delay the onset of fatigue (Davis, Jackson, et al. 1997; Davis, Welsh, et al. 1999).

Some sport drinks on the market, however, make claims that may not be validated by science (Coombes and Hamilton 2000); therefore, athletes would do well to shop wisely. In addition, sport drinks do not benefit athletes in high-intensity sports that require short bursts of speed and power, such as sprints, throws, and jumps because they don't sweat as much or exhaust as much glycogen stores (Powers et al. 1990). However, athletes who perform the intermittent high-intensity activity typical of most team sports can benefit from consuming sport drinks that offer a carbohydrate–electrolyte mixture (Welsh et al. 2002).

Dehydration usually results from intense training or competition in a moderate or hot environment. Athletes exercising intensely in the heat lose fluid in the form of sweat at a rate of two to three quarts (liters) per hour. Therefore, hydration is important for recovery after exercise or training. When an athlete is dehydrated, however, drinking water alone is insufficient to return his or her body to its preexercise state of hydration. In fact, drinking water alone tricks the body into thinking it is overhydrated and thus triggers the kidneys to increase urine output, which results in further fluid loss. However, studies show that when a higher concentration of sodium is ingested, as previously suggested, the amount of urine produced a few hours after exercise is lower (Maughan et al. 1993).

Following training, an athlete should drink a volume of fluid similar to or even greater than the amount lost through perspiration. This amount varies between athletes, but a relative amount can be calculated by weighing an athlete before and after training or competition. As a rule of thumb, an athlete should drink approximately 1.5 liters (quarts) of fluid for every kilogram (2.2 pounds) of weight lost. By combining proper hydration with adequate nutrition (in the form of drink or food, as well as appropriate nutritional supplements), the athlete begins the process of recovering and preparing for the vigor of training or competition that lies ahead.

Peri-Exercise Nutrition

In the training world, it is often said that a workout is only as good as the recovery that follows. This saying applies to nutrition. The high-intensity work of training for strength, speed, and endurance taxes the body's energy reserves, depleting glycogen stores and causing the breakdown of muscle tissue. However, taking in proper nutrition immediately after a workout quickly shifts the body from breakdown to regeneration.

In recent years, researchers, coaches, and sports medicine practitioners have focused attention on what has been called "peri-workout nutrition"—that is, nutrition during the hours immediately preceding and following an exercise session, as well as during the session itself (Hawley, Tipton, and Millard-Stafford 2006; Hoffman et al. 2010; Kraemer et al. 2006). This attention, for example, has finally resulted in a position statement by the International Society of Sports Nutrition (Kerksick 2008), as well as a document produced in common by North American sports medicine doctors and dieticians, stating that a special postworkout nutrition strategy can increase muscle recovery and adaptation to training (American College of Sports Medicine 2000).

Training causes a strong disturbance of the body's homeostasis, which results in important physiological changes. It has become increasingly clear that such alterations should be accounted for in an athlete's nutritional approach in order to maximize the quality of performance and accelerate and amplify the body's adaptation to training. Each muscular status—energy production, energy substrate restoration, protein breakdown, and protein synthesis—requires a particular intake of macronutrients (carbohydrate, protein, and fat). This differentiation means that getting the right nutrition at the right time can increase an athlete's recovery from exercise and improve his or her strength, power, and muscle-growth adaptations. Here, we adopt, with slight modification in terminology, the three phases of muscle status suggested by Ivy and Portman (2004): energetic, anabolic, and adaptive. The energetic state coincides with the training session, the anabolic state with the 45 minutes immediately following the session, and the adaptive state with the time between one training session and the next.

Research shows that during exercise (i.e., during the energetic phase), it is beneficial for an athlete to consume a mix of simple carbohydrate—300 to 400 milligrams per kilogram (2.2 pounds) of lean body mass (LBM), or, for an alactic session, half that dosage or none at all, depending on the training objective—and "fast" protein (whey isolate or, even better, hydrolyzed) at a ratio of 4 or 5 to 1. Doing so spares muscle glycogen (50 percent less glycogen utilization) (Haff et al. 2000), reduces muscle catabolism (i.e., reduces cortisol secretion), limits suppression of the immune system (which occurs mainly through glutamine depletion, which is also mediated by cortisol levels) (Bishop, Blannin, Walsh, et al. 2001), reduces muscle damage (decreases inflammatory markers by 50 percent) (Bishop, Blannin, Rand, et al. 1999; Ready, Seifert, and Burke 1999), increases muscle endurance, and speeds post-training recovery (Ivy et al. 2003).

These benefits can be extended in the anabolic phase, in which nutrition influences training effects (Tipton and Wolfe 2001), by taking the same mix immediately after a workout but at a higher dosage—600 to 800 milligrams of carbohydrate per kilogram of LBM (or half that dosage for an alactic session, depending on the training objective)—and a lower ratio (3:1) of carbohydrate to protein. Doing so helps sustain glycogen restoration—increasing the enzyme glycogen synthetase by 70 percent following a postworkout insulin spike (Zawadzki, Yaspelkis, and Ivy 1992)—in a period of high cellular insulin sensitivity (which begins to decline just 30 minutes after exercise and becomes "insulin resistance" after two hours). It also aids protein uptake and synthesis: +200 percent cellular amino

PRECOMPETITION MEAL TIPS

Athletes should eat a full meal three to four hours before a competition; eating closer to the event can cause gastrointestinal problems. When putting together a precompetition meal, use the following guidelines.

- The meal should consist of at least 50 percent complex carbohydrate to fuel the athlete for competition. He or she should stay away from simple carbohydrate, which is often contained, for example, in processed foods. Soft drinks (e.g., colas) should not even be placed on the table. Here is an example of a good precompetition meal: small to medium bowl of pasta with tomato sauce, 8-ounce (227-gram) piece of chicken or fish (low-fat protein source), and a side salad with a mixture of fresh vegetables.

- Athletes who feel hungry one to three hours before competition should not reach for a chocolate bar or candy. The sugar content of such items offers a quick pick-me-up, but the athlete's energy level will then drop quickly. In fact, such items, classified as high-glycemic foods (refer to table 5.1) leave the bloodstream almost as fast as they enter it and leave the athlete starving for energy. Lethargy is not a good feeling prior to competition! After the event, however, high-glycemic foods can be consumed to enhance glycogen storage (Burkes, Collier, and Hargreaves 1998).

- During competition, the athlete can drink a hypotonic or isotonic (depending on the environmental temperature) fast-carbohydrate drink with some fast protein or amino acids (as suggested earlier) to aid hydration status and keep blood glucose levels up, thus helping the athlete maintain power output throughout the competition (Fritzsche et al. 2000). During exercise, muscle cells can take up glucose from the bloodstream independent of insulin level; therefore, despite taking in a fast carbohydrate, the athlete is not at risk for reactive hypoglycemia (sudden drop in blood glucose due to an insulin spike). For long-lasting events (more than 45 minutes), the athlete can also add slower carbohydrate, such as isomaltulose and waxy maize.

- Both alcohol and caffeine can dehydrate the body. Alcohol also activates the detoxification system of the body for up to 48 hours. For this reason, athletes should avoid consuming alcohol within 48 hours of the start of competition. If the environmental temperature is particularly high and the event is of medium or long duration, caffeine should also be limited on the day of competition.

- Very fatty, greasy food is digested slowly and is hard on the digestive system. For this reason, fast food should be excluded from athletes' meal plans. Athletes should also be careful to eat foods that their bodies are accustomed to. The precompetition meal is not the time to try out new recipes or uncommon foods!

acid uptake and +25 percent of protein synthesis right after the training session (Biolo, Tipton, et al. 1997; Okamura et al. 1997; Biolo, Fleming, and Wolfe 1995; Tipton et al. 1999; Biolo, Williams, et al. 1999).

The postworkout period is the only time that an insulin spike does *not* suppress growth hormone levels (whereas it does suppress cortisol and reduce muscle protein catabolism) (Grizard et al. 1999; Bennet and Rennie 1991; Rennie and Millward 1983). This fact indicates that the body's physiological systems compensate for the alterations induced by training, both in terms of the energy substrates and the structural damage and adaptation.

Furthermore, a less known characteristic of the insulin spike is its capacity to increase blood flow to the muscles by 100 percent, thus aiding in the removal of metabolites and the delivery of nutrients and oxygen and thereby enabling faster recovery and adaptation.

Ivy and Portman (2004) distinguish between a rapid segment and a sustained segment of the adaptive (or, in their term, "growth") phase. The first segment lasts up to four hours after a workout and benefits from a further intake of carbohydrate (60 to 80 milligrams per kilogram of LBM) and protein (200 to 300 milligrams per kilogram of LBM) at two and four hours after training. The second segment, on the other hand, sees a return to the default macronutrient proportion of the diet. A daily protein intake up to 1.8 to 2. 5 grams per kilogram of LBM is recommended for power athletes. This protein dosage has been proven necessary for such athletes during high-intensity training phases (Lemon et al. 1997; Forslund et al. 2000). As Ivy and Portman have said, "many nutrition traditionalists . . . fail to incorporate in their programs some of the landmark studies showing how nutrition could have improved the sport performances of the last two decades. . . . This information abyss presents a true challenge for the serious strength athlete as he or she tries to navigate through hype or outdated thinking" (p. 83)

Fasting or delaying the postworkout meal by a few hours further exhausts the body, delays compensation, and insufficiently prepares the athlete for the next training session, which might occur within the next 24 hours. Although most trainees, especially endurance athletes, like to ingest a form of carbohydrate instead of protein after a strength training session, doing so does not support the high rate of protein synthesis that follows a workout (Borsheim et al. 2004). For instance, the high-volume and high-intensity training often performed by endurance athletes not only depletes the high-energy glycogen stores, but also promotes muscle breakdown. For this reason, it is important that endurance athletes also supplement their diets with protein right after training.

More advanced trainees benefit from preparing a mixture with fast carbohydrate (e.g., Vitargo S2) and fast protein (e.g., whey isolate or, even better, hydrolyzed whey—the di- and tripeptides of hydrolyzed protein are absorbed faster than free-form amino acids) to be consumed right after training. Recovery and adaptation can be further increased by including amino acids (e.g., L-glutamine, taurine, and L-leucine) and peptides (e.g., creatine); for directions, see the discussion of supplement usage later in this chapter.

Supplements

Phytonutrients, vitamins, essential amino acids, and essential fatty acids are necessary for normal physiological functioning but cannot be produced by the body itself. Therefore, it is necessary to get them either through the diet or in the form of a supplement. In addition, some amino acids are defined as "conditionally essential" because the need for them increases greatly in certain situations—for example, the need for glutamine during periods of intense training.

Unfortunately, the field of supplements has been the subject of a campaign of disinformation and deception unlike any other. This dubious distinction means that most of the information you hear or read about supplements is partially or completely false. Misinformation is misinformation regardless of where it comes from, so you must proactively distrust and verify by reading the scientific studies directly.

Not only that, but once you read the studies, consider the following factors: the study's funder (in some cases, a supplement manufacturer), the type of subject (human or animal), the number of subjects (the more the better), the characteristics of the subjects (sex, age, level of training, state of health), the type of study (preferably double-blind, meaning that the subjects did not know what they were taking and the control group was reversed at mid-study), the dosages used, the form of administration employed (e.g., oral, intravenous), and so on. You can find scientific studies at the PubMed website maintained by the (U.S.) National Institutes of Health (http://www.ncbi.nlm.nih.gov/pubmed/).This wonderful website provides an archive of the world's scientific knowledge, including scientific studies about training.

Table 5.4 shows a list of supplements for essential and nonessential nutrients that you can use to improve training and competition quality or speed up recovery and adaptation.

Table 5.4   Guidelines for Use of Common Sport Supplements per Training Objective

Supplement	What it is	Why to use it	When to use it	Dosage
Alpha lipoic acid, type R	Derivative of octanoic (fatty) acid; strong antioxidant	To improve cellular insulin sensitivity and reduce insulin response to meals	Daily	100 mg 3 or 4 times per day, including postworkout and before main meals
Omega-3 fatty acid	Essential fatty acid (EPA, DHA); anti-inflammatory	To improve cellular insulin sensitivity	Daily	1 g 3–5 times per day
BCAA	Branched-chain amino acid (essential)	To reduce muscle catabolism induced by heavy training sessions	On heavy training days	100–200 mg/kg of LBM, depending on diet (more for hypocaloric diets), to be taken before training
Creatine	Peptide synthesized from the amino acids arginine, glycine, and methionine	To increase cellular creatine stores used in anaerobic efforts; to increase cellular volume	Daily during intense strength, power, or speed phases	1.5 g before and after training; up to 100 mg/kg of LBM during hypertrophy phases
ZMA	Highly bioavailable form of zinc and magnesium	To increase sleep quality and make up for eventual deficiencies that might lead to lower levels of testosterone and growth hormone	During high-load phases or during the competitive phase	450 mg before sleeping
Caffeine	Alkaloid xanthine	To increase nervous system efficiency and speed up metabolism	Before competition or fat-loss training sessions	50–200 mg one hour before training or competition
L-tyrosine	Nonessential amino acid	To increase nervous system efficiency	Before competition or fat-loss training sessions	2–3 g one hour before training or competition

Supplement	What it is	Why to use it	When to use it	Dosage
Acetyl-L-carnitine	Acetylated peptide synthesized from the amino acids lysine and methionine	To increase nervous system efficiency and improve androgen receptor sensitivity	Before competition or intense training sessions	1–3 g one hour before training or competition
Beta-alanine	Nonessential amino acid	To buffer hydrogen ions	Daily during phases of anaerobic lactic work	1 g 3 times per day or 3 g one hour before training or competition
Vitargo S2	High-molecular-weight carbo-hydrate	To spare glycogen stores or restore them more rapidly after training	During and after high-intensity aerobic and mixed anaerobic–aerobic training sessions or as a postworkout carbohydrate of choice	10% solution during training, 400–800 mg/kg of LBM right after training
L-leucine	Essential amino acid	To increase protein synthesis or reduce catabolism	Daily during hypertrophy phases or during and after training	1–3 g mixed into protein shakes or 3–9 g distributed during peri-workout times
L-glutamine	Conditionally essential amino acid	To prevent depletion due to high-load sessions; to sustain protein synthesis and the immune system	Daily during high-intensity phases or on training days only	3–6 g distributed during peri-workout times or 3 g before sleeping
Taurine	Conditionally essential amino acid; inhibitory neurotransmitter	To increase parasympathetic system tone	After high-intensity training sessions, especially if stimulants, such as caffeine, acetyl-L-carnitine, and L-Tyrosine, have been used before the workout	1–2 g right after training

SUPPLEMENTS AND SPORT

In 2001, a study examined 634 nutritional supplements on the U.S. market and found that 94 contained ingredients included in the World Anti-Doping Agency's list of banned substances; another 66 contained "dubious" substances. Of course, we also know about cases of positive doping tests caused by supplements containing pro-hormones, which have been sold in the United States as "food supplements" since the early 2000s (Schanzer 2002).

This context helps us understand the aversion exhibited by many sport federations toward supplements in general. According to the study, supplements bought in Switzerland, Norway, France, Belgium, Spain, and Italy had the least probability of contamination or hidden ingredients.

This caveat does not mean that we must exclude all supplements produced in the United States. To the contrary, in the late 1990s and early 2000s, the brothers Bill and Shawn Phillips published several reviews of supplements on the U.S. market and gave a fairly accurate picture of how the various manufacturers operate and which ones can be trusted. If you cannot find these supplement reviews, please visit the following websites that deal with the analysis of food supplements: NSF (www.nsf.org) and ConsumerLab (www.consumerlab.com).

Reliable supplement providers tend to be large companies that have been in the business for a long time, do not produce pro-hormones, have a good reputation for product quality, do not invest most of their money in advertising campaigns based on extreme and glamorous statements, and offer products with a short list of ingredients. Examples include NOW Foods, Prolab, iSatori, MET-Rx, and EAS.

When analyzing a supplement's ingredients, bear in mind that they are listed in order of amount. Be aware also that a "proprietary blend" is usually not an effort to protect a mix of ingredients used at a precise ratio but a trick to make an important or expensive ingredient "jump the queue" when it is in fact contained in a small quantity. Thus, the product looks better but costs less.

6

Periodization as Planning and Programming of Sport Training

Periodization involves two basic concepts: periodization of the annual plan and periodization of biomotor abilities.

- Periodization of the annual plan involves dividing the program into units in order to better manage the training and adaptation processes and, if necessary, to ensure peak performance at major competitions. Annual plan periodization is particularly useful to coaches for the following reasons:

  - It helps coaches design a rationally structured training plan.

  - It enhances coaches' awareness of the time available for each phase.

  - It integrates, at appropriate times, technical and tactical loads, biomotor ability development loads, nutrition, and psychological techniques for the highest increment of the athlete's motor potential and peak performance.

  - It allows management of fatigue and planning of a higher volume of high-quality training.

  - It helps coaches plan a rational alternation of loading and unloading periods in the training phases, thus maximizing adaptation and performance while avoiding the accumulation of a critical level of fatigue and the onset of overtraining.

- Periodization of biomotor abilities allows athletes to develop their biomotor abilities (strength, speed, and endurance) to an optimal level as the basis for a higher level of sport performance. This form of periodization is based on the following premises:

  - Improvement in sport performance is based (especially for the high-level athlete) on increasing the athlete's motor potential.

- Morpho-functional adaptations (i.e., positive changes in the body structure and functions) require time, as well as alternation of work and recovery, in order to manifest themselves.

- The development of the biomotor abilities and the improvement of technical and tactical factors require a progressive approach in which the intensity of training stimuli is gradually increased on the basis of previously induced morphological and functional adaptations.

- An athlete cannot maintain peak performance for a prolonged or undefined time.

Planning, Programming, and Periodization

The terms *planning*, *programming*, and *periodization* are often used as if they were synonymous, but they are not. Planning is the process of arranging a training program into long and short phases in order to achieve training goals. Programming, in contrast, is the act of filling this structure with content in the form of training modalities. Periodization incorporates planning and programming—in other words, the structure of the annual plan and its content (consisting of training methods and training means) as it changes over time. Thus we can define the periodization of the annual plan as the structure of the training process and the periodization of biomotor abilities as the plan's content. In other words, each time we divide the year into phases and establish a sequence of development for each biomotor ability, we form a periodized plan.

Some critics of periodization state that it was created for individual sports that include a long preparation phase and a short competitive phase. Therefore, they assert, periodization is not applicable to modern team sports, which feature a short preparation period and a very long competitive period. This criticism would be true if the relevant factors could be put together in only one combination. In reality, however, we can design as many periodized plans as necessary for the range of possible situations we may encounter in the sport training process. Furthermore, if we were to analyze what these critics actually do, we would see that their plans still entail a division of the year into smaller periods and a periodization of biomotor abilities, thereby qualifying them as periodized plans.

Figure 6.1 lists the composing elements of every theory about planning the training process. Periodization itself is a wide methodological doctrine that includes many theoretical and methodological concepts.

In fact, before we discuss which planning and programming method is better suited for a certain sport, we should agree on terminology—and, even more important, on the very concepts that form the theory of the planning and programming of training.

Annual Plan Terminology

Leonid Matveyev's book *The Problem of Periodization of Sport Training* (1964) analyzed the training diary of Russian athletes who took part in the 1952 Olympic games. Unsurprisingly, in the same period, Tudor Bompa was already applying periodization of training with his athletes, including Mihaela Penes (gold medalist in the javelin throw at the 1964 Tokyo Olympics), and developing what would become his concept of the periodization of strength, which is detailed in this book. However, it was not until Bompa's popular work *Periodization: Theory and Methodology of Training* (1983) that periodization gained wide popularity, especially in North America.

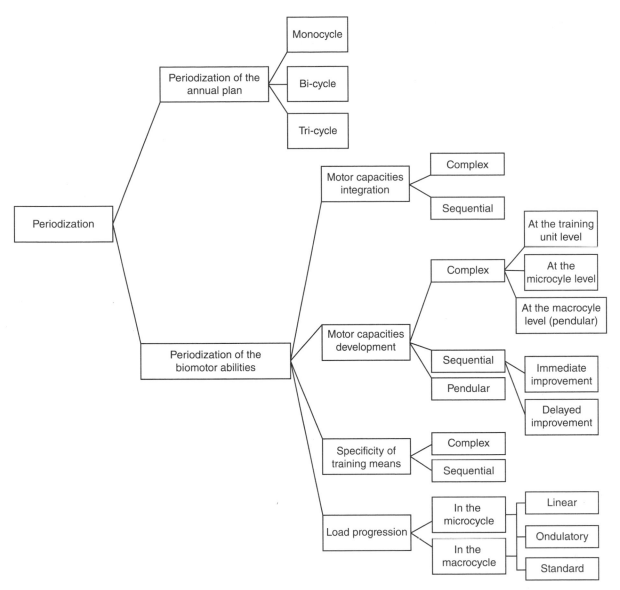

Figure 6.1 Scheme representing all composing units of every theory of the planning and programming of training.

Different from Soviet authors, who spoke of microcycle, mesocycle, and macrocycle—the latter being of various time lengths (six-month, annual, or four-year [Olympic cycle])—we use the following terminology (see figure 6.2):

- Annual plan (annual macrocycle for the Soviets): The year is divided into phases, subphases, macrocycles, and microcycles to better manage the training process. Annual plans are characterized by the number of competitive phases and are thus defined as monocyclical, bi-cyclical, or tri-cyclical.

- Phases (macrocycles for the Soviets): The three phases are preparation, competition, and transition.

	Yearly Plan					
Phases of training	Preparatory			Competitive		Transition
Sub-phases	General preparation	Specific preparation	Pre-competitive	Competitive		Transition
Macro-cycles						
Micro-cycles						

Figure 6.2 Division of an annual plan into its phases and cycles of training.

- Subphases: This further specification of the content of the phases includes general preparation, specific preparation, precompetition, competition, and transition. A subphase is made up of a group of macrocycles with the same training direction and whose length can vary from 1 week (for a short transition phase) to 24 weeks (for a long general preparation phase).

- Macrocycle (mesocycle for the Soviets): A macrocycle is a group of microcycles with the same training direction (according to the macrocycle and subphase) whose length can vary from 2 weeks (for a precompetitive unloading macrocycle, also called a taper macrocycle) to 6 weeks (for a long introductory macrocycle in general preparation) but are generally 3 or 4 weeks long.

- Microcycle: This is a cyclic sequence of training units that follow the macrocycle goals; its length can vary from 5 to 14 days but is usually 7 days long to match the week.

- Training unit: This is the single training session with pauses within the session shorter than 45 minutes.

Here we can make a distinction: The annual plan, phases, and subphases are tools used for planning, whereas the macrocycles, microcycles, and training units are tools used for programming. The former group allows trainers to draw up a long-term plan, and the latter group allows them to define in detail the content of the training process. Generally, the planning and programming process starts with the long-term tool (the annual plan) and ends with the shortest one (the training session). Thus the annual plan contains both elements of planning (e.g., phases and subphases) and elements of programming (e.g., macrocycles and microcycles depicting the periodization of biomotor abilities) and thereby addresses the whole training process (see figure 6.3). Note that intensity values refer to the overall training intensity, not to the dominant energy system.

The programming of the training process takes shape in the microcycle, through the use of methodological concepts such as the alternation of workloads and energy systems. Coaches can make use of training sessions and tests as feedback and feedforward elements to readily modify the program in order to individualize and maximize the training process.

Figure 6.3 — Complete annual plan for a sprinter preparing for the 2004 Olympics.

Date												
Month	Oct	Nov	Dec	Jan	Feb	Mar	Apr	May	June	July	Aug	Sept
Weekend (Domenica)	4 11 18 25	1 8 15 22	23 29 6 20 27	9 18 17 24 31	7 14 21 20 6	19 20 27	9 18 18 24 1	8 15 22 29	5 12 19 26	9 18 17 24 31	7 14 21 28	S

Competition HS Calendar
- National: (X July — National trials; X July — National trials)
- International (X): Florence indoor; Dartmund Ind. G.P.; Gont Ind. G.P.; Liovin Ind. G.P.; Karlruho Ind. G.P.; Athens Ind. G.P.; Club champc; Milan G.P.; Turin G.P.; Club clan, Fin.; Athens G.P.; Paris G.P.; Athens Olympic; Rikti G.P.

Test	X	X	X		X	X	X			X		X

Phases	Prep. I		Comp. I			Prep. II			Comp. II		Prep. III	Comp. III
Sub-phases	GP		SP	P-C	C	T / SP II	PEI		C II	T / SP III	PEII	C III

Macrocycles: 1 2 3 4 5 6 7 8 9 10 11 12 13 14 15 16 17

Microcycles: 1 2 3 4 5 6 7 8 9 10 11 12 13 14 15 16 17 18 19 20 21 22 23 24 25 26 27 28 29 30 31 32 33 34 37 38 39 40 41 42 43 44 45 46 47 48 49 50 51

Periodization of the biomotor abilities
- Strength: AA | MxS | Conv. to p. | Maint. | MxS | Conv. to p. | Maint. (COP) | MxS | Maint.
- Speed: Gen. sp. | Dev. Acc./max. speed | Dev. max. speed | (G.S. / D.M. Sp.) | Maint.
- Endurance: Gen. end. | Spec. enc. | Spec. end. | (G.E. / Sp End) | Maint.

Periodization of nutrition and psychological approach
- Psychology: Goal setting | Simulate competition strategies | Goal setting | Simulate competition strategies | Goal setting | Sim. competition strategies
- Nutrition: Bal. | High prot./carbs | High carbs/carbs | Bal. | High prot./carbs | High carbs/carbs | Bal. | H.p./c. | H.c./p.

Training factors
- Intensity: 5 4 3 3 3 4 3 2 1 3 2 1 3 2 1 1 3 1 1 2 1 3 1 1 3 2 1 3 2 1 3 1 1 3 1 1 1 1 1 4 1 1 5 2 3 4 5 3
- Volume: 5 4 3 2 1 3 2 1 2 2 4 2 2 2 4 3 4 4 4 3 4 3 4 3 4 3 3 4 3 3 3 4 3 4 3 4 4 4 4 2 4 2 3 3 4 5 3 4

Peaking index 1-5: 5 5 3 3 3 4 3 3 2 2 2 3 3 3 2 2 1 2 2 2 1 3 2 1 3 2 2 3 2 2 2 2 2 2 1 2 2 2 2 1 2 2 2 2 1 1 1 2

Legend:
- ■ Volume
- ○ Intensity
- ▲ Peaking index

Figure 6.3 Complete annual plan for a sprinter preparing for the 2004 Olympics.

91

Periodization of Biomotor Abilities

The goal of biomotor abilities training is to improve the athlete's performance on the basis of specialized morphological and functional adaptations. The most important feature of training the biomotor abilities is progressive overload. Even though an athlete's full motor potential is present in his or her genetic code, its expression requires the training process to be composed by general and specific means, not only for the principle of variety of training but also according to the trainability of the biomotor abilities themselves. For instance, trainability determines that endurance training for long-duration sport should be based mainly on specific work, which can represent up to 90 percent of the annual training time. By contrast, the more limited speed trainability requires major focus on general elements (such as strength and its various expressions).

Four elements differentiate each theory and methodology of the planning and programming of training in reference to the periodization of strength, speed, and endurance:

1. Integration of biomotor abilities
2. Development of each determinant biomotor ability throughout the plan
3. Degree of specificity of the training means throughout the plan
4. Load progression

Integration of Biomotor Abilities

When programming, the integration of biomotor abilities involves considering the dynamics by which the training of each biomotor ability affects the others, as well as the morphological and functional adaptations in response to the summation of stimuli. In the section of the annual plan dedicated to the periodization of biomotor abilities, you can understand the way that biomotor abilities are integrated by viewing the content of the three lines for strength, speed, and endurance for each macrocycle column (see figure 6.4).

Depending on how the biomotor abilities are integrated, it is possible to use one of two schemes: complex integration or sequential integration.

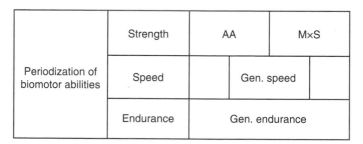

Periodization of biomotor abilities	Strength	AA	MxS
	Speed	Gen. speed	
	Endurance	Gen. endurance	

Figure 6.4 A vertical view of the annual plan depicts the integration of the biomotor abilities (in this case, anatomic adaptation, general speed, and general endurance during the general preparation phase).

Complex Integration

In this approach, strength, speed, and endurance are trained simultaneously during the whole year. That is, the load of each biomotor ability is distributed throughout the duration of the annual plan. This kind of integration is appropriate for all kind of sports, including those (such as team sports) in which the preparatory phase is short and the competitive phase is long without the need for a special peak of performance. It is the only method indicated for young athletes, who need a multilateral approach, and for inexperienced athletes in general.

Sequential Integration

In this approach, often referred to as block periodization, the workloads for strength, speed, and endurance, respectively, are concentrated into separate blocks that come one after another during the annual plan. Because the strength block is devoted almost completely to increasing that biomotor ability, the main problem with sequential integration lies in the challenge of retaining specific technique and specific biomotor abilities. For this reason, it is more easily applied by experienced speed and power athletes (not necessarily high level) who can better retain the other abilities.

Another possible limit of this planning method is that, during the speed or endurance block, there is no strength maintenance, which may lead to power loss if the competitive phase is long. A shorter version of sequential integration is indicated for racket sports and combat sports, where competitions are grouped into several periods throughout the year. In some sports, during the preparatory phase, coaches pursue the development of many aspects of physical training, such as aerobic power, maximum strength, muscular endurance, acceleration, and specific endurance. Each of these elements implies morphofunctional and psychological adaptations that sometimes conflict with each other. For instance, the adaptations required by the hypertrophy training (at both the skeletal muscle structure level and the neural level) are limited by the metabolic and neural costs of the endurance training. Therefore, it is advisable to establish the contribution of the two elements to the athlete's motor potential according to his or her sport and individual characteristics. This approach allows training to prioritize one element over the other and to develop the biomotor abilities with regard to the specific features of the sport itself without the need to clearly separate the training of a biomotor ability from the training of another and risking to detrain the latter.

Development of Biomotor Abilities

The term *development* addresses the way in which we want to train, or develop, a biomotor ability throughout the annual plan. In the section of the annual plan dedicated to the periodization of biomotor abilities, development is depicted by the horizontal line dedicated to each biomotor ability (see figure 6.5).

The development of biomotor abilities may be complex, sequential, or pendular. Each option is addressed in the following subsections.

Periodization of biomotor abilities	Strength	AA	M×S	Conversion to power	Maint.	Comp.	M×S	Conversion to P-E	Maint.	Comp.	M×S	Maint.	Taper	Comp.

Figure 6.5 A sequential development of strength within the annual plan.

Complex

In complex development of a biomotor ability, two or more qualities of the same ability are trained simultaneously—for example, maximum strength and power or muscular endurance. This approach can be used at different levels.

- Training unit: Maximum strength and power or muscular endurance are trained in a single training unit.
- Microcycle: Maximum strength and power or muscular endurance are trained in the same microcycle but in different training units.
- Macrocycle: Maximum strength and power or muscular endurance are trained throughout the macrocycle during dedicated microcycles.
- If two qualities are training alternatively during the macrocycle (e.g., a maximum strength microcycle followed by a power microcycle, followed again by a maximum strength microcycle, followed by another power microcycle), we have what is a called a "pendular" macrocycle.

Complex programming is used at the training unit level in only a few circumstances—for example, in youth training or amateur team sports, where a reduced number of weekly training units is required, and for maintenance of maximum and specific strength. When the complex development of a biomotor ability is of short duration (four to six weeks), the positive training effects are marked. On the other hand, such benefits quickly plateau.

For example, consider an amateur soccer team whose coach thinks that physical training is over by the end of the preparation phase. During the preparation phase, the team trains for development and integration of biomotor abilities through the complex approach. In other words, everything is trained simultaneously: power, muscular endurance, aerobic endurance, short anaerobic lactic power, and speed. When this training phase ends, however, the coach starts relying only on specific training, and the team slowly falls out of shape.

Sequential

In sequential development, as the name implies, the qualities of a biomotor ability are trained sequentially; for example, anatomical adaptation could be followed by maximum strength, which in turn could be followed by power. The sequence is such that each trained element promotes the development of the following one. For instance, maximum strength provides the basis for power, which in turn provides the basis for speed. The length of each training stimulus is determined by the time required to elicit the desired level of morpho-functional adaptation to the stimulus.

Figure 6.6 shows how each biomotor ability is developed to elicit the highest increase of a sprinter's motor potential. For a 100-meter sprinter, the specific strength is power endurance, and the specific mix of speed and endurance is speed endurance (lactic power). Once the anatomical adaptation macrocycle has been completed, maximum strength is trained to later maximize power. Acceleration is the specific base of technical and power output for maximum speed, and low volume aerobic power training helps the athlete recover for the following anaerobic work on the track.

In the following phase, power is trained as the neural base for power endurance and speed, and the endurance training becomes lactic tolerance training to create the metabolic adaptations upon which the athlete can maximize his or her specific endurance: lactic power. Then, maximum speed—and later, power endurance—are trained in order to create the physiological adaptations to maximize speed endurance. This example shows how the development and integration of biomotor abilities can be planned rationally to enable the ultimate performance.

Strength	MxS	P (maint.: MxS)	PE (maint.: MxS)	
Speed	Acceleration	Max speed		Speed endurance (lactic P)
Endurance	Intensive tempo (aerobic P)	Special endurance (lactic capacity)		

Key: maint. = maintenance, MxS = maximum strength, P = power, and PE = power endurance.

Figure 6.6 Morpho-Functional Adaptation Continuum for a 100-Meter Sprinter

Immediate and Delayed Improvement

The loading parameters for the sequential approach can be manipulated in such a way as to produce either immediate or delayed improvement. In the immediate-improvement approach, the indexes of the trained biomotor ability are improved at the end of the macrocycle. More specifically, the volume of the training stimulus enables improvement of the trained quality after a limited period of unload (usually one week). With this approach, it is also possible to work on speed and technical or tactical elements simultaneously with physical training.

In the delayed-improvement approach, on the other hand, the indexes of the trained biomotor ability are depressed at the end of the macrocycle but will improve later (this approach is also known as planned overreaching). Because the workload concentration in this approach temporarily decreases the specific functional parameters, it is necessary to temporarily separate this training from work on speed and technical or tactical elements. This separation allows the athlete to take advantage of the long-term effect of the physical workload concentration itself.

Pendular

In pendular development, two qualities of a biomotor ability are trained in alternative fashion. For example, a maximum strength macrocycle is followed by a power macrocycle, which is followed by another maximum strength macrocycle, which itself is followed by another power macrocycle. This approach is particularly indicated for racket sports, contact sports, and martial arts, for which a long maximum strength phase could negatively affect the power output of specific drills and the sometimes unpredictable competition schedule requires an athlete to not lower his or her readiness to compete too much.

Specificity of Training Means

Here again, we can distinguish between a complex approach and a sequential approach. The complex approach makes simultaneous and immediate use of both general and specific training means, at both moderate and high intensities. Because of the short preparation period and long competitive season, this approach is now common in team sports. By contrast, in the sequential approach, as the training potential of the chosen training means decreases over time, both the specificity and intensity of the training stimuli increase progressively. In this approach, each training means is used to exploit the morpho-functional adaptations induced by the previous ones (Verkhoshanskij 2008). This approach is particularly indicated to reach an athlete's motor potential for individual sports with long preparation periods.

Load Progression

Several sports have a consistent training load throughout the year, which is called a standard load. Some teams maintain 6 to 12 hours of training per week for the entire year with almost the same training contents throughout. Standard loading results in early improvement, followed by a plateau and then detraining during the competitive phase. On the other hand, despite being an effective way to progress the load over time for beginners, linear loading has been proven, both scientifically and empirically, to be an inferior way of applying progressive overload for intermediate and advanced athletes.

In fact, it is very unlikely that a biological system progresses in a mechanical or mathematical fashion over time. Instead, to elicit continuous and positive morpho-functional adaptations, a better approach is to implement a model that is cyclic, undulating, and self-adjusting. Such characteristics can—or better yet, should—be taken into consideration when designing a periodized plan.

Undulation at the Macrocycle Level

Undulation can be implemented at both the macrocycle level and the microcycle level. As shown in columns 1 and 2 of figure 6.7, the macrocycle can be undulated by alternating microcycles of different loads. Column 1 shows a sequence of medium-high, medium, high, and low weekly load, which is sometimes used by Cuban weightlifters. Column 2 shows a sequence of high, medium, medium-high, and low weekly load. The macrocycle can also be undulated by placing an unloading microcycle at the end of it. Column 3 shows this approach in a typical general preparation macrocycle of step loading (medium, medium-high, high, and low), and column 4 shows a typical specific preparation macrocycle of flat loading (high, high, low). The unloading microcycle placed at the end of the macrocycle results in a load undulation across macrocycles (see figure 6.8).

Undulation at the Microcycle Level

The undulation of load within a microcycle follows the very important methodological concepts of energy systems and load alternation (see figures 6.9 and 6.10). In planning competitive microcycles, we must also consider the need for postcompetition recovery and precompetition deloading (see figure 6.11).

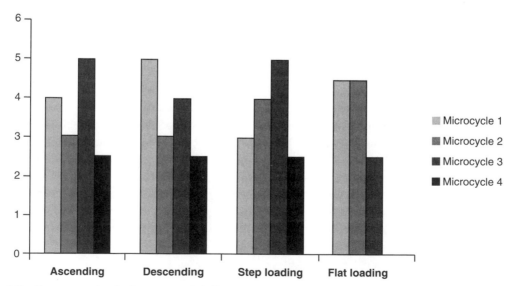

Figure 6.7   Four ways to design an undulating macrocycle.

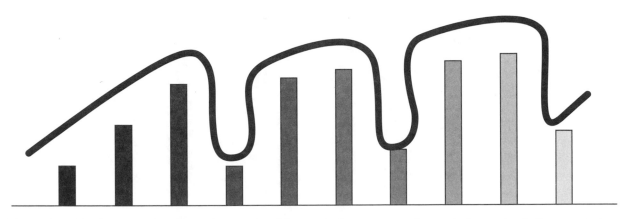

Figure 6.8 Placing an unloading microcycle at the end of a macrocycle maximizes adaptations and gives an undulatory quality to the load progression.

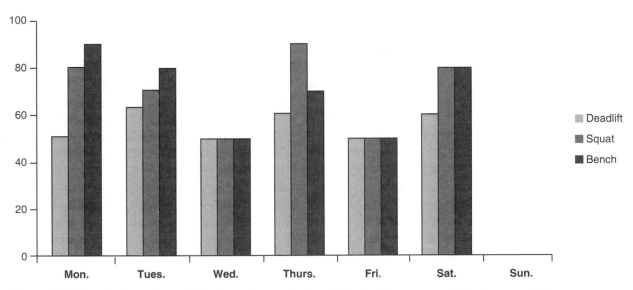

Figure 6.9 Load alternation within the microcycle in a high-frequency specialized powerlifting program.

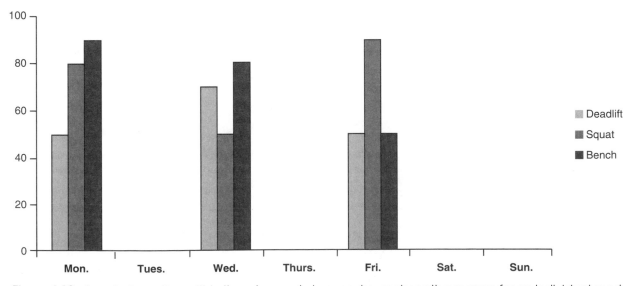

Figure 6.10 Load alternation within the microcycle in a maximum strength program for an individual sport.

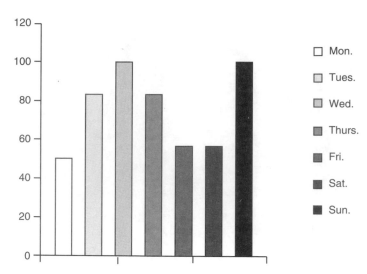

Figure 6.11 Alternation of the load within a competitive microcycle. The day after competition is low load to allow recovery, whereas the two days before competition are low load to reduce residual fatigue and allow better performance.

The self-adjusting training demand is met in multiple ways: constant monitoring of athletes, readiness to change the daily program according to their feedback, objective data collected during the training session, and testing at the end of each unloading microcycle placed at the end of a macrocycle. Periodization is not set in stone. The mechanistic rigidity often associated with periodization is probably based on the linear periodization of strength popularized in the United States in the 1980s, which required very long training periods during which the body was supposed to go through a mathematical progression. Such an approach has little to do with the more sophisticated and educated periodized strategies of the best coaches, who base their load determination on a continuous process of feedforward, feedback, and adjustment—as it should be.

Periodization is, in fact, a bundle of methodological concepts whose application we adapt to specific situations. For this reason, it can take many different forms. Coaches should be aware of the existence of various planning models, each of which is more indicated for certain sports and for certain athletes' developmental levels. On the programming side, coaches' training methodology and knowledge of exercise physiology should enable them to use their own intuition about how their athletes' bodies work and change in response to training stimuli, thus permitting them to foresee the desired morpho-functional adaptations. Nevertheless, achieving the best possible results requires constant monitoring, assessment, and adjustment of the program.

7

Laws and Principles of Strength Training for Sports

Proper application of training laws and principles ensures superior organization of training with the fewest possible errors. The seven laws of strength training (outlined in the following section) form the proper foundation for all strength training programs. The principles of training (addressed later in the chapter) outline the practical application of the laws in strength training programs.

A house is only as strong as its foundation. The seven basic laws of strength training work together to produce a strong, flexible, and stable athlete who can sustain the vigor required for sport. This result is achieved by developing the athlete's tendons, ligaments, and bones; strengthening the core; and adapting the body to the movements of the sport. The laws apply to all athletes, regardless of the physiological qualities of their chosen sport.

The principles of training promote a steady and specific increase in strength and other abilities by specifically adapting the program to the needs of the sport and, most important, to the physical capacity of the individual athlete. The principles work hand in hand with the laws in the quest to develop superior programs of strength. These principles—together with the periodization of strength and the integration of strength training with energy systems training—are essential to any successful training program.

Seven Laws of Strength Training

Any strength training program should be started by applying the seven laws of training to ensure adaptation and to the keep athlete free of injury. The laws are especially important for young or beginning athletes because they ensure the creation of a good base on which to build more specific training in later stages of the athlete's development.

Law 1: Develop Joint Mobility

In order to increase strength and mobility at the same time, most strength training exercises should be used for the entire range of motion of major joints, especially the knees, ankles, and hips. Good joint mobility prevents strain and pain around the joints; it also prevents stress injury. In particular, ankle mobility—that is, dorsal and plantar flexion, or bringing the toes toward and away from the calf—should be a major concern for all athletes, especially beginners. Athletes should start developing ankle mobility during prepubescence and pubescence so that in the latter stages of athletic development they need only maintain it.

Two great methods for improving flexibility are partner-assisted stretching and proprioceptive neuromuscular facilitation. In the case of myofascial adhesions—myofascia accounts for 41 percent of passive resistance to joint movement (Johns and Wright 1962)—effective methods include the use of foam rollers, Kelly Starrett's myofascia-releasing elastic band exercises, and a myofascia-releasing session with a certified practitioner. Myofascial release increases muscle flexibility and joint mobility without negatively affecting performance (Sullivan et al. 2013; McDonald et al. 2013; Healey et al. 2014). In fact, for peak performance, myofascia *must* be released before competition, especially in speed and power sports.

Law 2: Develop Ligament and Tendon Strength

Muscle strength improves faster than tendon and ligament strength. In addition, many training specialists and coaches overlook the strengthening of ligaments and tendons due to misuse of the principle of specificity or lack of a long-term vision. Yet most injuries occur not at the muscle but at the myotendinous junction. The reason is that without proper anatomical adaptation, vigorous strength training can injure the tendons and ligaments. With anatomical adaptation, however, tendons and ligaments grow strong. More specifically, training tendons and ligaments causes them to enlarge in diameter, thus increasing their ability to withstand tension and tearing.

Ligaments, which are made up of the fibrous protein collagen, play the important role of attaching articulated bones to each other across a joint. The collagen fibrils are arranged in varying degrees of folds to help resist an increase in load. The strength of a ligament depends directly on its cross-sectional area. A ligament may rupture when excessive force is directed at a joint. During regular exercise or activity, ligaments are easily elongated to allow movement in the joint to occur naturally. However, when a high load is applied, as in competition or training, ligament stiffness increases in order to restrict excessive motion in the joint. If the load is too great, the ligament is not able to withstand the stress and an injury can occur.

The best way to prevent such an injury is to properly condition the body to handle the stress. To adapt ligaments to handle the stress, and provide adequate time for regeneration, athletes can condition them through a cycle of loading and unloading, as in the anatomical adaptation phase of training. Progressively increasing the training load improves the viscoelastic properties of ligaments and allows them to better accommodate high tensile loads such as those used in dynamic movements, maximum strength training, and plyometrics.

Tendons, on the other hand, connect muscle to bone and transmit force from muscle to bone so that movement can occur. Tendons also store elastic energy, which is crucial to any ballistic movement, such as those used in plyometrics. The stronger the tendon is, the greater its capacity to store elastic energy. Therefore, powerful tendons are characteristic of sprinters and jumpers. Without strong tendons, they wouldn't be able to apply such great force against their bones to overcome the force of gravity.

Both ligaments and tendons are trainable. Their material and structural properties change as a result of training, leading to increased thickness, strength, and stiffness by up to 20 percent (Frank 1996). Ligaments and tendons are also capable of healing, although they might not recover to their preinjury capability.

With all this in mind, exercise, especially the type performed during the anatomical adaptation phase, can be considered an injury prevention method. If the strengthening of tendons and ligaments is disrupted, the athlete may experience a decline in tendons' ability to transmit force and in ligaments' ability to secure the anatomical integrity of joints. For steroid users, abusing this substance increases the muscle force at the expense of the ligaments' and tendons' material properties (Woo et al. 1994). More generally, increasing force without correspondingly strengthening the ligaments and tendons results in the ligament and tendon injuries experienced by so many professional American football players.

During spiking, the core muscles contract to stabilize the trunk so that the legs can perform an explosive takeoff and the arms hit the ball.

© AP Photo/Danny Moloshok

Law 3: Develop Core Strength

The arms and legs are only as strong as the trunk. Put another way, a poorly developed trunk provides only a weak support for hard-working limbs. Therefore, strength training programs should first strengthen the core muscles before focusing on the arms and legs.

Core muscles activate highly during jumps, rebounds, and plyometric exercises. They stabilize the body and serve as a link, or transmitter, between the legs and arms. Weak core muscles fail in these essential roles, thus limiting the athlete's ability to perform. Most of these muscles are dominated by slow-twitch fibers because of their supporting role in the body's posture and their continuous activation during arm and leg actions. They contract constantly, but not necessarily dynamically, to create a solid base of support for the actions of other muscle groups.

Many people complain of low-back problems yet do little to correct them. The best protection against low-back problems is well-developed back and abdominal muscles. This area of the body should not be neglected by coaches and athletes. At the same time, though core strength training is currently touted as a new theory with concomitant new exercises, some of them are in fact useless and even dangerous. This section provides our

IRRADIATION

When an athlete performs a strength exercise, many core muscles are activated and contract synergistically to stabilize the body and act as a support so that a limb can perform the exercise. This synergistic contraction is called activation overflow or irradiation (Enoka 2002; Zijdewind and Kernell 2001). The process is illustrated in the following examples.

Upright Rowing

The motion of upright rowing involves standing with the feet hip-width apart while the arms, holding a barbell, are lowered in front of the thighs. As the arms flex to lift the weight to and from the chest, the abdominal and back muscles, including the erector spinae (core muscles), contract to stabilize the trunk so that the arms can perform the action smoothly (an anti-flexion action in the sagittal plane). Without support from the core muscles to stabilize the trunk, the prime movers would not be very effective in performing the task.

While the exercise is performed, all the core muscles are activated (especially those of the back), are contracted (activation overflow), and, as a result, are strengthened. In fact, the level of muscle contraction can be higher during this exercise than during many body-weight exercises for core strength. Therefore, using it can better develop the core muscles (Hamlyn et al. 2007; Nuzzo 2008; Colado et al. 2011; Martuscello 2012).

Squatting and Deadlifting

During any leg action performed against resistance in the upright position, all core muscles are strongly activated to stabilize the trunk and use it as a support (Martuscello 2012). This activation also strengthens the muscles involved. In particular, heavy quarter squats (performed by elite athletes with a load three to four times body weight), for instance, elicit particularly strong contractions of the core muscles.

Spiking

One of the most dynamic athletic skills, volleyball spiking could not be properly performed without the direct support of the core muscles. During spiking, the core muscles contract to stabilize the trunk so that the legs can perform an explosive takeoff and the arms can hit the ball. The core muscles also fixate and stabilize the trunk in other situations where the arms and legs need to perform an athletic task; examples include running, jumping, throwing, medicine ball exercises, and various quick or agile foot movements. Indeed, the core is engaged by any strength or sport-specific exercise in which the core must contract in order to resist flexion or extension of the spine. As a result, the overall volume of specific core strengthening exercises can be reduced to a few sets of essential exercises per session.

point of view or school of thought regarding core training. We believe that excessively focusing on the core does nothing to promote an increase in performance but serves only as a means of distracting the athlete from performing a host of exercises that are integral to sport performance—those that work the prime movers of the sport.

The abdominal and back muscles surround the core area of the body with a tight and powerful support structure of muscle bundles running in different directions. If the abdominal muscles are poorly developed, the pelvis tilts forward, and lordosis (sway-back) develops at the lumbar area of the spine. The rectus abdominis, for example, runs vertically and keeps the spine from extending when the legs are fixed, as in sit-ups, to maintain good posture. The internal and external obliques help the rectus abdominis bend the trunk forward (spine flexion) and perform all twisting, lateral-bending, and trunk-rotating motions. They help an athlete recover from a fall in many sports and perform many actions in boxing, wrestling, and the martial arts. The anterior and lateral abdominal muscles perform delicate, precise trunk movements. These large muscles run vertically, diagonally, and horizontally.

Because many athletes have weak abdominal muscles in relation to their back muscles, general and specific abdominal muscle training is recommended. Isolating the abdominal muscles requires an exercise that flexes the spine but not the hips. Exercises that flex the hips are performed by the iliopsoas (a powerful hip flexor) and to a lesser extent by the abdominal muscles (which then work mostly isometrically to prevent spine extension in the sagittal plane). The most popular abdominal exercise is the sit-up, and the best sit-up position involves lying on the back with the calves resting on a chair or bench. This position works the abdominal muscles more effectively because the hips are already flexed.

The back muscles, including the deep back muscles along the vertebral column, are responsible for many movements, such as back extension and trunk extension and rotation. The trunk, in turn, acts as the transmitter and supporter of most arm and leg actions. The vertebral column also plays an essential role as a shock absorber during landing and takeoff actions.

Back problems can result from excessive, uneven stress on the spine or sudden movement in an unfavorable position. For athletes, back problems may result from wear and tear caused by improper positioning or forward tilting of the body. More specifically, disc pressure varies according to body position relative to external stress. For example, stress increases on the spine while lifting in seated positions or standing when the upper body swings, such as in upright rowing or elbow flexion. Sitting produces greater disc pressure than standing, and the least stress occurs when the body is supine or prone (as in bench presses or prone bench pulls). In many exercises that use the back muscles, abdominal muscles contract isometrically, stabilizing the body.

The iliopsoas is an essential muscle for hip flexion and running. Though not large, it is the most powerful hip flexor (other hip flexors are the rectus femoris, the sartorius, and the tensor fascia lata) and is responsible for swinging the legs forward during running and jumping. Well-developed hip flexors are required in sports performed on the ground or on the ice. These important muscles can be trained through exercises such as leg and knee lifts against resistance.

Law 4: Develop the Stabilizers

Prime movers work more efficiently with strong stabilizer, or fixator, muscles. Stabilizers contract, primarily isometrically, to stabilize a joint so that another part of the body can act. For example, the shoulders are immobilized during elbow flexion, and the abdominal muscles serve as stabilizers when the arms throw a ball. In rowing, when the trunk muscles act as stabilizers, the trunk transmits leg power to the arms, which then drive the blade through the water. A weak stabilizer, therefore, inhibits the contracting capacity of the prime movers.

Improperly developed stabilizers can also hamper the activity of major muscles. When placed under chronic stress, the stabilizers spasm, thus restraining the prime movers and reducing athletic effectiveness. This condition is often seen in volleyball players who suffer injury as a result of inadequate muscle strength and balance in the shoulder muscles (Kugler et al. 1996). At the shoulders, supra- and infraspinatus muscles rotate the arm. The simplest, most effective exercise to strengthen these two muscles is to rotate

STABILITY BALL TRAINING

Like everything in sport-specific training, the stability ball (also known as the Swiss ball or balance ball) is not new. It first hit the scene in the 1960s and has become very popular, especially in rehabilitative settings. Since the 1990s, it has also become popular in sport and fitness. Its popularity in the fitness field is understandable, given that the field is all about variety and excitement.

Many exercises performed on the stability ball provide good upper- and lower-body strength, flexibility, and of course core strength. However, the benefit of these exercises for athletes is overemphasized by some members of the sporting world, who claim that improvements in proprioception and balance translate to improvements in athletic performance. In reality, balance is not a limiting factor for performance; therefore, it is not in the same category as speed, strength, and endurance. In fact, the body will adapt to the unstable environment of sport through the stimulus of participating in the sport itself, as well as practicing technical and tactical drills related to the sport. Selected exercises can be performed on the ball, but they should be limited to the anatomical adaptation or transition phases of training, when general adaptation takes precedence over specific physiological adaptation.

Beyond these caveats, athletes and coaches should be well aware that performing a maximum strength phase on a stability ball can be very detrimental to athletic performance. The ball limits the amount of weight that the athlete can lift because more neural drive is used to stabilize the body as a whole, as well as the specific involved joints, thus reducing the activation of the fast-twitch muscle fibers of the prime movers. Therefore, the only stability ball exercises we recommend are those intended for training the abdominal muscles, which allow the athlete to fully stretch the abdominals before the concentric part of the exercise. Other muscle groups can be trained more effectively through other means.

Stability balls do have a time and place in training. Activation overflow explains how all muscles involved in a movement essentially communicate with each other and offer their help. Our bodies are extremely plastic and adapt wonderfully to traditional methods of training. And, most important in sports, an athlete's body performs better when it adapts better, thereby creating stability naturally.

the arm while holding a dumbbell. The resistance provided stimulates the two muscles stabilizing the shoulder. At the hips, the piriformis and gluteus medius muscles perform external (outward) rotation. To strengthen these muscles, the athlete should stand with the knees locked and lift the leg to the side with a strap connected to a cable machine.

Stabilizers also contract isometrically, immobilizing one part of the limb and allowing the other to move. In addition, they can monitor the state of the long bones' interactions in joints and sense potential injury resulting from improper technique, inappropriate strength, or spasms produced by poor stress management. If one of these conditions occurs, the stabilizers restrain the activity of the prime movers, thus avoiding strain and injury.

Thus stabilizers play important roles in athletic performance. However, some strength and conditioning coaches have recently exaggerated the training of the stabilizer muscles, especially through the use of proprioception training (also known as balance training). In fact, unstable surface training elicits high motor units activation due to co-contraction (simultaneous contraction of agonists and antagonists to stabilize a joint), which is not conducive to the neuromuscular adaptations required by speed and power athletes, who need "silent" (i.e., inactive) antagonists during powerful actions.

On the other hand, a number of studies have shown that proprioception training with balance boards does help provide stability to a formerly injured or unstable ankle (Caraffa et al. 1996; Wester et al. 1996; Willems et al. 2002). The theory is that if balance board training helps promote greater stability by increasing the proprioception and strength of the stabilizer muscles of an unstable structure, it will further strengthen and prevent injury to an already stable structure. This has to be proven, however, and in any case the real question is how much time should be devoted to exercises intended to strengthen the stabilizer muscles.

Certain studies show that proprioception training can decrease injury to the knee (Caraffa et al. 1996), whereas other studies disprove the benefits of proprioception training for injury prevention (Soderman et al. 2000). A recent review study, in particular, challenged flaws in the design and implementation of proprioception studies (Thacker et al. 2003). Furthermore, in the last 10 years, strength and conditioning coaches who have completely disregarded the use of balance boards or proprioception training for team sports (soccer and volleyball) have reported no increase in ankle or knee injuries.

Having said all this, balance board or Swiss ball training can be helpful during the early part of the preparatory phase (the anatomical adaptation phase). Unilateral exercises are certainly the best choice for improving joint stability while training the prime movers. Nevertheless, if proprioceptive strength is trained during the anatomical adaptation phase, the board or Swiss ball should be put away in the next phase to allow time for training with methods that directly enhance the athlete's physical stature and promote sport-specific strength, speed, and stamina. After all, even if exercises worked to improve an athlete's proprioception, the slow to intermediate nature of these exercises would never protect the joint from the fast and powerful movements performed in sport (Ashton-Miller et al. 2001). Preparing the stabilizers for movement is important; specifically, training for the movements of the sport with ideal sport-specific speed and power or endurance is vital to the athlete's performance and physical state.

Figure 7.1 shows a three-week split routine for a junior soccer player's anatomical adaptation macrocycle. Note the large use of unilateral exercises, the equal volume of work between agonists and antagonists, the sets' time under tension that falls in the lactic acid system capacity range (48 seconds to 80 seconds), the progressive increase of load, and the shorter duration of the macrocycle, typical for junior and master athletes. The following points provide a description of each column of the figure:

- Sets—Each number shows the set volume performed in a specific week. For example, 2-3-2 means that two sets are performed in the first week, three sets in the second week, and two sets in the third week.

- Reps—Each number shows the repetition volume performed in a specific week. For example, 20-15-12 means that 20 reps per set are performed in the first week, 15 reps per set in the second week, and 12 reps per set in the third week.

- Rest interval—Each number shows the rest interval taken between sets of an exercise in a specific week. For example, 1-1-1.5 means that one minute of rest is taken between sets in the first week, one minute in the second week, and one and a half minutes in the third week.

- Tempo—The first number depicts the duration in seconds of the eccentric phase, the second number depicts the pause between eccentric and concentric, and the third number depicts the duration of the concentric phase (an X means explosive).

- Load—These columns should be used to record the load used week by week for each set of each exercise.

EXERCISE	SETS	REPS	REST INTERVAL (MIN.)	TEMPO (SEC.)	LOAD 1st week	2nd week	3rd week
Workout A							
One-leg squat	2-3-2*	20-15-12*	1-1-1.5*	3-0-1**			
One-leg curl	2-3-2	20-15-12	1-1-1.5	3-0-X			
One-leg deadlift	2-3-2	20-15-12	1-1-1.5	3-0-1			
Quad glute extension	2-3-2	20-15-15	1-1-1.5	3-0-1			
Abductor machine	2-3-2	20-15-12	1-1-1.5	3-0-1			
Adductor machine	2-3-2	20-15-12	1-1-1.5	3-0-1			
Standing calf raise	2-3-2	20-15-12	1-1-1.5	2-2-1			
Crunch with weight	2-3-2	20-15-12	1	3-0-3			
Workout B							
Supine dumbbell press	2-3-2	20-15-12	1-1-1.5	3-0-1			
Dumbbell row	2-3-2	20-15-12	1-1-1.5	3-0-1			
Seated dumbbell press	2-3-2	20-15-12	1-1-1.5	3-0-1			
Dumbbell curl	2-3-2	20-15-12	1-1-1.5	3-0-1			
Front and side plank	2-2-1	30-30-45 (sec.)	0.5	Isometric			

*For each trio of numbers in this column, the first number applies to the first week, the second number to the second week, and the third number to the third week.

**For each trio of numbers in this column, the first number depicts the duration in seconds of the eccentric phase, the second number depicts the pause between eccentric and concentric, and the third number depicts the duration of the concentric phase (an X means explosive).

Figure 7.1 Sample Three-week Split Routine for the Anatomical Adaptation Macrocycle of a Junior Soccer Player

Law 5: Train Movements, Not Individual Muscles

The purpose of strength training in sports is load the joints' movements specifically used in performing the skills of a given sport. Athletes should resist training muscles in isolation, as is done in bodybuilding. From its very beginning, bodybuilding has promoted the concept of working muscles in isolation, a concept that has served this activity very well for generations. However, isolation exercises do not apply to sports, because athletic skills are multijoint movements performed in a certain order, forming what is called a kinetic (movement) chain.

For instance, a takeoff to catch a ball uses the following kinetic chain: hip extensions, then knee extensions, and finally ankle extensions, in which the feet apply force against the ground to lift the body. This powerful sequence, typical of so many sport actions, is called triple extension.

According to the principle of specificity, especially during the conversion (to specific strength) phase, body position and limb angles should resemble those needed for the specific skills to be performed. When athletes train for a movement, the muscles are integrated and strengthened to perform the action with more power. Therefore, athletes should not resort to weight training alone but should broaden their training routines by incorporating medicine balls, rubber cords (for water sports or to accommodate the resistance in power training with barbells), shots, and plyometric equipment. Exercises

Accelerating the body is a complex motor pattern. Knee extensors, hip extensors, and plantar flexors propel the body in concert with a vigorous action of the upper-body musculature.

performed with these instruments allow athletes to potentiate their athletic skills. Chapter 14 provides further examples of how these training instruments are used for better specific improvement.

Multijoint exercises, such as the squat, deadlift, bench press, military press, chin-up, Olympic lift, as well as throws and jumps, in sport training have been used since track-and-field athletes introduced them in the early 1930s, prior to the 1936 Olympic Games. Most athletes still follow this tradition. Such exercises are key to strength training efficiency and efficacy. A few isolation exercises (referred to as accessory exercises) can still be used to support hypertrophy of lacking muscles or to increase blood flow (necessary for tendons' health) and to support the muscle protein content of the prime movers during periods of low reps and very high loads in training.

In the end, don't ask, "Where is the program's biceps exercise?" Rather, ask yourself whether elbow flexion is part of the specific action required in the chosen sport and, if so, with what other movements it is integrated.

Law 6: Focus Not on What Is New but on What Is Necessary

In the past few years, the North American sport and fitness market has been invaded by many products that supposedly improve athletic performance. Often, however, they do not. In fact, an understanding of biomechanics and exercise physiology reveals that many products purported to improve strength, speed, and power may actually inhibit them. Two methods that have captured the minds of athletes, coaches, and trainers are balance training and overspeed training. Balance training is safe but also widely overused in the sport training industry. Overspeed training, on the other hand—along with many training devices used in an effort to enhance speed and power—jeopardizes an athlete's running technique and decreases the rate of force development.

In many cases, the preferred medium for promoting new ideas is the seminar. The speaker often shows new exercises and promises miraculous improvement. Not very often, however, does a speaker address the issues of anatomical and neuromuscular adaptation, which are central to performance improvement and should serve as the foundation for all sport-specific programs.

Certainly, it is important to have a good selection of exercises; however, an exercise is essential only if it targets the prime movers or the main muscle groups used in performing an athletic skill—no more, no less. It is immaterial, for example, whether the athlete uses a simple bench or a stability ball to perform bench presses. The essential goal is to perform the exercise with continuous acceleration through the range of motion. At the beginning of a bench press, fast-twitch muscle fibers are recruited to defeat inertia and the heavy load of the barbell. As the athlete continues to press the barbell upward, he or she should attempt to generate the highest possible acceleration. Under these conditions, the discharge rate is increased in the same fast-twitch muscle fibers. Maximum velocity, therefore, must be achieved toward the end of the action to coincide with the instant of releasing a ball or other athletic implement during sport performance.

Similarly, if a high level of strength adaptation is required in the leg muscles, then the athlete should squat, squat, and squat. The idea is to develop the greatest possible levels of strength and adaptation—in other words, to do what is necessary. Adding variety by implementing different exercises is fine as long as they target the same muscle group in the most specific way.

Law 7: Periodize Strength in the Long Term

Instead of focusing on a strength program's immediate returns in the form of maximal strength gains, strength and conditioning coaches should plan the strength training progression in a way that maximizes the athlete's motor potential over the long term. This emphasis means not using high loads as soon as possible with complex exercises that have not been technically mastered.

As stated in chapter 2, the base for general strength gains over time should be provided by *inter*muscular coordination training: explosive technique work with light to submaximal weights, never to concentric failure, planned after the anatomical adaptation or hypertrophy phase. On the other hand, *intra*muscular coordination training—work with submaximal to maximal weights, still possibly not to concentric failure, unless absolute strength is sought—peaks maximum strength but cannot be used for extended periods (no more than six weeks at a time).

Specific strength—be it power, power endurance, or muscle endurance—can be maximized only on the basis of a preceding and well-planned maximum strength phase. This requirement holds both at the annual plan level and the multiyear level. Figure 7.2 depicts an example of a sequence of intermuscular coordination and intramuscular coordination macrocycles for the increase of maximum strength in the annual plan; these macrocycles are placed before the specific strength (power) macrocycles. Figure 7.3 shows the strength progression for a four-year plan for a developing athlete.

AA 3+1	MxS 2+1 Intermuscular coordination loads used: 70 – >75%	MxS 2+1 Intermuscular coordination loads used: 75 – >80%	MxS 2+1 Intramuscular coordination loads used: 85 – >90%	P 2+1	P 2+1

Figure 7.2 Strength training progression in the annual plan for an individual sport where the specific strength is power.

Key: AA = anatomical adaptation, MxS (intermuscular coordination) = maximum strength (at loads of 70% to 80% of 1RM), MxS (intramuscular coordination) = maximum strength (loads of 85% to 90% of 1RM), P = power, 3+1 = macrocycle structure with 3 loading weeks plus 1 unloading week, and 2+1 = macrocycle structure with 2 loading weeks plus 1 unloading week.

Year 4	MxS (Intramuscular coordination)		Specific strength	
	AA	MxS (Intermuscular coordination)		
Year 3	MxS (Intermuscular-coordination)	MxS (Intramuscular coordination)		Specific strength
	AA	MxS (Intermuscular coordination)		
Year 2	MxS (Intermuscular coordination)		MxS (Intramuscular coordination)	Specific strength
	AA	Hypertrophy		MxS (Intermuscular coordination)
Year 1	MxS (Intermuscular coordination)			Specific strength
	AA		Hypertrophy	

Figure 7.3 Distribution and progression of strength training methods in a multiyear plan.

Key: AA = anatomical adaptation, MxS = maximum strength (intermuscular coordination at loads of 70% to 80% of 1RM) or maximum strength (intramuscular coordination at loads of 80% to 90% of 1RM).

Principles of Strength Training

The purpose of any strength training program is to produce a continual increase in the athlete's physical capacity. Strength training principles offer methods for adapting the body to the various loads used in training; they also provide guidelines for individualizing the program to the specific needs of the athlete and sport. Therefore, every strength training program should be built on principles.

Progressive Increase of Load

The principle of progressive increase of load is best illustrated by the legend of Milo of Croton in Greek mythology. To become the world's strongest man, Milo lifted and carried a calf every day beginning in his teenage years. As the calf grew heavier, Milo grew stronger. By the time the calf was a full-grown bull, Milo was the world's strongest man, thanks to long-term progression.

In more specific terms, training progressively elicits adaptations in the structure and functions of the athlete's body, thus increasing his or her motor potential and ultimately resulting in improved performance. Of course, the body reacts both physiologically and psychologically to the increased training load (that is, to the sum of the volume and intensity of all the training stimuli). Therefore, training also produces gradual changes in nervous reaction and functions, neuromuscular coordination, and psychological capacity to cope with stress. The entire process requires time and competent technical leadership.

As said in chapter 6, some coaches employ a consistent training load throughout the year, which is called a standard load. This approach may cause decreased performance during the late competitive phase because the physiological basis of performance has decreased and prevents consistent improvements (see figure 7.4). Superior adaptation and performance are produced only by steadily applying training load increments.

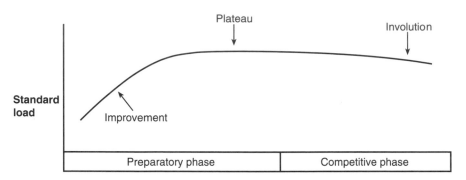

Figure 7.4 A standard load results in improvements only in the early part of the annual plan.

Another traditional strength training approach uses the overload principle. Early proponents of this principle claimed that strength and hypertrophy increase only if muscles work at their maximum strength capacity against workloads greater than those normally encountered (Hellebrand and Houtz 1956; Lange 1919). Contemporary advocates suggest that the load to exhaustion in strength training should be increased throughout the program (Fox, Bowes, and Foss 1989). Therefore, the curve of load increment can rise constantly (see figure 7.5).

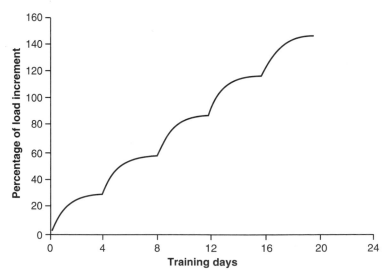

Figure 7.5 Load increments according to the overload principle.

Adapted from *Phys Ther Rev* 1956; 36(6): 371-383, with permission of the American Physical Therapy Association. Copyright © 1956 American Physical Therapy Association. APTA is not responsible for the translation from English.

Proponents of overloading suggest two ways to increase strength: (1) maximum loads to exhaustion, inducing strength gains, and (2) submaximal loads to exhaustion, inducing hypertrophy (a popular approach among bodybuilders). However, athletes cannot be expected to lift to exhaustion every time they work out. This is especially true from the specific preparation onward, when most of their energy must be directed to sport-specific activities and their bodies must be well recovered in order to optimally perform sport-specific skills.

In fact, such physiological and psychological strain leads to muscle tightness, impaired sport-specific technical proficiency, fatigue, exhaustion, injury, or overtraining. To be effective, a strength training program must follow the concept of periodization of strength, in which specific goals for each phase lead up to either peak performance at the year's major competitions or the best possible performance throughout a championship.

To achieve these goals, a more effective approach is step-type loading (see figure 7.6). The athlete's ability to tolerate heavy loads improves as the result of adaptation to stressors applied in strength training (Councilman 1968; Harre 1982). The step-type method requires a training load increase followed by an unloading phase during which the body adapts, regenerates, and prepares for a new increase.

The frequency of such unloading microcycles is determined by each athlete's needs, the rate of adaptation, and the competitive calendar. Training load increases are determined by the rate of the athlete's performance improvement; generally speaking, however, the intensity increase between steps (weeks) in a macrocycle commonly falls between 2 percent and 5 percent. An abrupt increase in training load may exceed the athlete's capacity to adapt and therefore affect his or her physiological balance.

The step-type approach does not necessarily mean increasing the load in each training session in a linear fashion. Furthermore, a single training session is insufficient to cause appreciable body adaptations. To achieve adaptation, the same exercise must be repeated several times in a week but at different intensities, followed by an increase in the following week.

In figure 7.6, let's say that each horizontal line represents a week, or microcycle, of training and that the load is applied on Monday. This load fatigues the body, but it is within the capability of the athlete. The body adjusts by Wednesday and adapts to the load over the next two days, and by Friday the athlete feels stronger and capable of lifting heavier loads. Thus fatigue is followed by adaptation and then a physiological rebound or improvement. This new level can be called a new ceiling of adaptation. By the next Monday, the athlete is physiologically and psychologically comfortable. This process is the

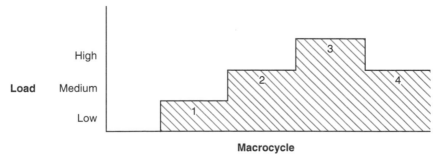

Figure 7.6 Illustration of a macrocycle, in which each column represents the weekly load, increasing in a step-like fashion.

reason that it is possible to either increase the strength training load linearly throughout the microcycle (if the loading parameters at the beginning of the macrocycle were well within the athlete's capacity) or undulate it (heavy on Monday, light on Wednesday, and medium-heavy on Friday).

The third step in figure 7.6 is followed by a lower step or unloading microcycle. A reduction in overall demand allows the body to regenerate and fully adapt. During the unloading week, the athlete recovers almost completely from the fatigue accumulated in the first three steps, replenishes energy stores, and relaxes psychologically. The body accumulates new reserves in anticipation of further increases in training load. Training performance usually improves following the unloading microcycle. Testing takes place at the end of the unloading microcycle.

The shorter the macrocycle is (for instance, a 2+1 structure, which entails two weeks of loading followed by an unloading week), the lower the increase from the beginning load. Thus a longer macrocycle may permit a larger increase, but it generally starts at a lower intensity. Longer macrocycles (3+1 or even 4+1 weeks) are used in the general preparation when the intensity at the beginning of the macrocycle is low, whereas shorter macrocycles are used from the specific preparation onward, as the training intensifies. It is, in fact, harder to sustain a prolonged increase of intensity when the intensity at the beginning of the macrocycle was already high. Although training load increases in steps, the load curve in the annual plan has a wavy shape that represents the ongoing increases and decreases of loading to stimulate and realize adaptations (see figure 7.7).

Although the step-loading method is applicable to every sport and athlete, two variations are possible—reverse step loading and flat loading—and they must be applied carefully and with discretion. In reverse step loading (see figure 7.8), the load decreases rather than increases from step to step. Some Eastern European weightlifters maintain that this form of loading (planning the heaviest loads immediately following a microcycle of low-intensity training) is more specific to their physiological needs. Reverse step loading has been

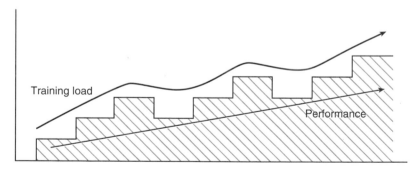

Figure 7.7 The curve of training load is undulatory (wavy arrow), whereas performance improves continuously (straight arrow).

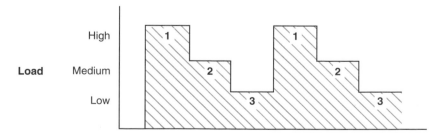

Figure 7.8 Reverse step loading as it used by some weightlifting schools.

used in weightlifting since the late 1960s but has not been accepted in any other sport. The reason is simple: The goal of strength training for sports is progressive adaptation—gradually increasing the athlete's training capabilities, and performance improvements are possible only when training capabilities have increased. Reverse loading should be used only during the peaking cycle prior to competition as a tapering method (see chapter 15). Endurance improvements are much better achieved by step loading, as the main factor is the volume, and it is better increased in a step-loading fashion throughout the year.

The flat loading pattern (see figure 7.9) is appropriate for advanced athletes with a strong strength training background, athletes who do not tolerate prolonged exposure to high-intensity training, and, generally, for power sports during the specific preparation phase. High-demand training is performed at the same level for two microcycles, followed by a low-load recovery week (three consecutive microcycles of high load cannot be performed due to the high level of accumulated fatigue). The two microcycles must involve high demand for either one or all elements—technical, tactical, speed, and endurance training. When planning the lower-intensity microcycle, all the elements must be of lower demand in order to facilitate relaxation and recovery.

The dynamics of the loading pattern for a well-trained athlete are a function of the training phase and the type of desired training adaptation. During the early part of the preparatory phase for all sports, the step loading pattern prevails, ensuring better progression (see figure 7.10). The flat loading pattern is better suited for the late preparatory phase, especially for power sports and for athletes competing at or beyond the national level. The step loading pattern is always preferred, however, for endurance sports, in which the development of endurance (cardiorespiratory and muscular) is particularly suited for long, progressive overload.

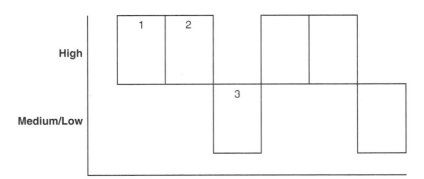

Figure 7.9 The flat loading pattern is usually employed during the specific preparation and competitive phases of power sports.

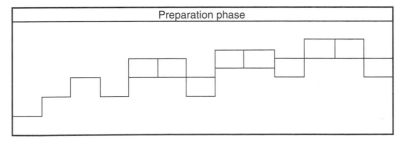

Figure 7.10 Suggested loading patterns for the preparation phase. Step loading is used at the beginning of the program since the load is increased progressively. After the first five weeks of progressive adaptation, flat step loading is used to ensure that training is very demanding and results in the specific adaptation necessary for performance improvement.

DEFINING AND UNDERSTANDING STRENGTH TRAINING LOAD PROGRESSION

Progressive overload is the favorite modality for eliciting morpho-functional adaptations through a progressive increase of muscular, metabolic, or neural stress over time. There are many ways to rationally progress the load and thereby elicit the desired adaptations, such as higher levels of hypertrophy, muscular endurance, maximum strength, or power. In order to understand these options, we must analyze the loading variables and how they influence the final training effect.

In the case of strength training, the training parameters are shown in figure 7.11.

Throughout a macrocycle, we can progress one or more of these parameters according to the training effects (adaptations) that we want to elicit. The parameters are described in detail in the following sections.

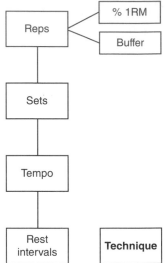

Figure 7.11 Strength training parameters.

Repetitions

The number of repetitions per set is very much linked to the percentage of 1-repetition maximum (1RM) used and the desired buffer (the difference between the number of repetitions performed in a set and the number that the athlete could perform to exhaustion at that percentage of 1RM). Throughout a macrocycle, we can either increase repetitions in order to increase endurance (more volume), keep repetitions the same while manipulating other parameters, or decrease repetitions to increase intensity (percentage of 1RM) or to unload or peak while maintaining or slightly reducing the intensity. In the latter two cases, we unload by increasing the buffer.

Throughout a macrocycle, we can decrease the buffer while maintaining the same number of repetitions. Doing so makes each workout progressively harder, while maintaining the same number of sets and reps (a preferred method by powerlifters that can also be used in other sports). We can also keep the buffer the same while increasing or decreasing one of the other parameters. Usually, we do not increase the buffer throughout a macrocycle, unless we are transitioning from a maximum-strength development macrocycle to a maximum-strength maintenance or a power macrocycle.

A high buffer allows for performing more technically correct repetitions because the load is less challenging, more explosive concentrics, and reduced residual fatigue. Thus high-buffer sets are used especially for intermuscular coordination work, for power development, and for unloading microcycles (see table 7.1). Buffer 0 means going to concentric failure, a preferred modality for hypertrophy training. Doing multiple 1 to 3 reps per set to failure or close to failure (5 percent buffer) elicits gains in relative strength that is an increase of strength without an accompanying increase of body weight. Going to failure or getting close to failure with a slightly higher time under tension per set and performing 3 to 6 reps will elicit gains in absolute strength that are gains in both strength and muscle size. Performing sets of 1 to 3 reps with a buffer of 10 to 20 percent will increase both maximum strength and power (what some call the "strength-speed method"). Performing 3 to 6 reps with a buffer of 25 to 40 percent will increase both maximum strength, via an improvement of the intermuscular coordination, and power (what some call the "speed-strength method"). We believe that terms such as *strength-speed* and *speed-strength* should be replaced by *power training with high loads* and *power training with low loads*, because in physics we have power, not strength-speed or speed-strength.

Table 7.1 The Relationship Between Load (Percentage of 1RM), Repetitions, Buffer, and the Training Effect

<table>
<tr><th rowspan="2"></th><th rowspan="2">% 1RM</th><th colspan="12">BUFFER</th></tr>
<tr><th colspan="2">0%</th><th colspan="2">5%</th><th colspan="2">10%</th><th colspan="2">15%</th><th colspan="2">20%</th><th colspan="2">25-40%</th></tr>
<tr><td rowspan="4">Intramuscular coordination</td><td>100</td><td>1*</td><td rowspan="2">Relative strength</td><td></td><td></td><td></td><td></td><td></td><td></td><td></td><td></td><td></td><td></td></tr>
<tr><td>95</td><td>2</td><td>1*</td><td rowspan="2">Relative strength</td><td></td><td></td><td></td><td></td><td></td><td></td><td></td><td></td></tr>
<tr><td>90</td><td>3</td><td>Absolute/ relative strength</td><td>2</td><td>1*</td><td rowspan="3">Maximum strength and power (high load)</td><td></td><td></td><td></td><td></td><td></td><td></td></tr>
<tr><td>85</td><td>5</td><td rowspan="2">Absolute strength</td><td>3</td><td>Absolute/ relative strength</td><td>2</td><td>1*</td><td rowspan="3">Maximum strength and power (high load)</td><td></td><td></td><td></td><td></td></tr>
<tr><td rowspan="7">Intermuscular coordination</td><td>80</td><td>6</td><td>5</td><td rowspan="2">Absolute strength</td><td>3</td><td>2</td><td>1*</td><td rowspan="3">Maximum strength and power (high load)</td><td></td><td></td></tr>
<tr><td>75</td><td>8</td><td rowspan="2">Hypertrophy</td><td>6</td><td>5</td><td>Absolute strength</td><td>3</td><td>2</td><td></td><td></td></tr>
<tr><td>70</td><td>12</td><td></td><td></td><td></td><td></td><td>5</td><td>Absolute strength</td><td>3</td><td></td><td></td></tr>
<tr><td>65</td><td></td><td></td><td></td><td></td><td></td><td></td><td></td><td></td><td></td><td></td><td>3*</td><td rowspan="4">Intermuscular coordination and power (low load)</td></tr>
<tr><td>60</td><td></td><td></td><td></td><td></td><td></td><td></td><td></td><td></td><td></td><td></td><td>3-5</td></tr>
<tr><td>55</td><td></td><td></td><td></td><td></td><td></td><td></td><td></td><td></td><td></td><td></td><td>3-5</td></tr>
<tr><td>50</td><td></td><td></td><td></td><td></td><td></td><td></td><td></td><td></td><td></td><td></td><td>3-6</td></tr>
</table>

*The numbers in this column refer to the number of repetitions.

Sets

Throughout a macrocycle, we can increase sets in order to increase work capacity and endurance (more volume). We can also keep the same number of sets to increase one of the other parameters or decrease the number of sets to unload or peak. The number of sets (volume) is the single most influential variable the on training's residual fatigue effect.

Tempo

Tempo is the duration of a full rep; therefore, it affects set duration. In turn, both the tempo of a single rep and the set duration directly influence the final training effect. For this reason, once the desired training effect and the corresponding rep tempo and set duration are established,

(continued)

it is advisable to keep them stable throughout the macrocycle. Changing them—for example, by performing the repetitions faster—might give the false impression of progressing when in fact the training effect is changed. Tempo is indicated with three or four numbers. The first number depicts the duration in seconds of the eccentric phase; the second number depicts the pause between eccentric and concentric; the third number depicts the duration of the concentric phase (an X means explosive); and the fourth number depicts the pause between the concentric and eccentric phase. For example, 3.1.X.0 for a squat means a descent of three seconds, followed by a pause of one second, followed by an explosive ascent and no pause before descending again. (King 1998)

Rest Interval

Like tempo and set duration, the rest interval directly influences the final training effect. We can increase the rest interval if the macrocycle moves toward a decrease in reps and an increase in intensity (percentage of 1RM). We can decrease the rest interval in order to increase endurance (more density). Or we can keep the rest interval the same while changing one or more of the other variables. When performing series of sets for power endurance and muscle endurance, reducing the rest interval between sets (while maintaining their power output) allows a densification that later translates into a higher mean power output for a longer duration.

Technique should also be considered; indeed, it should never be sacrificed for the sake of a false load progression. As Paul Chek has said, changing technique to grind out more reps or complete a heavy one is just "the world's fastest superset"—a potentially injurious and certainly deceiving action.

For an example of progression in parameters, see the program for the junior soccer player in the previous chapter (law 4).

Variety

Contemporary training requires the athlete to perform many hours of work. The volume and intensity of training sometimes increase yearly, and exercises are repeated numerous times. To reach high performance, any athlete who is serious about training must dedicate two to four hours each week to strength training, in addition to performing technical, tactical, and energy systems training.

Under these conditions, boredom and monotony can become obstacles to motivation and improvement. The best way to overcome these obstacles is to incorporate variety into training routines. Variety improves training response and positively affects an athlete's psychological well-being. In order to implement variety effectively, however, instructors and coaches must be well versed in strength training. A strength and conditioning coach should not, in fact, employ variety for variety's sake. Periodization of strength naturally includes rational variations of means and methods throughout the annual plan to elicit the best neuromuscular adaptations. The following guidelines will help you in designing strength training programs with sensible variations over the course of the annual plan.

- Progress from full range of motion (ROM) in the general preparation phase to sport-specific ROM in the late specific preparation phase and the competitive phase. Be mindful of the fact that full-ROM exercises cause more muscular tension than their partial counterparts; therefore, a low volume of such exercises should always be employed for maintaining maximum strength (Bloomquist et al. 2013; Hartmann et al. 2012; and Bazyler et al. 2014).

- Vary exercise selection by using more unilateral and dumbbell exercises during anatomical adaptation and compensation macrocycles.
- Vary loading by using the principle of progressive increase of load in training.
- Vary the type and speed of muscle contractions. The usual pattern goes from slow eccentrics (three to five seconds) and controlled concentrics (one to two seconds) in anatomical adaptation to slow eccentrics and fast concentrics (one second or less) in the hypertrophy and maximum strength macrocycles and then to fast eccentrics and explosive concentrics in macrocycles for power, power endurance, or muscle endurance short.
- Vary the method. Move from body weight, dumbbells, and machines during macrocycles for anatomical adaptation and hypertrophy to mainly barbells in macrocycles for maximum strength, conversion to specific strength, and maintenance.

Variety in exercise selection keeps the athlete motivated and the adaptation fresh. Problems can arise, however, when coaches and athletes substitute an exercise or change a method solely for the sake of doing something new. The principle of variety should be used only if the change or substitution keeps the athlete on the path of adaptation.

In addition, when athletes reach a high level of competition and fitness, certain exercises should never leave their regimen. Coaches can alter the load or method used in training but should always stick to the movements that best work the kinetic chain used in the sport or best elicit the threshold of stimulation needed for maximum gains. For example, although the leg press is an effective exercise for leg development, it does not cause the same neuromuscular drive as the squat. In fact, the squat is probably one of the single best exercises for lower-body maximum strength development, and it should never be replaced for the sake of relieving boredom.

Coaches and athletes should also remember that sport training is different from fitness training and that fitness ideals do not always work in sport training. For example, many strength training instructors preach that exercises should be altered every other week. However, though this approach may be beneficial when training personal training clients who require constant variety and excitement, it is not appropriate for athletes. Alternating of strength exercises for a given sport can be done only if the new exercise addresses the prime movers in that sport. In addition, introducing a new exercise (or training method, for that matter) causes muscle soreness and tightness, which in turn produces a transitory (two- to seven-day) loss of performance in sport-specific technical and tactical training. With this reality in mind, plan accordingly.

Because adaptation is a physiological requirement for athletic improvement, the same type of training and muscle groups must be targeted repeatedly in order to produce the highest degree of adaptation. Without constant increase in the adaptation of bodily systems, athletes see no visible improvement in their performance. Yes, repeating the same type of exercise day in and day out is very boring. But so is constantly repeating the technical skills of running, swimming, cycling, and rowing, to name a few. Yet nobody suggests to runners, swimmers, cyclists, and rowers that they alter their primary skill training because it is boring. Therefore, coaches should choose a number of exercises that have the same functional purpose but add variety to training. In this way, they can spice up the training program but keep in mind the main focus—the athlete's level of physiological adaptation.

Individualization

Contemporary training requires individualization. Each athlete must be treated according to his or her ability, potential, and strength training background. Coaches are sometimes tempted to follow the training programs of successful athletes, thus disregarding their particular athlete's needs, experience, and abilities. Even worse, they sometimes insert such programs into the training schedules of junior athletes, who are not ready, physiologically or psychologically, for such high loads.

Before designing a training program, the coach should assess the athlete. Even athletes who are equal in performance do not necessarily have the same work capacity. Individual work abilities are determined by several biological and psychological factors and must be considered in specifying the amount of work (volume), the load (intensity), and the type of strength training that an athlete performs. Work capacity is also affected by training background. Work demand should be based on experience. Even when an athlete exhibits great improvement, the coach must still be cautious in estimating training load (volume plus intensity). Thus, when assigning athletes of different backgrounds and experiences to the same training group, the coach should attend to individual characteristics and potential.

Another factor to consider when planning a training program is the athlete's rate of recovery. When planning and evaluating the content and stress of training, coaches should remember to assess demanding factors outside of training. They should be aware of the athlete's lifestyle and emotional involvements. Rate of recovery can also be affected by schoolwork and other activities. For help in monitoring the rate of recovery, coaches can use a heart rate variability monitoring device.

Sex-based differences also require consideration. Generally speaking, the total body strength of women is 63.5 percent of that of men. More specifically, the upper-body strength of women is, on average, 55.8 percent of that of men; the lower-body strength of women, however, is much closer to that of men, at an average of 71.9 percent (Laubach 1976). Women tend to have lower hypertrophy levels and lower work capacity than men do, mostly because their testosterone level is as much as 20 times lower (Wright 1980). Female athletes can follow the same training programs as male athletes without worrying about excessive bulky muscles. Women can apply the same loading pattern and use the same training methods as men without concern, except for when monitoring their recovery ability.

One study looked at sex-based differences in strength and muscle thickness changes following upper-body and lower-body resistance training. In both men and women, 12 weeks of total body resistance training resulted in a greater increase in muscle thickness in the upper body than in the lower body; it also produced similar time-course and proportionate increases in strength and muscle thickness for both men and woman (Evertsen et al. 1999). In other words, strength training is as beneficial for women as it is for men. In fact, strength gains for women occur at the same rate as men (Wilmore et al. 1978).

Strength training for women should be rigorously continuous, without long interruptions. Plyometric training should progress carefully over a long period to allow adaptation to occur. Because women generally tend to be physically weaker than men, improved and increased strength training can produce more visible gains in performance (Lephart et al. 2002). Further increases in strength from plyometric training promote greater power capabilities. As for training the energy systems, women can use the same training methods used by men.

One major issue involving sex difference is injury in sport. Female athletes often report a higher incidence of lower-body injuries, in particular to the knee joint. Studies have been conducted in an effort to explain this fact both physiologically and anatomically. For instance, when performing the kinematics and electromyographic activity of the one-leg squat, intercollegiate female athletes, as compared with their male counterparts, demonstrated less lateral trunk flexion and more ankle dorsiflexion, ankle pronation, hip adduction, hip flexion, and external rotation (Zeller et al. 2003). Furthermore, female athletes who participate in jumping and agility exercises tend to exhibit less muscular-stiffness protection of the knee than males do (Wojtys et al. 2003). Involuntarily, females allow their knees to drift inward (knock knees), which places more stress on the knee joint and can aggravate or strain the anterior cruciate ligament.

Although sex-specific planning is not entirely required, these differences indicate that time should be dedicated to improving maximum strength, in particular the strength of the lower body, in female athletes. In particular, increased strengthening of the quadriceps and hamstring at the end of the early preparatory phase can physiologically prepare the athlete for game-specific drills and power training, which place more stress on the knee joint and can lead to injury.

Specificity

To be effective and achieve greater adaptation, training must be designed to develop sport-specific strength. To do so, a strength and conditioning coach must make a simple performance model analysis of the sport for which the strength training program is being created. The analysis should take into account the ergogenesis (i.e., the energy contribution to the sporting event of each of the three energy systems), the specific joints' range of motion, the planes of movement, and the prime movers and their actions (eccentric, isometric, concentric). Training specificity is the most important mechanism for sport-specific neuromuscular adaptations.

Specificity and the Dominant Energy System

The coach should carefully consider the dominant energy system in the chosen sport. For instance, muscular endurance training is most appropriate for endurance sports such as rowing, long-distance swimming, canoeing, and speedskating (see chapters 3 and 14). The coach must also consider the specific muscle groups involved (the prime movers) and the movement patterns characteristic of the sport. Exercises should use the sport's key movement patterns. They must also improve the power of the prime movers. Normally, gains in power transfer to skill improvement.

Specificity Versus a Methodical Approach

The principle of specificity sprang from the idea that the optimal strength training program must be specific. Mathews and Fox (1976) developed this theory into a principle of training. According to this principle, an exercise or type of training that is specific to the skills of a sport results in faster adaptation and yields faster performance improvement. However, specificity should be applied only to advanced athletes during the competitive phase. These athletes devote a large portion of their annual strength training plan to train the dominant strength in their selected sport.

Misuse of specificity results in asymmetrical and inharmonious body development and neglects the antagonist and stabilizer muscles. Misuse can also hamper the development of the prime movers and result in injury. Overemphasizing specificity can result in narrow development of the muscles and one-sided, specialized muscle function. Therefore, compensation strength exercises should always be used in training, especially during the early preparatory phase and the transition phases of the annual plan. These exercises balance the strength of agonist and antagonist muscles.

Although specificity is an important principle, its long-term application can result in stressful, boring programs that lead to overtraining, overuse injury, and sometimes burnout. Therefore, specificity is best applied at appropriate times as part of a program based on a methodical, long-term approach. Such a program should have three main phases: the general and multilateral phase, the specialized training-specific phase, and the high-performance phase (refer to figure 7.3).

During the general-multilateral phase, strength training is performed in such a way that all muscle groups, ligaments, and tendons are developed in anticipation of future heavy loads and specific training. Such an approach will likely lead to an injury-free career. This phase may last one to three years, depending on the athlete's age and abilities. Throughout this phase, the coach needs to be patient. Overall multilateral development is a basic requirement for reaching a highly specialized level of training. Most of the maximum strength phase is dedicated to intermuscular coordination training (technique work with loads below 80 percent of 1RM).

After laying the foundation, the athlete begins the specialization phase, which continues throughout his or her career. During this phase, the strength training program does not address the specific needs of the sport through all phases of an annual plan. Rather, this program includes periodization of strength, which always starts with a buildup or anatomical adaptation phase (see the discussion of periodization of strength in law 7 in this chapter). Maximum strength training with loads above 80 percent is introduced in the annual periodization of strength.

The high-performance phase applies to athletes at the national and international levels. During this stage, specificity prevails from the latter part of the preparatory phase through the competitive phase of the annual plan. More time is now dedicated to the conversion-to-specific-strength phase than in earlier years.

Specificity of Exercises for Strength Training

When it comes to strength exercise selection for a sport, especially in the late preparatory phase, coaches must try to imitate the dynamic structure of the skill, as well as the spatial orientation or body position in relation to the surrounding environment. In other words, coaches should select exercises that place the body and limbs in positions similar to those used when performing the skill.

The angle between limbs or other body parts influences how a muscle contracts and which parts of it contract. Therefore, familiarity with these aspects (the specific joints' range or motion and prime movers muscle actions) is necessary for effective training.

To achieve maximum training specificity, an exercise must imitate the angle of the skill performed. For instance, the arm extensions used by shot-putters and American football linemen use the triceps muscles. One bodybuilding exercise that develops the triceps is the dumbbell elbow extension, which is performed either while bent over or in an erect position with the elbow above the shoulder. However, such exercises isolate the triceps from the other muscles involved in shot-putting and tackling and consequently are not very effective for these athletes. A better option for them is the incline bench press performed at an angle of 30 to 35 degrees, which is similar to the angle used in the selected sports. This exercise also works the other active muscles, such as the pectoral muscles and the deltoids.

SPECIFICITY AND FUNCTIONAL TRAINING

Specific strength is often confused with functional strength. The term *functional strength* is fairly recent. It refers to exercises performed on various equipment, such as balls, ABS (plastic) pipes with foam, and proprioceptive platforms, all of which are designed to create a more difficult environment in order to increase participation by small and deep stabilizing muscles (Staley 2005, 22). However, can we think that Olympic and world championship events have been won, and world records set, without the athletes having worked on specific strength, or not having done so in an optimal manner, until the year 2000?

In fact, specific strength and functional strength are not synonymous. Training for the specific strength needed in a given sport involves replicating the specific modality of force expression needed in the chosen event, both neurally and metabolically. This training is achieved by using exercises that mimic the action of the kinetic chains in the specific motor skills (including specific joints' range of motion and force vector). Particular emphasis is placed on the prime movers, without disturbing the motor patterns required for the sport's technique.

In contrast, the term *functional strength*, rather than referring to the physiological and biomechanical parameters of the specific event or motor skill, is more commonly considered as indicating the manner in which strength is trained—that is, its training means: free weights or cables, unilateral training, and possibly standing and through more than one plane of motion. (Exceptions to this definition are found in propaedeutic exercises and some core stability exercises.) In other words, in order to talk about specific strength training, the essential starting points are the biomechanical—and in particular the physiological—parameters of the event. Functional training, in contrast, is simply defined by the use of exercises with the characteristics just listed.

To state that the exercise selection fully defines the degree of functionality of a strength training program is, obviously, methodologically wrong, but it is also true that the best functionalists apply the concept of periodization of strength to their planning. In addition, not only do they take into account the biomechanics when selecting exercises, but also they consider the physiology when choosing load parameters, despite preferring certain exercises and methods. We should, however, ask ourselves to what extent certain functional training methods are appropriate in order to reach the levels of maximum strength development needed in certain power sports (e.g., one-leg squat grabbing a suspension training belt). At this point, it should be clear that periodization of strength is a more comprehensive concept than functional training, and specific strength is grounded on biomechanics an physiology, rather than exercise novelty, variation, or simple skill mimicking.

Program Design

8

Manipulation of Training Variables

To create successful strength training programs, coaches and athletes manipulate several training variables, mainly volume and intensity. Both the volume and the intensity of training, as well as its frequency, change according to the competition schedule and the objective of training. More specific factors within the categories of volume and intensity include load, which is generally expressed as a percentage of 1-repetition maximum (1RM); buffer; repetitions; sets; tempo of execution; and rest intervals between sets. Manipulating these specific variables alters the volume, intensity, degree of effort, and density of training—and, consequently, the training effect.

Strength training programs must also include a mix of general and sport-specific exercises. As a rule of thumb, the early part of the yearly training program, which can include three to six months of preparatory training, should include a higher volume of training with low proportion of sport-specific exercises. As the competitive season approaches, however, the intensity of training is stressed, the volume is decreased, and sport-specific exercises become a major part of the program.

Training Volume

Volume, or the quantity of work performed, can be measured either in terms of the weight lifted per training session, per microcycle, or per macrocycle or in terms of the total number of sets or reps performed per training session, per microcycle, per macrocycle, or per year. Instructors, coaches, and athletes should keep records of the tonnage (total weight) lifted or the sets and reps performed per session or per training phase to help them plan future training volumes.

Training volume varies based on the sport's particular physical demands, the athlete's strength training background, and the type of strength training performed. For example, athletes attempting to develop muscular endurance use a high volume of training because of the many reps they perform. Maximum strength training, on the other hand, results in

Weightlifters' ability to endure continually higher training loads enables them to meet the strength requirements of their sport.

lower tonnage and density, despite the high load, because of the lower number of total reps and the longer rest intervals. A medium training volume is typical for athletes in sports that require power, because the load is low to medium.

Overall training volume becomes more important as athletes approach high performance. There are no shortcuts. Athletic performance requires high weekly training frequency, which, in turn, may result in greater training volume. As athletes adapt to a higher volume of training, they experience better recovery and a higher level of structural and neural adaptation. This increase in work capacity can later translate into better handling of the intensification phases, as well as better performance overall.

As seen in table 7.3 in the previous chapter, which addresses multiyear planning of strength training, once optimal volume has been reached the main stressor for mature athletes should be intensity. Work capacity is acquired over time; therefore, in order to increase training volume by increasing training frequency, it is necessary at first to lower the volume per training unit. This reduction is achieved by dividing the previous total volume of the microcycle by the new, higher number of training units. Increasing the number of training units while maintaining the same weekly training volume allows the work to be intensified thanks to increased recovery as the volume and duration per unit decrease. As a result, greater adaptations are possible (Bompa and Haff 2009).

Later, the volume per session can be increased, if necessary. For example, suppose that your objective is to increase strength training from three to four training units per microcycle and that your starting point is a microcycle with three strength training sessions, each with 8 tons of volume (thus 24 tons of total volume per microcycle). In this situation, here are an incorrect method and a correct method.

- Incorrect method: Add a training unit of 8 tons, thus abruptly increasing the total volume of the microcycle from 24 to 32 tons (an increase of 25 percent).

- Correct method: Divide the total volume of 24 tons by the new total of four training units. The total microcycle volume remains unchanged at 24 tons, but the volume of the single sessions is reduced to 6 tons each (a decrease of 25 percent), thus allowing a greater average intensity and better recovery. The volume per session can be increased later if need be.

Strength training volume depends on the athlete's biological makeup, the specifics of the sport, and the importance of strength in that sport. Mature athletes with a strong strength training background can tolerate higher volumes, but volume should not be increased for its own sake. Rather, it should be increased if the specific situation requires it—and never at the expense of the quality of sport-specific training.

Because biomotor abilities training (increase of the athlete's motor potential) must be integrated with sport-specific training (specific performance), our starting point should be the least training volume that is effective at increasing the indexes of a certain biomotor ability. As a principle, during general preparation the volume of biomotor abilities training can be such as to temporarily affect the specific performance. During specific preparation, there should a correlation between the increase of a biomotor ability's indexes and the specific performance. And during the competitive phase, biomotor abilities training should be such as to allow maintenance, slight improvement, or peaking of the specific performance.

A dramatic or abrupt increase in volume can be detrimental, irrespective of the athlete's sport or ability, resulting in fatigue, uneconomical muscular work, and possibly injury. These pitfalls can be avoided by implementing a progressive plan with an appropriate method of monitoring load increments. Here are a few rules of thumb.

a. The duration of a session should not exceed 75 minutes unless it is a high-volume, maximum-strength session with long rest intervals or a muscle-endurance-long session for an ultra-endurance athlete.

b. The volume of an anatomical adaptation session should fall between 16 and 32 total sets; a hypertrophy session between 16 and 24 (and less than one hour in duration); a maximum strength session between 16 and 24; a power session between 10 and 16; and a power endurance or muscle-endurance-short session between 4 and 12.

c. Once the sets' volume is established, it should not vary more than 50 percent within a macrocycle—for example, 2 sets per exercise in the first microcycle, 3 sets per exercise in the second and third microcycles, 2 sets in the fourth (unload) microcycle.

The total volume depends on several factors, and the determinant is the importance of strength to the sport. For instance, international-class weightlifters often plan 33 short tons (30 tonnes) per training session and approximately 44,000 short tons (40,000 tonnes) per year. For other sports, the volume differs drastically (see table 8.1). Power and speed sports require a much higher volume than boxing does; in sports in which muscular endurance is dominant, such as rowing and canoeing, the volume of strength per year can be three to six times higher.

Training Intensity

In strength training, intensity is expressed as a percentage of load or 1-repetition maximum. It is an indicator of the strength of the nervous stimuli employed in training, and it is determined by the degree to which the central nervous system (CNS) is called into action. Stimulus strength depends on load, speed of movement, and variation of rest intervals between reps. Training load, expressed as intensity percentage of 1RM, refers to the mass or weight lifted. Strength training employs the intensity zones and loads presented in table 8.2.

A supermaximum load exceeds one's maximum strength (1RM). In most cases, loads between 100 and 120 percent of 1RM can be used by applying the eccentric (yielding to the force of gravity) or isometric (maximal contraction without joint movement) method.

Table 8.1 Suggested Guidelines for Volume (in Tonnes) of Strength Training per Year

| Sport or event | VOLUME PER MICROCYCLE IN TRAINING PHASES | | | VOLUME PER YEAR | |
	Preparatory	Competitive	Transition	Minimum	Maximum
Shot put	24–40	8–12	4–6	900	1,450
Football	30–40	10–12	6	900	1,400
Baseball, cricket	20–30	8–10	2–4	850	1,250
Downhill skiing	18–36	6–10	2–4	700	1,250
Long and triple jumps	20–30	8–10	2	800	1,200
Rowing	30–40	10–12	4	900	1,200
Kayaking, canoeing	20–40	10–12	4	900	1,200
Wrestling	20–30	10	4	800	1,200
Swimming	20	8–10	2–4	700	1,200
High jump	16–28	8–10	2–4	620	1,000
Triathlon	16–20	8–10	2–4	600	1,000
Cycling	16–22	8–10	2–4	600	950
Ice hockey	15–25	6–8	2–4	600	950
Speedskating	14–26	4–6	2–4	500	930
Lacrosse	14–22	4–8	2–4	500	900
Basketball	12–24	4–6	2	450	850
Javelin	12–24	4	2	450	800
Volleyball	12–20	4	2	450	600
Sprinting	10–18	4	2	400	600
Gymnastics	10–16	4	4	380	600
Rugby	10–20	4–6	4	320	600
Squash	8–12	4	4	350	550
Figure skating	8–12	2–4	2	350	550
Tennis	8–12	2–4	2	350	550
Boxing, martial arts	8–14	3	1	380	500
Golf	4–6	2	1	250	300

Table 8.2 Intensity Value and Load Used in Strength Training

Intensity value	Load	% of 1RM	Type of contraction	Method	Adaptations
1	Supermax	>105	Eccentric or isometric	Maximum strength	Intramuscular coordination
2	Max	90–100	Eccentric-concentric		
3	Heavy	85–90	Eccentric-concentric	Maximum strength and power (high load)	
4		80–85	Eccentric-concentric		
5	Medium	70–80	Eccentric-concentric		Intermuscular coordination
6		50–70	Eccentric-concentric	Power (low load)	
7	Low	30–50	Eccentric-concentric		

Only a few athletes with a robust strength training background should use supermaximum loads. Such loads should be employed for limited time periods and only for some muscle groups, in particular those muscle groups whose eccentric loading is high during the sport-specific activity (for instance, the hamstrings during sprinting or the quads during landing or changing directions). Most other athletes should be restricted to loads of no more than 100 percent of 1RM.

Maximum load can range from 90 to 100 percent of 1RM, heavy load from 80 to 90 percent, medium load from 50 to 80 percent, and low load from 30 to 50 percent. Each intensity zone elicits slightly different neuromuscular adaptations (see chapter 2) and necessitates a precise progression. Intensities above 90 percent should be used sparingly, especially to concentric failure, for their testosterone-lowering effect (Häkkinen and Pakarinen 1993; Izquierdo et al. 2006) despite their additional positive neuromuscular adaptations. The only weightlifting schools that supported frequent use of loads above 90 percent were the Bulgarians, the Turks, and the Greeks—groups that were, not surprisingly, plagued by an exceptionally high incidence of positive doping tests (Bulgaria had 3 positives at the 2000 Olympics, 3 before the 2004 Olympics, and 11 before the 2008 Olympics; Greece had 11 positives before the 2008 Olympics; both teams had zero medals at the 2008 Beijing Olympics and 2012 London Olympics; and Turkey had 48 positives in 2013).

Testing the 1RM every three or four weeks at the end of a macrocycle is usually enough to reap the benefits of the 90 percent to 100 percent intensity range. Over the years, Western strength training authors have often supported the use of concentric failure (with no buffer) as a required condition for strength gains. In reality, as can be seen from the information presented in chapter 2 (Neuromuscular Response to Strength Training), all of the performance-enhancing neuromuscular adaptations (except for the highest hypertrophic effect [Burd et al. 2010]) occur without the need for concentric failure. This view is further supported by the strength training load and repetition distribution of elite weightlifters and powerlifters; most of their strength training uses 70 percent to 90

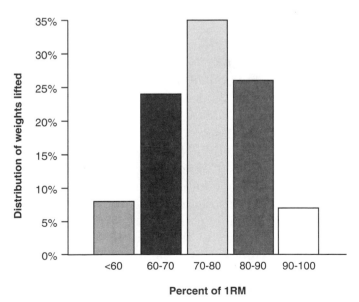

Figure 8.1 The distribution of weights lifted by USSR weightlifting team members during preparation for the 1988 Olympic Winter Games (one year of direct observation).

Adapted from "Preparation of National Olympic Team in Weight Lifting to the 1988 Olympic Games in Seoul," Technical report #1988-67, All-Union Research Institute of Physical Culture, Moscow, 1989.

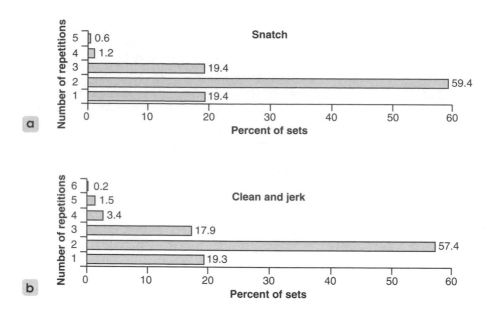

Figure 8.2 Percentage of sets with various numbers of lifts in the training of elite athletes.

Reprinted, by permission, from V.M. Zatsiorsky, 1992, "Intensity of strength training facts and theory: Russian and Eastern European approach," *National Strength and Conditioning Association Journal* 14(5): 46-57.

percent and low reps and is never carried to concentric failure (see figures 8.1 and 8.2 and tables 8.3 and 8.4).

Table 8.3, in particular, provides an example of the load distribution among training zones used by the former Russian national powerlifting coach Boris Sheiko, one of the most successful coaches in powerlifting history. Table 8.4 shows the reps-per-set guidelines of the USSR Junior National (1975 to 1980) and Senior National (1980 to 1985) weightlifters under coach Alexander Prilepin (1979). Prilepin's athletes won 85 international medals, including Olympic medals, and set 27 world records.

Furthermore, as an athlete becomes objectively strong (thus neuromuscularly efficient), he or she can tolerate a less frequent exposure to maximum loads (see figure 8.3).

Load should relate to the type of strength being developed and, more important, to the sport-specific combination resulting from the blending of strength with speed or of strength with endurance. Details about training these sport-specific combinations are presented in chapter 14. For general guidelines about the load to use in developing each of these combinations, see table 8.5. The load is not the same through all training phases. Rather, periodization alters the load according to the goals of each training phase. As shown in the table, the load ranges from 30 percent to more than 100 percent of 1RM, and the corresponding intensities are shown in the second row of the table. The rows below that indicate the sport-specific combinations and the suggested load for each.

Periodization incorporates proper planning for all of the performance abilities needed in the chosen sport. For instance, training for a middle-distance runner addresses training distance covered, sessions per week, and of course volume of work (e.g., sets and reps) performed in each strength training session. The more reps and sets an athlete performs in a session, the greater the volume of work. Volume and intensity are very closely related and represent the quantity and quality of work. One is not more important than the other; both should be strategically manipulated in training to produce a desired effect.

Table 8.3 Intensity and Volume Fluctuations for the Sheiko Squat and Deadlift

SHEIKO SQUAT

Macrocycle	1									
Microcycle	1		2		3		4			
Intensity (% of 1RM)	Volume		Volume		Volume		Volume		Total lifts	Zone
50%	5	5	5	10	3	5	5	5	90	Zone 4
55%					5					
60%	10	4	4	9	3	4	4	4		
65%					4				84	Zone 3
70%	25	6	6	22	3	6	6	6		
75%		15			6				104	Zone 2
80%			10	10	12	18	15	18		
85%					8				8	Zone 1

SHEIKO DEADLIFT

Macrocycle	1					
Microcycle	1	2	3	4		
Intensity	Volume	Volume	Volume	Volume	Total lifts	Zone
50%	3	7	6	3	46	Zone 4
55%	4					
60%	3	7	10	3		
65%	4		8		46	Zone 3
70%	6	14	8	6		
75%	24	12			74	Zone 2
80%	4	16	6	12		
85%				6	12	Zone 1
90%			6			

Reprinted, by permission, from P. Evangelista, 2010, "La programmazione della forza - criteri di scelta e analisi degli schemi di allenamento," a workshop for the Tudor Bompa Institute Italia, May 23, 2010.

Table 8.4 Reps-per-Set Guidelines of the USSR Junior National (1975 to 1980) and Senior National (1980 to 1985) Teams

% of 1RM	Reps per set	Optimal total	Range
55–65	3–6	24	18–30
70–75	3–6	18	12–24
80–85	2–4	15	10–20
>90	1–2	7	4–10

Adapted from A.S. Vorobyev and M.S. Prilepin, 1979, "Comparative effectiveness of the different types of loadings applied in the weightlifters training," "International Weightlifting Journal, Vol. 1, Sofia, Bulgaria: 7-9.

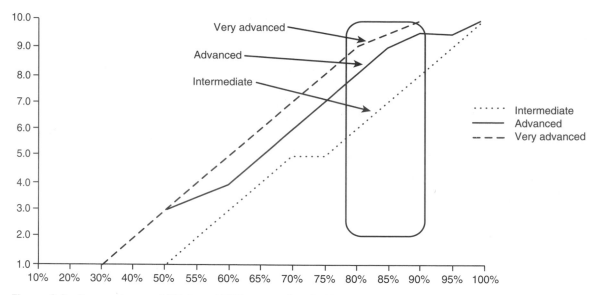

Figure 8.3 Percentage of 1RM and RPE according to the athlete's level.

Reprinted, by permission, from P. Evangelista, 2010, "La programmazione della forza - criteri di scelta e analisi degli schemi di allenamento," a workshop for the Tudor Bompa Institute Italia, May 23, 2010.

Table 8.5 Relationship Between Load and Different Types and Combinations of Strength

% of 1RM	>105	100	90		80	70	60	50	40	30
Intensity	Supermax	Max	Heavy		Medium		Low			
Type of strength	Maximum strength			Strength and power (high load)			Power (low load)			
							Muscle endurance			
Sport-specific strength combinations	Landing and reactive power	███	███							
	Throwing power			███	███					
	Takeoff power			███	███	███				
	Starting power			███	███	███				
	Deceleration power			███	███	███				
	Acceleration power				███	███	███			
	Power endurance				███	███	███	███		
	Muscle endurance short					███	███	███		
	Muscle endurance medium						███	███	███	
	Muscle endurance long							███	███	███

As with most body systems, a dose response exists between the total volume of work and the level of adaptation. Beginning strength trainers or athletes initially benefit from a low volume, such as one or two sets, but eventually plateau and require greater stimulation in order to experience further adaptation. Therefore, it is not surprising to have athletes perform the squat for multiple sets (such as six to eight) or 50-plus reps, depending on the desired physiological effect. Keep in mind that the term *intensity*, as used in the sporting world, is strictly a representation of a percentage of load used in training. In other words, the only true way to increase intensity is to increase the load.

For instance, suppose that an athlete performs two reps for the first set of a lift at 90 percent of 1RM and then, after a four-minute rest, completes three reps to failure at the same load. From set 1 to set 2, the athlete has not increased the intensity. The volume has been increased, along with the stress inflicted on the muscle, but the load has remained at 90 percent; therefore, the intensity has not changed.

Trainers and coaches must be careful not to correlate intensity with the muscular feeling that occurs following a set. As a rule of thumb, the more sets the athlete performs, the lower the number of reps, and vice versa. For instance, during a maximum strength phase, an athlete might perform six sets of three reps with an increase load from 70 percent to 80 percent of 1RM; however, during the hypertrophy phase, the same athlete might perform only three sets of 10 reps with a load of 65 percent of 1RM.

Athletes' training programs should always be individualized, and coaches and trainers should look for signs of fatigue. One of the biggest problems in the sport training world is the sacrifice of quality for quantity. Planning should be used only as a guideline for program design. That is, it should not be written in stone; instead, session-by-session progress and setbacks should be noted and used in revising the training program. Coaches should watch for the point at which an athlete is no longer capable of performing the suggested number of reps for a specific load or of performing the desired number of reps explosively and with sound technique. This judgment is critical, especially in the maximum strength phase of training, when the primary goal is to achieve nervous system adaptations.

Table 8.6 shows a hypothetical training log for an athlete performing the squat at maximum strength with no buffer (a method to simultaneously elicit strength and hypertrophy

Table 8.6 Comparison of Suggested Plan to Actual Program for Squat Training

SET	SUGGESTED Load (% of 1RM)	Reps	Rest interval (min.)	ACTUAL Load (% of 1RM)	Reps	Rest interval (min.)
1	80	5–6	3	80	6	3
2	84	4–5	4	84	5	4
3	87	3–4	4	87	4	6*
4**	87	3–4	4	87	2*	5*
5	90	2–3	4	87*	2	5*
6	90	2–3	4	87*	1+1* (spot required to complete rep)	5*

*Differs from suggested program.
**Exercise should have been terminated following the fourth set.

adaptations, also known as the absolute strength method). The athlete decided to complete the program that the coach designed and recorded the number of reps per set. Despite resting for a longer interval following the fourth set, however, the athlete was not able to complete the desired number of reps. To fulfill the repetition requirement, the fifth and sixth sets required a decrease in load. By making this decrease, the athlete in essence performed many wasted sets that will negatively influence recovery, physiological effect, and possibly sport-specific training. Instead, the athlete should have ended the exercise following the diminished performance of the fourth set.

Number of Exercises

The key to an effective training program is adequate exercise selection. It is difficult to establish an optimum number of exercises, and, desiring to develop more muscle groups, some coaches select far too many. The resulting program is overloaded and fatiguing. Instead, the number and types of exercise must be selected according to the age and performance level of the athlete, the needs of the sport, and the phase of training.

Age and Performance Level

One of the main objectives of a training program for juniors or beginners is the development of a solid anatomical and physiological foundation. For strength training, the coach should select many exercises (nine to twelve) that address the primary muscle groups. Such a program may last one to three years, depending on the athlete's age and the expected age for achieving high performance.

On the other hand, the main training objective for advanced athletes is to reach the highest possible level of performance. Therefore, their strength programs, especially during the competitive phase, must be specific, with only a few exercises (two to six) directed at the prime movers.

Needs of the Sport

Strength training exercises, particularly for elite athletes, should meet the specific needs of the chosen sport and address the prime movers dominant in that sport. For example, an elite high jumper may need to perform only three or four exercises to adequately strengthen all prime movers. A wrestler or American football player, on the other hand, may need to perform six to nine exercises to accomplish the same goal. And all sprinting athletes should do one exercise for the hip extensors with the knee straight (hamstrings), one exercise for the hip extensors with flexed knee (glutes), one exercise for the knee extensors (quads), and one exercise for the plantar flexors (calves). Therefore, the more prime movers used in a sport, the more exercises are needed. However, it may be possible to lower the number by using well-selected multijoint exercises.

Phase of Training

After the transition phase, a new annual plan should be used to start building the foundation for future training. In a general strength training program, anatomical adaptation is desirable early in the preparatory phase. For such a program to involve most muscle groups, the number of exercises has to be high (nine to twelve), regardless of the specifics of the chosen sport.

As a program progresses, the number of exercises is reduced, culminating in the competitive phase, in which the athlete performs only two to six very specific exercises that are essential to the sport. For instance, an American football, hockey, basketball, or volleyball player will perform perhaps nine or ten exercises during the preparatory phase but only four to six during the league season. By being selective, coaches can increase training efficiency and lower the athlete's overall fatigue.

Strength training is done *in addition to* technical and tactical training. In short, an inverse relationship exists between the load used in training and the number of exercises per training session. A decrease in the number of exercises indicates that the athlete is training for the specifics of the sport. As the number of exercises decreases, the number of sets per exercise increases. In this way, more workload is placed on the specific prime movers of the sport in order to optimize the muscles' strength, and power for competition. Once the competitive season begins, progressive adaptation is set aside, and a low number of exercises and moderate set increments are used to maintain physiological adaptation.

Even though the upper body is only minimally involved in some sports (such as soccer, many track-and-field events, and cycling), many strength programs emphasize exercises for the upper body. In addition, many physical education instructors, still influenced by bodybuilding theories, suggest far too many exercises for athletes. In reality, athletes who use a high number of exercises decrease the number of sets targeted to each prime mover. This approach leads to very low training adaptation and therefore very low training effect.

The desired result—high training adaptation and therefore improvement of performance—is possible only when athletes perform more sets for the chosen kinetic chain. The coach has the option of spreading all required sets for the fundamental exercises across more sessions throughout the microcycle or concentrating them in a few sessions. The first option allows the athlete to perform shorter sessions and include more accessory exercises, whereas the second option may require longer sessions and a reduction in accessory exercises.

Order of Exercises

The first determinant in exercise order is motor complexity. In fact, complex, multijoint exercises—those that normally target the prime movers in a kinetic sequence similar to the specific sport action—should always be performed first in a workout, when the nervous system is fresh. Thus, when selecting the number of exercises, strength and conditioning coaches should consider the prime movers involved in performing the skills of the sport and place the exercises in the order of their motor complexity.

Again, strength training for sport has been unduly influenced by the training methodologies of bodybuilding. Many strength training books and articles, for example, propose exercising the small-muscle groups first and then the large-muscle groups. However, this approach results in fatiguing the small-muscle groups, which leaves athletes unable to effectively train the large-muscle groups. The large-muscle groups are the prime movers in the sport, and it is extremely important that the prime movers be trained in a unfatigued state.

Another overused training method from the world of bodybuilding is the preexhaustion method. Using this method, trainees exhaust the prime movers with single-joint exercises (such as leg extensions) before executing multijoint exercises (such as the squat). Although this theory may be useful to bodybuilders, current research challenges its usefulness in sport (Augustsson et al. 2003).

Therefore, sport trainers should avoid using this method even during the hypertrophy phase of training. Instead, the main exercises in strength training programs for sport should be multijoint exercises in which the major prime movers work together. Single-joint exercises can be used during the early preparatory phase, such as during anatomical adaptation, but should be phased out in the later stages of training. Training for sport is all about optimizing strength, power, and endurance—not improving the aesthetic appeal of the athlete.

Specific strength exercises that resemble a sport-specific motor pattern repeat similar motions, thus giving the exercises a learning component. Imitation of technical skills also involves the chain of muscles in a pattern similar to their involvement in the sport. For instance, it makes sense for a volleyball player to perform half squats and toe raises together because spiking and blocking require the same moves. Therefore, the chain of muscles involved is acting in the same sequence as in jumping. A volleyball player, then, is concerned not with whether the small-muscle groups or the large-muscle groups are involved first but only with mimicking the sport-specific motion and involving the chain of muscles in the same way as in spiking and blocking.

Two options are available for choosing the order in which to perform the exercises prescribed by the coach: vertical and horizontal. First, the athlete may follow the order of exercises in sequence from the top down—a vertical sequence or strength circuit—as listed on the daily program sheet. This method leads to better recovery for the muscle groups involved. In fact, by the time the first exercise is performed again, the muscles have fully recovered. To ensure better recovery, exercises should alternate either between antagonist muscle groups or between upper and lower body. If all parts of the body are exercised, the following order is suggested: lower body push, upper body push, lower body pull, upper body pull, and so on.

For the second option, the athlete may perform all the sets for the first exercise, then move to the next exercise—a horizontal sequence. If the buffer used is low or nonexistent (if sets are taken to, or close to, concentric failure), or if the rest intervals are inadequate, this sequence may cause great local fatigue by the time all sets are performed for one exercise. As a result, it may produce hypertrophy rather than power or maximum strength, and, in the case of maximum strength sessions with lengthy rest intervals, the total duration of the sessions may become excessive. One solution is to couple antagonistic muscle groups and do one set each alternatively; this method, referred to as jump sets, is a hybrid of the vertical and horizontal sequences. It halves the session's duration and doubles the recovery between sets of the same exercise. Table 8.7 shows how the jump-sets method results in a shorter workout with the same training volume.

Number of Reps and Tempo

Speed of execution—that is, tempo—is an important parameter of loading in strength training, yet it is not necessarily properly understood. For example, it is considered common knowledge in bodybuilding circles that loads over 85 percent of 1RM are lifted slowly, but this is not necessarily so. Power athletes trained to lift explosively can be fast with weights up to 95 percent of 1RM and express high levels of power output even with such high loads.

It all comes down to training the nervous system to activate and fire all of the motor units in the shortest time. This effect can be achieved by periodizing the strength training program, going from intermuscular coordination training (moderate and heavy loads lifted explosively) to intramuscular coordination training (maximum loads lifted explosively,

Table 8.7 Comparison of Sample Exercise Sequence Arrangements

HORIZONTAL SEQUENCE					STRENGTH CIRCUIT					JUMP SETS				
Sequence	Exercise	Sets	Reps	Rest interval (min.)	Sequence	Exercise	Sets	Reps	Rest interval (min.)	Sequence	Exercise	Sets	Reps	Rest interval (min.)
A	Squat	5	3	3	A1	Squat	5	3	1.5	A1	Squat	5	3	1.5
B	Bench press	5	3	3	A2	Bench press	5	3	1.5	A2	Bench press	5	3	1.5
C	Stiff-leg deadlift	4	3	3	A3	Stiff-leg deadlift	4	3	1.5	B1	Stiff-leg deadlift	4	3	1.5
D	Bent-over row	4	3	3	A4	Bent-over row	4	3	1.5	B2	Bent-over row	4	3	1.5
E	Standing calf raise	3	6	2	A5	Standing calf raise	3	6	1.5	C1	Standing calf raise	3	6	1.5
F	Military press	3	6	2	A6	Military press	3	6	1.5	C2	Military press	3	6	1.5
G	Weighted crunch	3	6	2	A7	Weighted crunch	3	6	2	D	Weighted crunch	3	6	2
Session duration	70 min.				Session duration	50 min.				Session duration	50 min.			
Rest between sets of same exercise	2–3 min.				Rest between sets of same exercise	14 min.				Rest between sets of same exercise	3 min.			

or at least with the intent to move them explosively) (Behm and Sale 1993). Refer back to table 2.2.

For development of maximum strength (i.e., working at 70 to 100 percent of 1RM), the number of reps is very low (one to five); see also table 7.1. For exercises to develop power (i.e., working at 50 to 80 percent of 1RM), the number of reps is low to moderate (1 to 10, performed dynamically). For muscular endurance of short duration, 10 to 30 reps will work, whereas muscular endurance of medium duration requires 30 to 60 nonstop reps, and muscular endurance of long duration requires an even higher number of reps—up to 200. Instructors who regard 20 reps as adequate for enhancing muscular endurance may find the suggested number of reps shocking. However, the performance of 20 reps makes only an insignificant contribution to overall performance in sports that require muscular endurance of medium or long duration, such as rowing, kayaking, canoeing, long-distance swimming, and cross-country skiing.

Table 8.8 shows the relationship between load and repetitions possible performed to failure by two different types of athletes. The table also shows that 1RM conversion tables are virtually useless, because they do not take into account the individual characteristics of the athlete, who could be at one of the extremes of the neural–metabolic continuum.

Table 8.8 Relationship Between Percentage of 1RM and Possible Repetitions to Failure for Neurologically Efficient Athletes Versus Metabolically Efficient Athletes

% of 1RM	HIGH NEUROMUSCULAR-EFFICIENCY ATHLETE (POWER) Reps	HIGH METABOLIC-EFFICIENCY ATHLETE (ENDURANCE) Reps
100	1	1
95	1–2	2–3
90	3	4–5
85	5	6–8
80	6	10–12
75	8	15–20
70	10	25–30
65	15	40–50
60	20	70–90
50	25–30	90–110
40	40–50	120–150
30	70–100	150–200

Speed is critical in strength training. For the best training effects, the speed of execution, at least in the concentric phase, must be fast and explosive for most types of work. The key to proper execution of speed is the way in which the athlete applies force against resistance. For instance, when an American football player, a thrower, or a sprinter lifts a heavy load (over 90 percent of 1RM), the motion may look slow, but the force against the resistance is applied as fast as possible. Otherwise, the nervous system does not recruit and fire at high frequency all the motor units necessary to defeat resistance. Only fast and vigorous application of force trains the voluntary recruitment of fast-twitch muscle fibers. in fact, a recent study demonstrated that performing the concentric action of a lift at the maximal intended velocity versus half that velocity elicited a maximum strength increase over six weeks that was double that of the slow lifting as well as an increase in velocity with all loads (Gonzalez-Badillo et al. 2014).

For this reason, the speed of contraction plays a very important role in strength training. To achieve explosive force, the athlete must concentrate on activating the muscles quickly, even when the barbell is moving slowly. Most of the time, however, the bar should in fact move fast. Only a high speed of contraction performed against a heavy load (over 70 percent of 1RM) rapidly recruits the fast-twitch fibers and results in increased maximum strength and power capability.

The physiological response to strength training is also affected by repetition tempo, which relates directly to the length of time that the muscle is under tension during a set; see table 8.9. For this reason, the speed of movement should vary from phase to phase. The appropriate tempo for each phase of the strength training program is indicated in table 8.10.

Moderate speeds in the concentric phase increase the metabolic stress and the muscular force expression throughout the range of motion and can be used to increase the hypertrophic response to training. Moderate speeds can be used during the anatomical

Table 8.9 Training Effects According to Variation of Tempo

MUSCLE ACTION	ECCENTRIC PHASE		ISOMETRIC BETWEEN ECCENTRIC AND CONCENTRIC PHASES*		CONCENTRIC PHASE		ISOMETRIC BETWEEN CONCENTRIC AND ECCENTRIC PHASES*	
TEMPO	Slow (3 to 5 sec.)	Fast (< 1 sec.)	Absent	Present (1 to 5 sec.)	Slow (2 to 3 sec.)	Fast (< 1 sec.)	Absent	Present (1 to 2 sec.)
TRAINING EFFECTS	More hypertrophy	Less hypertrophy	Less hypertrophy	More hypertrophy	More hypertrophy	More max strength	More metabolic stress	More fast-twitch fiber recruitment
	More max strength	More cyclic starting strength	More cyclic starting strength	More acyclic starting strength	More metabolic stress	More neural stress		

*Pushing exercises.

Table 8.10 Suggested Tempo per Training Phase

	Eccentric phase	Isometric between eccentric and concentric phases*	Concentric phase	Isometric between concentric and eccentric phases*	Example of suggested tempo
AA	Slow	Present or absent	Slow or fast	Absent	3.0.2.0
Hyp.	Slow	Present or absent	Fast	Absent	4.1.1.0
MxS	Slow	Present or absent	Fast	Absent or present	3.0.X.1
P	Fast	Absent (cyclic), present (acyclic)	Fast	Absent or present	1.0.X.0
PE	Fast	Absent (cyclic), present (acyclic)	Fast	Absent	1.0.X.0
MES	Fast	Absent	Fast	Absent	1.0.1.0
MEM	Moderate	Absent	Fast	Absent	2.0.1.0
MEL	Moderate	Absent	Moderate	Absent	2.0.1.0

Key: AA = anatomical adaptation, Hyp. = hypertrophy, MEL = muscle endurance long, MEM = muscle endurance medium, MES = muscle endurance short, MxS = maximum strength, P = power, and PE = power endurance.
*Pushing exercises.

adaptation phase of training because they allow more motor control and higher times under tension. The athlete can spend about three or four seconds in the eccentric portion of the lift, pause for one second for the transition from eccentric to concentric, and then spend two seconds in the concentric portion. For the rest of the annual plan, however, athletes should perform the concentric actions for strength exercises fast or explosively because the vast majority of sport actions require fast concentric contractions.

The intended speed of contraction should be as fast as possible during the phases focused on maximum strength, power, power endurance, and muscle endurance short. During the maximum strength phase, athletes should slowly perform a three- to four-second eccentric action followed by an explosive concentric action. The transition from the eccentric action to the concentric action can be manipulated during this phase. The best way to maximize concentric strength is, in fact, to remove any reflexive or elastic qualities developed during the eccentric phase of the lift by pausing for one or two seconds before performing a further concentric lift. Such methods should be used in the early part of the maximum strength phase.

Let's take the bench press as an example. When performing the bench press, extending the arms forms the concentric portion of the lift, and returning the barbell to chest level and stretching the chest muscles forms the eccentric portion. Generally speaking, an athlete slowly flexes the arms to bring the bar to the chest before quickly returning the bar to the starting position and starting the cycle again. On the other hand, the eccentric portion of the lift can increase the force of the concentric lift that follows if the eccentric portion is also executed quickly, thus eliciting what is called the myotatic (stretch) reflex. This reflex is the reason that plyometric training is so popular in sport. In essence, plyometric training improves sport performance by heightening the physiological properties of the prime movers for quick and explosive concentric actions.

As an athlete quickly lowers the bar to the chest, neural mechanisms in the muscles are heightened and elastic energy is stored in the tendons and used during the concentric or lifting portion of the exercise. Thus, a true increase in pure concentric force generation can be achieved by briefly pausing after the eccentric lift and making the upward motion of the bar a pure concentric lift without any positive influence from the eccentric action. This approach allows standardization of the range of motion for each rep by preventing the athlete from cheating or rebounding the weight. Because it encourages better technique, it improves intermuscular coordination.

The approach can also be used to help an athlete break through a strength plateau. The coach should decide whether the main focus is voluntary concentric strength maximization or imitation of the sport-specific neuromuscular pattern (usually an eccentric–concentric action). Eventually, the focus should be switched from the former to the latter, during the maximum strength phase.

Tempo is strictly linked to set duration; it represents the time under tension per rep, which, when multiplied by the number of reps in a set, determines the set's set duration. Each training phase has an ideal way to perform each rep depending on the training effect pursued in that phase. This specificity applies as well to set duration, which is related to the energy system involved. The training effect for different set durations is presented in table 8.11.

Number of Sets

A set is the number of reps per exercise followed by a rest interval. The number of sets depends on the number of exercises and the strength combination. The number of sets per exercise decreases as the number of exercises increases because otherwise the workout would get too voluminous. There is also an inverse relationship between the number of reps per set and the number of sets per exercise. For example, for a rower, canoeist, or cross-country skier attempting to develop muscular endurance of long duration, the key element is the number of reps per set. Because the number of reps is high, these athletes have difficulty performing more than three sets.

The number of sets also depends on the athlete's ability and training potential, the number of muscle groups to be trained, and the training phase. For instance, a high jumper

Table 8.11   Set Duration and Training Effects

Set duration	Training effect
2 to 12 seconds	Strength improvement without hypertrophy gains (relative strength) and power
15 to 25 seconds	Strength improvement with hypertrophy gains (absolute strength)
30 to 60 seconds	Hypertrophy
6 to 15 seconds (series of sets) 15 to 30 seconds (sets)	Power endurance
15 to 60 seconds (series of sets) 30 to 120 seconds (sets)	Muscle endurance short
1 to 4 minutes (series of sets) 2 to 8 minutes (sets)	Muscle endurance medium
More than 8 minutes	Muscle endurance long

or diver in a specialized training program may use three to five exercises for four to six sets each. A higher number of exercises would require fewer sets, which would entail obvious disadvantages. Consider a hypothetical high jumper who uses eight exercises involving several muscle groups of the legs, upper body, and arms. For each exercise or muscle group, the athlete performs work of 880 pounds (about 400 kilograms). Because the athlete can perform only four sets, the total amount of work per muscle group is 3,520 pounds (about 1,600 kilograms). If the number of exercises is reduced to four, however, the athlete can perform, say, eight total sets for a total of 7,040 pounds (about 3,200 kilograms) per muscle group. Thus the athlete can double the total work on the prime movers by decreasing the total number of exercises and increasing the number of sets.

The number of sets performed per training session also depends on the training phase. During the preparatory (preseason) phase—and in particular the anatomical adaptation phase, when most muscle groups are trained—more exercises are performed with fewer sets. As the competitive phase approaches, however, training becomes more specific, and the number of exercises decreases while the number of sets increases. Finally, during the competitive phase (season), when the purpose of training is to maintain a certain level of strength or a given strength combination, everything is reduced, including the number of sets, so that the athlete's energy is spent mostly on technical and tactical work or sport-specific training.

In team sports where the competitive season is very long, the athlete performs only a few sets per exercise (two, three, or at most four) in order to reduce residual fatigue and the chance of negative influence on recovery and specific performance. A well-trained athlete in an individual sport, on the other hand, can perform three, six, or even eight sets. Certainly, it makes sense to perform a high number of sets. The more sets the athlete performs of a fundamental exercise for the prime movers, the more work the athlete can perform, ultimately leading to higher strength gains and improved performance.

Rest Interval

Energy, of course, is necessary for strength training. During training, an athlete uses mainly the fuel of a given energy system according to the load employed and the duration of the activity. During high-intensity strength training, energy stores can be greatly taxed and even completely exhausted. Therefore, in order to complete the work, athletes must take a rest interval to replenish depleted fuel before performing another set.

In fact, the rest interval between sets or training sessions is as important as the training itself. The amount of time allowed between sets determines, to a great extent, how much energy can be recovered before the following set. Therefore, careful planning of the rest interval is critical in avoiding needless physiological and psychological stress during training.

The duration of the rest interval depends on several factors, including the combination of strength being developed, the load employed, the tempo, the set duration, the number of muscles involved, and the athlete's level of conditioning. The athlete's body weight must also be considered because heavy athletes with larger muscles tend to regenerate at a slower rate than lighter athletes do.

Rest Intervals Between Sets

The rest interval is a function of the load employed in training and the type of strength being developed, especially in relation to the buffer (see table 8.12).

Table 8.12 Suggested Guidelines for Rest Intervals Between Sets

Intensity zone	Load	% of 1RM	Concentric failure (no buffer) or close to it (low buffer)	Rest interval (minutes)	Far from concentric failure (high buffer)	Rest interval (minutes)
1	Supermax	>105	Relative strength	4–8	—	—
2	Max	90–100		3–6	Max strength (90%–95% of 1RM)	2–4
3	Heavy	85–90	Absolute strength	2–4	Max strength and power (high load)	2–3
4		80–85				
5	Medium	70–80	Hypertrophy	1–3		1–3
6		50–70	Muscle endurance	0.5–2	Power (low load)	
7	Low	30–50				

During a rest interval, the high-energy compounds adenosine triphosphate (ATP) and creatine phosphate (CP) are replenished proportionately to the duration of the rest interval. When the rest interval is calculated properly, creatine phosphate can be restored fully or almost fully and lactic acid accumulates more slowly, thus enabling the athlete to maintain a high power output for the entire workout. If the rest interval is shorter than one minute, lactic acid concentration gets high; when the rest interval is shorter than 30 seconds, lactate levels are so high that even well-trained athletes find them difficult to tolerate. A proper rest interval, on the other hand, reduces the accumulation and facilitates the removal of lactic acid from the muscles.

Some sports require athletes to tolerate lactic acid; examples include short-distance running, swimming, rowing, canoeing, some team sports, boxing, and wrestling. Strength training for athletes in these sports should take into consideration the following factors.

- A 30-second rest restores about 50 percent of depleted ATP-CP.
- Using a one-minute rest interval for several sets of 15 to 20 reps is insufficient to restore the muscle's energy substrates and enable a high power output (see table 8.13).
- Fatigue accumulated during maximum strength exercise followed by too short a rest interval results in a reduced discharge rate of motor neurons, which reduces speed. This effect does not occur following a three-minute rest interval (Bigland-Ritchie et al. 1983); in fact, a rest interval of three minutes or longer allows almost complete ATP-CP restoration.
- A longer rest interval (over three minutes) results in greater improvement of hamstring strength (Pincivero, Lephart, and Karunakara 1997).
- Sets taken to concentric failure require far more recovery time than sets not taken to concentric failure. For instance, a set of 5 reps with a 70 percent of 1RM load (15 percent buffer) might require one to two minutes to repeat the set with the same power output, whereas the same load taken to failure with 12 to 15 reps might require more than five minutes to repeat the same mean power output, which is certainly lower than the 5 reps set (see figure 8.4). Furthermore, after an athlete works to failure, a four-minute rest interval is insufficient to eliminate lactic acid from the working muscles or to replenish all of the energy requirements, such as glycogen.

In addition, power output and metabolic profile differ considerably between the following two options: five sets of 10 reps taken to concentric failure versus ten sets of 5 reps not taken to concentric failure using the same load as a percentage of 1RM (Gorostiaga et al. 2012). Not going to failure resulted in higher mean power output, a higher ATP level after the last set (6 versus 4.9 millimoles), a higher PC level (14.5 versus 3.1 millimoles), and a lower lactate level (5.8 versus 25 millimoles); see figure 8.4 and table 8.13.

The degree to which ATP-CP is replenished between sets depends on the duration of the rest interval—the shorter the rest interval, the less ATP-CP is restored and, consequently, the less energy is available for the next set. Therefore, one consequence of an

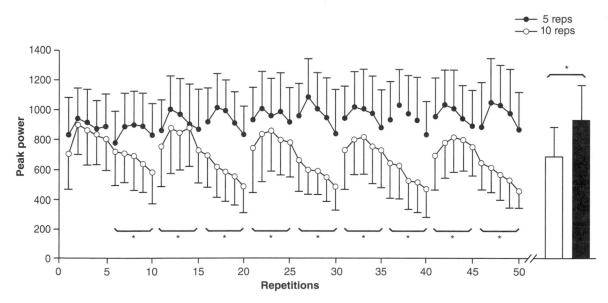

Figure 8.4 Power output comparison for each repetition of five sets of 10 reps taken to failure versus ten sets of 5 reps not taken to failure.

Table 8.13   Metabolic Response to Five Sets of 10 Reps Taken to Failure Versus Ten Sets of 5 Reps Not Taken to Failure

	10 REPS			5 REPS		
	Pre	Post 1st series	Post final series	Pre	Post 1st series	Post final series
ATP	6.46 ± 0.56	6.42 ± 0.57	4.90 ± 0.39	6.58 ± 0.35	6.19 ± 0.59	6.09 ± 0.41
ADP	0.86 ± 0.03	0.91 ± 0.10	0.92 ± 0.11	0.86 ± 0.04	0.89 ± 0.08	0.87 ± 0.08
AMP	0.07 ± 0.04	0.09 ± 0.03	0.09 ± 0.04	0.08 ± 0.04	0.08 ± 0.03	0.08 ± 0.03
TAN	7.37 ± 0.59	7.42 ± 0.67	5.91 ± 0.44	7.52 ± 0.36	7.16 ± 0.66	7.04 ± 0.49
IMP	0.01 ± 0.00	0.08 ± 0.11	0.87 ± 0.69	0.01 ± 0.00	0.01 ± 0.00	0.01 ± 0.02
PCr	21.0 ± 8.86	7.75 ± 5.53	3.15 ± 2.88	19.5 ± 4.06	11.68 ± 7.82	14.47 ± 7.24
Cr	8.93 ± 4.96	25.45 ± 3.80	22.90 ± 6.89	8.40 ± 3.25	16.97 ± 6.33	15.57 ± 5.01
PCr + Cr	29.91 ± 5.19	34.55 ± 6.23	26.06 ± 8.44	27.90 ± 3.65	30.56 ± 6.19	30.15 ± 8.46
La	1.70 ± 1.18	17.20 ± 3.50	25.01 ± 8.09	2.02 ± 1.05	7.10 ± 2.54	5.80 ± 4.62
Energy change	0.933 ± 0.006	0.927 ± 0.004	0.909 ± 0.014	0.932 ± 0.007	0.927 ± 0.006	0.928 ± 0.006

Key: ATP = adenosine triphosphate; ADP = adenosine diphosphate; AMP = adenosine monophosphate; TAN = total adenine nucleotide; IMP = inosine monophosphate; PCr = phosphocreatine; Cr = creatine; La = lactate

Reprinted, by permission, from E.M. Gorostiaga, I. Navarro-Amézqueta, J.A. Calbet, et al., 2012. "Energy metabolism during repeated sets of leg press exercise leading to failure or not," *PLOS One* 7(7): doi 10.1371/journal.pone.0040621. © 2012 Gorostiaga et al.

inadequate rest interval between sets is an increased reliance on the lactic acid system for energy. If the rest interval is too short, the lactic acid system provides most of the energy needed for subsequent sets. Reliance on this energy system results in lower power output and increased lactic acid accumulation in the working muscles, which leads to pain and fatigue, thus impairing the athlete's ability to train effectively.

Thus, unless the athlete is training for hypertrophy or lactate tolerance, a longer rest interval is required in order to maintain power output and combat excessive lactic acid accumulation.

A second consequence of an inadequate rest interval is local muscular and CNS fatigue. Most research findings point to the following possible causes and sites of fatigue.

Motor Neuron

The nervous system transmits impulses to muscle fibers through the motor neuron. A nerve impulse possesses a certain degree of frequency. Higher frequency of nerve impulses means stronger muscle contraction, which gives the athlete more ability to lift heavy loads or apply force rapidly for a sprint. The discharge frequency of nerve impulses is greatly affected by fatigue; specifically, as fatigue increases, the force of contraction decreases as a result of lower discharge rate (Ranieri and Di Lazzaro 2012; Taylor, Todd, and Gandevia 2006). Therefore, longer rest intervals (up to eight minutes) are necessary for CNS recovery during the maximum strength phase.

Neuromuscular Junction

The neuromuscular junction is the nerve attachment on the muscle fiber that relays nerve impulses to the working muscle. Fatigue at this site results largely from increased release of chemical transmitters (i.e., neurotransmitters) from the nerve endings (Tesch 1980). The electrical properties of a nerve usually return to normal levels if an athlete rests for a two- to three-minute interval after performing a set. However, after performing powerful contractions, such as those typical of maximum strength training with maximal loads or speed or speed-endurance training, sufficient recovery may require a rest interval of longer than five minutes.

Contractile Mechanisms

The muscle's contractile mechanisms (actin and myosin) can also be sites of fatigue and performance breakdown. Specifically, the increased acidity caused by repeated muscular contraction, especially at high intensity, decreases the peak tension—or the ability of a muscle to contract maximally—and affects the muscle's ability to react to the nerve impulses (Fox, Bowes, and Foss 1989; Sahlin 1986). The contracting muscle is also fatigued by the depletion of muscle glycogen stores, which occurs during prolonged exercise (more than 30 minutes) (Conlee 1987; Karlsson and Saltin 1971; Sahlin 1986). Other energy sources, including glycogen from the liver, cannot fully cover the working muscle's energy demands.

The CNS can also be affected by local muscle fatigue; in fact, this result is typical of sets taken to concentric failure. During training, chemical disturbances occur inside the muscle that affect its potential to perform work (Bigland-Ritchie et al. 1983; Hennig and Lomo 1987). When the effects of these chemical disturbances are signaled back to the CNS, the brain sends weaker nerve impulses to the working muscle, which decreases its working capacity in an attempt to protect the body. During an adequate rest interval of three to five minutes, the muscles are allowed to recover almost completely. The brain then senses the lack of danger and sends more powerful nerve impulses to the muscles, which results in better muscular performance.

Strength Training Frequency

The duration and frequency of rest intervals between strength training sessions depend on the athlete's conditioning and ability to recover, the training phase, and the energy source used in training. Well-conditioned athletes always recover faster, especially as training progresses toward the competitive phase, when they are supposed to reach their highest physical potential. Normally, strength training follows technical or tactical training, and if athletes tax the same energy system and fuel (e.g., glycogen) during technical and strength training, the next training of this type must be planned for two days later because 48 hours are required for full restoration of glycogen (Fox, Bowes, and Foss 1989; Piehl 1974). Even with a carbohydrate-rich diet, glycogen levels do not return to normal in less than two days.

If athletes perform only strength training, as some do on certain days during the preparatory phase, the restoration of glycogen occurs faster—55 percent in 5 hours and almost 100 percent in 24 hours. This faster restoration means that strength training can be planned more frequently. In the case of a strength training session during which multiple sets of low reps not taken to failure followed by adequate rest intervals are performed, glycogen restoration is not even a concern, as the energy system mainly involved would be the anaerobic alactic ATP-CP system.

The planning of strength training sessions should also take into account the time required for recovery of muscle protein. Untrained subjects who take part in resistance training programs that include a combination of concentric and eccentric actions show muscle fiber breakdown (protein breakdown) that can persist as long as 48 hours after the bout of strength training (Gibala et al. 1995). The good news is that the concomitant net increase in the synthesis of muscle protein is greater than the breakdown. Protein synthesis, or the rebuilding of muscle fibers, following a strength training session can be further increased by ingesting a mix of carbohydrate and protein immediately following the session. Muscle protein recovery also likely happens faster in trained athletes.

Finally, probably the most important factor to consider in planning strength training sessions is nervous system fatigue. Scheduling high-intensity workouts on back-to-back days does not allow proper time for neural recovery. For instance, many athletes perform maximum strength training on Monday followed by plyometric training on Tuesday. Because both sessions tax similar neural pathways, recovery time between the two is inadequate, and injury or signs of overtraining may appear unless the training uses a very low volume of both kinds of session.

Overall, then, scientific research overwhelmingly argues that recovery after a strength or aerobic training session must be adequate to allow time for all body systems to regenerate and adapt to the stimulus before being introduced to a similar or more aggressive training session of the same nature. In the circle of training, recovery plays as vital a role as the stimulus applied in training. Specifically, energy fuel must be restored, the nervous system must recover, and the net protein balance (synthesis minus breakdown) must remain positive in order to achieve progressive increases in muscular strength, power, endurance, or size.

The process can be simplified by designing training programs according to the energy systems used. Chapter 3 provides an in-depth discussion of the role of energy systems in training and the amount of time needed for recovery and regeneration following a training session.

Restoration of Phosphates

As seen in the discussion of energy systems in chapter 3, adenosine triphosphate is the energy currency of the body, and creatine phosphate is used to form new ATP from the ADP that results from ATP metabolism. The body's energy substrates, such as the phosphates and glycogen, are lowered by the fatigue that is slowly brought on by lifting weights or performing high-level metabolic activity. The body then recovers and replenishes energy supplies to preexercise conditions (or higher) through the restoration of phosphates and glycogen.

As shown in table 8.14, phosphagens (ATP-CP) restoration reaches 50 percent in the first 30 seconds of recovery and 100 percent within three to five minutes. This pattern explains why a three- to five-minute rest is needed between sets of high-intensity resistance training, such as lifting heavy weights for four to eight reps or sprinting for 50 meters. For instance, during a sprint workout, if the rest intervals between 50-meter repetitions are insufficient (say, one or two minutes only), the workout will become progressively more lactic, thus shifting from a speed training session to a lactate tolerance session (Janssen 2001).

Table 8.14 Time Course of ATP-CP Restoration

Time (min.)	% of restoration
0.5	50
1	75
1.5	87.5
2	93.7
2.5	96.8
3	98.3
3.5	99
4	99.4
4.5	99.8
5	100

Beginning a set without proper phosphates recovery does not allow the athlete to maintain power output throughout the set or from one set to the next. Therefore, in the maximum strength phase of training, athletes should rest for three to five minutes before performing more sets with the same muscle group, unless they use a high buffer. For maximum recovery when exercising at very high intensity and with a low buffer, athletes should use the vertical method of training—moving to the next exercise after each set. In other words, the athlete completes one set of each suggested exercise before returning to the first exercise for the second set. This pattern allows ample time for phosphates recovery in the muscle.

Activity During the Rest Interval

When recovering between high-intensity intermittent (lactic) bouts of exercise, performance in subsequent bouts is affected more positively by engaging in aerobic activity at approximately 20 percent of $\dot{V}O_2$max than by than stretching or passive rest (Dorado, Sanchis-Moysi, and Calbet 2004). To facilitate faster recovery between sets, athletes could also perform relaxation exercises (such as shaking the legs, arms, and shoulders) or light massage, both of which speed up recovery. In addition, athletes can perform diversionary activities that involve the unfatigued muscles in light contractions, which have been reported to facilitate faster recovery of the prime movers (Asmussen and Mazin 1978).

Static stretching should *not* be performed for the muscles that are going to be trained in a strength or power session unless it is placed at the beginning of a long warm-up routine that implies an escalation of intensity, because it may acutely inhibit their power output (Power et al. 2004; Cramer et al. 2005; Nelson et al. 2005; Yamaguchi et al. 2006; Samuel et al. 2008; La Torre et al. 2010). The purpose of stretching exercises is to artificially lengthen a muscle where the myosins and actins are overlapped. The sooner the muscles reach their anatomical length, the faster they start their recovery and regeneration process, thus more easily eliminating the metabolites accumulated during training. Static stretching addressing the muscles used should be planned for the end of the training session.

Strength Training Loading Patterns

One of the most popular strength training loading patterns is the pyramid. Its structure, shown in figure 8.5, implies that the load increases progressively to a higher intensity while the number of reps decreases proportionately. The physiological advantage of using the pyramid is that it prepares the nervous system for higher tensions in a gradual way, thus stabilizing technique and lowering inhibitory mechanisms. To facilitate the highest level of strength adaptation, athletes should avoid going to concentric failure in any set and should use a range of 10 percent to 15 percent in the loading pattern from the first set to the last set of the pyramid. Any range greater than 15 percent does not optimize strength gains.

Another pattern, the double pyramid, consists of two pyramids, one of which is inverted on top of the other. The number of reps decreases from the bottom up in the first pyramid, then increases again in the second pyramid. Conversely, the load gets higher as the reps decrease, then lower as the reps increase again (see figure 8.6).

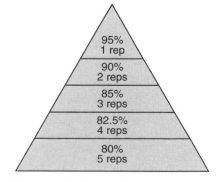

Figure 8.5 Pyramid loading pattern. In this case, a 5 percent buffer is used, so there is no concentric failure for any of the sets.

Although the double pyramid has its merits, some cautions are necessary. Most proponents of this pattern suggest reaching concentric failure in all sets. In this approach, however, by the time the final sets are performed, both the CNS and the muscles involved may be exhausted, in which case these sets will not produce the expected benefits.

To the contrary, because the fatigue will impair the recruitment of the fast-twitch fibers, the last sets in this loading pattern result in muscle hypertrophy rather than development of strength or power. Increases in power, in particular, can be obtained only when an athlete is in a unfatigued state, which generally occurs at the beginning of a session immediately following the warm-up. However, if both maximum strength and hypertrophy training are planned in the same training session (the absolute strength method), the double pyramid may be an acceptable solution because it allows a high total time under tensions for the fast-twitch muscle fibers.

For an improved variant of the double pyramid, the skewed pyramid is suggested (see figure 8.7). In this approach, the load is constantly increased throughout the session, except during the last set, when it is lowered (e.g., 80 percent, 85 percent, 90 percent, 95 percent, and 80 percent). Lowering the load in that last set (i.e., the back-off set) and taking it to failure has been proven to retain muscle hypertrophy when the majority of high-intensity, low-rep sets would only stimulate relative strength (Goto et al. 2004). This method could be used during the strength maintenance phase of the annual plan.

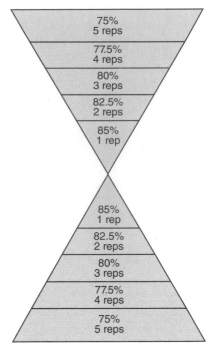

Figure 8.6 Double-pyramid loading pattern. The progression over time can involve keeping the same sets and reps scheme yet increasing the intensity by 2.5 percent of 1RM each microcycle, thus lowering the buffer from between 10 percent and 15 percent to 2.5 percent over the entire maximum strength phase.

One of the best loading patterns for maximizing strength gains is the flat pyramid (see figure 8.8). It develops maximum strength and also elicits some hypertrophy specific to fast-twitch fibers, thanks to the higher number of total reps performed at high loads. This loading pattern starts with a warm-up set of, say, 50 percent of 1RM, followed by intermediary sets at 60 percent, 70 percent, and 75 percent, then stabilizes the load at 80

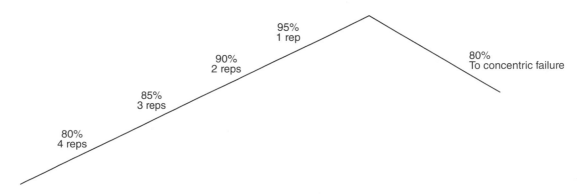

Figure 8.7 Skewed pyramid loading pattern.

148

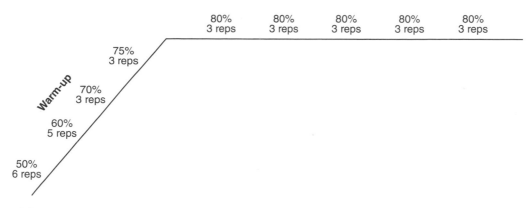

Figure 8.8 Flat pyramid loading pattern.

percent for the entire workout. The physiological advantage of the flat pyramid is that by using a load of only one intensity level, the best neuromuscular adaptation for maximum strength is achieved without confusing the body with several intensities.

In traditional pyramids, on the other hand, the load often varies from 70 percent to 100 percent. Load variations of such magnitude cross three levels of intensity: medium, heavy, and maximum. Despite the fact that the load necessary to produce gains in maximum strength falls between 70 percent and 100 percent, each intensity zone (70 percent to 80 percent, 80 percent to 90 percent, and 90 percent to 100 percent) elicits slightly different neuromuscular adaptations (see chapter 2) and necessitates a precise progression. In fact, the volume spent in each intensity zone determines the main neuromuscular adaptations. Therefore, a traditional pyramid that uses a load of 70 percent to 100 percent may result in gains in both power and maximum strength, and, while this may be of general benefit to athletes, it does not maximize gains in either area.

Variations of the flat pyramid are certainly possible and necessary, as long as the load stays within the intensity range required for the desired neuromuscular adaptations in a specific macrocycle (70 percent to 80 percent for intermuscular coordination, 80 percent to 90 percent for intramuscular coordination). One such modification can be made by keeping all work sets at the same number of repetitions while increasing the load (thus lowering the buffer) from set to set. Figure 8.9 depicts the progression of such a loading pattern over three maximum strength macrocycles.

When seeking to maximize strength gains in intermediate and advanced athletes, wave loading is an excellent pattern. As its practical application is a bit more complex than the pyramids, we tend not to use the wave loading pattern with beginners but rather reserve it for later stages of athletic development. For a 14-week progression, see figure 8.10. Wave loading involves two or three waves, usually composed of three work sets, in which the load is increased progressively while the number of reps decreases. The same pattern of load and reps used for the first wave is repeated in the following wave(s).

The physiological advantage of wave loading hinges on the fact that a latter wave is potentiated by the higher-intensity sets of a former wave, thus increasing the power output at the same percentage of 1RM. It also leaves power athletes fresher for high-intensity sets, because they don't need to do all of the more voluminous sets before the low-rep sets, as it happens for other loading patterns. Some proponents of wave loading have suggested exploiting the neural potentiation of the first wave by increasing the load in the second wave. Although this approach can be used to elicit gains in both strength and hypertrophy, we prefer to progress the load from week (microcycle) to week, thus increasing strength and power and leaving more energy for sport-specific activity.

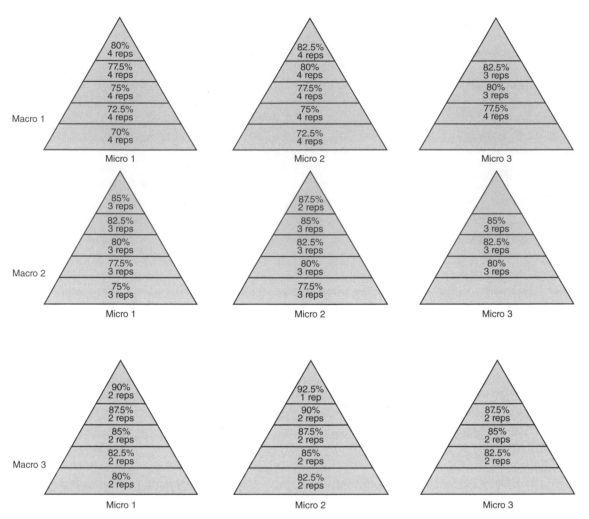

Figure 8.9 Load and repetition progression in three 2+1 maximum-strength macrocycles using the modified flat pyramid loading pattern with a descending buffer. This kind of programming is used by power athletes whose specific activity also strongly taxes the nervous system.

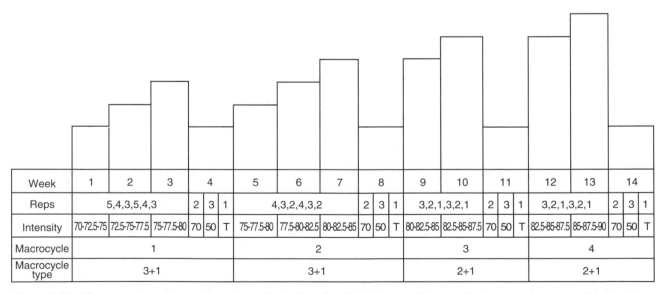

Week	1	2	3	4	5	6	7	8	9	10	11	12	13	14
Reps	5,4,3,5,4,3			2	3	1	4,3,2,4,3,2			2	3	1	3,2,1,3,2,1			2	3	1	3,2,1,3,2,1			2	3	1
Intensity	70-72.5-75	72.5-75-77.5	75-77.5-80	70	50	T	75-77.5-80	77.5-80-82.5	80-82.5-85	70	50	T	80-82.5-85	82.5-85-87.5	70	50	T	82.5-85-87.5	85-87.5-90	70	50	T
Macrocycle	1				2				3			4		
Macrocycle type	3+1				3+1				2+1			2+1		

Figure 8.10 The wave loading pattern is particularly suited for intermediate and advanced power athletes. Here is a 14-week progression with three repetition schemes throughout the macrocycles.

Training Program Design

All training programs must be planned, designed, and measured in order to assess whether the training objective has been achieved. The following steps remove any confusion from the process of designing a program and assessing its significance to the athlete's level of development.

Analysis of the Sport's Performance Model

Analyze the contribution of each biomotor ability and determine the most specific qualities to train.

Endurance

1. Use scientific literature to determine the contribution of each energy system to the sport activity (at the competitive level of the team or athlete):
   - Anaerobic alactic (ATP-CP)
   - Anaerobic lactic (LA)
   - Aerobic (O_2)
2. Evaluate whether an activity is continuous or intermittent.
3. Determine the working intensity zones for endurance and the progression to be used throughout the training program.
4. Choose the methods to use in each macrocycle and the progression of training means.

Speed

1. Evaluate the number, intensity, and duration of sprints or quick actions.
2. Consider the differences between, and the contribution of, each of the following qualities of speed: alactic speed (acceleration, maximum speed), lactic speed short (repeated sprint ability, or RSA), and lactic speed long (speed endurance). Note: lactic speed long (speed endurance) is an expression of lactic power in which speed is maintained for more than eight seconds. In contrast, lactic speed short (repeated sprint ability or RSA) is an expression of alactic capacity in which sprints under six seconds are repeated with partial recovery until they become an expression of lactic power short, which also heavily engages aerobic power during short rest intervals to restore phosphates through aerobic phosphorylation.
3. Evaluate the type (active or passive) and duration of recovery between sprints or fast actions.
4. Evaluate whether speed is expressed linearly or nonlinearly.
5. Choose the methods to use in each macrocycle and the progression of training means.

Strength

1. Select the type of strength. Determine which of the following qualities of strength are specific to the event: power; power endurance; or muscle endurance short, medium, or long. The increase of the chosen quality or qualities will be the ultimate goal of the entire periodization of strength. Remember that for the endurance types of strength (of a more metabolic nature), the morpho-functional adaptations to training require longer exposure to the stimuli than is the case for the neural adaptations.

This factor directly affects the length of the conversion phase, and therefore the time remaining for other phases, as the program designing process works backward from the end point.

2. Determine the appropriate duration of the anatomical adaptation period based on the athlete's characteristics (including his or her athletic development stage and strength training experience) and the time available for an introductory phase.

3. Decide whether or not to implement a period devoted to hypertrophy in light of the characteristics of the athlete and of the sporting event.

4. Select the exercises to use in training. Strength and conditioning coaches should select training exercises according to the specifics of the sport, the athletes' needs, and the phase of training. Each athletic skill is performed by prime movers, which can differ from sport to sport, depending on the specific skill requirements. Therefore, coaches must first identify the prime movers, then select the strength exercises that best involve those muscles. At the same time, they must consider the athlete's needs, which depend on his or her background and individual strengths and weaknesses.

   Because the weakest link in a chain always breaks first, compensation exercises (also referred to as accessory exercises) should be selected to strengthen the weakest muscles. The selection of exercises is also phase specific. Normally, during the anatomical adaptation phase, most muscle groups are employed to build a better and more multilateral foundation. As the competitive phase approaches, training becomes more specific, and exercises are selected specifically to involve the prime movers. Thus, coaches must analyze the sport movements in order to determine exercises and loading parameters. The following factors should be considered:

   • Planes on which the movements take place (sagittal, frontal, transverse)

   • Force expressed at various joint angles within the sport-specific range of motion (i.e., the zone that must be most affected by the development of the specific strength)

   • Muscle groups producing the movements (i.e., the prime movers, which also must be most affected by the development of the specific strength)

   • Muscle actions (concentric, eccentric, isometric)

5. Choose the methods to use in each macrocycle and the progression of training means. Details about training methods and progression are provided in chapters 11 through 15.

Analysis of the Tradition of Training in a Sport

Analyze the training tradition of the chosen sport. Over the years, coaches have found solutions mostly based on practicality rather than science. Equipped with the latest knowledge and your practical experience, you can find the ideal starting point to overcome such tradition.

Analysis of the Athlete

To determine the current state of training, you need to test the athlete's degree of development of each biomotor ability or its qualities, possibly in relation to the means that you will use in the training program. Consider test results and the athlete's competitive level in order to establish the training load progression and the performance goals for every biomotor ability in each phase of the year.

TESTING THE 1 REPETITION MAXIMUM (1RM)

Some coaches believe that testing for 1RM is dangerous—that lifting 100 percent can result in injury. However, it is not dangerous for trained athletes to lift 100 percent once every three or four weeks. Most injuries occur during training and competition, not during testing. Sometimes the body of an athlete is subjected to forces up to five times his or her body weight during the sporting activity, so testing maximum strength should not constitute a safety concern. Consider, as well, that testing is performed at the end of the unloading microcycle of a macrocycle, when the athlete has recovered from the fatigue of the previous loading microcycles. However, a test for 1RM must follow a thorough, progressive warm-up, such as the one suggested here (in kilograms) for the squat (projected 1RM at 150 kilograms):

1st set: 20 kilograms × 10 reps, 30-second rest interval, 13 percent of 1RM

2nd set: 60 kilograms × 4 reps, 60-second rest interval, 40 percent of 1RM

3rd set: 80 kilograms × 2 reps, 90-second rest interval, 53 percent of 1RM

4th set: 100 kilograms × 2 reps, 2-minute rest interval, 67 percent of 1RM

5th set: 120 kilograms × 1 rep, 2-minute rest interval, 80 percent of 1RM

6th set: 130 kilograms × 1 rep, 3-minute rest interval, 87 percent 1RM

7th set: 140 kilograms × 1 rep, 4-minute rest interval, 93 percent 1RM

8th set: 145 kilograms × 1 rep, 5-minute rest interval, 97 percent 1 RM

9th set: 150 kilograms × 1 rep, 6-minute rest interval, 100 percent 1RM

First, determine the athlete's degree of strength training. Maximum strength is the highest load that an athlete can lift in one repetition (1RM). Before designing a maximum strength or power program, a coach should know each athlete's maximum strength at least in the dominant exercises. An athlete's individual data are valid only for a certain cycle of training, usually a macrocycle, because the degree of training changes continuously. The 1RM test should be performed only by athletes with some experience in strength training and only after macrocycles involving some exposure to loads equal to or greater than 70 percent of 1RM. This is especially true for beginners. You should also test muscle strength balance around the joints that are most important for the sport (using submaximal weights of 3RM to 8RM) and test sport-specific strength at the beginning of the year to enable monitoring of its progression and to get information about the dynamics of adaptation to your training programs.

All the preceding steps give you a clear picture of the athlete's level of athletic development and degree of training in each biomotor ability. You can use this information to determine the type and number of exercises, the loading pattern, the percentage of 1RM, the number of reps, and the number of sets to prescribe for a macrocycle training program. The program cannot, however, be the same for each macrocycle. Training demand must increase progressively so that the athlete adapts to a larger workload, which translates into increased strength. Coaches should test athletes in order to redetermine their 1RM before each new macrocycle in order to ensure that progress is achieved in maximum strength and that the new load is related to the gains made in strength.

It is also possible to use one or more sport-specific power or conditioning tests to gain an idea of the athlete's sport-specific athletic shape throughout the whole training process.

Record the information. In order to do so effectively, one must understand the notation used in a training program chart to express load, number of reps, and number of sets. Load is noted as a percentage of 1RM, and athletes must be tested, especially during the preparatory phase at the end of each macrocycle. Knowing an athlete's 1RM allows the coach to select the percentage to use in training according to the training goals of each phase. Notation of load, number of reps, and number of sets is expressed as follows: The numerator (e.g., 80) refers to the load as a percentage of 1RM, the denominator (e.g., 5) represents the number of reps, and the multiplier (e.g., 4) indicates the number of sets. The advantage of expressing load as a percentage of 1RM is that when working with a larger group of athletes, such as a football team, the coach does not have to calculate the weight for each player; rather, each athlete uses his or her personal 1RM as the basis for calculating weight, which may vary from player to player. Thus individualization is built into this method.

SAMPLE NOTATION FOR A STRENGTH TRAINING PROGRAM

Any strength training program should be written on a sheet of paper or in the training journal. Table 8.15 illustrates a sample format for a strength training program. The first column lists the exercises in sequential order. The second column specifies the load, number of reps, and number of sets. The last column indicates the rest interval to be taken following each set.

Table 8.15 Sample Strength Training Program Format

Exercise	Load/reps/sets (load as % of 1RM)	Rest interval (minutes)
1. Squat	80/4 × 4	3
2. Bench press	85/3 × 4	3
3. Deadlift	70/3 × 4	2
4. Lat machine	60/5 × 3	1.5
5. Crunches	Body weight/15 × 3	1

Exercise Prescription

The 656 muscles distributed throughout the human body are capable of performing a great variety of movements. All athletic skills and actions are performed by muscles as a result of contraction. Therefore, if an athlete wants to improve a skill or physical performance, he or she must concentrate on training the muscles that perform the action—the prime movers.

The process of prescribing exercises for a given muscle group (or groups) must be based on phase-specific considerations. During the anatomical adaptation phase, exercises must be selected that develop most muscle groups—both agonist and antagonist—to build a stronger base for the training phases to follow. As the competitive phase approaches, exercises become very specialized and are prescribed specifically for the prime movers (see table 8.16; The asterisks indicate the relative volume dedicated to each group of exercises).

Table 8.16 Periodization of Exercise Prescription Throughout the Annual Plan

Type of exercise	Anatomical adaptation	Max strength (early prep)	Max strength (late prep)	Conversion to specific strength
Unilateral	*****	***	***	**
Bilateral	***	*****	*****	*****
Full range of motion	*****	*****	***	**
Specific range of motion	—	—	****	*****

Exercise prescription should be based not on exercises borrowed from weightlifting or bodybuilding but on an understanding of how the muscles produce a movement. Especially from the late preparatory phase onward, an exercise is good for an athlete in a given sport if it follows the principle of specificity. This means it must involve the prime movers and the synergistic muscles used in performing the skills of that particular sport or event.

Coaches often turn to bodybuilding for exercise ideas without understanding the differences between bodybuilding and other sports. One difference lies in the type of method—analytic or compound—used to determine how an exercise achieves a specific training goal. Bodybuilders use the analytic method for high muscle definition. They analyze each muscle's individual action and movement, then train each muscle in isolation to achieve the best size development.

In sport, however, the compound method should be used because it involves not just an individual muscle but all muscles of the joint (or joints) necessary to produce an athletic skill. Exercises should also involve the muscles and joints in a sequence similar to that used in performing the needed skills. For instance, to train the muscles involved in starting in sprinting, athletes should use squats, lunges, and step-ups rather than the leg extension machine.

In many cases, athletes and coaches rate the success of a strength training program according to the amount of muscle the athlete builds (hypertrophy). However, aside from exceptions such as American football linemen, shot-putters, and heavyweight boxers and wrestlers, constant increase in muscle size is not a desirable effect for most athletes. Power and speed sports—or sports with quick, explosive action (e.g., baseball, football, hockey, most track-and-field events, volleyball)—rely on nervous system training, which includes many power exercises and moderate to high loads (greater than 70 percent of 1RM) that result in neural adaptation (Enoka 1996; Sale 1986; Schmidtbleicher 1992). For most sports, neural adaptation in strength training means increasing power and the speed of the contraction without increasing muscle mass—in other words, increasing relative strength and power.

Higher neural adaptation is achieved by carefully selecting training methods and exercises. Researchers and international-class coaches share similar views about what represents the specificity of strength training. These views can be summarized as follows.

- Strength training methods must be specific to the speed of contraction used in the sport (Coyle et al. 1991; Kanehisa and Miyashita 1983). This requirement means that from the second half of the preparatory phase through the competitive phase,

155

coaches should select methods that specifically increase the speed of contraction and therefore the level of power.

- Training methods and exercises must increase the contraction force in the intended direction of movement. This requirement means selecting exercises according to the muscles used to perform the technical skills of a given sport (the prime movers). Therefore, bodybuilding exercises waste time, especially during the second part of the preparatory and throughout the competitive phases.

- Training methods must increase activation of the prime movers. For this reason, selected exercises must be sport specific and primarily engage the prime movers.

- Training methods must increase the discharge rate of motor neurons (Hortobagyi et al. 1996) or stimulate the muscles to perform an athletic action with power and high speed. Motor neurons innervate, stimulate, and arouse the muscles. The more specific the training method and exercises are, the better the nervous system is trained to perform quick and powerful athletic movements.

- Motor unit recruitment and firing rate increase with higher loads and faster contractions (De Luca et al. 1982). Training methods that enhance maximum strength and power are the only ones that increase fast-twitch muscle fiber recruitment and the firing rate of motor units.

- Exercise action must be performed along the neural pathway used in the sport (Häkkinen 1989). More specifically, exercises must be selected so that contractions are performed in the same activation sequence that occurs during performance of the relevant sport skills. If an exercise does not realistically simulate, or is not specific to, a technical skill, the result is lower exercise transfer and lower performance improvement.

- Neural adaptation that results from training for specificity of strength increases the number of voluntarily activated motor units. This capability transfers from general to specific exercises. Well-selected training methods, such as maximum strength methods and power training, activate more motor units. As a result, an athlete can perform sport-specific skills with higher speed of contraction and more power.

9

The Microcycle Short-Term Plan

A successful strength training program should be part of a long-term training plan and not implemented only during certain parts of the annual plan. Nor should strength training be performed just for the sake of it. If (and only if) properly implemented, strength training helps protect athletes from injury, delays the onset of fatigue, and enables the athlete to generate the high level of power output required for optimal sport performance. In order to be effective, however, strength training must meet the objectives of the particular training phase and mesh with the overall plan.

Because a training program is a methodical, scientific strategy for improving performance, it should be well organized and well designed. An effective training program incorporates the principles of periodization of strength throughout the year. Whether short-term or long-term, the training program also reflects the coach's methodological knowledge and takes into account the athlete's background and physical potential.

A good training plan is simple, objective, and flexible so that it can match the athlete's physiological adaptation and performance improvements. Planning theory, however, is very complex, and this book discusses planning only as it pertains to strength training. Further information can be found in *Periodization: Theory and Methodology of Training* (Bompa 2009). In this chapter we address the organization of the training session plan and the microcycle; in the next chapter we cover the annual plan for the periodization of strength Refer to the periodization sections in chapter 10 for more sport-specific information.

Training Session Plan

The training session is the main tool for organizing the daily workout program. To achieve better management and organization, the training session can be structured into four main segments. The first two (introduction and warm-up) prepare the athlete for the main part, in which the concerted training takes place, and the last part (cool-down) returns the athlete to the normal physiological state.

Introduction

During the introduction to a training session, the coach or instructor shares with the athletes the training objectives for the day and how they are to be achieved. The coach also organizes the athletes into groups and gives them necessary advice regarding the daily program.

Warm-Up

The specific purpose of the warm-up is to prepare athletes for the program to follow. During the warm-up, body temperature is raised, which appears to be one of the main factors in facilitating performance. The warm-up stimulates the activity of the central nervous system (CNS), which coordinates all systems of the body, speeds up motor reactions through faster transmission of nerve impulses, improves the biomechanical performance of the motor system, increases the contraction speed and peak power that muscles can produce, and improves coordination (Enoka 2002; Wade et al. 2000). The elevation of body temperature also warms up and facilitates the stretching of muscles, myofascia, and tendons, thus preventing or reducing ligament sprains and tendon and muscle strains. Warmed-up muscle tissue is able to accommodate higher-velocity stretches before the tendon–bone coupling experiences damage (Enoka 2002).

The warm-up for strength training includes two parts: general and specific. The general warm-up (5 to 10 minutes) involves light jogging, cycling, or step-ups, followed by calisthenics and dynamic stretching exercises to increase blood flow, which raises body temperature. This activity prepares the muscles and tendons for the planned program. During the warm-up, athletes should also prepare mentally for the main part of the training session by visualizing the exercises and motivating themselves for the strain of training. The specific warm-up (3 to 5 minutes) is a short transition to the working part of the session. In this portion, athletes prepare themselves for a successful workout by performing multiple sets of a few reps (5 down to 1 or 2 as the load increases) on the equipment to be used and employing gradually heavier loads leading to those planned for the day (which means fewer warm-up sets for high-rep sets, more warm-up sets for heavier sets of fewer reps).

Main Part

The main part of the training session is dedicated to the concerted training program, in which training objectives are accomplished, including strength training. In most sports, technical and tactical work are the main objectives of training, and strength development is a secondary priority. First-priority activities are performed immediately after the warm-up, followed by strength training. Frequently, the sport-specific activity preceding the strength training session functions as a general warm-up so that the athlete can directly begin performing the warm-up sets of the first exercise. The types of training to be performed in a given day depend on the phase of training as well as the training objectives. Table 9.1 provides sample options for sequencing your training for several training sessions.

The training program must be based on scientific principles, and the fundamental guidelines are provided by the dominant energy systems in the chosen sport. When dis-

Table 9.1 Sample Sequence Options for Training Sessions

Session 1	Session 2	Session 3	Session 4
1. Warm-up 2. Alactic technical skills 3. Speed 4. Maximum strength or power	1. Warm-up 2. Lactic technical and tactical skills 3. Power endurance	1. Warm-up 2. Aerobic tactical skills 3. Muscular endurance	1. Warm-up 2. Alactic tactical skills 3. Power

cussing certain combinations for both the training session and the microcycle, coaches and athletes should remember the following key points.

- In sports characterized by short-duration (less than 10-second) explosive actions, power is the most specific quality of strength. Examples include sprinting, jumping, and throwing events in track and field; sprinting in cycling; ski jumping; free-style skiing; diving; pitching and batting; American football throwing; any takeoff or quick change of direction in a team sport; and quick limb actions in boxing, wrestling, and the martial arts.

- Speed endurance (15- to 50-second) activities characterized by fast actions interspersed with quick changes of direction, jumps, and short rest intervals tend to rely on power endurance or muscle endurance short. These actions include 50-meter to 100-meter swimming; 200-meter to 400-meter events in track and field; 500-meter speedskating; tennis; figure skating; and many game elements in team sports.

- Prolonged activities performed against any type of resistance (be it gravity, ground, water, snow, or ice) depend on mainly muscular endurance. These activities include rowing; swimming events longer than 100 meters; kayaking and canoeing; cross-country skiing; and certain elements of team, combat, and racket sports. Therefore, strength coaches must carefully analyze their sport and decide the proportions in which their athletes need to be exposed to power, power endurance, and muscular endurance.

Cool-Down

Whereas the warm-up serves as a transition from the normal biological state of daily activities to high-intensity training, the cool-down is a transition with the opposite effect: It brings the body back to its normal functions. Therefore, athletes should not leave for the showers immediately after the last exercise. Instead, during a cool-down of 10 to 20 minutes, they can perform activities that facilitate faster regeneration and recovery from the strains of training.

As a result of training, especially intensive work, athletes build up high amounts of lactic acid, and their muscles are exhausted, tense, and rigid. To overcome this fatigue and speed up the recovery process, they should perform relaxation and stretching exercises. Specifically, at the end of the training, they should perform 5 to 10 minutes of low-intensity, continuous aerobic activity that causes the body to continue perspiring (intensity zone 6; see chapter 3), followed by 5 to 10 minutes of stretching. Doing so improves general recovery and the removal of metabolites through their passage from the muscle cells to the circulatory system, thus reducing body temperature, heart rate, and blood pressure (Moeller et al. 1985; Hagberg et al. 1979).

In addition, the cool-down lowers the level of cortisol, which can otherwise disturb night rest and remain at high levels up to 24 hours following training, thereby delaying the recovery process and the adaptations to training, and it lowers catecholamines, particularly adrenaline and noradrenaline (Jezova et al. 1985). Cool-down activities also reduce the athlete's emotional tension, thus favoring recovery even at a mental level (Jezova et al. 1985). Finally, stretching in particular allows the muscles to go back to their anatomical length and restores the joint range of motion, a process that otherwise may require up to 24 hours.

Once the cool-down has begun to dissipate the results of fatigue, it is fundamental to speed up recovery and training adaptations by starting the restoration of energy substrates. This topic is discussed in detail in chapter 5. For now, we underline the fact that the rates of recovery and adaptation are determined not only by the type of training performed but also by the athlete's training level, his or her internal load (i.e., residual fatigue; see chapter 4) at the end of the session, and his or her nutritional interventions (Bompa and Haff 2009).

Training Session Models

Many sports require technical and tactical training, as well as training for maximum speed, speed endurance, and aerobic endurance—all of which tax different energy systems. How can these components of training be combined without producing a high degree of fatigue and without the adaptation of one element interfering with the improvement of the others? These concerns can be addressed in one of two ways: (1) combine training components so that the athlete taxes only one energy system per training session or (2) alternate the energy systems in each microcycle so that the athlete trains according to the prevailing energy system(s) in the particular sport. The following sections describe training session models that tax the various energy systems used in sports.

Model Training Taxing the Anaerobic Alactic System

1. Warm-up
2. Technical training of short duration
3. Maximum speed and agility training (two to eight seconds)
4. Maximum strength training
5. Power training

The order of activities in this model was established based on the physiological and mental needs of the athlete. Training must focus first on activities that require more nervous system concentration, mental focus, and thus a fresh mind—in other words, technique, speed, or both. Maximum speed should be trained before maximum strength because gains in maximum strength and power have been found to be more effective when preceded by maximum-velocity sprints (Baroga 1978; Ozolin 1971).

This particular training model is applicable to team sports including American football, soccer, baseball, softball, and cricket; sprinting, jumping, and throwing events in track and field; diving; racket sports; the martial arts; contact sports; and other sports in which the anaerobic alactic system is dominant. Although there are two strength training options, we suggest using only one type according to the phase of training. However, this does not exclude the possibility of using both.

The duration of a strength training session in this model depends both on the importance of strength in the sport and on the training phase. During the preparatory phase, a strength training session can last 45 to 75 minutes. In the competitive phase, it is much shorter (20 to 40 minutes), and the work is dedicated primarily to maintaining strength gained during the preparatory phase. Exceptions to this basic rule are made for throwers in track and field, linemen in American football, and wrestlers in the heavyweight category, who require more time for strength training (60 to 90 minutes).

Model Training Taxing the Anaerobic Lactic System

1. Warm-up
2. Technical or tactical training of medium duration (10 to 60 seconds)
3. Training for speed endurance and agility of longer duration (between 15 and 50 seconds) or short reps (3 to 10 seconds) with short rest intervals
4. Training for power endurance or muscular endurance of short duration

This model is suggested for any sport in which the anaerobic lactic system is taxed (10 to 60 seconds of activity burst). Thus, tactical training, especially in the form of prolonged but intensive drills, can be followed by a combination of strength training in which a certain degree of lactic endurance is used—either power endurance or muscular endurance of short duration. Applying this model once or twice a week is beneficial to athletes in most sports that use the anaerobic lactic energy system, such as in 50- to 100-meter swimming, track and cycling; 200 to 800 meters in track and field; as well as team, racket, and contact sports and the martial arts.

Model Training Taxing Both the Anaerobic and Aerobic Systems

1. Warm-up
2. Technical or tactical training of long duration (between 1.5 and 8 minutes)
3. Training for muscular endurance of medium duration

Aerobic endurance includes endurance of medium duration that involves both the anaerobic lactic acid system and the aerobic system. Aerobic system training is generally of a long duration and dedicated to training strictly the aerobic system with little adaptation of the anaerobic system. The model depicted previously combines tactical training of medium duration (1.5 to 8 minutes) with muscular endurance of medium duration, both of which tax the anaerobic lactic system, but mostly the athlete's aerobic endurance or ability to delay the onset of fatigue. This model is good for specialized training sessions for team, racket, and contact sports and the martial arts, in which the scope of training is to stress the last part of the game or match.

Model Training Taxing the Aerobic System

1. Warm-up
2. Aerobic endurance training
3. Training for muscular endurance of long duration

The previous model is most effective for sports in which aerobic endurance is either dominant or very important to achieving the expected athletic performance. These sports include distance running, triathlon, road cycling, cross-country skiing, rowing, canoeing, kayaking, mountain cycling, and marathon canoeing. For these sports, muscular endurance is trained at the end of the session because the resulting fatigue may affect the athlete's ability to achieve the objectives of aerobic training.

Model Training to Develop Power and Agility in Fatigue

1. Warm-up
2. Technical and tactical training taxing the aerobic system
3. Power and agility training

Quite often, the result of a competition is decided in the final minutes. Athletes must be trained for such conditions in order to generate greater power and quickness, display a high level of agility at the end of the competition, and, as a result, perform at a higher level. The most efficient way to enhance these abilities is to train

Developing power and agility under fatigued conditions requires power and agility training to be placed at the end of a session after the technical and tactical training has taxed the aerobic system.

athletes under conditions of fatigue similar to those that they will encounter in competition. Training sessions geared toward meeting this objective should first fatigue the athlete via metabolic conditioning (intensity zone 3 or 4), followed by 20 to 30 minutes of high-intensity power and agility drills. These drills can be both specific and nonspecific. Another option, especially for racket sports, martial arts, boxing, and wrestling, is to use muscular endurance training for 20 to 30 minutes, followed by power and agility drills of high intensity. This model is good for specialized training sessions for team, racket, and contact sports and the martial arts in which the scope of training is to stress the last part of the game or match.

Planning the Microcycle

The microcycle, or weekly training program, is probably the most important planning tool. Throughout the annual plan, the nature and dynamics of microcycles change according to the phase of training, the training objectives, and the physiological and psychological demands faced by the athlete. A macrocycle, on the other hand, is a training plan composed of two to six weeks or microcycles.

Load Increments

Throughout macrocycles, the load in strength training is increased depending on the type of cycle and training phase. The work within each macrocycle follows a step-type progression. From an intensity standpoint, microcycles follow the principle of progressive increase of load in training. As illustrated in table 9.2, *a* through *c*, the load is progressively increased during the first three cycles, which are followed by a regeneration cycle in which the load is decreased to facilitate recuperation and replenishment of energy. Then a maximum strength test is performed before another macrocycle begins. Based on this model, suggested load increments are provided in the tables using the notation system described in chapter 8, in which the nominator indicates the load as a percentage of 1RM, the denominator indicates the number of reps, and the multiplier indicates the number of sets. The following are three possible modalities of load progression,

- In table 9.2*a*, the volume stays the same, intensity increases, the buffer for the main working sets decreases, and a 1RM test is performed at the end of the fourth (unloading) microcycle.

Table 9.2*a* Macrocycle: Volume Stays the Same and the Intensity of the Main Working Sets Increase by 2.5 Percent Each Week*

Training load	$\frac{70}{6}1\ \frac{75}{4}1\ \frac{80}{3}3$	$\frac{70}{6}1\ \frac{75}{4}1\ \frac{82.5}{3}3$	$\frac{70}{6}1\ \frac{75}{4}1\ \frac{85}{3}3$	Day 1 $\frac{70}{2}4$	Day 2 $\frac{50}{3}3$ $\frac{80}{1}1$	Day 3 1RM test
Microcycle	1	2	3	4 (unloading)		

*The load suggested in each microcycle refers to the work per day, which can be repeated two to four times per week depending on the training goals.

- In table 9.2*b*, the volume of sets stays the same, the number of reps decreases, the intensity increases, the buffer stays the same, and a 1RM test is performed at the end of the fourth microcycle.

Table 9.2*b* Macrocycle: Volume Decreases While Mean Intensity* Increases by 5 percent Each Week**

Training load	$\frac{70}{6}1\ \frac{75}{4}1\ \frac{80}{3}3$	$\frac{75}{5}1\ \frac{80}{3}1\ \frac{85}{2}3$	$\frac{80}{3}1\ \frac{85}{2}1\ \frac{90}{1}3$	Day 1 $\frac{70}{2}4$	Day 2 $\frac{50}{3}3$ $\frac{80}{1}1$	Day 3 1RM test
Microcycle	1	2	3	4		

*Mean intensity = ((intensity1 × reps × sets) + (intensity2 × reps × sets) + (intensity3 × reps × sets))/total reps. In this case: ((70×6×1) + (75×4×1) + (80×3×3))/(6+4+9) = 75.8%; (75×5×1) + (80×3×1) + (85×2×3))/(5+3+6) = 80.3%; ((80×3×1) + (85×2×1) + (90×1×3))/(3+2+3) = 85%.

**The load suggested in each microcycle refers to the work per day, which can be repeated one to two times per week depending on the training goals.

• In table 9.2c, the volume increases, and the intensity and the buffer stay the same.

Table 9.2c Macrocycle: Volume of the Main Working Sets Increases by One Unit Each Week*

				Day 1	Day 2 $\frac{50\ 3}{3}$	Day 3
Training load	$\frac{70}{6}$ 1 $\frac{75}{4}$ 1 $\frac{80}{3}$ 3	$\frac{70}{6}$ 1 $\frac{75}{4}$ 1 $\frac{80}{3}$ 4	$\frac{70}{6}$ 1 $\frac{75}{4}$ 1 $\frac{80}{3}$ 5	$\frac{70}{2}$ 4	$\frac{80}{1}$ 1	1RM test
Microcycle	1	2	3	4 (unloading)		

*The load suggested in each microcycle refers to the work per day, which can be repeated one to two times per week depending on the training goals.

As shown, the work, or the total load in training, is increased in steps, with the highest load occurring in microcycle 3. To increase the work from microcycle to microcycle, the coach has three options: increase the load while decreasing the buffer (table 9.2a), increase the load while keeping the same buffer, thus lowering the reps per set (table 9.2b), or increase the number of main work sets from microcycle 1 to microcycle 3 (table 9.2c).

The approach can be chosen to suit the needs of different classifications of athletes. For example, young athletes have difficulty tolerating a high number of sets. It is true that they should have a high number of exercises that develop the entire muscular system and adapt the muscle attachments on the bones (i.e., the tendons) to strength training. However, it is difficult to tolerate performing a high number of exercises and a high number of sets at the same time. Therefore, it is advisable to opt for a high number of exercises at the expense of the number of sets.

Microcycle 4 represents a regeneration week in which volume is lowered and buffer increased to reduce the fatigue resulting from the first three steps, to replenish the energy stores, and to promote psychological relaxation.

Again, in athletics, strength training is subordinate to technical and tactical training. Consequently, the load of strength training per week should be calculated in light of the overall volume and intensity of training.

Before discussing strength training options per microcycle, it is important to mention that the total work per week is also planned according to the principle of progressive increase of load in training. Figures 9.1 through 9.3 illustrate three microcycles, each of which is suggested for each of the conventional steps referred to earlier.

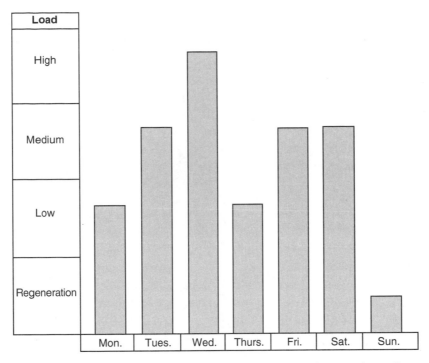

Figure 9.1 Low-workload microcycle with one high-load day and several medium- and low-load days (Sunday is a rest day).

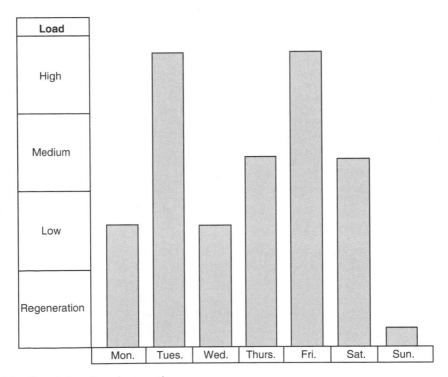

Figure 9.2 Medium-intensity microcycle.

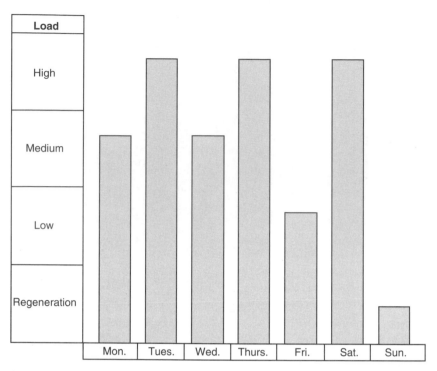

Figure 9.3 High-workload microcycle with three high-intensity training days.

Number of Strength Training Sessions per Microcycle

The number of strength training sessions per microcycle depends on the following factors: the athlete's classification, the importance of strength in the chosen sport, and the phase of training.

Athlete's Classification

Young athletes should be introduced to strength training progressively. At first, they can be exposed to one to two short strength training sessions per microcycle following technical or tactical work. Progressively, over a period of two to four years, this exposure can be increased to three or four sessions. Senior athletes competing at national or international competitions can take part in three or four strength training sessions per week, mainly during the preparatory phase.

Importance of Strength in the Sport

Strength training may hold more or less importance in a particular sport depending on the sport's relevant skills, dominant abilities, and energy system requirements. For example, strength is less important in a sport in which aerobic endurance is clearly dominant, such as marathon running. On the other hand, strength plays a crucial role in sports in which power is dominant, such as American football and track-and-field throwing events. When strength is less important, one or two strength training sessions per week may suffice. When it is more important, strength training must be done at least three times per microcycle, especially during the preparatory phase.

Phase of Training

The number of strength training sessions also depends on the phase of training. Depending on the sport, two to four sessions per microcycle should be performed during the preparatory phase, and one to three sessions per microcycle should be performed during the competitive phase.

Athletes who perform four strength training sessions per week will have to perform some sessions on consecutive days. In such circumstances, coaches have two options: (1) train the same muscle groups in every session but alternate intensities—maximum strength one day and power the next—or (2) split the exercises for upper body and for lower body to achieve faster recovery. With the first option, some form of intensity alternation is necessary because it would be impossible for the same muscle groups to fully recover if the same loading parameters were used for two sessions within 24 hours or, even worse, four sessions within 96 hours.

In sport, strength training is performed in addition to technical and tactical training. For maximum effectiveness—and for the most economical use of energy—strength training exercises must be chosen to stress mainly the prime movers. When we talk about strength training for sports, to increase effectiveness, the number of strength training exercises in a workout should be reduced as much as possible, especially after the anatomical adaptation phase. This reduction allows the athlete to perform more sets and forces the prime movers to contract many times. The outcome is more strength and power development for the required muscles. A special concern, though, is represented by multiplanar (i.e., acting on multiple planes of movement) sports, such as team sports, contact sports, and martial arts. For this sport, a higher number of exercises has to be employed to address, for instance, the high force demands in the transverse plane.

Types of Strength and Restoration of Energy Systems

Some proponents suggest that strength training should be planned on "easy" days. From a physiological standpoint, this thought does not make much sense. To some extent, the majority of sports require training of most, if not all, of the motor abilities of speed, strength, and endurance. Each ability uses and depends on a particular energy system, and the systems differ in their rate of recovery and restoration of fuel.

The full restoration of glycogen starts after 5 minutes of rest, but it might take up to 48 hours to be completed, depending on the sport-specific training and the type of strength training performed in a day. In fact, glycogen can be fully restored given an appropriate dietary intake of carbohydrate in 24 hours after an intermittent activity and 48 hours after a highly taxing metabolic session (Hermansen and Vaage 1977). It takes about 48 hours after continuous intensive work but only about 24 hours after intermittent activity, such as strength training (Brooks, Brauner, and Cassens 1973; Fox, Bowes, and Foss 1989). Following high-intensity strength or speed training sessions in which the CNS is also taxed, complete nervous system recovery may take 48 hours. And after maximum-intensity efforts that highly stress the CNS, such as a 100-meter race or a powerlifting competition, the athlete may need up to seven days of lower loading in order to repeat the same level of performance, which indicates full regeneration of all the physiological systems involved.

As explained in chapter 5, the time course of substrate restoration is heavily influenced by the quality and timing of food intake, as well as by the extent of damage to the myofibrils caused during the training session (Bompa and Haff 2009). The rate of regeneration from low-intensity aerobic activities is much faster—approximately eight hours. Restoration of energy stores and nervous system recovery may be sped up by aerobic compensation sessions or lower-intensity tactical work. These types of training day can be considered easy and can be planned after the hardest days of the week or after competition.

The largest effect of a training session falls, of course, on the energy system that is mainly trained during the session; the other two systems are affected to a lesser extent. This fact means that the trained energy system requires more recovery time than the others do. For instance, whenever an anaerobic system is trained first in a given week, it is possible to train the aerobic system the next day, then the other anaerobic system (the one not trained on the first day), and finally the first anaerobic one again. When the aerobic system is trained first, it can be followed by the anaerobic alactic system. Anaerobic alactic exercises, in fact, need less support from the aerobic system than do anaerobic lactic exercises because the former induces a lower oxygen debt than the latter.

Therefore, especially in power and speed sports, a microcycle should alternate between the anaerobic and aerobic systems. Here are three options, depending on the sport and the training phase:

Alactic-Aerobic-Lactic-Aerobic-Alactic-Aerobic-rest

Alactic-Aerobic-Lactic-Aerobic-Alactic-Lactic-rest

Alactic-Lactic-Aerobic-Alactic-Lactic-Aerobic-rest

In the case of long-aerobic-endurance sports, on the other hand, the training menu is limited in terms of energy systems alternation. Therefore, the aerobic system is trained daily at various intensities.

Let's assume that a coach plans intensive training sessions on Monday, Wednesday, and Friday and easy days on Tuesday and Thursday. Because the intensive days are separated by 48 hours—and especially because an easy day is scheduled during those 48 hours—glycogen can reach full restoration and the CNS can recover before the next planned intensive day. This dynamic changes drastically, however, if the coach schedules intensive strength training sessions on the easy days. In that case, the athlete taxes the anaerobic energy systems on the easy days as well as on the intensive days, thus taxing the nervous system and the glycogen stores every day.

As a result, strength training becomes an obstacle to restoration. This pattern complicates the ratio of energy expenditure to restoration and the recovery of the nervous system—a state of affairs that can bring the athlete to fatigue or even exhaustion. And it is only a short step from exhaustion to overtraining.

Consequently, strength training must be planned on the same days as technical and tactical training or speed and power training—that is, on the anaerobic days. In this approach, the athlete heavily taxes the glycogen stores and the nervous system, but the overall training program does not interfere with recovery and regeneration before the next high-intensity training, which is scheduled for 48 hours later. As a guideline for organizing a microcycle, table 9.3 shows activities grouped by energy system and thus possibly trained on three different days.

In addition to determining the sequence of training sessions within a microcycle, we must also consider the sequence of training means within the sessions themselves. In fact, certain training objectives can be achieved only in the right circumstances—namely,

Table 9.3   Classification of Training Methods According to the Main Energy System Taxed (Ergogenesis)

Anaerobic alactic day	Anaerobic lactic day	Aerobic day
1. Technical skills (1–10 seconds) 2. Tactical skills (5–10 seconds) 3. Acceleration and maximum speed 4. Maximum strength and power	1. Technical skills (10–60 seconds) 2. Tactical skills (10–60 seconds) 3. Speed endurance (10–60 seconds) 4. Power endurance, muscle endurance short	1. Long-duration technical skills (>60 seconds) 2. Long- and medium-duration tactical skills (>60 seconds) 3. Aerobic endurance 4. Muscle endurance medium and long

Table 9.4   Training Objectives and Fatigue State

Athlete's residual fatigue	Training objectives*
Absent (fresh)	Technique, tactic (learning), acceleration, maximum speed, power
Low	Technique, tactic, acceleration, speed endurance, maximum strength, power, power endurance
Moderate	Special endurance, aerobic power, muscle endurance short and medium
High (fatigued)	Aerobic capacity, technical and tactical refinement under specific conditions, muscular endurance long

*Training objectives that require minimal residual fatigue should be trained after an easy day and placed first in the sequence of a training session.

when the athlete's level of residual fatigue is adequate for the development, retention, or refinement of certain biomotor abilities. Table 9.4 shows the acceptable level of residual fatigue for training certain biomotor abilities.

The following tables provide examples of strength training programs related to other athletic activities and to the dominant energy systems. Table 9.5 suggests a microcycle for individual speed and power sports (sprints and jumps in track and field) in which energy systems are alternated. Strength training is consistently planned on days when other types of activity tax the same energy system. For instance, drills for speed training, which tax the anaerobic alactic system, are followed by training for power. In addition, each day of anaerobic activity (Monday, Wednesday, and Friday) is followed by a day when aerobic training is taxed in the form of tempo running (100 to 200 yards or meters at 60 percent of maximum speed for 8 to 20 reps).

Table 9.6 illustrates how the energy systems and the specifics of strength can be alternated for a sport in which aerobic endurance is dominant, such as rowing, kayaking, canoeing, cycling, triathlon, cross-country skiing, or a swimming event of more than 400 meters. Each time aerobic endurance is trained, the only type of strength training proposed is muscular endurance. When anaerobic training is planned (Tuesday), it is followed by power endurance, which taxes the same system (anaerobic lactic).

Table 9.5   Alternation of Energy Systems for Speed- and Power-Dominant Individual Sports

Monday	Accelerations Maximum speed Maximum strength or power
Tuesday	Tempo running
Wednesday	Accelerations Speed endurance Power endurance
Thursday	Tempo running
Friday	Accelerations Maximum speed Maximum strength or power
Saturday	Tempo running

Table 9.6   Alternation of Energy Systems for Aerobic-Endurance-Dominant Sports

Monday	Aerobic endurance Muscular endurance
Tuesday	Anaerobic endurance Power endurance
Wednesday	Aerobic endurance Compensation
Thursday	Mixed training Power endurance
Friday	Aerobic endurance Muscular endurance
Saturday	Aerobic endurance Compensation

Two taxing days of training (Monday and Tuesday) are followed by a lighter aerobic training day for compensation and to supercompensate the glycogen stores depleted the day before. The same approach is used again in the second part of the cycle.

For sports with high-complexity training (technical, tactical, and physical), the alternation of energy systems and strength training could follow the model presented in table 9.7. Examples include all team sports, the martial arts, and racket sports. Every day, all proposed activities tax the same energy system. Obviously, no more than three of the suggested training activities may be planned, which for strength training may mean choosing either maximum strength or power.

On Tuesday, an anaerobic lactic day can be planned (tactical and specific endurance training). To tap the same energy system, the strength training program should consist of activities aimed at developing power endurance or muscle endurance short. Wednesday is a compensation day of less demanding technical and tactical training. For the remaining three training days, the same sequence pattern is used (AL-LA-O$_2$).

Table 9.7 Alternation of Energy Systems for High-Complexity Sports

Monday	Alactic technical skills Speed Maximum strength or power
Tuesday	Lactic tactical skills Speed endurance short Power endurance or muscle endurance short
Wednesday	Aerobic technical and tactical skills Compensation
Thursday	Alactic technical and tactical skills Speed Maximum strength or power
Friday	Lactic technical and tactical skills Speed endurance short Power endurance or muscle endurance short
Saturday	Technical and tactical skills Compensation

During the competitive phase, the approach used to maintain strength training depends strictly on the competition schedule. There are three possibilities: one competition per week, two competitions per week, or one tournament per week.

Table 9.8 presents types of activity to plan between two competitions that fall at the ends of consecutive weeks. Because the typical days of competition vary from sport to sport, we have numbered the training sessions rather than specifying a day of the week

Table 9.8 Suggested Training Program for a Microcycle Falling Between Two Competitions

Day	Type of activity	Loading pattern
1	Competition	High
2	Day off (recovery and regeneration)	Off
3	Technical skills Longer-duration tactical drills Aerobic power	Low to medium
4	Technical and tactical skills Alactic capacity and agility Maximum strength and power	High
5	Technical and tactical skills High-intensity model training	Medium-high
6	Technical and tactical skills Speed and agility Power	Low
7	Tactical skills Model training	Low
8	Competition	High

for each session. The postcompetition day is intended for recovery and regeneration, to remove fatigue from the systems, and to ready the athlete to resume training on the next day.

As in other microcycles, the suggested training programs consider the physiological need to alternate and thus tax mostly one energy system per day. As a result, maximum strength training is planned on days when the anaerobic alactic system is taxed and has the scope of strength maintenance. Certainly, the suggested maximum strength training is short and uses selected exercises specific to the sport for which the athlete is training. The workload of training must be subdivided into low-, medium-, and high-intensity days. Planning the training sessions accordingly helps the athlete better manage the demands and stress associated with training and competition. Keep in mind the need for alternation between training, unloading, competition, and recovery before resuming training again.

Table 9.9 illustrates a microcycle with three competitions over a week—a situation common in team sports where the team plays championship and cup simultaneously or the championship itself requires two game a week. Under such conditions, the maintenance of strength is slightly different—one day of maximum strength and one for power, power endurance, or muscular endurance. On day 5, the postcompetition day, we suggest activities that can stimulate recovery and regeneration, such as massage, stretching, sauna, and low-intensity training. To best accommodate these activities, day 5 can be divided into two parts (for those athletes who can afford free time): recovery and regeneration in the morning and short, low-intensity technical and tactical training in the afternoon. On precompetition days, athletes engage in tactical training similar to the activities they will meet the next day in competition.

Table 9.10 illustrates a microcycle for sports that use weekend tournaments (such as Friday, Saturday, and Sunday). Because such tournaments can be organized either a few weeks apart or repeated for several weeks in a row (e.g., high school and university competitions), the same structure can be used for one week or more. Coaches will want to make changes in the microcycle based on their athletes' specific conditions, level of

Table 9.9 Suggested Strength Training Program for a Microcycle With Three Competitions

Day	Type of activity	Loading pattern
1	Competition	High
2	Day off (recovery and regeneration)	Off
3	Technical and tactical skills Alactic speed Power training	Medium
4	Competition	High
5	Recovery and regeneration Technical and tactical skills	Low
6	Technical and tactical skills Alactic speed Maximum strength	High
7	Tactical skills Model training	Low
8	Competition	High

Table 9.10 Suggested Strength Training Program for a Microcycle for a Weekend Tournament

Day	Type of activity	Loading pattern
Monday	Day off (recovery and regeneration)	Off
Tuesday	Technical and tactical skills Longer-duration drills	Medium
Wednesday	Technical and tactical skills Alactic speed and agility training Power	Medium to high
Thursday	Technical and tactical skills Model training	Low
Friday	Competition	High
Saturday	Competition	High
Sunday	Competition	High

fatigue, and classification, as well as other factors, such as travel and the feasibility of organizing daily training sessions.

On Thursday, coaches should organize a tactical training to model the strategies that their athletes will use for the duration of the tournament. Coaches who have time for a short training session during the tournament can even use very low intensity activities, say, in the morning, to mimic the strategies that their athletes will use in an afternoon or evening competition.

Integration of Microcycles Into Macrocycles

A microcycle should not be an isolated entity; rather, it should be integrated thoughtfully into the larger macrocycle. This integration should always occur. See chapters 11 through 15 for more discussion of integrating different training phases and methods into a continuous training concept.

The integration of different types of microcycle into a macrocycle depends on the training phase, the athlete's classification, the athletes' strength training background, and the type of macrocycle. Two types of macrocycles are used during the preparatory phase: the step macrocycle and the flat macrocycle. Step loading is useful in developmental macrocycles. Consisting of progressive increases in load, step loading is less stressful and therefore more applicable to the early part of the preparatory phase. The step macrocycle is advisable to be used all year long for entry-level and intermediate athletes and endurance athletes, whereas it can be limited to the early general preparation for more advanced athletes in power sports.

The flat macrocycle subjects athletes to a higher average level of training volume, intensity, or both and thereby challenges their level of adaptation even more. It is suggested for advanced athletes with extensive training backgrounds or simply for macrocycles where the training is very intense or specific, thus requiring more frequent unloading. In fact, it is suggested to use a 2+1 structure for flat loading instead of the 3+1 normally used in step loading.

As illustrated in figure 9.4, the height of the each block reflects the demand training. The letter L indicates a loading microcycle, and the letter U indicates an unloading microcycle,

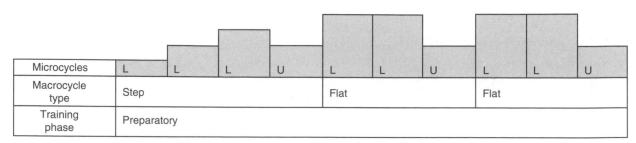

Microcycles	L	L	L	U	L	L	U	L	L	U
Macrocycle type	Step				Flat			Flat		
Training phase	Preparatory									

Figure 9.4 Step and flat macrocycles within the preparatory phase.

which is placed at the end of each macrocycle for recovery purposes. During the competitive phase, the integration of microcycles into macrocycles depends directly on the competition schedule. Therefore, because the schedule varies by the sport, so, too, does the structure of the macrocycle. As an example, let us consider the competitive phase for an individual sport. The macrocycle, shown in table 9.11, consists of a postcompetition recovery and regeneration microcycle to eliminate fatigue before resuming normal training. This microcycle is followed by two developmental microcycles, which are used to train the athlete in order to further improve or retain the specific biomotor abilities. Next comes a precompetition peaking microcycle, in which the volume of training is reduced dramatically (up to a 60 percent reduction), while the intensity is reduced only slightly, in order to peak for the competition.

Table 9.11 The Structure of a Macrocycle for the Competitive Phase of an Individual Sport

Type of microcycle	Postcompetition: recovery and regeneration	Developmental	Developmental	Precompetition peaking	C
Number of strength training sessions per microcycle	1or 2 (toward the end of the microcycle)	2–4	2–4	1 (in the early days of the microcycle)	

C = competition

Strength training can normally be performed during developmental microcycles to ensure that detraining doesn't affect the athlete's ability to reach peak performance at the end of the competitive phase, when championship competitions are scheduled.

The structure of a macrocycle differs for team sports, in which each week represents an opportunity to compete, sometimes twice. As a result, strength training must be implemented according to the microcycles exemplified in this chapter, especially in figures 9.1 through 9.3. Because team sports have such a high number of competitions, the scope of strength training programs must be to maintain specific strength gains made during the preparatory phase. This approach avoids detraining. Moreover, thanks to the physiological benefits from maintaining high levels of specific strength, athletes' levels of athletic competence are maintained throughout the entire competitive season.

10

The Annual Plan

The annual training plan is as important a tool for achieving long-term athletic goals as the microcycle is for achieving short-term athletic goals. An organized and well-planned annual training plan is a requirement for maximizing the athlete's motor potential improvements. To be effective, it must be based on the concept of periodization and employ its training principles as guiding precepts. One primary objective of training is for the athlete to reach peak performance at a specific time, usually for the main competition of the year. For the athlete to achieve this high level of performance, the entire training program must be properly periodized and planned so that the development of skills and motor abilities proceeds logically and methodically throughout the year.

Periodization consists of two basic components. The first component, periodization of the annual plan, addresses the various training phases throughout the year. The second component, periodization of the biomotor abilities, addresses the development of biomotor abilities training to increase the athlete's motor potential. In particular, the periodization of strength structures strength training to maximize its effectiveness in meeting the needs of the specific sport.

Periodization of the Annual Plan

The first component of periodization consists of breaking down the annual plan into shorter, more manageable training phases. Doing so enhances the organization of training and allows the coach to conduct the program systematically. In most sports, the annual training cycle is divided into three main phases of training: preparation (preseason), competitive (season), and transition (off-season). Each training phase is further subdivided into cycles.

The duration of each training phase depends heavily on the competition schedule, as well as the time needed to improve skills and develop the dominant biomotor abilities. During the preparation phase, the coach's primary objective is to develop athletes' physiological foundations. During the competitive phase, it is to strive for perfection according to the specific demands of competition.

Figure 10.1 illustrates the periodization of the annual plan into phases and cycles of training. This particular plan has only one competitive phase, so athletes have to peak only once during the year; such a plan is called a monocycle or single-peak annual plan. Of course, not all sports have only one competitive phase. For example, track and field, swimming, and several other sports have indoor and outdoor seasons or two major competitions for which athletes must peak. This type of plan is usually called a bi-cycle or double-peak annual plan (see figure 10.2). Advanced athletes competing at international level, on the other hand, have to peak up to three times a year. Think of the most individual sports athletes that have to peak for the winter championship, summer championship (that usually functions as national selection trials), and, finally, for the world championship or the Olympics. In that case, we speak of a tri-cyclical annual plan.

Phases of training	Preparatory			Competitive			Transition
	Yearly plan						
Sub-phases	General preparation		Specific preparation	Pre-competitive	Competitive		Transition
Macro-cycles							
Micro-cycles							

Figure 10.1 Periodization of a monocycle.

Annual plan					
Preparatory (I)	Competitive (I)	Transition (I)	Preparatory (II)	Competitive (II)	Transition (II)

Figure 10.2 Periodization of a bi-cycle.

Periodization of Strength

Coaches should be more concerned with deciding what kind of physiological response or training adaptation will lead to the greatest improvement than with deciding what drills or skills to work on in a given training session or phase. Once they have made the first decision, they will have an easier time selecting the appropriate type of work to produce the desired development. Only by considering these overriding physiological factors can coaches choose an approach that results in the best training adaptation and ultimately leads to increases in physiological capacity and improved athletic performance.

Such an innovative approach is facilitated by periodization. Recall from chapter 1 that the purpose of strength training for sports is not the development of strength for its own sake. Rather, the goal is to maximize power, power endurance, or muscular endurance, according to the needs of the chosen sport. This chapter demonstrates that the best approach for achieving that goal is the periodization of strength, with its specific sequence of training phases.

As illustrated in figure 10.3, periodization of strength includes seven phases with specific strength training objectives. Training phases are conventionally divided by a vertical bar, illustrating where one phase ends and another begins. However, the type of strength training does not change from one phase to another as abruptly as the chart implies. To the contrary, a smoother transition can be made from one type of strength to another one (e.g., from maximum strength to power).

Preparation				Competitive		Transition
Anatomical adaptation	Hypertrophy if necessary	Maximum strength	Conversion to specific strength (power; power endurance; or muscular endurance short, medium, or long)	Maintenance of maximum strength and specific strength	Cessation of strength training	Compensation training

Figure 10.3 Periodization of Strength for a Monocycle

Phase 1: Anatomical Adaptation

Periodization of strength has become very popular worldwide, and many training specialists and authors have discussed and written about this very efficient strength training concept. However, in their attempt to be different or to claim originality, some authors suggest a periodization of strength plan that starts with hypertrophy training. This might be acceptable in bodybuilding, but it is definitely not acceptable in strength training for sports. In fact, except for some throwers in track and field and some position players in American football, hypertrophy or muscle size is not a determining factor in high-performance athletics.

To the contrary, athletes in most sports—such as basketball, soccer, and swimming, not to mention sports divided into weight-class categories—are extremely reluctant to increase nonfunctional muscle hypertrophy. Furthermore, to maximize hypertrophy, athletes must work each set to exhaustion, which at times may result in a high level of discomfort that negatively affects the sport-specific training or even causes injury. For this reason, the original model of periodization of strength starts with an anatomical adaptation phase.

Following a transition phase, during which athletes usually do very little strength training, it is scientifically and methodologically sound to start a strength program aimed at adapting the anatomy for the heavy loads to follow. The main objectives of this phase are to involve most muscle groups and to prepare the muscles, ligaments, tendons, and joints to endure the subsequent lengthy and strenuous training phases. Strength training programs should not focus on only the legs or arms; they should also focus on strengthening the core area—the abdominal muscles, the low back, and the spinal column musculature. These sets of muscles work together to ensure that the trunk supports the legs and arms during all movements and also act as shock-absorbing devices during the performance of many skills and exercises, especially landing and falling.

Additional objectives for anatomical adaptation are to balance strength between the flexors and extensors surrounding each joint; to balance the two sides of the body, especially the legs and arms; to perform compensation work for the antagonist muscles; and to strengthen the stabilizer muscles (see the Exercise Prescription section in chapter 8). The volume of strength training must be balanced between muscle functions (see figure 10.4)—in other words, between agonists and antagonists around a joint. Failing to do so may result in postural imbalances and injuries.

In some cases, balanced development between agonist and antagonist muscles is impossible because some agonist muscles are larger and stronger than others. For instance, the knee extensors (quadriceps) are stronger than the knee flexors (hamstrings). The same is true for the ankle plantar flexors (gastrocnemii) and extensors (tibialis anteriori). The knee extensors and ankle plantar flexors are exposed to more training because activities such as running and jumping are used heavily in most sports. Professionals in the field, however, must be aware of the agonist-to-antagonist ratios and attempt to maintain them through training. If they neglect to do so and instead constantly train the agonists—the prime movers of given sport skills—the imbalance will likely result in impaired performance due both to neural inhibition of force expression of the prime movers and to injuries (for example, rotator cuff injuries in baseball).

The transition and anatomical adaptation phases are ideal for balanced development of antagonist muscles because they occur at a time in the training cycle when there is no pressure from competition. Little information exists about the agonist-to-antagonist ratios, especially for the high-speed limb movements typical of sports. Table 10.1 provides some information on the subject for low, isokinetic speeds. This information should be used only as a guideline for maintaining these ratios, at least during the anatomical adaptation and transition phases.

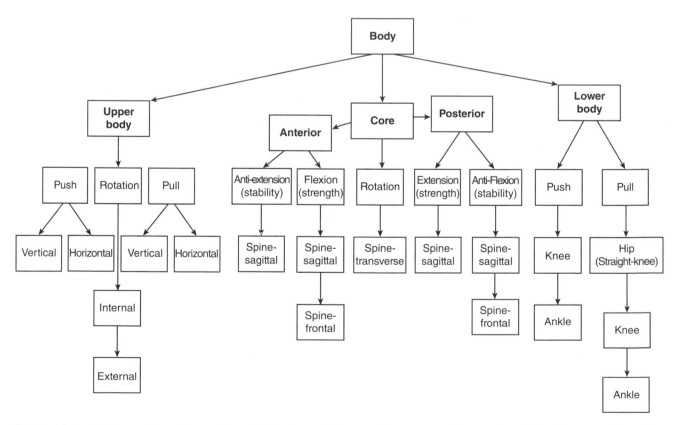

Figure 10.4 One way to achieve muscular balance is to use the same volume of work for the agonist and antagonist muscles around a joint.

Table 10.1 Agonist-to-Antagonist Ratios for Slow Concentric Isokinetic Movements

Joint	Strength training	Ratio
Ankle	Plantar flexion (gastrocnemius, soleus) to dorsiflexion (tibialis anterior)	3:1
Ankle	Inversion (tibialis anterior) to eversion (peroneus)	1:1
Knee	Extension (quadriceps) to flexion (hamstrings)	3:2
Hip	Extension (spinal erectors, gluteus maximus, hamstrings) to flexion (iliopsoas, rectus femoris, tensor fascia latae, sartorius)	1:1
Shoulder	Flexion (anterior deltoids) to extension (trapezius, posterior deltoids)	2:3
Shoulder	Internal rotation (subscapularis, latissimus dorsi, pectoralis major, teres major) to external rotation (supraspinatus, infraspinatus, teres minor)	3:2
Elbow	Flexion (biceps) to extension (triceps)	1:1
Lumbar spine	Flexion (abdominals) to extension (spinal erectors)	1:1

Reprinted, by permission, from D. Wathen, 1994, Muscle balance. In *Essentials of strength training and conditioning*, edited for the National Strength and Conditioning Association by T.R. Baechle (Champaign, IL: Human Kinetics), 425.

Throughout the anatomical adaptation phase, the goal is to involve most, if not all, muscle groups in a multilateral program. Such a program should include a high number of exercises (9 to 12) performed comfortably without pushing the athlete. Remember, vigorous strength training always develops the strength of the muscles faster than the strength of the muscle attachments (tendons) and joints (ligaments). Consequently, apply such programs too early often result in injuries to these tissues.

In addition, when large-muscle groups are weak, the small muscles have to take over the strain of the work. As a result, the small-muscle groups may become injured more quickly. Other injuries occur because insufficiently trained muscles lack the force to control landings, absorb shock, and balance the body quickly to be ready to perform another action (not because of a lack of landing skills). This is the reason why plyometric training is introduced gradually after two or three weeks of anatomical adaptations, using low-intensity jumps and bound to reach the highest intensities right after the maximum strength phase when a solid base of muscular strength has been laid down.

The duration of the anatomical adaptation phase depends on the length of the preparation phase, the athlete's background in strength training, and the importance of strength in the given sport. A long preparation phase, of course, allows more time for anatomical adaptation. Logically, athletes who have a weak strength training background require a much longer anatomical adaptation phase. This phase fosters progressive adaptation to training loads and improves the ability of muscle tissue and muscle attachments to withstand the heavier loads of the phases that follow.

Young or inexperienced athletes need eight to ten weeks of anatomical adaptation training. In contrast, mature athletes with four to six years of strength training require no more than two or three weeks of this phase. Indeed, for these athletes, a longer anatomical adaptation phase likely provides no significant additional training effect.

Phase 2: Hypertrophy

In some sports, an increase in muscle size is a very important asset. However, as mentioned throughout this text, hypertrophy training, which is extremely popular in bodybuilding, is overused in the sporting world. When applied to strength training for sports, hypertrophy training must extend beyond the old definition of training to exhaustion. Specifically, it can be used as a primer for the maximum strength phase to follow by adapting the body to using progressively heavier loads.

During this phase, athletes can use two different approaches: hypertrophy I and hypertrophy II. Hypertrophy I is often used with athletes who require a distinct increase in muscle size and strength. It relies on using loads between 15RM (i.e., 15 reps to failure) and 10RM with little rest (60 to 90 seconds maximum) between sets. If bodybuilding techniques such as rest-pause and drop sets are used during this phase to increase the tension and protein synthesis within the musculature, the load used is between 8RM and 5RM, because these techniques further increase the total time under tension per set.

Hypertrophy II involves a more hybrid kind of work between hypertrophy and maximum strength that prepares the fast-twitch muscle fibers for the hard work to follow during the maximum strength training phase. Hypertrophy II increases absolute strength by eliciting both neural and structural adaptations. This phase uses loads from 8RM to 5RM with longer but not complete rest intervals (90 to 120 seconds).

For both hypertrophy I and hypertrophy II, the time devoted and the loads are determined by the athlete's age, physical development, and strength training experience. At the end of the hypertrophy phase, a maximum strength test is performed in order to plan the training percentage of the first maximum strength macrocycle.

Phase 3: Maximum Strength

The main objective of this phase is to develop the highest possible level of strength. This goal can be achieved only by using heavy loads in training: 70 percent to 90 percent of 1-repetition maximum (1RM) or, less often, 90 percent to 100 percent.

We like to divide the maximum strength phase into distinct two parts: maximum strength I and II. Maximum strength I works mainly on the intermuscular aspect of maximum strength adaptations. It is composed of one or two 3+1 macrocycles in which the load for the main strength exercises increases from 70 percent to 80 percent of 1RM. Maximum strength II works mainly on the intramuscular aspect of maximum strength adaptations. It is composed of one or two 2+1 macrocycles in which the load for the main strength exercises increases from 80 percent to 90 percent of 1RM (see figures 10.5 through 10.8).

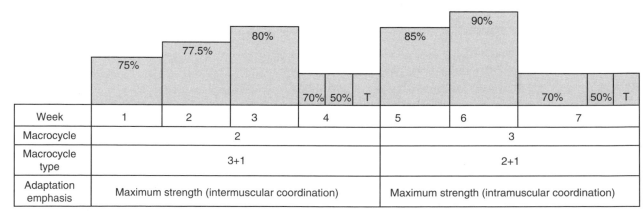

Figure 10.5 Suggested load progression for a seven-week maximum strength phase (the latter part of the unloading week is devoted to finding the new 1RM on which to base the next cycle).

Key: T = maximum strength testing.

Figure 10.6 chart:

Week	1	2	3	4	5	6	7	8
Load	75%	77.5%	80%	70% / 50% / T	82.5%	85%	90%	70% / 50% / T
Macrocycle	1				2			
Macrocycle type	3+1				3+1			
Adaptation emphasis	Maximum strength (intermuscular coordination)				Maximum strength (intramuscular coordination)			

Figure 10.6 Suggested load progression for an eight-week maximum strength phase (the latter part of the unloading week is devoted to finding the new 1RM on which to base the next cycle).

Key: T = maximum strength testing.

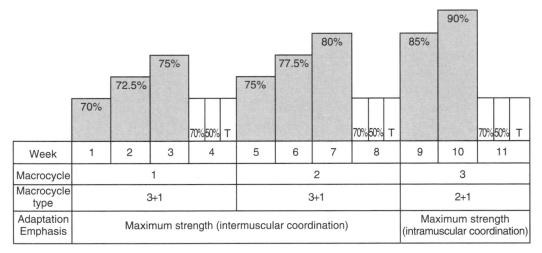

Week	1	2	3	4	5	6	7	8	9	10	11
Load	70%	72.5%	75%	70% / 50% / T	75%	77.5%	80%	70% / 50% / T	85%	90%	70% / 50% / T
Macrocycle	1				2				3		
Macrocycle type	3+1				3+1				2+1		
Adaptation Emphasis	Maximum strength (intermuscular coordination)								Maximum strength (intramuscular coordination)		

Figure 10.7 Suggested load progression for an 11-week maximum strength phase (the latter part of the unloading week is devoted to finding the new 1RM on which to base the next cycle).

Key: T = maximum strength testing.

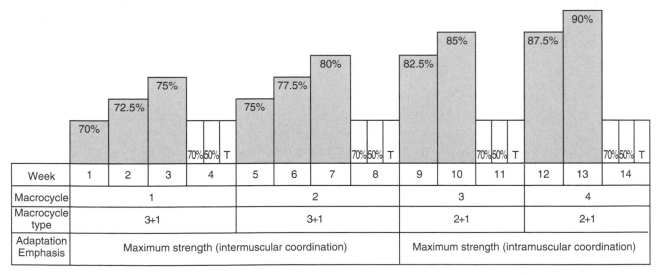

Week	1	2	3	4	5	6	7	8	9	10	11	12	13	14
Load	70%	72.5%	75%	70% / 50% / T	75%	77.5%	80%	70% / 50% / T	82.5%	85%	70% / 50% / T	87.5%	90%	70% / 50% / T
Macrocycle	1				2				3			4		
Macrocycle type	3+1				3+1				2+1			2+1		
Adaptation Emphasis	Maximum strength (intermuscular coordination)								Maximum strength (intramuscular coordination)					

Figure 10.8 Suggested load progression for a 14-week maximum strength phase (the latter part of the unloading week is devoted to finding the new 1RM on which to base the next cycle).

Key: T = maximum strength testing.

The duration of this phase, roughly from one to three months, is a function of the chosen sport or event and the athlete's needs. A shot-putter or American football player may need a lengthy phase of slightly more than three months, whereas an ice hockey player may need only one or two months to develop this type of strength. The load can be increased in a three- or four-week macrocycle (2+1 or 3+1), and it usually progresses by 2 percent to 5 percent per microcycle. Macrocycles for the intermuscular coordination type of maximum strength use loads up to 80 percent of 1RM and can be either 2+1 or 3+1 but are usually 3+1. Macrocycles for the *intra*muscular coordination type of maximum strength use loads above 80 percent and mostly the 2+1 format, because of their higher mean intensity.

This phase is characterized by a higher number of sets with a lower number of exercises. The duration of this phase also depends on whether the athlete follows a monocycle or bi-cycle annual plan. For obvious reasons, young athletes may have a shorter maximum strength phase with lower loads (intermuscular coordination work only).

Most sports require either power (e.g., for jumps and throws in track and field), power endurance (e.g., for sprints in track and field), muscular endurance (e.g., for 800- to 1,500-meter swimming), or all three (e.g., for rowing, canoeing, wrestling, combat sports, martial arts, and some team sports). Each of these types of specific strength is affected by the level of maximum strength. For instance, without a high level of maximum strength, an athlete cannot reach high levels of power. Because power is the product of force and velocity, it is logical to develop maximum strength first, then convert it to power.

Phase 4: Conversion to Specific Strength

The main purpose of this phase is to convert gains in maximum strength into competitive, sport-specific combinations of strength. Depending on the characteristics of the chosen sport or event, maximum strength must be converted into power; power endurance; or muscular endurance short, medium, or long. By applying an adequate training method for the type of strength sought and using training methods specific to the selected sport (for example, speed training), athletes gradually convert maximum strength into power.

Throughout this phase, depending on the needs of the sport and the athlete, a certain level of maximum strength must be maintained (usually employing both sport-specific range and full-range-of-motion exercises). If not, power may decline (due to detraining of neuromuscular qualities) toward the end of the competitive phase. This is certainly the case for professional players in American football, soccer, and baseball, because each of these sports has such a long season.

For sports in which power or muscular endurance is the dominant strength, the appropriate method must be dominant in training. When both power and muscular endurance are required, the training time and methods should adequately reflect the optimal ratio between these two abilities. For instance, for a wrestler, the ratio should be almost equal; for a canoeist in a 500-meter program, power should dominate; and for a rower, muscular endurance should dominate. In team sports, martial arts, wrestling, boxing, and most other power-dominant sports, coaches should combine power training with exercises that lead to the development of agility and quick reaction and movement times during the conversion phase. Only this type of approach prepares athletes for the sport-specific requirements of competition.

The duration of the conversion phase depends on the ability that needs to be developed. Conversion to power can be achieved in four or five weeks of specific power training. On the other hand, conversion to muscular endurance requires as many as six to eight weeks because both the physiological and the anatomical adaptations to such demanding work take much longer.

Phase 5: Maintenance

The tradition in many sports is to eliminate strength training when the competitive season starts. However, athletes who do not maintain strength training during the competitive phase experience a detraining effect with the following repercussions.

- Muscle fibers decrease to their pretraining size, resulting in a strength and power loss (Staron, Hagerman, and Hikida 1981; Thorstensson 1977).

- Loss of strength also results from decreases in motor unit recruitment. The athlete fails to voluntarily activate the same number of motor units as before, which causes a net decrease in the amount of force that can be generated (Edgerton 1976; Hainaut and Duchatteau 1989; Houmard 1991).

- Power decreases ensue because the rate of force production depends on the firing rate.

- Detraining becomes evident after four weeks, when athletes begin to be unable to perform skills requiring strength and power as proficiently as they did at the end of the conversion phase (Bompa 1993a).

As the term suggests, the main objective of strength training during this phase is to maintain the standards achieved during the previous phases. Once again, the program followed during this phase is a function of the specific requirements of the chosen sport. Such requirements must be reflected in the training ratio between maximum strength and the specific strength. For instance, a shot-putter may plan two sessions to train for maximum strength and two to train for power, whereas a jumper may consider one for maximum strength and two for power. Similarly, a 100-meter swimmer may plan one session to train for maximum strength, one for power, and one to train for muscular endurance short, whereas a 1,500-meter swimmer may dedicate the entire strength program to perfecting muscular endurance long.

For team sports, ratios should be calculated according to the role of strength in the particular sport; in addition, they should be position specific. For instance, a pitcher should perform maximum strength and power equally while also doing compensation work to avoid rotator cuff injury. Similarly, distinctions should be made between linemen and wide receivers in American football and sweepers, midfielders, and forwards in soccer. Linemen and wide receivers should spend equal time on maximum strength and power but use different percentages of 1RM (linemen use a lower velocity of the application of force in their specific activity). Soccer players have to maintain both power and power endurance short—that is, the ability to repeat numerous power actions with incomplete rest.

Between one and four sessions per week must be dedicated to maintaining the required strength qualities, depending on the athlete's level of performance and the role of strength in skill performance. Studies show that at least one strength maintenance session per week is necessary to maintain most of the strength gains and the power output reached during preparation (Graves et al. 1988; Wilmore and Costill 2004; Rønnestad et al. 2011).

Compared with the preparation phases, the time allocated to the maintenance of strength in the maintenance phase is much lower. Therefore, the coach has to develop a very efficient and specific program. For instance, two to (at most) four exercises involving the prime movers will enable the athlete to maintain previously reached strength levels. As a result, the duration of each strength training session will be short—20 to 40 minutes.

Phase 6: Cessation

As the main competition of the year approaches, most of the athlete's energy must be directed to the main sport-specific biomotor ability or mix of biomotor abilities. Again, the purpose of the cessation phase is to conserve the athlete's energy for competition and peak his or her sport-specific biomotor abilities. For this reason, the strength training program should end at least three to fourteen days before the main competition. The exact timing depends on multiple factors:

Donovan Bailey after his 100-meter victory at the 1996 Olympics.

- *The athlete's sex*—female athletes, who retain strength gains less easily than males do, should usually maintain strength training until three days before competition.

- *The chosen sport*—A longer cessation phase, one to two weeks long, may result in improved alactic speed performance due to overshooting of the fast-twitch Type IIx muscle fibers. For long endurance sports for which strength is not as important as for anaerobic sports, strength training can be ended two weeks before the main competition for the year.

- *Body type*—Heavier athletes tend to retain both adaptations and residual fatigue longer and therefore should end strength training earlier than lighter athletes.

Phase 7: Compensation

Traditionally, the last phase of the annual plan has been inappropriately called the "off-season"; in reality, it represents a transition from one annual plan to another. The main goal of this phase is to remove fatigue acquired during the training year and replenish the exhausted energy stores by decreasing both volume (through a decrease in frequency) and intensity of training. During the months of training and competition, most athletes are exposed to numerous psychological and social stressors that drain their mental energy. During the transition phase, athletes can relax psychologically by getting involved in various physical and social activities that they enjoy.

The transition phase should last no longer than four weeks for serious athletes. A longer phase results in detraining effects, such as the loss of most training gains, especially strength gains. The detraining that results from neglecting strength training in

DETRAINING

Strength can be improved or maintained only if an adequate load or training intensity is administered continually. When strength training is decreased or ceased, as often happens during competitive or long transition phases, a disturbance occurs in the biological state of the muscle cells and bodily organs. This disturbance results in a marked decrease in the athlete's physiological well-being and work output (Fry, Morton, and Keast 1991; Kuipers and Keizer 1988).

Decreased or diminished training can leave athletes vulnerable to "detraining syndrome" (Israel 1972). The severity of strength loss depends on the elapsed time between training sessions. Many organic and cellular adaptation benefits may be degraded, including the protein content of myosin.

When training proceeds as planned, the body uses protein to build and repair damaged tissues. When the body is in a state of disuse, however, it begins to catabolize or break down protein because it is no longer needed (Appell 1990; Edgerton 1976). As this process of protein degradation continues, some of the gains made during training are reversed. Testosterone levels, which are important for strength gains, have also been shown to decrease as a result of detraining, which may, in turn, diminish the amount of protein synthesis (Houmard 1991).

Total abstinence from training is associated with a range of symptoms, including a rise in psychological disturbances, such as headache, insomnia, a feeling of exhaustion, increased tension, increased mood disturbance, lack of appetite, and psychological depression. An athlete may develop any one of these symptoms or a combination of two or more. The symptoms all have to do with lowered levels of testosterone and beta-endorphin, a neuroendocrine compound that is the main forerunner of euphoric postexercise feelings (Houmard 1991).

Detraining symptoms are not pathological and can be reversed if training resumes shortly. If training is discontinued for a prolonged period, however, athletes may display symptoms for some time. This pattern indicates the inability of the human body and its systems to adapt to the state of inactivity. The length of time needed for these symptoms to incubate varies from athlete to athlete, but they generally appear after two to three weeks of inactivity and vary in severity.

Coaches of athletes involved in speed- and power-dominant sports must be aware of the fact that when muscles are not stimulated with strength or power training activities, muscle fiber recruitment is disrupted (Wilmore and Costill 2004). This disruption results in a deterioration of performance. Costill reported that strength gained during a 12-week program decreased by 68 percent as a result of 12 weeks of strength training interruption; this is a substantial loss for some athletes, especially those in speed- and power-dominant sports. In contrast, subjects who kept performing at least one strength training session per week retained all of the strength they had gained in the 12 weeks of training.

The decrease in muscle fiber cross-sectional area is quite apparent after a few weeks of inactivity. The fastest rate of muscle atrophy, especially the degradation of contractile protein, takes place in the first two weeks. These changes result from lower glycogen content in the muscle, and especially from protein breakdown, as a result of inhibition of the cellular anabolic pathways (Kandarian and Jackman 2006; Zhang et al. 2007). In addition, the tendons' tensile strength diminishes as a consequence of atrophy in collagen fiber, and the ligaments' total collagen mass diminishes as well (Kannus et al. 1992).

(continued)

DETRAINING *(continued)*

Slow-twitch fibers are usually the first to lose their ability to produce force. Fast-twitch fibers are generally least affected by inactivity. In fact, when exposed to lactic training, fast-twitch glycolytic muscle fibers of Type IIx (more precisely, their myosin-heavy chains) take on the characteristics of fast-twitch oxidative glycolytic fibers of Type IIa (Andersen et al. 2005). Yet they regain their faster characteristics when training volume is greatly reduced. This is not to say that atrophy does not occur in these fibers—it just takes a little longer than in slow-twitch fibers.

After an initial increase due to rebound in fast-twitch fibers, speed is affected by longer detraining because the breakdown of muscle protein and the loss of neural adaptation decrease the power capabilities of muscle contractions. The loss in power becomes more pronounced as a result of diminished motor recruitment. The reduction in nerve impulses to the muscle fibers makes muscles contract and relax at slower rates. Reduction in the strength and frequency of these impulses can also decrease the total number of motor units recruited during a series of repeated contractions (Edgerton 1976; Hainaut and Duchatteau 1989; Houmard 1991).

Detraining also affects aerobic-dominant sports. Coyle and colleagues (1991) observed that an 84-day training stoppage did not affect glycolytic enzyme activity but did decrease the activity of oxidative enzymes by 60 percent. This finding demonstrates that anaerobic performance can be maintained longer than aerobic performance, although both lactic capacity and aerobic power are affected by decreases in muscle glycogen of up to 40 percent that result from at least four weeks of detraining (Wilmore and Costill 2004).

the off-season can be detrimental to athletes' rate of performance improvement in the following year.

Athletes and coaches should remember that strength is hard to gain and easy to lose. Athletes who perform no strength training at all during the transition phase may experience decreased muscle size and considerable power loss (Wilmore and Costill 1993). Because power and speed are interdependent, such athletes also lose speed. Some authors claim that the disuse of muscles also reduces the frequency of discharge rate and the pattern of muscle fiber recruitment; thus, strength and power loss may be the result of not activating as many motor units.

Although physical activity volume is reduced by 50 percent to 60 percent during the transition phase, athletes should find time to work on the maintenance of strength training. Specifically, it can be beneficial to work on the antagonists, stabilizers, and other muscles that may not necessarily be involved in the performance of the sport-specific skills. Similarly, compensation exercises should be planned for sports in which an imbalance may develop between parts or sides of the body—for example, pitching, throwing events, archery, soccer (work the upper body more), and cycling.

Variations in the Periodization of Strength Model

The periodization of strength example presented earlier in this chapter (see figure 10.3) was helpful for illustrating the basic concept, but it cannot serve as a model for every situation or every sport. Each individual or group of athletes requires specific planning and programming based on training background, sex, and the specific characteristics of the chosen sport or event. This section of the chapter explains variations of periodization of strength and offers follow-up illustrations of specific periodization models for certain sports and events.

Some sports, and some positions in team sports, require strength and heavy muscle mass. For instance, it is advantageous for throwers in track-and-field events, linemen in American football, and heavyweight wrestlers and boxers to be both heavy and powerful. These athletes should follow a unique periodization model with a long phase of training planned to develop hypertrophy (see chapter 12). Developing hypertrophy first seems to increase force potential faster, especially if followed by maximum strength and power development phases, which are known to stimulate the activation and firing rate of fast-twitch muscle fiber.

Figure 10.9 shows a periodization model for heavy and powerful athletes. The traditional anatomical adaptation phase is followed by a hypertrophy phase of at least six weeks, which in turn is followed by maximum strength training and conversion to power. During the maintenance phase, these athletes should dedicate time to preserving maximum strength and power that will also preserve the hypertrophy gains obtained in the previous stages. The annual plan concludes with compensation training specific to the transition phase.

Because the preparation phase in power sports can be very long (e.g., in U.S. and Canadian college football), the coach may decide to build even more muscle mass. To this end, another model can be followed—see figure 10.10—in which phases of hypertrophy are alternated with phases of maximum strength. The numbers above each phase in figure 10.10 and some of the following tables indicate the duration of that phase in weeks.

Figure 10.11 illustrates a periodization with a longer preparation phase and pendular alternation between maximum strength and power macrocles. The longer preparation

Prep.				Comp.	T
AA	Hyp.	MxS	Conv. to P	Maint.: P, MxS	Compens.

Key: AA = anatomical adaptation, comp. = competitive, compens. = compensation, conv. = conversion, hyp. = hypertrophy, maint. = maintenance, MxS = maximum strength, P = power, prep. = preparation, and T = transition.

Figure 10.9 Periodization Model for Athletes Requiring Hypertrophy

Prep.								Comp.	T
3 AA	7 Hyp.	6 MxS	3 Hyp.	3 MxS	3 Hyp.	3 MxS	4 Conv. to P	16 Maint.: P, MxS	4 Compens.

Key: AA = anatomical adaptation, comp. = competitive, compens. = compensation, conv. = conversion, hyp. = hypertrophy, maint. = maintenance, MxS = maximum strength, P = power, prep. = preparation, and T = transition.

Figure 10.10 Variation of Periodization for Development of Hypertrophy and Maximum Strength

Prep.							Comp.	T
7 AA	6 MxS	3 P	6 MxS	3 P	3 MxS	4 P	16 Maint.: P, MxS	4 Compens.

Key: AA = anatomical adaptation, comp. = competitive, compens. = compensation, maint. = maintenance, MxS = maximum strength, P = power, prep. = preparation, and T = transition.

Figure 10.11 Periodization Model for Athletes Requiring Frequent Alternations of Strength Training Emphasis

phase assumes either a summer sport or a sport played during the winter and early spring. The pendular alternation between maximum strength and power is indicated for sports (e.g., racket and combat sports) characterized by a few concentrated competitions throughout the year, which means that a longer maximum strength phase could be detrimental to sport-specific skills.

Furthermore, similar variations of power and maximum strength phases are necessary because gains in power are faster if muscles are trained at various speeds of contraction (Bührle 1985; Bührle and Schmidtbleicher 1981). Both power and maximum strength training train the fast-twitch fibers. In addition, maximum strength training results in motor unit recruitment patterns that display high levels of force, and power training increases the frequency or speed at which the muscles carry out the work. Anyone who has witnessed the performance of a shot-putter, javelin thrower, or hammer thrower can appreciate the force and speed characteristics involved. Macrocycles alternating maximum strength and power can also be employed by power athletes such as sprinters and jumpers in track and field at a more advanced stage of development.

If the same methods and loading pattern are maintained for longer than two months, especially by athletes with a strong strength training background, the pattern of fiber recruitment becomes standard, eventually reaching a plateau. At that point, no drastic improvement can be expected. Thus bodybuilding methods defeat their purpose in sports in which speed and power are dominant abilities. This reality explains why several of the figures in this chapter propose a sequence of maximum strength and power macrocycles.

In addition, the importance of maximum strength phases should not be underestimated because any deterioration in maximum strength affects the athlete's ability to maintain power or muscle endurance at the desired level throughout the competitive phase. In sports in which athletes must peak twice a year (e.g., swimming and track and field), a bi-cycle annual plan is optimal. Figure 10.12 presents the periodization of strength plan for a double-peak (bi-cycle) annual plan.

OCT.	NOV.	DEC.	JAN.	FEB.	MAR.	APR.	MAY	JUNE	JULY	AUG.	SEPT.
Prep. I			Comp. I			T	Prep. II		Comp. II		T
AA	MxS		Conv. to P	Maint.		AA	MxS	Conv. to P	Maint.	Compens.	

Key: AA = anatomical adaptation, comp. = competitive, compens. = compensation, conv. = conversion, maint. = maintenance, MxS = maximum strength, P = power, prep. = preparation, and T = transition.

Figure 10.12 Periodization Model for a Bi-Cycle Annual Plan

For sports with three competitive phases, athletes must peak three times a year. Examples include wrestling, boxing, and international-level swimming and track and field, which feature a winter season, an early summer season ending with national championships or trials, and a late summer season ending with the world championship or Olympics. The annual plan for such sports is called a tri-cycle plan, and a periodization model for this plan is presented in figure 10.13.

For sports with a long preparation phase—such as softball, American football, and track cycling—figure 10.14 shows a periodization option with two peaks: an artificial peak at the end of April and a real peak (e.g., for the football season) during the fall. This model was developed at the request of a football coach who wanted to improve his players' maximum strength and power. The model was very successful, both with the football

	OCT.	NOV.	DEC.	JAN.	FEB.	MAR.	APR.	MAY	JUNE	JULY	AUG.	SEPT.
	Prep. I			Comp. I		T	Prep. II	Comp. II			Prep. III	Comp. III	T
Periodization of strength	3	9		4	6	1	6	4	6	1	2	3	3
	AA	MxS		Conv. to P	Maint.: P and MxS	AA	MxS	Conv. to PE	Maint.: PE and MxS		AA	MxS, PE	Maint.: PE and MxS	Compens.

Key: AA = anatomical adaptation, comp. = competitive, compens. = compensation, conv. = conversion, maint. = maintenance, MxS = maximum strength, P = power, PE = power endurance, prep. = preparation, and T = transition.

Figure 10.13 Periodization Model for a Tri-Cycle Annual Plan

DEC.	JAN.	FEB.	MAR.	APR.	MAY	JUNE	JULY	AUG.	SEPT.	OCT.	NOV.
Prep.					T	Prep. II		Comp.			T
AA	MxS		Conv. to P	AA	MxS			Conv. to P	Maint.: P, MxS	Compens.	

Key: AA = anatomical adaptation, comp. = competitive, compens. = compensation, conv. = conversion, maint. = maintenance, MxS = maximum strength, P = power, prep. = preparation, and T = transition.

Figure 10.14 Double-Peak Periodization

players and with cycling sprinters; all of the athletes increased their maximum strength and power to the highest levels ever. This new approach for a typical monocycle sport was based on the following reasons:

- A very long preparation phase with heavy loading and little variety was considered too stressful and therefore of dubious physiological benefit.
- A double-peak periodization offers the advantage of planning two phases for maximum strength training and two for power training. American football linemen followed a slightly different approach, in which hypertrophy training preceded the maximum strength phase. The benefits expected by the coach were realized: an increase in overall muscle mass, an increase in maximum strength, and the highest level of power ever achieved by his players.

Periodization Models for Sports

To make this book practical and readily applicable, it includes several sport-specific periodization models for strength. For each model, we include five factors that indicate the physiological characteristics for the relevant sport:

- Dominant energy system(s)
- Ergogenesis (percentage of each energy system's contribution to final performance)
- Main energy substrate(s)
- Limiting factor(s) for performance
- Objective(s) for strength training

Strength training should be linked to the sport-specific energy system(s). Doing so makes it relatively easy to decide the strength training objectives. For instance, for sports in which the anaerobic alactic system is dominant, the limiting factor for performance is power. On the other hand, sports dominated by the anaerobic lactic system or the aerobic system always require a certain component of muscular endurance.

In this way, coaches can better train their athletes physiologically and, as a result, improve their performance. For example, increments in power should never be expected if the training applies bodybuilding methods. The phrase "limiting factor(s) for performance" means that the desired performance cannot be achieved unless those factors are developed at the highest possible level. More specifically, good performance is limited or hindered if the athlete possesses only a low level of the required sport-specific combination of strength.

The following examples cannot cover all possible variations for each sport. To develop such a model, one would have to know the specific competition schedule, as well as the competition level and objectives of the individual athlete. Thus, for example, for sports such as track and field and swimming, the periodization models are designed around the main competitions in winter and summer.

SPRINTING

A sprinter requires frequent strides that are long and powerful. His or her velocity correlates directly with the amount of force applied during the very short ground contact of each step (200 milliseconds out of the blocks and 80 milliseconds at maximum velocity). For the 60-meter event, endurance is not as important as acceleration because the sprinter needs to move as fast as possible over a short distance. For the 100-meter and 200-meter events, however, speed endurance (lactic power) is fundamental; in fact, it makes the difference between elite and sub-elite sprinters. A sample periodization model for sprinters is presented in figure 10.15.

- Dominant energy system: 60-meter—anaerobic alactic; 100-meter and 200-meter—anaerobic lactic
- Ergogenesis: 60-meter—80% alactic, 20% lactic; 100-meter—53% alactic, 44% lactic, 3% aerobic; 200-meter—26% alactic, 45% lactic, 29% aerobic
- Main energy substrate(s): 60-meter—creatine phosphate; 100-meter and 200-meter—creatine phosphate and glycogen
- Limiting factors: 60-meter—acceleration power; 100-meter and 200-meter—power endurance; all—starting power, reactive power
- Training objectives: 60-meter—power; 100-meter and 200-meter—power endurance; all—maximum strength

Periodization	Oct.	Nov.	Dec.	Jan.	Feb.	Mar.	Apr.	May	June	July	Aug.	Sept.
	Prep. I			Comp. I		T / Prep. II			Comp. II	T / Prep. III	Comp. III	T
Strength	3 AA	9 MxS		4 Conv. to P	7 Maint.: P and MxS	1 AA / 5 MxS	4 Conv. to PE		6 Maint.: PE and MxS	1 AA / 3 MxS, PE	4 Maint.: PE and MxS	4 Compens.
Energy systems	O_2 P	Lactic cap., alactic P, and O_2 P		Alactic and lactic P		Alactic P and lactic cap.	Alactic and lactic P			Alactic P and lactic cap.	Alactic and lactic P	Games play

Aerobic (O_2) training for a sprinter represents the cumulative effect of tempo training (repetitions of 600-meter, 400-meter, and 200-meter).

Key: AA = anatomical adaptation, cap. = capacity, comp. = competitive, compens. = compensation, conv. = conversion, maint. = maintenance, MxS = maximum strength, O_2 = aerobic, P = power, PE = power endurance, prep. = preparation, and T = transition.

Figure 10.15 Periodization Model for Sprinters

THROWING EVENTS: SHOT PUT, DISCUS, HAMMER, AND JAVELIN

Training for throwing events in track and field requires great power (based on improvement of maximum strength) and hypertrophy (especially for shot put and to some degree for discus). Specifically, a high level of muscular strength is required in the legs, torso, and arms for generating acceleration through the range of motion and maximum throwing power. A sample periodization model for throwing events is presented in figure 10.16.

- Dominant energy system: anaerobic alactic
- Ergogenesis: 95% alactic, 5% lactic
- Main energy substrate: creatine phosphate
- Limiting factor: throwing power
- Training objectives: maximum strength, power

Periodization	Oct.	Nov.	Dec.	Jan.	Feb.	Mar.	Apr.	May	June	July	Aug.	Sept.
	Prep. I			Comp. I			T	Prep. II		Comp. II			T
Strength	3 AA	5 Hyp.	6 MxS, hyp.	3 Conv. to P	8 Maint.: MxS, hyp., P	2 A A	3 Hyp.	4 MxS, hyp.	2 Conv. to P	10 Maint.: MxS, P		3 Compens.
Energy systems	Lactic and alactic cap.	Alactic P and cap.				Alactic P	Alactic P and cap.					Games play

Hypertrophy training follows AA and must be maintained during the maximum strength macrocycles but at a ratio of one hypertrophy set for every three maximum strength sets (the back-off set method can be used in this case).

Key: AA = anatomical adaptation, cap. = capacity, comp. = competitive, compens. = compensation, conv. = conversion, hyp. = hypertrophy, maint. = maintenance, MxS = maximum strength, P = power, prep. = preparation, and T = transition.

Figure 10.16 Periodization Model for Throwing Events

LONG SPRINTING AND MIDDLE-DISTANCE RUNNING

Long sprinters and middle-distance runners are fast runners who can also tolerate a large buildup of lactic acid during the race. Good performance requires the ability to respond quickly to changes in running pace. Therefore, these athletes need both good aerobic power and good lactic capacity, as well as lactic acid tolerance. A sample periodization model is presented in figure 10.17.

- Dominant energy systems: anaerobic lactic, aerobic
- Ergogenesis: 400-meter—12% alactic, 50% lactic, 38% aerobic; 800-meter—6% alactic, 33% lactic, 61% aerobic; 1,500-meter—2% alactic, 18% lactic, 80% aerobic
- Main energy substrates: creatine phosphate, glycogen
- Limiting factor(s): starting power (400-meter); acceleration power (400-meter); muscle endurance short (400-meter, 800-meter elite level); muscle endurance medium (800-meter, 1,500-meter)
- Training objectives: maximum strength (all); power endurance (400-meter); muscle endurance short (400-meter, 800-meter); muscle endurance medium (800-meter, 1,500-meter)

Periodization	Oct.	Nov.	Dec.	Jan.	Feb.	Mar.	Apr.	May	June	July	Aug.	Sept.
	Prep. I			Comp. I		T	Prep. II		Comp. II			T
Strength	3 AA	6 MxS	5 Conv. to ME	6 Maint.: ME, MxS		1 A A	6 MxS	6 Conv. to ME	15 Maint.: ME, MxS			4 Compens.
Energy systems	O_2 P		Lactic cap., O_2 P, lactic P, alactic P			O_2 P		Lactic cap., O_2 P, lactic P, alactic P				O_2

The suggested order of energy systems training also implies training priorities per training phase.

Key: AA = anatomical adaptation, cap. = capacity, comp. = competitive, compens. = compensation, conv. = conversion, maint. = maintenance, ME = muscle endurance, MxS = maximum strength, O_2 = aerobic, P = power, prep. = preparation, specific str. = specific strength, and T = transition.

Figure 10.17 Periodization Model for Long Sprinting and Middle-Distance Running

LONG-DISTANCE AND MARATHON RUNNING

High aerobic capacity is an essential physical attribute of distance runners. In fact, it is necessary to maintain a steady, fast pace throughout the long race. Glycogen and free fatty acid are the fuels used to produce energy for the race. For a sample periodization model, see figure 10.18.

- Dominant energy system: aerobic
- Ergogenesis: 10,000-meter—3% lactic, 97% aerobic; marathon—100% aerobic
- Main energy substrates: glycogen, free fatty acid
- Limiting factor: muscular endurance long
- Training objectives: muscular endurance long (all), power endurance (10,000-meter).

Periodization	Oct.	Nov.	Dec.	Jan.	Feb.	Mar.	Apr.	May	June	July	Aug.	Sept.
	Prep.							Comp.			T	
Strength	8 AA		6 MxS, P	6 MEM, MxS, PE		8 Conv. to MEL		14 Maint.: MEL, MxS, PE			Compens.	
Energy systems	O_2 cap.			O_2 cap., O_2 P		O_2 cap., O_2 P, lactic cap.					Alternative activites	

MxS < 80% of 1RM

Key: AA = anatomical adaptation, cap. = capacity, comp. = competitive, compens. = compensation, conv. = conversion, maint. = maintenance, MEL = muscle endurance long, MEM = muscular endurance medium, MxS = maximum strength, O_2 = aerobic, P = power, PE = power endurance, prep. = preparation, and T = transition.

Figure 10.18 Periodization Model for Long-Distance and Marathon Running

SPRINT SWIMMING

Sprint swimmers use mainly the lactic acid system. They must generate quick, powerful strokes to move efficiently through the water for an extended period of time. For a sample periodization model, see figure 10.19, which presents a bi-cycle for a nationally ranked sprinter.

- Dominant energy systems: anaerobic lactic, aerobic, anaerobic alactic
- Ergogenesis: 50-meter—20% alactic, 50% lactic, 30% aerobic; 100-meter—19% alactic, 26% lactic, 55% aerobic
- Main energy substrates: creatine phosphate, glycogen
- Limiting factors: power (all), power endurance (50-meter), muscular endurance short (100-meter)
- Training objectives: maximum strength (all), power endurance (50-meter), muscular endurance short (100-meter)

Periodization	Sept.	Oct.	Nov.	Dec.	Jan.	Feb.		Mar.		Apr.	May	June	July	Aug.
	Prep. I				Comp. I		T	Prep. II			Comp. II			T
Strength	4 AA	8 MxS		4 Conv. to specific str.	8 Maint.: specific str., MxS		2 AA	6 MxS		4 Conv. to specific str.	7 Maint.: specific str., MxS =			7 Compens.
Energy systems	O_2 cap.	Lactic cap., O_2 P	Lactic P, O_2 P, lactic cap., alactic P	Lactic P, alactic P, O_2 compens.			O_2 P, lactic cap.	Lactic P, O_2 P, lactic cap., alactic P		Lactic P, alactic P, O_2 compens.				O_2 cap.

The order of energy systems training per phase also represents the priority of training for that phase.

Key: AA = anatomical adaptation, cap. = capacity, comp. = competitive, compens. = compensation, conv. = conversion, maint. = maintenance, MxS = maximum strength, O_2 = aerobic, P = power, prep. = preparation, specific str. = specific strength, and T = transition.

Figure 10.19 Periodization Model for a National-Class Sprinter in Swimming (Bi-Cycle)

LONG-DISTANCE SWIMMING

Long-distance swimmers must train for muscular endurance. A long race taxes the aerobic energy system, and proper muscular endurance training gives the swimmer an endurance edge. For a sample periodization model, see figure 10.20. The model assumes two competitive phases—one beginning in January and the other beginning in late spring.

- Dominant energy system: aerobic
- Ergogenesis: 10% lactic, 90% aerobic
- Main energy substrates: glycogen, free fatty acid
- Limiting factor: muscular endurance long
- Training objectives: muscular endurance medium, muscular endurance long

Periodization	Sept.	Oct.	Nov.	Dec.	Jan.	Feb.	Mar.	Apr.	May	June	July	Aug.
	Prep. I				Comp. I		T	Prep. II		Comp. II		T
Strength	3 AA	3 MxS	3 MEM	3 MxS	6 Conv. to MEL	6 Maint.: MEL, MxS	3 AA	4 MxS	6 Conv. to MEL	7 Maint.: MEL, MxS		4 Compens.
Energy systems	O_2 cap.	O_2 cap., O_2 P	O_2 P, O_2 cap.	O_2 P, lactic cap., O_2 cap.			O_2 cap., O_2 P	O_2 P, O_2 cap.	O_2 P, lactic cap., O_2 cap.			O_2 compens.

Key: AA = anatomical adaptation, cap. = capacity, comp. = competitive, compens. = compensation, conv. = conversion, maint. = maintenance, MEL = muscle endurance long, MEM = muscular endurance medium, MxS = maximum strength, O_2 = aerobic, P = power, prep. = preparation, and T = transition.

Figure 10.20 Periodization Model for a National-Class Long-Distance Swimmer

SHORT-DISTANCE SWIMMING BY A MASTER ATHLETE

The dominant training factor for a master athlete is power. Developing both power and maximum strength requires a long preparation phase. For a sample periodization model for a master swimmer, see figure 10.21. The model assumes only one competitive phase—from May through late August.

- Dominant energy systems: anaerobic lactic, anaerobic alactic, aerobic
- Ergogenesis: 50-meter—18% alactic, 45% lactic, 37% aerobic; 100-meter—15% alactic, 25% lactic, 60% aerobic
- Main energy substrates: creatine phosphate, glycogen
- Limiting factors: power (all), power endurance (50-meter), muscular endurance short (100-meter)
- Training objectives: maximum strength (all), power endurance (50-meter), muscular endurance short (100-meter)

Periodization	Oct.	Nov.	Dec.		Jan.	Feb.	Mar.	Apr.	May	June	July	Aug.	Sept.
	Prep.								Comp.			Transition	
Strength	8 AA		4 MxS	3 P	4 MxS	3 P	4 MxS	6 Conv. to PE	12 Maint.: PE, MxS			8 Compens.	
Energy systems	O_2 cap., O_2 P		O_2 P, O_2 cap.		Lactic cap., O_2 P	Lactic P, O_2 P, lactic cap., alactic P		Lactic P, alactic P, O_2 P				O_2 cap.	

Key: AA = anatomical adaptation, cap. = capacity, comp. = competitive, compens. = compensation, conv. = conversion, maint. = maintenance, MxS = maximum strength, O_2 = aerobic, P = power, PE = power endurance, and prep. = preparation.

Figure 10.21 Periodization Model for a Master Athlete (Short-Distance) Swimmer

CYCLING: ROAD RACING

Road racing overwhelms the aerobic system. The only times that cyclists tax the anaerobic energy system are during steep climbing and at the finish of the race. Cyclists must be prepared to work hard over a long distance, generating constant rotations per minute to maintain speed and power against the resistance of the pedals, the environment, and the terrain. For a sample periodization model, see figure 10.22.

- Dominant energy system: aerobic
- Ergogenesis: 5% lactic, 95% aerobic
- Main energy substrates: glycogen, free fatty acid
- Limiting factors: muscular endurance long, power endurance
- Training objectives: muscular endurance long, power endurance, maximum strength

Periodization	Nov.	Dec.	Jan.	Feb.	Mar.	Apr.	May	June	July	Aug.	Sept.	Oct.
	Prep.						Comp.					T
Strength	4 AA	6 MxS		6 MEL	3 MxS	9 Conv. to MEL	13 Maint.: MEL, PE, MxS					6 Compens.
Energy systems	O$_2$ cap.		O$_2$ P, O$_2$ cap., lactic cap.									O$_2$ cap.

Key: AA = anatomical adaptation, cap. = capacity, comp. = competitive, compens. = compensation, conv. = conversion, maint. = maintenance, MEL = muscle endurance long, MxS = maximum strength, O$_2$ = aerobic, PE = power endurance, prep. = preparation, and T = transition.

Figure 10.22 Periodization Model for Road Racing

TRIATHLON

Triathlon, which requires proficiency in three athletic skills, presents a great challenge to both physical and psychological endurance. Paramount to success in triathlon is the body's efficiency in using the main fuel-producing source: free fatty acid. For a sample periodization model, see figure 10.23.

- Dominant energy system: aerobic
- Ergogenesis: 5% lactic, 95% aerobic
- Main energy substrates: glycogen, free fatty acid
- Limiting factor: muscular endurance long
- Training objectives: muscular endurance long, maximum strength

Periodization	Oct.	Nov.	Dec.	Jan.	Feb.	Mar.	Apr.	May	June	July	Aug.	Sept.
	Prep.						Comp.					T
Strength	4 AA	8 MxS		12 Conv. to MEL			20 Maint.: MEL, MxS					4 Compens.
Energy systems	O_2 cap.	O_2 cap., O_2 P		O_2 P, O_2 cap., lactic cap.								O_2 cap.

The suggested order of energy systems training also implies training priorities per training phase.

Key: AA = anatomical adaptation, cap. = capacity, comp. = competitive, compens. = compensation, conv. = conversion, maint. = maintenance, MEL = muscle endurance long, MxS = maximum strength, O_2 = aerobic, prep. = preparation, and T = transition.

Figure 10.23   Periodization Model for Triathlon

CANOEING AND KAYAKING: 500 AND 1,000 METERS

Flatwater sprints are all about speed and specific endurance. In order to move quickly to the finish line, the racer must quickly pull the paddle against the resistance of the water. For a sample periodization model, see figure 10.24.

- Dominant energy systems: aerobic, anaerobic lactic, anaerobic alactic
- Ergogenesis: 500-meter—16% alactic, 22% lactic, 62% aerobic; 1,000-meter—8% alactic, 10% lactic, 82% aerobic
- Main energy substrates: creatine phosphate, glycogen
- Limiting factors: muscular endurance, power endurance, starting power
- Training objectives: power endurance, maximum strength, muscular endurance short and medium

Periodization	Oct.	Nov.	Dec.	Jan.	Feb.	Mar.	Apr.	May	June	July	Aug.	Sept.
	Prep.							Comp.				T
Strength	5 AA	6 MxS	4 PE	1 T	6 MxS	3 MES	3 MxS	7 Conv. to MEM	13 Maint.: MEM, MxS			4 Compens.
Energy systems	O_2 cap.	O_2 cap., O_2 P, lactic cap.	O_2 P, O_2 cap., alactic P, lactic cap.	O_2 P	O_2 P, lactic cap., alactic P, O_2 cap.		O_2 P, lactic P, alactic P, O_2 cap.					O_2 cap.

The order of energy systems training represents the order of priority in a given training phase.

Key: AA = anatomical adaptation, cap. = capacity, comp. = competitive, compens. = compensation, conv. = conversion, MES = muscle endurance short, MEM = muscle endurance medium, maint. = maintenance, MxS = maximum strength, O_2 = aerobic, P = power, PE = power endurance, prep. = preparation, and T = transition.

Figure 10.24 Periodization Model for Canoeing and Kayaking (500 and 1,000 Meters)

CANOEING AND KAYAKING: MARATHON

Unlike sprints, marathon races require muscular endurance of long duration. In addition, a racer must have a well-developed aerobic energy system to endure the length of the race. For a sample periodization model, see figure 10.25.

- Dominant energy system: aerobic
- Ergogenesis: 5% lactic, 95% aerobic
- Main energy substrates: glycogen, free fatty acid
- Limiting factor: muscular endurance long
- Training objectives: muscular endurance long, power endurance, maximum strength

Periodization	Nov.	Dec.	Jan.	Feb.	Mar.	Apr.	May	June	July	Aug.	Sept.	Oct.
	Prep.						Comp.					T
Strength	6 AA	6 MxS	3 MEM	3 MxS	12 Conv. to MEL				18 Maint.: MEL, MxS			4 Compens.
Energy systems	O_2 cap.	O_2 cap., O_2 P		O_2 P, O_2 cap., lactic cap.								O_2 cap.

Key: AA = anatomical adaptation, cap. = capacity, comp. = competitive, compens. = compensation, conv. = conversion, maint. = maintenance, MEL = muscle endurance long, MEM = muscular endurance medium, MxS = maximum strength, O_2 = aerobic, P = power, prep. = preparation, and T = transition.

Figure 10.25 Periodization Model for Canoeing and Kayaking (Marathon)

SKIING: ALPINE

Alpine skiers must be able to react quickly to the course flags. Over the long preparation phase, maximum strength development alternates with power development. For a sample periodization model, see figure 10.26.

- Dominant energy systems: anaerobic lactic, anaerobic alactic
- Ergogenesis: 10% alactic, 40% lactic, 50% aerobic
- Main energy substrates: creatine phosphate, glycogen
- Limiting factors: reactive power, power endurance
- Training objectives: maximum strength, power endurance, muscle endurance short

Periodization	May	June	July	July	Aug.	Sept.	Oct.	Nov.	Dec.	Jan.	Feb.	Mar.	Apr.
	Prep.							Comp.					T
Strength	4 AA	8 MxS	3 PE	6 MxS	3 PE	3 MxS		6 Conv. to MES	15 Maint.: MES, MxS, PE				4 Compens.
Energy systems	O$_2$ cap.	O$_2$ P, lactic cap.		Lactic P, lactic cap., O$_2$ P									Alternative activities

The aerobic training (O$_2$) can be the cumulative effect of longer-duration specific drills.

Key: AA = anatomical adaptation, cap. = capacity, comp. = competitive, compens. = compensation, conv. = conversion, maint. = maintenance, MES = muscle endurance short, MxS = maximum strength, O$_2$ = aerobic, P = power, PE = power endurance, prep. = preparation, and T = transition.

Figure 10.26 Periodization Model for Alpine Skiing

SKIING: CROSS-COUNTRY AND BIATHLON

Cross-country races require strong aerobic endurance. Maximum strength is converted to muscular endurance toward the end of the preparation phase so that the skier is primed to withstand the demands of a long race. For a sample periodization model, see figure 10.27.

- Dominant energy system: aerobic
- Ergogenesis: 5% lactic, 95% aerobic
- Main energy substrates: glycogen, free fatty acid
- Limiting factor: muscular endurance long
- Training objectives: muscular endurance long, power endurance, maximum strength

Periodization	May	June	July	Aug.	Sept.	Oct.	Nov.	Dec.	Jan.	Feb.	Mar.	Apr.
	Prep.								Comp.			T
Strength	6 AA	8 MxS	7 MEL	3 MxS	11 Conv. to MEL				13 Maint.: MEL			4 Compens.
Energy systems	O_2 cap.	O_2 cap., O_2 P	O_2 cap., O_2 P, lactic cap.									O_2 cap.

The suggested order of energy systems training also implies training priorities per training phase.

Key: AA = anatomical adaptation, cap. = capacity, comp. = competitive, compens. = compensation, conv. = conversion, maint. = maintenance, MEL = muscle endurance long, MxS = maximum strength, O_2 = aerobic, P = power, prep. = preparation, and T = transition.

Figure 10.27 Periodization Model for Cross-Country and Biathlon Skiing

FIGURE SKATING

In order to complete the required jumps, figure skaters must develop powerful takeoff (concentric) strength and landing (eccentric) strength. They also need strong anaerobic and aerobic energy systems, especially for long programs. For a sample periodization model, see figure 10.28.

- Dominant energy systems: anaerobic lactic, aerobic
- Ergogenesis: 40% alactic, 40% lactic, 20% aerobic
- Main energy substrates: creatine phosphate, glycogen
- Limiting factors: takeoff power, landing power, reactive power, power endurance
- Training objectives: power, power endurance, maximum strength

Periodization	May	June	July	Aug.	Sept.	Oct.	Nov.	Dec.	Jan.	Feb.	Mar.	Apr.
	Prep.							Comp.				T
Strength	8 AA		4 MxS	4 P	4 MxS	4 P	4 MxS	4 PE	10 Maint., P, PE, MxS			6 Compens.
Energy systems	O_2 cap., O_2 P			Lactic cap., O_2 P		Lactic P, O_2 P, alactic P		Lactic P, alactic P, O_2 P				Alternative activies

The aerobic training (O_2) is achieved by performing specific drills, lines, and repetitions. The suggested order of energy systems training also implies training priorities per training phase.

Key: AA = anatomical adaptation, cap. = capacity, comp. = competitive, compens. = compensation, maint. = maintenance, MxS = maximum strength, O_2 = aerobic, P = power, prep. = preparation, and T = transition.

Figure 10.28 Periodization Model for Figure Skating

GOLF

The paramount factors in this popular sport are the golfer's power in hitting the ball off the tee and his or her precision in putting on the green. Good aerobic endurance helps any player cope with the fatigue of the sport and therefore improve concentration and effectiveness, especially during the last holes. For a sample periodization model, see figure 10.29.

- Dominant energy system: anaerobic alactic
- Ergogenesis: 100% anaerobic alactic
- Main energy substrates: creatine phosphate
- Limiting factors: power, mental concentration, aerobic endurance
- Training objectives: power, maximum strength

Periodization	Oct.	Nov.	Dec.	Jan.	Feb.	Mar.	Apr.	May	June	July	Aug.	Sept.
	Prep.						Comp.					T
Strength	6 AA	5 MxS	1 T	8 MxS, P	2 T	4 Conv. to P	20 Maint.: P, MxS					6 Compens.
Energy systems	O$_2$ cap.			O$_2$ P								O$_2$ cap.

Key: AA = anatomical adaptation, cap. = capacity, comp. = competitive, compens. = compensation, conv. = conversion, maint. = maintenance, MxS = maximum strength, O$_2$ = aerobic, P = power, prep. = preparation, and T = transition.

Figure 10.29 Periodization Model for Golf

ROWING

Rowing requires aerobic endurance and the ability to generate powerful strokes against water resistance. The athlete should also develop strong starting power and muscular endurance. For a sample periodization model, see figure 10.30.

- Dominant energy systems: anaerobic lactic, aerobic
- Ergogenesis: 10% alactic, 15% lactic, 75% aerobic
- Main energy substrates: creatine phosphate, glycogen
- Limiting factors: muscular endurance medium and short, starting power
- Training objectives: muscular endurance medium, muscle endurance short, maximum strength

Periodization	Sept.	Oct.	Nov.	Dec.	Jan.	Feb.	Mar.	Apr.	May	June	July	Aug.
	Prep.							Comp.				T
Strength	6 AA	6 MxS		4 MES	4 MxS	4 MEM	4 MxS	6 MEM	10 Maint.: MEM, MES, MxS			4 Compens.
Energy systems	O_2 cap.	O_2 cap., O_2 P		O_2 P, lactic cap., alactic P, O_2 cap.	O_2 P, lactic P, lactic cap., alactic P, O_2 cap.			O_2 P, lactic cap., alactic P, lactic P, O_2 cap.				

The suggested order of energy systems training also implies training priorities per training phase.

Key: AA = anatomical adaptation, cap. = capacity, comp. = competitive, compens. = compensation, maint. = maintenance, MEM = muscular endurance medium, MES = muscular endurance short, MxS = maximum strength, O_2 = aerobic, P = power, prep. = preparation, and T = transition.

Figure 10.30 Periodization Model for Rowing

BASEBALL, SOFTBALL, AND CRICKET

The dominant ability in these three sports is power displayed in the specific drills of batting and pitching, reaction, and high acceleration. Any restriction placed on training during long preparation phases, especially in professional baseball, may reduce the amount of preparation time, and the long competition schedule can lead to fatigue or injury. Since power and acceleration depend greatly on the ability to recruit the highest possible number of fast-twitch muscle fibers, maximum strength is a very important ability in these athletes' quest for success. Maintaining power and maximum strength helps players succeed throughout the season. For a sample periodization model for an elite baseball team, see figure 10.31. For a sample model for an amateur baseball, softball, or cricket team, see figure 10.32.

- Dominant energy system: anaerobic alactic
- Ergogenesis: 95% alactic, 5% lactic
- Main energy substrates: creatine phosphate
- Limiting factors: throwing power, acceleration power, reactive power
- Training objectives: maximum strength, power

Periodization	Dec.	Jan.	Feb.	Mar.	Apr.	May	June	July	Aug.	Sept.	Oct.	Nov.
	Prep.			Precomp.		Comp.						T
Strength	4 AA	10 MxS		6 Conv. to P	26 Maint.: power, MxS							6 Compens.
Energy systems	O$_2$ P, lactic cap.	Alactic P, lactic P short										O$_2$ compens.

The metabolic training represents the cumulative effect of tempo training and specific tactical drills. The suggested order of energy systems training also implies training priorities per training phase. Since the competition phase is very long, detraining of strength may occur; therefore, players must maintain power and maximum strength.

Key: AA = anatomical adaptation, cap. = capacity, comp. = competitive, compens. = compensation, conv. = conversion, maint. = maintenance, MxS = maximum strength, O$_2$ = aerobic, P = power, prep. = preparation, and T = transition.

Figure 10.31 Periodization Model for an Elite Baseball Team

Periodization	Nov.	Dec.	Jan.	Feb.	Mar.	Apr.	May	June	July	Aug.	Sept.	Oct.
	Prep.						Comp.					T
Strength	4 AA	6 MxS	4 P	4 MxS	4 P	4 MxS	4 P	16 Maint.: P, MxS				6 Compens.
Energy systems	O$_2$ P, lactic cap.	Alactic P, lactic P short										O$_2$ compens.

Key: AA = anatomical adaptation, cap. = capacity, comp. = competitive, compens. = compensation, maint. = maintenance, MxS = maximum strength, O$_2$ = aerobic, P = power, prep. = preparation, and T = transition.

Figure 10.32 Periodization Model for an Amateur Baseball or Softball Team

BASKETBALL

Basketball requires players to be strong, agile, and capable of quick acceleration, deceleration, and changes of direction. Proper strength and power training prepares a basketball player for the rigors of the season. For a sample periodization model for a college basketball team, see figure 10.33. For a sample model for an elite basketball team, see figure 10.34.

- Dominant energy systems: anaerobic alactic, anaerobic lactic, aerobic
- Ergogenesis: 60% alactic, 20% lactic, 20% aerobic
- Main energy substrates: creatine phosphate, glycogen
- Limiting factors: takeoff power, acceleration power, power endurance
- Training objectives: maximum strength, power, power endurance

Periodization	July	Aug.	Sept.	Oct.	Nov.	Dec.	Jan.	Feb.	Mar.	Apr.	May	June
	Prep.				Comp.							T
Strength	4 AA	8 MxS		8 Conv. to P	26 Maint.: P, MxS							6 Compens.
Energy systems	O_2 P, lactic cap., alactic P	Lactic cap., alactic P, O_2 P		Lactic P short, alactic P, O_2 P								O_2 compens.

Key: AA = anatomical adaptation, cap. = capacity, comp. = competitive, compens. = compensation, conv. = conversion, maint. = maintenance, MxS = maximum strength, O_2 = aerobic, P = power, prep. = preparation, and T = transition.

Figure 10.33 Periodization Model for a College Basketball Team

Periodization	Aug.	Sept.	Oct.	Nov.	Dec.	Jan.	Feb.	Mar.	Apr.	May	June	July
	Prep.				Comp.							T
Strength	3 AA	8 MxS		7 Conv. to P	28 Maint.: P, MxS							6 Compens.
Energy systems	O_2 P, lactic cap., alactic P	Lactic cap., alactic P, O_2 P		Lactic P short, alactic P, O_2 P								O_2 compens.

Aerobic training (O_2) represents the cumulative effect of tempo running during the anatomical adaptation phase and the specific drills for O_2 training during the other training phases (two to five minutes nonstop). The suggested order of energy systems training also implies training priorities per training phase.

Key: AA = anatomical adaptation, cap. = capacity, comp. = competitive, compens. = compensation, conv. = conversion, maint. = maintenance, MxS = maximum strength, O_2 = aerobic, P = power, prep. = preparation, and T = transition.

Figure 10.34 Periodization Model for an Elite Basketball Team

WATER POLO

Water polo requires high energy expenditure, using the aerobic system, interspersed with fast acceleration and powerful shooting actions. Passing and shooting precision are essential skills to learn during the many hours of training. For a sample periodization model, see figure 10.35.

- Dominant energy systems: anaerobic lactic, aerobic
- Ergogenesis: 10% alactic, 30% lactic, 60% aerobic
- Main energy substrate: glycogen
- Limiting factors: muscular endurance medium, power endurance, acceleration power, shooting power
- Training objectives: muscular endurance medium, power endurance, maximum strength

Periodization	Aug.	Sept.	Oct.	Nov.	Dec.	Jan.	Feb.	Mar.	Apr.	May	June	July
	Prep.							Comp.			T	
Strength	4 AA	8 MxS		6 PE	4 MxS	6 Conv. to MEM		16 Maint.: MEM, MxS, PE			8 Compens.	
Energy systems	O_2 cap., O_2 P	O_2 P, lactic cap., alactic P, O_2 cap.			O_2 P, lactic P, alactic P, O_2 cap.		O_2 P, lactic cap., alactic P				O_2 cap.	

O_2 training implies also using tactical drills of longer duration (two to four minutes).

Key: AA = anatomical adaptation, cap. = capacity, comp. = competitive, compens. = compensation, conv. = conversion, maint. = maintenance, MEM = muscular endurance medium, MxS = maximum strength, O_2 = aerobic, P = power, PE = power endurance, prep. = preparation, and T = transition.

Figure 10.35 Periodization Model for a National League Water Polo Team

AMERICAN FOOTBALL: LINEMEN

Linemen must be able to react explosively when the ball is put into play. They must also withstand an opponent's strength. Therefore, in order to build bulk, a hypertrophy phase is included. For a sample periodization model for college football linemen, see figure 10.36. For a sample model for elite football linemen, see figure 10.37.

- Dominant energy systems: anaerobic alactic, anaerobic lactic
- Ergogenesis: 70% alactic, 30% lactic
- Main energy substrates: creatine phosphate, glycogen
- Limiting factors: starting power, maximum strength
- Training objectives: maximum strength, hypertrophy, power

Periodization	Mar.	Apr.	May	June	July	Aug.	Sept.	Oct.	Nov.	Dec.	Jan.	Feb.
	Prep.						Comp.				T	
Strength	4 AA	6 Hyp.		9 MxS		6 Conv. to P	20 Maint.: MxS, P				7 Compens.	
Energy systems	Lactic cap., alactic P	Alactic P, lactic cap.	Alactic P, lactic P short								O_2 P, alactic P	

Key: AA = anatomical adaptation, cap. = capacity, comp. = competitive, compens. = compensation, conv. = conversion, hyp. = hypertrophy, maint. = maintenance, MxS = maximum strength, P = power, prep. = preparation, and T = transition.

Figure 10.36 Periodization Model for College Football Linemen

Periodization	Apr.	May	June	July	Aug.	Sept.	Oct.	Nov.	Dec.	Jan.	Feb.	Mar.
	Prep.				Comp.							T
Strength	2 AA	10 Hyp.		6 MxS	4 Conv. to P	22 Maint.: MxS, P						6 Compens.
Energy systems	Lactic cap., alactic P		Alactic P, lactic P short									O_2 P, alactic P

Key: AA = anatomical adaptation, cap. = capacity, comp. = competitive, compens. = compensation, conv. = conversion, hyp. = hypertrophy, maint. = maintenance, MxS = maximum strength, P = power, prep. = preparation, and T = transition.

Figure 10.37 Periodization Model for Elite Football Linemen

AMERICAN FOOTBALL: WIDE RECEIVERS, DEFENSIVE BACKS, TAILBACKS

Unlike linemen, these players require speed and agility rather than muscular bulk. For a sample periodization model for college football wide receivers, defensive backs, and tailbacks, see figure 10.38. For a sample model for players at these positions in professional football, see figure 10.39.

- Dominant energy systems: anaerobic alactic, anaerobic lactic
- Ergogenesis: 60% alactic, 30 % lactic, 10% aerobic
- Main energy substrates: creatine phosphate, glycogen
- Limiting factors: acceleration power, reactive power, starting power
- Training objectives: power, maximum strength

Periodization	Mar.	Apr.		May	June	July	Aug.	Sept.	Oct.	Nov.	Dec.	Jan.	Feb.
	Prep.							Comp.					T
Strength	4 AA	4 MxS	3 P	3 MxS	3 P	3 MxS	4 P	22 Maint.: P, MxS					6 Com- pens.
Energy systems	O_2 P, lactic cap., alactic P	Lactic cap., alactic P, O_2 P		Lactic P, alactic P, O_2 P				Alactic P, lactic P					O_2 P, alactic P

Key: AA = anatomical adaptation, cap. = capacity, comp. = competitive, compens. = compensation, maint. = maintenance, MxS = maximum strength, O_2 = aerobic, P = power, prep. = preparation, and T = transition.

Figure 10.38 Periodization Model for College Football Wide Receivers, Defensive Backs, and Tailbacks

Periodization	Apr.	May	June	July			Aug.	Sept.	Oct.	Nov.	Dec.	Jan.	Feb.	Mar.
	Prep.							Comp.						T
Period. of strength	2 AA	6 MxS	3 P	3 MxS	3 P	3 MxS	4 Conv. to P	22 Maint.: P						6 Com- pens.
Period. of energy systems	O_2 P, lactic cap., alac-tic P	Lactic cap., alactic P, O_2 P	Lactic P, alactic P, O_2 power					Alactic P, lactic P						O_2 P, alactic P

Key: AA = anatomical adaptation, cap. = capacity, comp. = competitive, compens. = compensation, conv. = conversion, maint. = maintenance, MxS = maximum strength, O_2 = aerobic, P = power, prep. = preparation, and T = transition.

Figure 10.39 Periodization Model for Pro Football Wide receivers, Defensive Backs, and Tailbacks

SOCCER

The most popular sport in the world is a game of great technical and physical demands, in which the result is determined by power, speed, agility, and specific endurance. The accompanying figures provide sample periodization models for an amateur American soccer team (figure 10.40), a professional American soccer team (figure 10.41), a European season for an amateur soccer team (figure 10.42), a European season for a professional soccer team (figure 10.43), and a European season for a goalkeeper (figure 10.44).

- Dominant energy systems: aerobic, anaerobic lactic, anaerobic alactic
- Ergogenesis: alactic 2%, lactic 23%, aerobic 75%
- Main energy substrates: creatine phosphate, glycogen
- Limiting factors: power, starting power, power endurance short, acceleration power, deceleration power, reactive power
- Training objectives: power, maximum strength

Periodization	Oct.	Nov.	Dec.	Jan.	Feb.	Mar.	Apr.	May	June	July	Aug.	Sept.
	Prep.						Comp.				T	
Strength	4 AA	8 MxS		4 P, MxS	2 T	6 Conv. to P	20 Maint.: P, MxS				8 Compens.	
Energy systems	O_2 cap., O_2 P	O_2 P, alactic P		O_2 P, alactic P, lactic P short	O_2 P	Alactic P, lactic P short, O_2 P					Compens.	

The energy systems can be trained via tempo training, interval training, or repetition training, as well as by means of specific drills and short-sided matches. The order of energy systems listed for each phase also represents the priority of training in that training phase.

Key: AA = anatomical adaptation, cap. = capacity, comp. = competitive, compens. = compensation, conv. = conversion, maint. = maintenance, MxS = maximum strength, O_2 = aerobic, P = power, prep. = preparation, and T = transition.

Figure 10.40 Periodization Model for an Amateur Soccer Team

Periodization	Aug.	Sept.	Oct.	Nov.	Dec.	Jan.	Feb.	Mar.	Apr.	May	June	July
	Prep.		Comp. I			T	Comp. II					T
Strength	2 AA	6 MxS, P	12 Maint.: P, MxS			2 T	20 Maint.: P, MxS				6 Compens.	
Energy systems	O_2 cap., O_2 P	O_2 P, alactic P, lactic P short, O_2 compens.	Alactic P, lactic P short, O_2 P, O_2 compens.			O_2 P	Alactic P, lactic P short, O_2 P, O_2 compens.				O_2 cap.	

Key: AA = anatomical adaptation, cap. = capacity, comp. = competitive, compens. = compensation, maint. = maintenance, MxS = maximum strength, O_2 = aerobic, P = power, prep. = preparation, and T = transition.

Figure 10.41 Periodization Model for a Professional Soccer Team

Periodization	Aug.	Sept.	Oct.	Nov.	Dec.	Jan.	Feb.	Mar.	Apr.	May	June	July
	Prep. I		Comp. I		T	Prep. II	Comp. II					T
Strength	2 AA	4 MxS, P	13 Maint.: P, MxS,		1 Cess.	3 MxS, P	19 Maint.: P, MxS					10 Compens.
Energy systems	O₂ cap., O₂ P	O₂ P, alactic P, lactic P short, O₂ compens.	Alactic P, lactic P short, O₂ P, O₂ compens.		Cess.	Alactic P, lactic P short, O₂ P, O₂ compens.						Games, O₂ cap.

Key: AA = anatomical adaptation, cap. = capacity, cess. = cessation, comp. = competitive, compens. = compensation, maint. = maintenance, MxS = maximum strength, O₂ = aerobic, P = power, prep. = preparation, and T = transition.

Figure 10.42 Periodization Model for an Amateur Soccer Team (European Season)

Periodization	July	Aug.	Sept.	Oct.	Nov.	Dec.	Jan.	Feb.	Mar.	Apr.	May	June
	Prep. I		Comp. I		T	Prep. II	Comp. II					T
Strength	2 AA	6 MxS, P	15 Maint.: P, MxS		1 Cess.	3 MxS, P	19 Maint.: P, MxS					6 Compens.
Energy systems	O₂ cap., O₂ P	O₂ P, alactic P, lactic P short, O₂ compens.	Alactic P, lactic P short, O₂ P, O₂ compens.		Cess.	Alactic P, lactic P short, O₂ P, O₂ compens.						O₂ cap.

Key: AA = anatomical adaptation, cap. = capacity, cess. = cessation, comp. = competitive, compens. = compensation, maint. = maintenance, MxS = maximum strength, O₂ = aerobic, P = power, prep. = preparation, and T = transition.

Figure 10.43 Periodization Model for a Professional Soccer Team (European Season)

Periodization	Aug.	Sept.	Oct.	Nov.	Dec.	Jan.	Feb.	Mar.	Apr.	May	June	July
	Prep. I	Comp. I			T	Prep. II	Comp. II					T
Strength	2 AA	6 MxS, P	15 Maint.: P, MxS		1 Cess.	3 MxS, P	19 Maint.: P, MxS					6 Compens.
Energy systems	Alactic P, O₂ compens.				Cess.	Alactic P, O₂ compens.						Games, O₂ cap.

Key: AA = anatomical adaptation, cap. = capacity, cess. = cessation, comp. = competitive, compens. = compensation, maint. = maintenance, MxS = maximum strength, O₂ = aerobic, P = power, prep. = preparation, and T = transition.

Figure 10.44 Periodization Model for a Soccer Goalkeeper (European Season)

RUGBY

Rugby is a game of high energy, power, and intricate skills performed in rhythm. For a sample periodization model for an amateur rugby team, see figure 10.45. For a sample model for a professional rugby team, see figure 10.46.

- Dominant energy systems: anaerobic alactic, lactic, aerobic
- Ergogenesis: 10% alactic, 30% lactic, 60% aerobic
- Main energy substrates: creatine phosphate, glycogen
- Limiting factors: power, power endurance, acceleration power
- Training objectives: power, maximum strength

Periodization	Sept.	Oct.	Nov.	Dec.	Jan.	Feb.	Mar.	Apr.	May	June	July	Aug.
	Prep.						Comp.				T	
Strength	4 AA	12 MxS			8 Conv. to P		20 Maint.: P, MxS				8 Compens.	
Energy systems	O_2 cap., O_2 P	O_2 P, alactic P, lactic P short, O_2 compens.			Alactic P, lactic P short, O_2 P, O_2 compens.						O_2 cap.	

O_2 training refers mostly to performing specific tactical drills of longer duration (three to five minutes nonstop). The suggested order of energy systems training also implies training priorities for each training phase. Power endurance is also trained performing lactic power short drills.

Key: AA = anatomical adaptation, cap. = capacity, comp. = competitive, compens. = compensation, conv. = conversion, maint. = maintenance, MxS = maximum strength, O_2 = aerobic, P = power, prep. = preparation, and T = transition.

Figure 10.45 Periodization Model for an Amateur Rugby Team

Periodization	July	Aug.	Sept.	Oct.	Nov.	Dec.	Jan.	Feb.	Mar.	Apr.	May	June
	Prep.			Comp.							T	
Strength	3 AA	8 MxS		4 Conv. to P	31 Maintain.: P, MxS						6 Compens.	
Energy systems	O_2 cap., O_2 P	O_2 P, alactic P, lactic P short, O_2 compens.		Alactic P, lactic P short, O_2 P, O_2 compens.							O_2 cap.	

Key: AA = anatomical adaptation, cap. = capacity, comp. = competitive, compens. = compensation, conv. = conversion, maint. = maintenance, MxS = maximum strength, O_2 = aerobic, P = power, prep. = preparation, and T = transition.

Figure 10.46 Periodization Model for a Professional Rugby Team

HOCKEY

Important elements in this sport include acceleration and quick changes of direction. Training should focus on refining skills and developing power and both aerobic and anaerobic endurance. For a sample periodization model, see figure 10.47.

- Dominant energy systems: anaerobic lactic, aerobic
- Ergogenesis: 10% alactic, 40% lactic, 50% aerobic
- Main energy substrates: creatine phosphate, glycogen
- Limiting factors: acceleration power, deceleration power, power endurance
- Training objectives: maximum strength, power, power endurance

Periodization	June	July	Aug.	Sept.	Oct.	Nov.	Dec.	Jan.	Feb.	Mar.	Apr.	May
	Prep.				Comp.							T
Strength	4 AA	6 MxS	4 P	4 MxS	4 Conv. to PE	24 Maintenance: P, PE, MxS						6 Compens.
Energy systems	O_2 cap., O_2 P, alactic P	Lactic cap., O_2 P, alactic P		Alactic and lactic P short, O_2 P								O_2 cap.

Key: AA = anatomical adaptation, cap. = capacity, comp. = competitive, compens. = compensation, conv. = conversion, maint. = maintenance, MxS = maximum strength, O_2 = aerobic, P = power, PE = power endurance, prep. = preparation, and T = transition.

Figure 10.47 Periodization Model for Ice Hockey

VOLLEYBALL

A volleyball player must react quickly and explosively off the ground in order to spike, block, or dive. Maximum strength and power are required for carrying a player through the long competitive phase with stable performance and confidence. For a sample periodization model for American college volleyball, see figure 10.48. For a sample model for a European season, see figure 10.49.

- Dominant energy systems: anaerobic alactic, anaerobic lactic
- Ergogenesis: 70% alactic, 20% lactic, 10% aerobic
- Main energy substrates: creatine phosphate, glycogen
- Limiting factors: reactive power, takeoff power, power
- Training objectives: power, maximum strength

Periodization	June	July	Aug.	Sept.	Oct.	Nov.	Dec.	Jan.	Feb.	Mar.	Apr.	May
	Prep.					Comp.					T	
Strength	4 AA	6 MxS	4 P	4 MxS	4 P	22 Maint.: MxS, P					8 Compens.	
Energy systems	O_2 P, alactic P, lactic P short	Alactic P, lactic P short									Alternative activities (e.g., beach volleyball)	

The suggested order of energy systems training also implies training priorities per training phase.

Key: AA = anatomical adaptation, cap. = capacity, comp. = competitive, compens. = compensation, maint. = maintenance, MxS = maximum strength, O_2 = aerobic, P = power, prep. = preparation, and T = transition.

Figure 10.48 Periodization Model for Volleyball (American Season)

Periodization	Aug.	Sept.	Oct.	Nov.	Dec.	Jan.	Feb.	Mar.	Apr.	May	June	July
	Prep.			Comp.	T	Comp				T		
Strength	2 AA	4 MxS	4 Conv. to P	9 Maint.: MxS, P	2 AA	21 Maint.: MxS, P				10 Compens.		
Energy systems	O_2 P, alac-tic P, lactic P short	Alactic P, lactic P short								Alternative activies (e.g., beach volleyball)		

The suggested order of energy systems training also implies training priorities per training phase.

Key: AA = anatomical adaptation, cap. = capacity, comp. = competitive, compens. = compensation, conv. = conversion, maint. = maintenance, MxS = maximum strength, O_2 = aerobic, P = power, prep. = preparation, and T = transition.

Figure 10.49 Periodization Model for Volleyball (European Season)

BOXING

Boxers must be able to attack and react quickly and powerfully to an opponent's attack throughout the duration of the match. They require both aerobic and anaerobic energy. For a sample periodization model, see figure 10.50.

- Dominant energy systems: anaerobic lactic, aerobic
- Ergogenesis: 10% alactic, 40% lactic, 50% aerobic
- Main energy substrates: creatine phosphate, glycogen
- Limiting factors: power endurance, reactive power, muscular endurance medium
- Training objectives: power endurance, maximum strength, muscular endurance medium

Period-ization	Sept.	Oct.	Nov.	Dec.		Jan.	Feb.	Mar.	Apr.		May	June	July	Aug.
	Prep. I		Specific prep. I	Match	T	Prep. II	Specific prep. II	Match	T	Prep. III	Specific prep. III		Match	T
Strength	3 AA	6 MxS, P	3 Conv. to MEM	2 Maint.: MEM, MxS	2 AA	4 MxS, P	4 Conv. to MEM	4 Maint.: MEM, MxS	2 AA	3 MxS, P	3 Conv. to MEM	8 Maint.: MEM, MxS		Compens.
Energy systems	O_2 cap.	O_2 P, alactic P, lactic cap.	Lactic cap., O_2 P, alactic P		O_2 cap.	O_2 P, alactic P, lactic cap.	Lactic cap., O_2 P, alactic P		O_2 cap.	O_2 P, alactic P, lactic cap.	Lactic cap., O_2 P, alactic P			O_2 compens.

Maximum strength training is performed at 70 percent to 80 percent of 1RM for two of the three phases and 80 to 90 percent for the third phase. For heavyweights, use loads of 80 percent to 90 percent of 1RM for the second and third phases. Aerobic (O_2) training should include specific boxing drills performed nonstop for two to five minutes. The suggested order of energy systems training also implies training priorities for each training phase.

Key: AA = anatomical adaptation, cap. = capacity, compens. = compensation, conv. = conversion, maint. = maintenance, MEM = muscular endurance medium, MxS = maximum strength, O_2 = aerobic, P = power, prep. = preparation, and T = transition.

Figure 10.50 Periodization Model for Boxing

RACKET SPORTS: TENNIS, RACQUETBALL, SQUASH, AND BADMINTON

Racket sports involve fast and reactive play in which success is determined by reaction time and quick, precise changes of direction. For a sample periodization model for an amateur tennis player, see figure 10.51. For a sample model for a professional player, see figure 10.52. For a sample model for racquetball, squash, and badminton, see figure 10.53.

- Dominant energy systems: alactic, aerobic, anaerobic lactic
- Ergogenesis: tennis—50% alactic, 20% lactic, 30% aerobic; squash—40% alactic, 20% lactic, 40% aerobic; badminton—60% alactic, 20% lactic, 20% aerobic
- Main energy substrates: creatine phosphate, glycogen
- Limiting factors: power, reactive power, power endurance
- Training objectives: power, power endurance, maximum strength

Periodization	Oct.	Nov.	Dec.	Jan.	Feb.	Mar.	Apr.	May	June	July	Aug.	Sept.
	Prep.					Comp.					T	
Strength	6 AA	8 MxS, P		6 Conv. to PE		24 Maint.: P, PE, MxS					8 Compens.	
Energy systems	O_2 P, lactic cap.	Lactic cap., alactic P, O_2 P		Alactic P, lactic P short, O_2 P							O_2 compens.	

Key: AA = anatomical adaptation, cap. = capacity, comp. = competitive, compens. = compensation, conv. = conversion, maint. = maintenance, MxS = maximum strength, O_2 = aerobic, P = power, PE = power endurance, prep. = preparation, and T = transition.

Figure 10.51 Periodization Model for an Amateur Tennis Player

Period-ization	1	2	3	4	5	6	7	8	9	10	11	12	
	Prep. I		Comp. I	T	Prep. II	Comp. II	T	Prep. III	Comp. III	T	Prep. IV	Comp. IV	T
Strength	4 AA	6 MxS, PE	4 Maint.: PE, MxS	2 AA	4 MxS, PE	4 Maint.: PE, MxS	2 AA	6 MxS, PE	4 Maint.: PE, MxS	2 AA	4 MxS, PE	4 Maint.: PE, MxS	6 Compens.
Energy systems	O_2 P, lactic cap.	Lactic cap., alactic P, O_2 P	Alactic P, lactic P short, O_2 P	O_2 P, lactic cap.	Lactic cap., alactic P, O_2 P	Alactic P, lactic P short, O_2 P	O_2 P, lactic cap.	Lactic capacity, alactic P, O_2 P	Alactic P, lactic P short, O_2 P	O_2 P, lactic cap.	Lactic cap., alactic P, O_2 P	Alactic P, lactic P short, O_2 P	O_2 cap.

This model assumes a program with four major tournaments. Since dates for major tournaments vary, the months of the year are numbered rather than named. Aerobic (O_2) training means specific drills of longer duration performed nonstop (three to five minutes). The suggested order of energy systems training also implies the priority of training for each training phase.

Key: AA = anatomical adaptation, cap. = capacity, comp. = competitive, compens. = compensation, maint. = maintenance, MxS = maximum strength, O_2 = aerobic, P = power, prep. = preparation, and T = transition.

Figure 10.52 Periodization Model for a Professional Tennis Player

Periodization	1	2	3	4	5	6	7	8	9	10	11	12	
	Prep. I			Comp. I	T	Prep. II		Comp. II	T	Prep. III		Comp. III	T
Strength	3 AA	6 MxS	3 PE	4 Maint.: P, MxS	2 AA	6 MxS	4 PE	4 Maint.: PE, MxS	2 AA	3 MxS	3 PE	4 Maint.: PE, MxS	8 Compens.
Energy systems	O_2 P, lactic cap.	Lactic cap., alactic P, O_2 P		Alactic P, lactic P short, O_2 P	O_2 P, lactic cap.	Lactic cap., alactic P, O_2 P		Alactic P, lactic P short, O_2 P	O_2 P, lactic cap.	Lactic cap., alactic P, O_2 P		Alactic P, lactic P short, O_2 P	O_2 compens.

Because competition dates vary by geographical region, months are numbered rather than named. This model is a tri-cycle. The order of energy systems training also represents the priority of training in a given phase. Aerobic training (O_2) can be done via tempo training and by performing specific drills.

Key: AA = anatomical adaptation, cap. = capacity, comp. = competitive, compens. = compensation, maint. = maintenance, MxS = maximum strength, O_2 = aerobic, P = power, prep. = preparation, and T = transition.

Figure 10.53 Periodization Model for Racquetball, Squash, and Badminton

MARTIAL ARTS

Martial artists need flexibility, power, agility, and quick reflexes based on energy supplied by all three energy systems. Figure 10.54 shows a sample periodization model for martial arts without a considerable endurance component. Figure 10.55 shows a sample for martial arts *with* a considerable endurance component.

- Dominant energy systems: anaerobic alactic, anaerobic lactic, aerobic
- Ergogenesis: 50% alactic, 30% lactic, 20% aerobic
- Main energy substrates: creatine phosphate, glycogen
- Limiting factors: starting power, power endurance, reactive power, muscular endurance short
- Training objectives: power, maximum strength, power endurance, muscular endurance short

Periodization	June	July	Aug.	Sept.	Oct.	Nov.	Dec.	Jan.		Feb.	Mar.	Apr.	May
	Prep. I						Comp. I	T	Prep. II			Comp. II	T
Strength	4 AA	12 MxS			8 Conv. to P		4 Maint.: P, MxS	2 AA	8 MxS		4 Conv. to P	4 Maint.: P, MxS	6 Compens.
Energy systems	O_2 cap.	O_2 P, lactic cap., alactic P			Alactic P, lactic P, O_2 P			O_2 cap.	O_2 P, lactic cap., alactic P		Alactic P, lactic P, O_2 P		Alternative activities

Metabolic training can be done via specific drills. The suggested order of energy systems training also implies training priority for each training phase.

Key: AA = anatomical adaptation, cap. = capacity, comp. = competitive, compens. = compensation, conv. = conversion, maint. = maintenance, MxS = maximum strength, O_2 = aerobic, P = power, prep. = preparation, and T = transition.

Figure 10.54 Periodization Model for Martial Arts Without a Considerable Endurance Component

Periodization	June	July	Aug.	Sept.	Oct.	Nov.	Dec.	Jan.		Feb.	Mar.	Apr.	May
	Prep. I						Comp. I	T	Prep. II			Comp. II	T
Strength	4 AA	8 MxS	4 P	4 MxS	6 Conv. to MEM	3 Maint.: MEM, MxS		2 AA	8 MxS		4 Conv. to MEM	3 Maint.: MEM, MxS	6 Compens.
Energy systems	O_2 cap.	O_2 P, lactic cap., alactic P			O_2 P, alactic P, lactic P			O_2 cap.	O_2 P, lactic cap., alactic P		O_2 P, alactic P, lactic P		Alternative activities

Metabolic training can be done via specific drills. The suggested order of energy systems training also implies training priority for each training phase.

Key: AA = anatomical adaptation, cap. = capacity, comp. = competitive, compens. = compensation, conv. = conversion, maint. = maintenance, MEM = muscular endurance medium, MxS = maximum strength, O_2 = aerobic, P = power, prep. = preparation, and T = transition.

Figure 10.55 Periodization Model for Martial Arts With a Considerable Endurance Component

WRESTLING

A wrestler's success is determined by technique and tactical skills, as well as power, power endurance, and flexibility. For a sample periodization model, see figure 10.56.

- Dominant energy systems: anaerobic alactic, anaerobic lactic, aerobic
- Ergogenesis: 30% alactic, 30% lactic, 40% aerobic
- Main energy substrates: creatine phosphate, glycogen
- Limiting factors: power, power endurance, flexibility
- Training objectives: power, power endurance, maximum strength, muscular endurance short

Periodization	1	2	3	4	5	6	7	8	9	10	11	12
	Prep. I			Comp. I		T	Prep. II		Comp. II		T	
Strength	4 AA	10 MxS, P, PE		8 Maint.: P, PE, MxS		2 Compens.	4 AA	6 MxS, P, MES	10 Maint.: P, MES, MxS		8 Compens.	
Energy systems	O_2 cap.	O_2 P, lactic cap., alactic P		O_2 P, alactic P, lactic P		O_2 cap.	O_2 cap.	O_2 P, lactic cap., alactic P	O_2 P, alactic P, lactic P		O_2 compens.	

This is a bi-cycle geared to national championships and an international competition. Aerobic (O_2) training can be achieved via sport-specific drills of longer duration (two to three minutes). The suggested order of energy systems training also implies training priorities for each training phase.

Key: AA = anatomical adaptation, cap. = capacity, comp. = competitive, compens. = compensation, maint. = maintenance, MES = muscular endurance short, MxS = maximum strength, O_2 = aerobic, P = power, PE = power endurance, prep. = preparation, and T = transition.

Figure 10.56 Periodization Model for Wrestling

Periodization of Loading Pattern per Training Phase

Loading patterns in training are not standard or rigid. Just as they vary according to the sport or level of performance, they also change according to the type of strength sought in a given training phase. To make this concept easier to understand and implement, figures 10.57 through 10.63 show how it is applied in several sports. The examples illustrate the dynamics of loading pattern per training phase for a monocycle in amateur baseball, softball, or cricket (figure 10.57), for college basketball (figure 10.58), for American college football linemen (figure 10.59), for an endurance-dominant sport such as canoeing (figure 10.60), and for bi-cycles for sprinting in track and field (figure 10.61), and sprint and long-distance swimming (figures 10.62 and 10.63).

The charts indicate (from top to bottom) the number of weeks planned for a particular training phase, the type of training sought in that phase, and the loading pattern (high, medium, or low). Even if your chosen sport is not addressed in the examples, you will be able to apply the concept to your own case once you understand it. In addition, the examples are so varied that they are applicable through association.

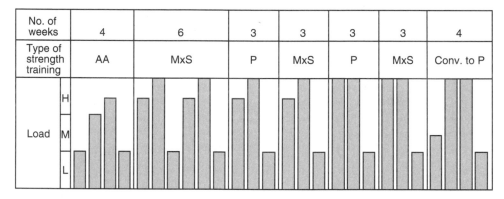

Figure 10.57 Variations of loading pattern for strength training phases for an amateur baseball, softball, or cricket team. To maximize the level of power development, the last three macrocycles involve two adjacent high loads followed by regeneration cycles (low loads).

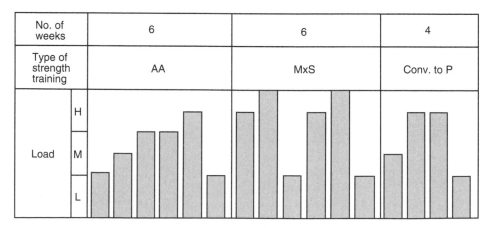

Figure 10.58 Suggested loading pattern for a college basketball team in which the preparation phase must be performed from early July through late October.

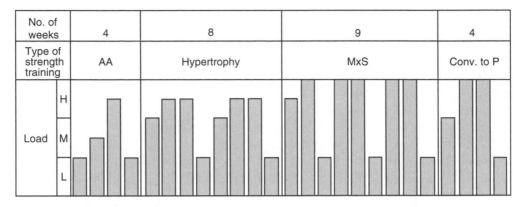

Figure 10.59 Variations of loading pattern for periodization of strength in American college football linemen. A similar approach can be used with throwers in track and field and for the heavyweight category in wrestling.

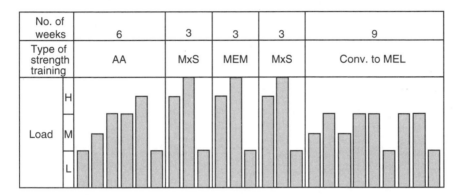

Figure 10.60 Variations of loading pattern for marathon canoeing, in which muscular endurance long is the dominant ability. A similar approach can be used for cycling, Nordic skiing, triathlon, and rowing.

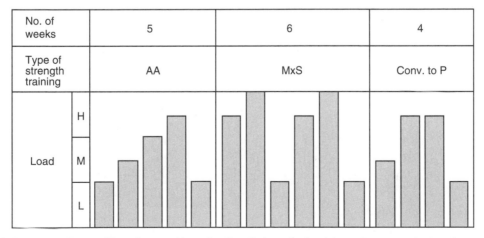

Figure 10.61 Variations of loading pattern for the first part of a bi-cycle annual plan for sprinting in track and field.

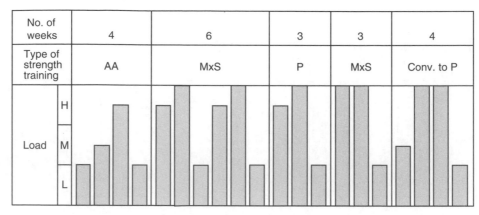

No. of weeks		4	6	3	3	4
Type of strength training		AA	MxS	P	MxS	Conv. to P

Figure 10.62 Variations of loading pattern for a sprinter in swimming (first part of a bi-cycle annual plan). Training demand for the last two phases is high, since the load is high for two adjacent weeks.

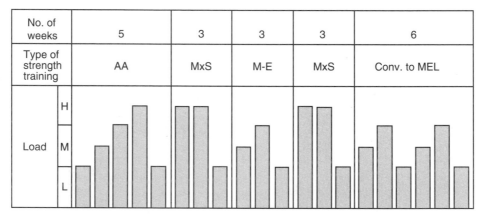

No. of weeks		5	3	3	3	6
Type of strength training		AA	MxS	M-E	MxS	Conv. to MEL

Figure 10.63 Variations of loading pattern for a long-distance swimming event. The load for maximum strength should not exceed 80 percent of 1RM. Similarly, the load for muscular endurance is low (30 percent to 40 percent), but the number of repetitions is very high (see training parameters for the MEL in chapter 14).

Periodization Effects on the Force–Time Curve

In chapter 2, we analyze the force–time curve and pointed out the various components of strength it depicts. We also show how different loads affect the neuromuscular system's adaptations and explain how an athlete needs to train the nervous system to display the highest amount of force in the shortest amount of time. Because of the influence of bodybuilding, strength training programs often include a high number of reps (12 to 15) performed to exhaustion. Such programs mainly develop muscle size, not quickness of contraction. As illustrated in figure 10.64, the application of force in sports is performed very quickly—specifically, in a period lasting from a bit less than 100 milliseconds to 200 milliseconds. The only type of strength that stimulates the highest development of such quick application of force is a sequential application of maximum strength training and power training (Verkhishansky 1997).

However, the opposite is true if training employs a variant of bodybuilding work. In that case, the repetitions per set are higher than for maximum strength and power training, so the force application takes longer (more than 250 milliseconds). Therefore, it is not specific to the needs of most sports. Because the application of force in sports is usually very fast, the main purpose of strength training for sports is to shift the force–time curve to the left—or as close as possible to the typical sport-specific time of force application (less than 200 milliseconds)—through the use of maximum strength and power training applied sequentially. See figure 10.65.

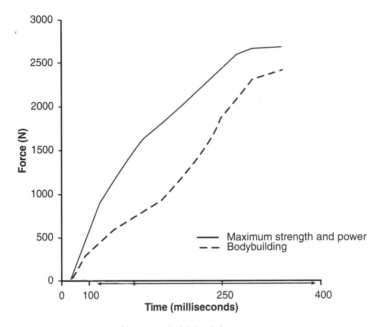

Figure 10.64 The force–time curve of two weight training programs.

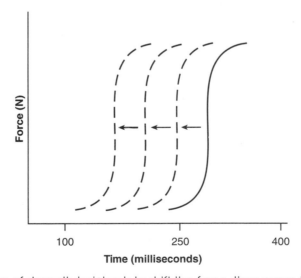

Figure 10.65 The purpose of strength training is to shift the force–time curve to the left.

This shift toward the sport-specific time of application of force is not achieved quickly. Indeed, the whole point of periodization of strength is to use phase-specific strength training to shift the force–time curve to the left—that is, to decrease execution time—before the start of major a competition. This is when athletes need the quick application of strength and when they benefit from gains in power.

As explained earlier, each training phase of the periodization of strength focuses on certain objectives. By plotting the force–time curve for each training phase, both coaches and athletes can see from another angle how the curve is influenced by training. Figure 10.66 shows the periodization of strength when a hypertrophy phase is included. Certainly, only athletes in some sports use this model, whereas those in many other sports exclude hypertrophy from the annual plan.

As figure 10.66 shows, the type of program performed during the anatomical adaptation phase has little effect on the force–time curve. At most, it may shift it slightly to the right (i.e., increase execution time). Typical hypertrophy training methods make the curve shift to the right because each set is performed to exhaustion, and thus the power output of per rep gets lower and lower. Therefore, the resulting gains in muscle size do not translate into gains in the fast application of strength.

In contrast, the use of heavy loads from the maximum strength phase onward results in explosiveness during the conversion of maximum strength to power, thus shifting the curve to the left as desired. As this type of strength training is continued during the maintenance phase, the curve should remain to the left.

A high level of power, or explosiveness, cannot be expected before the start of the competitive phase. Power is maximized only as a result of implementing the conversion phase; therefore, a high level of power should not be expected during the hypertrophy phase or even during the maximum strength phase. However, gains in maximum strength are vital if increments in power are expected from year to year, because power is a function of maximum strength. Periodization of strength, then, offers the best road to success for both muscular endurance and power development.

Preparatory				Competitive
AA	Hypertrophy	MxS	Conv. to P	Maintenance
100 250 400	100 250 400	100 250 400	100 250	100 250
Remains unchanged	Shifts to the right	Shifts to the left	Shifts to the left	Remains shifted to the left

Figure 10.66 Influence of the specifics of training for each phase on the force–time curve.

Part
III

Periodization of Strength

Phase 1: Anatomical Adaptation

11

All athletes involved in competitive sports follow a yearly program intended to enable peak performance in major competition. Peak performance requires athletes to build a proper physiological foundation, and one key factor in doing so is strength training. Therefore, strength training is an essential element in a coach's quest to produce good athletes.

General athletic training must be planned and periodized in a way that ensures performance improvement from phase to phase and enables peak performance during the competitive season. The same is true of strength training. Like general athletic ability and skill, strength can be refined through various methods and phases of training to create the desired final product: sport-specific strength.

As illustrated in table 10.3, strength training should be performed throughout the annual plan according to the concept of periodization of strength. As explained in more detail elsewhere in this book, each sport requires a certain combination of types of strength, which provides the key part of the physiological basis for performance. Athletes can transform strength into a sport-specific quality by applying the periodization of strength and by using training methods specific to the needs of each strength training phase. Thus, an athlete's training methods must change as the training phase changes.

This chapter and the next four discuss all available training methods as they relate to the periodization of strength. Each training phase is treated separately in order to show which method best suits a particular phase and the needs of athletes. The discussions also address positive and negative aspects of most methods and how to apply them, as well as training programs using particular methods.

Circuit Training and the Anatomical Adaptation Phase

During the early stages of strength training, especially with entry-level athletes, almost any strength training method or program results in strength development to some degree. As the athlete develops a strength foundation, however, the coach should create a specific, periodized strength training program to maximize the athlete's natural abilities. Coaches must bear in mind the fact that each athlete possesses a unique rate of adaptation to a given method—and therefore a different rate of improvement.

Strength training is a long-term proposition. Athletes reach their highest performance level not after four to six weeks of a strength training program but rather during the competitive phase, which comes months after the anatomical adaptation (AA) phase. The goal of the AA phase is to progressively adapt the muscles, and especially their attachments to bone (tendons), so that they can cope more easily with the heavier loads used in the ensuing training phases. As a result, the overall training load must be increased without causing the athlete to experience much discomfort.

The simplest method to consider for anatomical adaptation is circuit training, mainly because it provides an organized structure and alternates muscle groups. Circuit training can be used not only to develop the foundation of strength for future training phases but also to develop nonspecific cardiorespiratory endurance by combining strength and endurance training.

Some authors suggest that combining aerobic endurance with strength training during the same phase may seriously compromise the development of maximum strength and power. Their claim is that strength training is incompatible with long-distance aerobic training because fast-twitch fibers may adapt to behave like slow-twitch fibers. These studies scientifically validate the theory that adaptation in speed and power sports is negatively affected by combining a long duration and slow aerobic activity (one hour or longer) with maximum strength or hypertrophy training on the same day. Short-term adaptation suffers.

However, athletes in sports for which both strength and aerobic endurance are equally important (e.g., soccer, rowing, kayaking, canoeing, and cross-country skiing) have no choice but to train both during the preparatory phase. In addition, the argument against such combined training is based mostly on research that was conducted for just a few weeks, whereas training is a long-term endeavor. Has the full adaptation to such training actually occurred? Indeed, some research suggests the opposite—that a certain compatibility exists between strength and endurance training performed at the same time (see chapter 1). In fact, as shown by the following examples, the type of endurance training suggested in this text for the AA phase differs considerably from long and slow-duration activities.

Circuit training was first proposed by Morgan and Adamson (1959) of Leeds University as a method for developing general fitness. Their initial circuit training routine consisted of several stations arranged in a circle (hence the term *circuit training*) so as to work muscle groups alternately from station to station. As circuit training grew in popularity, other authors began to modify it.

A wide variety of approaches can be used in a circuit training routine, such as body weight, surgical tubing, medicine balls, light implements, dumbbells, barbells, and strength training machines. A circuit may be short (6 to 9 exercises), medium (10 to 12 exercises), or long (13 to 15 exercises) and may be repeated a certain number of times, depending on the number of exercises involved—the more exercises, the fewer circuit repetitions. The number of circuits should be no more than two for a long circuit and no more than four for a short circuit. The number of reps per station should start higher (say, at 20) and decrease over time (say, down to 8 to 10). Fewer reps (5 or 6) can be used for the fundamental exercises starting with a very high buffer that is decreased over time.

In determining the number of reps per station, the number of circuit repetitions, and the load, the coach must consider the athlete's work tolerance and fitness level. Total workload during the anatomical adaptation phase should not be so high as to cause the athlete pain or great discomfort. Athletes themselves should help determine the amount of work to perform.

Circuit training is a useful, though not magical, method for developing the foundation of strength during the anatomical adaptation phase. Other training methods (e.g., jump sets, as explained in chapter 8) can be equally beneficial if they alternate the muscle groups.

As shown in the following examples, the training methodology used for the anatomical adaptation phase must be adapted to the physiological profile of the sport (e.g., speed or power versus endurance) and the needs of the athlete. The methodology must also develop most muscles used in the chosen sport. More specifically, in line with the overall purpose of the preparatory phase—and particularly the goal of anatomical adaptation—exercises should be selected to develop the core area of the body as well as the prime movers.

The alternation of muscle groups in circuit training facilitates recovery. The rest interval can be 30 to 90 seconds between stations and one to three minutes between circuits. Circuit training also enables a wide variety of routines to be created because most gyms contain many apparatuses, workstations, and strength training machines. This variety constantly challenges an athlete's skills while also keeping him or her interested.

Program Design for the Circuit Training Method

Circuit training may be used from the first week of the anatomical adaptation phase. The coach should select the workstations according to the equipment available. Athletes should follow a certain progression, depending on their classification and training background. Younger athletes with little or no strength training background should start with exercises using their own body weight or lower loads (e.g., medicine balls, small dumbbells, empty barbells). Over time, they can progress the load using medicine balls, barbells, and strength machines. Again, exercise during this phase must be selected to involve most muscle groups, irrespective of the needs of the specific sport; in other words, the coach should implement a multilateral approach. However, the prime movers should also be targeted. After all, they are the engines for effective performance of sport-specific skills.

The three circuits presented in figure11.1 do not come close to exhausting the available possibilities in a gym, but they are typical for entry-level or junior athletes. Young athletes who are new to circuit training may want to split circuits into two phases. As adaptation occurs, an athlete can begin progressively adding exercises from phase 2 to the end of phase 1 until he or she can perform all of the exercises nonstop. Start with two groups of four, as presented in circuit B; as the athlete adapts to the program, bring the fifth exercise into phase 1, and so on. This approach keeps the athlete motivated to reach the goal, and it keeps his or her body open to new challenges and levels of adaptation.

Entry-level athletes should individualize the number of reps by working up to the point of feeling either slight discomfort or discomfort per se. *Slight discomfort* can be translated as uneasiness. *Discomfort*, on the other hand, refers to the threshold at which the athlete is maintaining good technique but must stop the exercise due to pain.

Circuit A: body weight	1. Squat to parallel 2. Push-up 3. Bent-knee sit-up 4. Quad hip extension 5. Back extension 6. Toe raise 7. Plank
Circuit B: body weight (combination of two minicircuits)	Phase 1 1. Squat to parallel 2. Push-up (wide stance) 3. Bent-knee sit-up 4. Quad hip extension Phase 2 1. Push-up (narrow stance) 2. Back extension 3. Toe raise 4. Front plank
Circuit C: dumbbells and medicine ball	1. Squat to parallel 2. Floor press 3. Quad hip extension 4. Bent-over row 5. Toe raise 6. Military press 7. Upright row 8. Medicine ball forward throw 9. Jump squat 10. Medicine ball overhead throw 11. Bent-knee sit-up 12. Plank

Figure 11.1   Sample Circuit Training Programs

Table 11.1 shows how to plan a circuit training program, including duration, frequency of training sessions per week, and other parameters for both novice and experienced athletes. As you can see, training parameters for experienced athletes are quite different from those for novices. For example, it makes good sense for a novice athlete to use a longer anatomical adaptation phase because he or she needs more time for adaptation itself and for creating a good base for the future. On the other hand, extending this phase much longer than four weeks does not produce visible gains for an experienced athlete.

Similar differences apply to the number of stations per circuit. Because novice athletes must address as many muscle groups as realistically possible, they use more stations, and their circuits are longer. Advanced athletes, however, can reduce the number of stations to focus on exercises for the prime movers, on compensation, and on core exercises, thus resulting in shorter circuits that are repeated more times.

Both load and the total physical demand per circuit must be increased progressively and individually. The example shown in figure 11.2 illustrates that both the load and the pattern of increase differ between novice and experienced athletes. Of course, as the number of repetitions goes down, the load goes up, and the load changes from cycle to cycle. For exercises performed against resistance, lower loads are used for entry-level athletes, and slightly heavier loads are used for advanced athletes.

Table 11.1 Training Parameters for Circuit Training

Training parameter	Novice athlete	Experienced athlete
Duration of anatomical adaptation	6–10 weeks	2–4 weeks
Load (if applicable)	20 reps down to 8 throughout the entire phase	12–15 reps down to 8 throughout the entire phase
Buffer	1 or 2 reps short of exhaustion	1 rep short of exhaustion or to exhaustion
No. of stations per circuit	10-15	6-9
No. of circuits per session	2 or 3*	3 or 4*
Total time of circuit training session	35–60 minutes	40–60 minutes
Rest interval between exercises	30–90 seconds	30–120 seconds
Rest interval between circuits	2–3 minutes	1–2 minutes
Frequency per week	2 or 3	3 or 4

*Higher figure for the lower number of stations; lower figure for both the higher and lower number of stations.

Novice athlete (performing sets to *slight discomfort*)	20 reps, 2 circuits	15 reps, 3 circuits	12 reps, 2 circuits	15 reps, 2 circuits	12 reps, 3 circuits	10 reps, 2 circuits
Experienced athlete (performing sets to *discomfort*)	15 reps, 2 circuits	12 reps, 3 circuits	12 reps, 2 circuit	10 reps, 3 circuits	8 reps, 3 circuits	8 reps, 2 circuits
Microcycle	1	2	3	4	5	6

Figure 11.2 Suggested Pattern for Load Increments During Circuit Training for Novice and Experienced Athletes

Standard Training Program During the Anatomical Adaptation Phase

Circuit training is not the only possible way to organize strength training during the anatomical adaptation phase. In fact, a standard, horizontal execution strength training program can be used as well. In a horizontal approach all the planned warm-ups and work sets of an exercise are performed before switching to the next one in the program. As long as the methodological characteristics of the anatomical adaptation phase are respected (such as starting with a high number of exercises, short rest intervals, and a higher number of reps per set, and progressing to lower number of reps and higher loads over the course of the phase), the horizontal approach is just as valid as the circuit training and actually more indicated for intermediate and advanced athletes.

The following list shows how to plan a standard training program during the anatomical adaptation phase, including duration, frequency of training sessions per week, and other parameters that are valid for intermediate and advanced athletes.

Training Parameters for Standard Training

Duration (of anatomical adaptation): 2 to 4 weeks

Load: 12 to 20 reps down to 6 to 8 throughout the entire phase

Buffer: 1 rep short of exhaustion or to exhaustion

Number of exercises: 6 to 8

Number of sets: 2 to 4

Total time of training session: 40 to 60 minutes

Rest interval between exercises: 30 to 120 seconds

Frequency per week: 3 or 4

Figures 11.3 through 11.7 illustrate standard and circuit training in various sports for four and seven weeks of anatomical adaptation training. A seven-week cycle gives the athlete time to build a stronger base and offers the physiological benefits of longer and better adaptation. These programs should be adapted to each athlete's classification and abilities.

Toward the end of the anatomical adaptation phase, the load reached allows athletes to make an immediate transition to the maximum strength phase, as shown in figure 11.3. This approach can be used for all athletes except those requiring increased muscle mass, such as throwers and American football linemen. For these athletes, a hypertrophy phase must be planned between the AA phase and the MxS phase. Figure 11.4 illustrates a four-week anatomical adaptation program appropriate for athletes with a very short preparatory phase, especially those in racket and contact sports that require three or four major peaks per year. Because this AA phase is so short, the load in training is increased very quickly to ready the athlete for the maximum strength phase. Detraining poses less of a concern in these sports because their transition phase is much shorter than those of most other sports (see figure 11.4). Figure 11.5 illustrates standard strength training for team sports with a high-endurance component; in fact, cardio repetitions are placed both

Exercise	WEEK						
	1	2	3	4	5	6	7
1. Leg press	2×15	3×12	3×10	2×10	3×8	3×6	2×6
2. Chest press	2×15	3×12	3×10	2×10	3×8	3×6	2×6
3. Dumbbell stiff-leg deadlift	2×15	3×12	3×10	2×10	3×8	3×6	2×6
4. Military press	2×15	3×12	3×10	2×10	3×8	3×6	2×6
5. Leg curl	2×12	3×10	3×8	2×8	3×8	3×6	2×5
6. Upright row	2×15	3×12	3×10	2×10	3×8	3×6	2×6
7. Toe raise	2×15	3×12	3×10	2×10	3×8	3×6	2×6
8. Bent-knee sit-up	2×12	3×12	3×15	2×15	3×18	3×20	2×20
LOADING PATTERN							
			High			High	
		Medium			Medium		
	Low			Low			Low

Figure 11.3 Example of a Standard Strength Training Program for the Anatomical Adaptation Phase

Exercise	WEEK 1	2	3	4	Rest interval
1. Rope skipping	3 min.	2×3 min.	4×2 min.	2×2 min.	30 sec.
2. Squat	2×10	3×8	3×6	2×5	2 min.
3. Bench press	2×10	3×8	3×6	2×5	2 min.
4. Back hyperextension	2×15	3×12	3×10	2×8	2 min.
5. Front lat pull-down	2×10	3×8	3×6	2×5	2 min.
6. Toe raise	2×15	3×12	3×10	2×8	1 min.
7. Ab crunch	2×15	3×20	3×30	2×30	1 min.
8. Trunk side bend (each side)	2×10	3×8	3×6	2×5	1 min.
9. Medicine ball chest throw (4 kg)	2×8	3×8	3×10	2×8	1 min.
10. Low-impact plyometrics	2×10	3×10	3×12	2×12	1 min.

LOADING PATTERN

Week 1: Low — Week 2: Medium — Week 3: High — Week 4: Low

Figure 11.4 Sample Suggested Standard Training for Sports With a Short Preparatory Phase

Rope skipping aids in cardiorespiratory training.

Exercise	WEEK 1	2	3	4	5	6	7	Rest interval
1. Cardio	10 min.	10 min.	2×5 min.	2×5 min.	3×3 min.	4×2 min.	2×2 min.	1 min.
2. One-leg squat	2×15	3×12	3×10	2×10	3×8	3×6	2×6	2 min.
3. Dumbbell press	2×15	3×12	3×10	2×10	3×8	3×6	2×6	1 min.
4. One-leg curl	2×12	3×12	3×10	2×10	3×8	3×6	2×5	2 min.
5. Dumbbell row	2×15	3×15	3×12	2×12	3×10	3×8	2×8	1 min.
6. Toe raise	2×15	3×15	3×12	2×12	3×10	3×8	2×8	1 min.
7. Ab crunch	2×20	3×20	3×25	2×20	3×25	3×30	2×25	1 min.
8. Medicine ball backward throw (4 kg)	2×6	3×8	3×10	2×8	3×10	3×10	2×8	2 min.
9. Low-impact plyometrics	2×8	3×10	3×12	2×10	3×12	3×12	2×10	1 min.
10. Power ball side throw (10 kg)	2×6	3×8	3×10	2×8	3×10	3×10	2×8	1 min.
11. Cardio	5 min.	7 min.	7 min.	2×5 min.	3×3 min.	3×3 min.	2×2 min.	1 min.

LOADING PATTERN

Week 1: Low — Week 2: Medium — Week 3: High — Week 4: Low — Week 5: Medium — Week 6: High — Week 7: Low

Figure 11.5 Sample Suggested Standard Training Program for Team Sports in Which Cardiorespiratory Endurance is an Important Component

The cardio component in this example could include any of various options (e.g., running, using a stair stepper, riding a bicycle ergometer).

at the beginning and at the end of the strength workout. Figure 11.6 illustrates a circuit training program with a higher number of unilateral lower-body exercises for athletes in team sports such as soccer, basketball, rugby, lacrosse, water polo, and hockey. Figure 11.7 illustrates standard training for baseball, softball, and racket sports. To enable maximum adaptation in these sports, certain specific exercises are introduced early on in the AA phase for trunk and hip rotation—specifically, abdominal rainbows, incline trunk rotations, and power ball side throws.

Exercise	Tempo	REPS					
		Week 1	Week 2	Week 3	Week 4	Week 5	Week 6
1. One-leg press	3.0.1	20	15	12	10	8	6
2. Dumbbell press	3.0.1	20	15	12	10	8	6
3. One-leg hip bridge	3.0.1	20	15	12	10	8	6
4. Dumbbell row	3.0.1	20	15	12	10	8	6
5. One-leg semi-stiff deadlift	3.0.1	20	15	12	10	8	6
6. Dumbbell press	3.0.1	20	15	12	10	8	6
7. Standing calf raise	3.0.1	20	15	12	10	8	6
8. Upright row	3.0.1	20	15	12	10	8	6
9. Bent-knee sit-up	3.0.1	20	15	12	10	8	6
10. Front plank	—	45 sec.	60 sec.	75 sec.	75 sec.	90 sec.	60 sec. with weight
No. of circuits		2	3	2	2	3	2
Rest interval between exercises		1 min.					
Rest interval between circuits		2 min.		No rest interval	2 min.		No rest interval
Workout duration (approximate)		50 min.	65 min.	40 min.	35 min.	50 min.	30 min.

LOADING PATTERN

	High			High	
Medium			Medium		
		Low			Low

Figure 11.6 Sample Suggested Circuit Training Program for Team Sports

Exercise	WEEK							Rest interval
	1	2	3	4	5	6	7	
1. Side or diagonal lunge (each side)	2×15	3×12	3×10	2×10	3×8	3×6	2×6	2 min.
2. Cable cross-over	2×15	3×12	3×10	2×10	3×8	3×6	2×6	1–2 min.
3. Back extension	2×15	3×15	3×12	2×12	3×10	3×8	2×8	1–2 min.
4. Front lat pull-down	2×15	3×12	3×10	2×10	3×8	3×6	2×6	2 min.
5. Dumbbell external rotator	2×15	3×15	3×12	2×12	3×10	3×8	2×8	1 min.
6. Toe raise	2×15	3×15	3×12	2×12	3×10	3×8	2×8	1–2 min.
7. Bent-knee sit-up	2×20	3×20	3×25	2×20	3×25	3×30	2×25	2 min.
8. Ab rainbow (each side)	2×20	3×20	3×25	2×20	3×25	3×30	2×25	1–2 min.
9. Power ball side throw (10 kg)	2×6	3×8	3×10	2×8	3×10	3×10	2×8	1–2 min.
10. Low-impact plyometrics	2×8	3×10	3×12	2×10	3×12	3×12	2×10	2–3 min.

LOADING PATTERN

		High			High	
	Medium			Medium		
Low			Low			Low

Figure 11.7 Sample Suggested Standard Training Program for Baseball, Softball, and Racket Sports

PREVENTING INJURIES IN THE ANATOMICAL ADAPTATION PHASE

Injury during sport training affects the future of many athletes. For example, in the year 2000 alone, more than 150,000 injuries occurred in soccer in the United States. As if that were not enough, injuries are most common in the team sports that attract young athletes. The good news is that many of these injuries can be prevented by introducing strength training with the purpose of promoting injury prevention. For this reason, continual education is extremely important, especially for coaches who work with young athletes whose bodies are in the process of maturing. For these athletes, strengthening exercises that use body weight should be as much a part of the training program as are the technical and tactical skills of their chosen sport.

Unfortunately, in most training programs for young adults, muscle strengthening is overemphasized and injury prevention is overlooked. More specifically, programs often omit the training of ligaments and tendons for injury prevention simply because the anatomical adaptation phase is nonexistent. In such cases, improper periodization of strength, starting with a stressful hypertrophy phase, often results in a higher incidence of injury. And here is another reason that connective tissue adaptation should be included in every strength training program: The integrity of the ligament–joint apparatus can become a limiting factor in the performance of many athletes, especially those who possess only a superficial strength training background.

Coaches should remember that, unlike muscle tissue adaptation, which takes only a few days, connective tissue (ligament and tendon) adaptation often takes several weeks (McDonagh and Davies 1984). This time requirement is why we suggest a longer anatomical adaptation phase for most athletes. AA training must focus not only on strengthening the muscles but also (and most important) on progressively strengthening the connective tissues for the purpose of injury prevention. Recognizing this reality serves coaches well during the maximum strength training phase, when the load is very challenging even for advanced athletes.

Another important element in the quest to prevent injury is good flexibility exercise performed religiously both at the beginning of the warm-up and during the cool-down. The joints emphasized should be sport specific. As part of the ankle mobility routine, the range of motion of the Achilles tendon can be improved through stretching (specifically, through dorsiflexion—bringing the toes toward the tibia).

Finally, contrary to what coaches and physiotherapists used to say, athletes should avoid knee circles (the knee is designed to work mainly in the sagittal plane). In addition, in recent years, more and more spine specialists have suggested avoiding lumbar spine mobility exercises, especially when they involve flexion or rotation, in order to avoid damaging the intervertebral discs.

Phase 2: Hypertrophy

Many people think that the larger a person is, the stronger that person is. This is not always the case. For example, a weightlifter may be capable of lifting heavier loads than a larger, bulkier bodybuilder can lift. For this reason, athletes should seek an increase of lean body mass that is functional for their sport, as some hypertrophy, especially of the fast-twitch muscle fibers, contributes to an increase in force expression.

As the preceding distinctions imply, bodybuilding hypertrophy and sport-specific hypertrophy differ in important ways. In bodybuilding hypertrophy, the bodybuilder generally uses loads of 60 percent to 80 percent of 1-repetition maximum (1RM) for sets of 8 to 15 reps taken to failure. Some bodybuilders, however, attribute their success to using fewer reps and high training loads taken beyond failure with forced and negative reps, while others believe in performing as many reps as possible (usually up to 20). Given that all these types of bodybuilders are massively built and share similar records and numbers of wins, we may infer that in professional bodybuilding, it is not only training that makes a difference.

In any case, athletes and coaches of other sports must keep in mind that the purpose of bodybuilding is not optimal performance but optimal symmetry and maximal muscle mass. Aesthetical symmetry, however, is irrelevant to many sports, in which function is the main priority. And although bodybuilders do increase muscle mass, the functionality of that mass is questionable, whereas functionality—that is, improved performance—is the goal of training in other sports.

Sport-Specific Hypertrophy

Hypertrophy training is intended for athletes whose sport performance will be helped by an increase in muscle size. To name a few, such athletes include football linemen, shot-putters, and discus throwers (for a detailed periodization-of-strength model for your sport, refer to chapter 10.)

Sprinter Kim Collins, 2003 World Indoor (60 meters) silver medalist and World Outdoor (100 meters) gold medalist, did not need huge muscles to be among the fastest men on earth.

For athletes, the enlargement of muscle size (hypertrophy) should be achieved by applying a sport-specific training methodology. In other words, whereas bodybuilding focuses on enlarging overall musculature, hypertrophy training for sports focuses mainly on increasing the size of the specific prime movers without neglecting the neural component of force expression.

This kind of hypertrophy—sport-specific hypertrophy—is achieved by means other than bodybuilding methods. Specifically, training for sport-specific hypertrophy requires heavy loads with minimal rest and high number of sets to increase the density (thickness) of, and amount of protein in, the prime movers. This way, hypertrophy training for sports is long lasting because the increase in muscle size is based on the increase in strength.

To simplify hypertrophy training, we have broken it down into two phases: hypertrophy I and hypertrophy II. Hypertrophy I uses various bodybuilding techniques to optimize muscle exhaustion and growth, whereas hypertrophy II refers to sport-specific hypertrophy. Since we have discussed hypertrophy II at some length here and in chapter 10, this section offers in-depth explanation of hypertrophy I methods.

When incorporating hypertrophy I methods into a training program, athletes and coaches should be cautious. Specifically, they must take into consideration the athlete's physical maturity and the timing in relation to the yearly training program. During the early preparatory season, hypertrophy I bodybuilding methods work very well to help stimulate the highest increase lean muscle mass. Late in the preparatory season, however, sport-specific hypertrophy II techniques should be implemented. Regardless of which method of hypertrophy is employed in training, the majority of the program should consist of multijoint exercises, such as squats, leg presses, bench presses, back rows, chin-ups, dips, and core exercises to stimulate hormonal response and muscle growth and strengthen the prime movers integrated in a complex kinetic chain, as happens in sporting activities. Isolation exercises should be kept to a minimum.

The hypertrophy phase can last six to eight weeks depending on the needs of the athlete and the sport or event. And again, if both hypertrophy I and II training methods are used, hypertrophy I should be used early in the preparatory season. The total length of the preparatory phase is also important because the longer it is, the more time the athlete has to work on hypertrophy, as well as maximum strength.

The end of the hypertrophy phase does not mean that an athlete who needs to build muscle mass must stop this training. As illustrated in the example for a lineman in figure 12.1, hypertrophy training can be maintained and even further developed during the maximum strength phase. Depending on the needs of the athlete, the proportion between maximum strength training and hypertrophy training can be three to one, two to one, or even one to one. During the maintenance phase, however, only certain athletes—such as shot-putters and linemen in American football—should continue hypertrophy training, and then only during the first half. As the most important competitions approach, power and maximum strength training should prevail.

Preparatory				Competitive
3 AA	6 Hyp.: 3 or 4 sessions	6 MxS: 2 or 3 sessions Hyp.: 1 or 2 sessions	5 Conv. to P: 2 sessions MxS: 1 session Hyp.: 1 session	Maint.: P, MxS, hyp.

Key: AA = anatomical adaptation, conv. = conversion, hyp. = hypertrophy, maint. = maintenance, MxS = maximum strength, and P = power.

Figure 12.1 Suggested Proportions of Hypertrophy, Maximum Strength, and Power Training for American Football Linemen

Program Design for Sport-Specific Hypertrophy Training

Once the anatomical adaptation phase has readied the connective tissue (tendons and ligaments), hypertrophy training can begin with a test for 1RM. in that case, the 1RM test must be performed at the end of the last microcycle (unloading) of the anatomical adaptation phase. Athletes then start with a 60 percent load, or one that allows them to perform 12 reps. The load is then increased in each microcycle until it reaches a level at which the athlete can perform only 6 reps. For training parameters of the hypertrophy phase, see table 12.1.

To achieve maximum training benefits, the athlete must reach the highest number of reps possible in each set. This means reaching a degree of exhaustion that prevents him or her from doing another rep even when applying maximum contraction. Without performing each set to exhaustion, the athlete does not achieve the expected level of muscle hypertrophy because the first reps do not produce enough stimulus to maximize muscle mass. The key element in hypertrophy training is not just exhaustion per set but the cumulative effect of exhaustion in the total number of sets. This cumulative exhaustion stimulates the chemical reactions and protein metabolism necessary for optimal muscle hypertrophy.

Hypertrophy exercises should generally be performed at low to moderate speed in order to maximize the muscles' time under tension. However, athletes in speed- or power-dominant sports are strongly advised against slow concentric speed of execution,

Table 12.1 Training Parameters for the Hypertrophy Phase

Duration of hypertrophy phase	6–8 weeks
Load	60%–80% of 1RM
No. of exercises	6–9
No. of reps per set	12 down to 6
No. of sets per session	10–12 (split*) or 18–24 (full body)
Rest interval	2–5 minutes
Speed of execution	Slow eccentric (3 to 5 seconds), possible pause between eccentric and concentric (1 to 5 seconds), fast concentric (1 second or less—explosive)
Frequency per week	2–4 times

*Exercises for the lower body are trained on separate days from the exercises for the upper body. A usual split routine for sports during the hypertrophy phase is as follows: Monday: lowery body; Tuesday: upper body; Wednesday: rest; Thursday: lower body; Friday: upper body; Saturday and Sunday: rest.

especially if the hypertrophy phase is longer than six weeks. The primary reason for this advice is that the neuromuscular system adapts to slow execution and therefore does not stimulate the recruitment of fast-twitch muscle fibers that is crucial for speed- and power-dominant sports.

As compared with bodybuilding, hypertrophy training for sports involves fewer exercises in order to focus mainly on the prime movers rather than on all muscle groups. The benefit of this approach is that more sets are performed per exercise (three to six, or even as many as eight), thus stimulating better muscle hypertrophy for the prime movers.

Depending on the microcycle, the rest interval between sets can vary from two to five minutes. The closer the athlete gets to switching to a maximum strength phase of training, the longer the rest interval must be between sets. For instance, in a six- to eight-week hypertrophy phase of training, the first three (or four) weeks can be used to stimulate maximum hypertrophy gains by using short rest periods (60 to 90 seconds between sets), and the last three or four weeks can use longer rest periods.

At the end of a training session, an athlete should stretch the muscles that he or she has worked. Because of the many contractions, the muscles shorten. This results in reduced muscle range of motion and decreased quickness of contraction, which in turn affects the joint positioning and overall body posture, as well as neurally facilitates the agonist and neurally inhibits the antagonist, reducing, over time, overall performance ability of the affected muscles. In addition, a shortened muscle has a slower rate of regeneration because only the normal biological length facilitates active biochemical exchanges. These exchanges provide nutrients to the muscles and remove metabolic wastes, thus facilitating better recovery between sets and after training sessions.

Figure 12.2 shows a sample eight-week program developed for a heavyweight wrestler. The program suggested in each box is repeated three times per week. Figure 12.3 shows a sample six-week program for a female college volleyball player who has a relatively large disproportion between height and weight. Figure 12.4 shows a sample six-week program for a power and speed athlete who wants to gain muscle mass. The first eight exercises for the lower body are performed on days 1 and 4, and the next eight exercises for the upper body are performed on days 2 and 5. Figure 12.5 shows

VARIATIONS OF HYPERTROPHY TRAINING METHODS

The main factors responsible for hypertrophy are not fully understood, but researchers increasingly believe that increased muscle size is stimulated mainly by 1) the mechanical stress to the muscle fibers (Owino et al. 2001; Goldspink 2005; Ahtiainen et al. 2001; Liu et al. 2008; Hameed et al. 2008; Roschel et al. 2011; Goldspink 2012; Schoenfeld 2012), mainly determined by the load used, the total time under tension, especially of the eccentric phase, and the total volume in terms of reps; 2) the metabolic stress (Sjogaard 1985; Febbraio and Pedersen 2005; Hornberger et al. 2006), mainly determined by the set duration that should be preferable in the anaerobic lactic energy system domain (30 to 60 seconds), and, again, the total volume in terms of reps. Because taking a set to concentric failure represents the main element of success in achieving muscle hypertrophy, several variations of the original bodybuilding method have been developed. Most of them pursue same objective: When exhaustion is reached, a few more reps must be performed through hard work. The expected result is greater muscle growth, or increased hypertrophy. Of all the variations (there are more than 20), the following ones are most representative.

- *Split routine*—Athletes perform two or three exercises per muscle group. Because they address every muscle of the body, they may be in the gymnasium for almost two hours to finish the entire program. Even if athletes have the energy to do this, the physiological response to such endurance does not favor the maximization of hypertrophy. The solution is to divide the total volume of work into parts and address one part of the body on each day—thus the term *split routine*. This approach means that even if an athlete trains four times per week, any given muscle group is worked only twice per week.

- *Forced repetitions*—As an athlete performs a set to concentric failure, a partner assists by providing sufficient support to enable one or two more reps.

- *Rest-pause*—An athlete reaches concentric failure in a set, then rests only 10 to 20 seconds before starting again until concentric failure is reached (usually after one to three reps). This approach increases the set's duration and the hypertrophic stimulus.

- *Drop sets*—An athlete reaches concentric failure in a set, then quickly lowers the load by 5 percent to 10 percent (depending on how many more reps the trainer expects the athlete to perform, or whether an additional drop set is programmed), starts again, and continues until concentric failure. This technique also increases the set's duration and the hypertrophic stimulus.

The initial load in the rest-pause and drop-set approaches can be higher than in the usual bodybuilding programs because the set's duration is increased via micropauses (in rest-pause) or small deloading (in drop sets). This characteristic makes these two techniques particularly useful for athletes' hypertrophy because it increases the fast-twitch muscle fibers' time under tension during a set. Bodybuilding books and magazines often refer to many other methods, some of which are said to work miracles for athletes. Coaches and athletes should take care to distinguish the fine line that separates fact from fantasy.

Exercise	Tempo	WEEK								Rest interval
		1	2	3	4	5	6	7	8	
Deadlift	3.1.1	2×12	3×12	3×10	2×10	3×8	3×6	3×5	2×5	2 min (weeks 1-4) 3 min (weeks 5-8)
Bench press	3.0.X	2×12	3×12	3×10	2×10	3×8	3×6	3×5	2×5	2 min (weeks 1-4) 3 min (weeks 5-8)
Squat	3.2.X	2×12	3×12	3×10	2×10	3×8	3×6	3×5	2×5	2 min (weeks 1-4) 3 min (weeks 5-8)
Pulley row	3.0.X	2×12	3×12	3×10	2×10	3×8	3×6	3×5	2×5	2 min (weeks 1-4) 3 min (weeks 5-8)
Hip thrust	3.0.1	2×12	3×12	3×10	2×10	3×8	3×6	3×5	2×5	1 min (weeks 1-4) 2 min (weeks 5-8)
Floor press	3.0.X	2×12	3×12	3×10	2×10	3×8	3×6	3×5	2×5	1 min (weeks 1-4) 2 min (weeks 5-8)
Good morning	3.0.X	2×12	3×12	3×10	2×10	3×8	3×6	3×5	2×5	1 min (weeks 1-4) 2 min (weeks 5-8)
Farmer's walk (weight on one side; time in sec)	—	30+30 × 2 sets	40+40 × 2 sets	50+50 × 2 sets	30+30 × 2 sets	40+40 ×2 sets	50+50 ×2 sets	60+60 × 2 sets	40+40 ×2 sets	1 min

LOADING PATTERN

1	2	3	4	5	6	7	8
		High				High	
	Medium				Medium		
Low				Low	Low		Low

Figure 12.2 Sample Training Program for a Heavyweight Wrestler in the Hypertrophy Phase

All sets are taken to failure, so the weight might be adjusted downward in the second set in order to fulfill the required number of reps per set.

a sample hypertrophy program designed in jump set format to save time. Figure 12.6 shows a sample split routine (upper/lower) where bodybuilding intensification methods are employed to further elicit hypertrophy. When such methods are employed, a lower number of sets per session must be planned because they heavily tax both the muscles and the CNS. In the following figures, you find the repetitions decreasing from week to week. Each decrease of repetitions corresponds to an increase of load so that each set is taken to failure. Because of the residual fatigue, the load might be adjusted downward in the second and third set to fulfill the required number of reps per set.

Bodybuilding workouts, even those using the split routine, are very exhausting; often, in fact, 120 to 180 reps are performed in a single training session. Such high muscle loading requires a long recovery. Because of the type of work specific to bodybuilding, the ATP-CP and glycogen stores are greatly taxed after a demanding training session. Although ATP-CP is restored very quickly, liver glycogen (if tapped) requires 40 to 48 hours to replenish. Thus, heavy workouts to complete exhaustion should not be performed more than two times per microcycle for the same muscle groups (for intensity variations, refer to the discussion of microcycle planning in chapter 9).

Some may argue that athletes who use the split routine train a given group of muscles on every second day, thus leaving 48 hours between the two training sessions, which

Phase 2: Hypertrophy

Exercise	Tempo	WEEK						Rest interval
		1	2	3	4	5	6	
Half squat	3.0.X	2×12	3×12	3×10	2×10	3×8	3×6	1 min (weeks 1-4) 2 min (weeks 5-8)
Incline dumbbell press	3.0.X	2×12	3×12	3×10	2×10	3×8	3×6	1 min (weeks 1-4) 2 min (weeks 5-8)
Dumbbell walking lunges	3.0.1	2×20	2×15	2×12	1×12	3×10	3×8	1 min (weeks 1-4) 2 min (weeks 5-8)
Mid-pronated lat pull-down	3.0.X	2×12	3×12	3×10	2×10	3×8	3×6	1 min (weeks 1-4) 2 min (weeks 5-8)
Back hyperextension	3.0.X	2×12	2×12	2×10	1×10	2×8	2×6	1 min (weeks 1-4) 2 min (weeks 5-8)
Dumbbell shoulder press	3.0.X	2×12	3×12	3×10	2×10	3×8	3×6	1 min.
Standing calf raise	3.0.1	2×12	2×12	3×10	2×10	2×8	2×6	1 min.
Dumbbell triceps extensions	3.0.1	2×12	2×12	2×10	1×10	2×8	2×6	1 min.
Dumbbel external rotator	3.0.2	2×12	2×12	2×10	1×10	2×8	2×6	1 min.
Crunch with weight	3.0.1	2×12	2×12	2×10	1×10	2×8	2×8	1 min.

LOADING PATTERN					
		High			High
	Medium			Medium	
Low			Low		

Figure 12.3 Sample Training Program for a Female College Volleyball Player in the Hypertrophy Phase
All sets are taken to failure, so the weight might be adjusted downward in the second set in order to fulfill the required number of reps per set.

is sufficient for the restoration of energy fuels. However, though this may be true for local muscle stores, it ignores the fact that when muscle glycogen is exhausted, the body starts tapping the glycogen stores in the liver. If the liver source is tapped every day, 24 hours may be insufficient to restore glycogen. This deficit may result in the overtraining phenomenon. Moreover, many of the routines and methods used by bodybuilders, such as four- or five-day split routines or two workouts per day, do not allow for nervous system recovery or the recruitment of the fast-twitch muscle fibers that are integral to sport performance.

In addition to exhausting energy stores, constant intense training puts wear and tear on the contractile proteins, exceeding their anabolism (the myosin's protein-building rate). Such overloading can cause the muscles involved to no longer increase in size; in other words, there may be no gains in hypertrophy.

When this happens, coaches should reassess the application of the overloading principle and start using the step-type method, as suggested by the principle of progressive increase of load in training. They should also consider inserting an unloading microcycle more frequently in order to facilitate regeneration, which is just as important as training.

Exercise	Tempo	Week 1 Days 1 and 4	Week 2 Days 1 and 4	Week 3 Days 1 and 4	Week 4 Days 1 and 4	Week 5 Days 1 and 4	Week 6 Days 1 and 4	Rest interval
Squat (day 1) or deadlift (day 4)	3.2.1	2×8	3×8	3×6	2×6	3×5	4×5	2 min (weeks 1-4) 3 min (weeks 5-8)
Hip thrust	3.0.X	2×12	3×12	3×10	2×10	3×8	3×6	1 min (weeks 1-4) 2 min (weeks 5-8)
Back hyperex-tensions	3.0.1	2×12	3×12	3×10	2×10	3×8	3×6	1 min (weeks 1-4) 2 min (weeks 5-8)
Leg curls	3.0.X	2×8	3×8	3×6	2×6	3×5	4×5	1 min (weeks 1-4) 2 min (weeks 5-8)
Standing calf raise	3.1.1	2×12	3×12	3×10	2×10	3×8	3×6	1 min.
Crunches with weight	3.0.1	2×12	3×12	3×12	2×10	3×8	3×6	1 min.

Exercise	Tempo	Week 1 Days 2 and 5	Week 2 Days 2 and 5	Week 3 Days 2 and 5	Week 4 Days 2 and 5	Week 5 Days 2 and 5	Week 6 Days 2 and 5	Rest interval
Bench press	3.0.X	2×12	3×12	3×10	2×10	3×8	3×6	2 min (weeks 1-4) 3 min (weeks 5-8)
Mid-pronated lat pull-down	3.0.X	2×12	3×12	3×10	2×10	3×8	3×6	2 min (weeks 1-4) 3 min (weeks 5-8)
Military press	3.0.X	2×12	3×12	3×10	2×10	3×8	3×6	1 min (weeks 1-4) 2 min (weeks 5-8)
Dumbbell curls	3.0.1	2×8	3×8	3×6	2×6	3×5	4×5	1 min.
French press	3.0.1	2×12	3×12	3×10	2×10	3×8	3×6	1 min.
Land mine (reps, left and right)	—	12+12	14+14	16+16	14+14	16+16	18+18	1 min.
Farmer's walk (time in seconds, left and right)	—	30+30	40+40	50+50	40+40	50+50	60+60	1 min.

LOADING PATTERN

		High			High
	Medium			Medium	
Low			Low		

Figure 12.4 Sample Training Program for an Ice Hockey Player in the Hypertrophy Phase

All sets are taken to failure, so the weight might be adjusted downward in the second set in order to fulfill the required number of reps per set.

Phase 2: Hypertrophy

Sequence*	Exercise	Tempo	Rest interval	Week 1	Week 2	Week 3	Week 4	Week 5	Week 6
A1	Squat	4.1.1	2 min.	3×12	4×10	2×10	3×8	4×6	2×6
A2	Hip thrust	3.0.1	2 min.	3×12	4×10	2×10	3×8	4×6	2×6
B1	Bench press	3.1.1	2 min.	3×12	4×10	2×10	3×8	4×6	2×6
B2	Barbell row	3.0.1	2 min.	3×12	4×10	2×10	3×8	4×6	2×6
C1	Semi-stiff-leg deadlift	4.0.1	1 min.	2×12	2×10	1×10	2×8	2×6	1×6
C2	Standing calf raise	4.1.1	1 min.	2×12	2×10	1×10	2×8	2×6	1×6
D1	Narrow dip	3.0.1	1 min.	2×12	2×10	1×10	2×8	2×6	1×6
D2	Dumbbell curl	3.0.1	1 min.	2×12	2×10	1×10	2×8	2×6	1×6
E	Weighted crunch	3.0.3	1 min.	2×12	2×10	1×10	2×8	2×6	1×6

LOADING PATTERN					
	High			High	
Medium			Medium		
		Low			Low

*Jump set format: Do one set of exercise A1, take rest interval, do one set of exercise A2, take rest interval, and repeat the sequence. Then pass to next pair (B1 and B2), and continue until finished.

Figure 12.5 Sample Loading Pattern for a Six-Week Training Program for a Heavyweight Wrestler in the Hypertrophy Phase

All sets are taken to failure, so the weight might be adjusted downward in the second set in order to fulfill the required number of reps per set.

A workout is only as good as an athlete's ability to recover from it. Athletes can perform lower-volume split sessions—working two or three muscle groups for a total of 12 to 18 sets, tapping less into the liver's glycogen, and generating less muscle breakdown (catabolism)—up to four times per week with at least 72 hours of recovery between trainings of the same muscle group. For example, an athlete could devote Monday and Thursday to the lower body and Tuesday and Friday to the upper body.

Because improperly used bodybuilding techniques can handicap most athletes, they are used sparingly in sport training. Even so, bodybuilding methods may benefit some athletes in a certain phase of strength development. For instance, because bodybuilding is relatively safe and employs moderately heavy loads, some novice athletes can use its methods, provided that they do work just short of exhaustion in each set (i.e., use a low buffer of one or two reps). The techniques may also benefit athletes who want to move up a weight class in sports such as boxing, wrestling, and the martial arts.

Exercise	Tempo	Week 1 Days 1 and 4	Week 2 Days 1 and 4	Week 3 Days 1 and 4	Week 4 Days 1 and 4	Week 5 Days 1 and 4	Week 6 Days 1 and 4	Rest interval
Leg press	3.2.1	2×8	2×8+ds	2×6+ds	2×8	3×5	4×5	2 min (weeks 1-4) / 3 min (weeks 5-8)
Dumbbell walking lunges	3.0.X	2×10	2×12+rp	2×14+rp	2×10	3×8	3×6	2 min.
Semi-stiff legs deadlift	3.0.1	2×12	3×10	3×8	2×10	3×8	3×6	1 min (weeks 1-4) / 2 min (weeks 5-8)
Leg curls	3.0.X	2×8	2×8+rp	2×6+rp	2×6	3×5	4×5	2 min.
Standing calf raise	3.1.1	2×8	2×+ds	2×6+ds	2×10	3×8	3×6	2 min.
Crunches with weight	3.0.1	2×12	3×12	3×10	2×10	3×8	3×6	1 min.

Exercise	Tempo	Week 1 Days 2 and 5	Week 2 Days 2 and 5	Week 3 Days 2 and 5	Week 4 Days 2 and 5	Week 5 Days 2 and 5	Week 6 Days 2 and 5	Rest interval
Bench press	3.0.X	2×8	2×+ds	2×6+ds	2×6	3×5	4×5	2 min (weeks 1-4) / 3 min (weeks 5-8)
Pulley rows	3.0.X	2×8	2×8+ds	2×+ds	2×6	3×5	4×5	2 min (weeks 1-4) / 3 min (weeks 5-8)
Dumbbell shoulder press	3.0.X	2×12	3×10+ds	3×8+ds	2×10	3×8	3×6	1 min (weeks 1-4) / 2 min (weeks 5-8)
Dumbbell curls	3.0.1	2×8	2×8+rp	2×6+rp	2×6	3×5	4×5	1 min.
Cable push-downs	3.0.1	2×12	3×10+ds	3×8+ds	2×10	3×8	3×6	1 min.
Plank (sec.)	—	40	50	60	40	60	70	—

LOADING PATTERN

		High			High
	Medium			Medium	
Low			Low		

Key: ds = drop sets; rp = rest pause.

Figure 12.6 Sample Split Routine Using Bodybuilding Intensification Methods to Elicit Hypertrophy

All sets are taken to failure, so the weight might be adjusted downward in the second set in order to fulfill the required number of reps per set.

13

Phase 3: Maximum Strength

Nearly every sport requires strength, but what each sport really calls for is sport-specific strength. In creating sport-specific strength, an important role (if not the determinant one) is played by maximum strength. The specific role played by maximum strength varies between sports, and this role determines the length of the maximum strength training phase for a given sport. The more important the role is—for example, it is quite important for throwers in track and field and for American football linemen—the longer the maximum strength phase is. Similarly, the phase is shorter for sports (e.g., golf, table tennis) in which maximum strength contributes less to final performance. For these reasons, the coach must know the physiology behind the increase of maximum strength as well as the methods to apply during each training phase to maximize the final outcome: the highest possible level of specific strength.

Physiology of Strength Training

Until a few years ago, we believed that strength was determined mainly by the muscles' cross-sectional area (CSA). For this reason, weight training was used to increase "engine size"—in other words, to produce muscular hypertrophy. Now, we see it differently. CSA remains the single best predicting factor of an individual's strength, but the main factors responsible for strength increase (especially in nonbeginner athletes) are in fact the neural adaptations to strength training, such as improvements in inter- and intramuscular coordination and disinhibition of inhibitory mechanisms (refer back to chapters 2 and 7 for further explanation on the neural adaptations to strength training).

In a nutshell, an athlete's ability to generate high forces depends to a great extent on the following factors:

- Intermuscular coordination—ability to synchronize all muscles of a kinetic chain involved in an action

- Intramuscular coordination—capacity to voluntarily recruit as many motor units as possible and send nerve impulses at high frequency
- Hypertrophy—the diameter or cross-sectional area of the muscle involved

Improving intermuscular coordination—that is, muscle groups' coordination—depends strictly on learning (technique), which requires many reps of the same exercise using a moderate load (40 percent to 80 percent of 1-repetition maximum [or 1RM]) and performed explosively with perfect technique (MxS-I). Intramuscular coordination—the capacity to recruit fast-twitch fibers—depends on training content, in which high loads (80 percent to 90 percent of 1RM) are moved explosively (MxS-II). Both of these types of strength training, MxS-I and MxS-II, activate the powerful fast-twitch motor units.

Overall muscle mass depends on the duration of the hypertrophy phase, but an athlete does not necessarily have to develop large muscles and high body weight to become significantly stronger. Throughout maximum strength and power training, athletes learn to better coordinate the relevant muscle groups and use loads that result in higher recruitment of fast-twitch muscle fiber (loads greater than 80 percent of 1RM). As a result, by using the methods outlined in this chapter for the maximum strength phase, athletes can improve their maximum strength with some gains in functional muscle mass.

Of the three types of muscle contraction, eccentric contractions create the highest tension (up to 140 percent of concentric 1RM strength). The second-highest tension is created by isometric contractions (up to 120 percent of concentric 1RM strength). Still, concentric strength must be developed at the highest levels because most sport actions are concentric. Indeed, the direct application of other forms of contraction—isometric and especially eccentric—directly benefits athletic performance by supporting further improvements in concentric force.

Exercises used to develop maximum strength should never be performed under conditions of exhaustion, as they are in bodybuilding, except when the goal is to achieve absolute strength gains (strength plus hypertrophy). Because maximum strength training engages maximum activation of the central nervous system—including factors such as concentration and motivation—it improves intermuscular and intramuscular coordination. High CNS adaptation (e.g., improvement of neuromuscular coordination) also results in adequate inhibition of the antagonist muscles. This result means that when maximum force is applied, these muscles are coordinated in such a way that the antagonists do not contract to oppose the movement.

The CNS normally prevents the activation of all the motor units available for contraction. Eliminating this inhibition is one of the main objectives of MxS-II training—that is, intramuscular coordination training with loads above 80 percent of 1RM. This reduction in CNS inhibition is accompanied by an increase in strength that results in the greatest improvement in specific performance potential.

Training Methods for the Maximum Strength Phase

Throughout the maximum strength (MxS) phase a number of training methods can be used. The most commonly employed methods entail the use of moderately heavy (MxS-I) and heavy (MxS-II) loads, applied in this sequence. In certain circumstances, the eccentric method, the isometric method or the Maxex method can supplement the former, basic methods. In the following sections, you will find a discussion about what these methods are and how to implement them within a periodized training plan.

Please note that all of these methods are percentage-based, meaning that the load indicated is a percentage of the 1RM. For this reason, before the beginning of the maximum strength phase (be it at the end of the anatomical adaptation phase or the hypertrophy phase when present) and at the end of each macrocycle that constitutes it, the 1RM for the main exercises must be tested. The 1RM test serves the double purpose of assessing the maximum strength improvement of the athlete and as a base for the calculation of the training loads for the following macrocycle (refer to chapter 8 for further instructions on how to test the 1RM).

Submaximum (MxS-I) and Maximum (MxS-II) Loads Methods

In periodization of strength for sports, the submaximum and maximum load methods are probably the most effective ways to develop maximum strength. Improving maximum strength is paramount for most sports for the following reasons:

- The increases in voluntary motor unit activation results in high recruitment of fast-twitch muscle fibers that transfers to any sport activity.

- Maximum strength is the determinant factor in increasing power. As such, it enables the athlete to reach a high neural output for sports in which speed and power are dominant.

- Maximum strength is also a critical element in improving muscular endurance, especially of short and medium duration.

- Maximum strength is important for sports in which relative strength is crucial, such as martial arts, boxing, wrestling, sprinting, and jump events in track and field, and most team sports. Relative strength is the proportion between maximum strength and body weight, meaning that the higher the relative strength is, the better the performance will be.

Submaximum and maximum load methods positively influence athletes in speed- and power-dominant sports by increasing the muscle size and recruitment of more fast-twitch fibers. Although large increases in muscle size are possible for athletes who are just starting to use these methods, they are less likely in athletes with longer training backgrounds, though they too will steadily put on small amounts of functional muscle mass as their training loads increase over time. The greatest gains in maximum strength, however, result from better muscle group coordination and increased recruitment of fast-twitch motor units.

The loads used for maximum strength development—70 percent to 90 percent of 1RM for only one to five reps—result in sets of short duration and, combined with complete rest intervals, allow complete restoration of ATP. As a result, the ATP deficiency and the depletion of structural protein are too low to strongly activate the protein metabolism that stimulates hypertrophy. Consequently, when used with sufficient rest intervals, such loads result in an increase in maximum strength but not so much in hypertrophy unless total volume (i.e., high total time under tension) is high enough.

The submaximum and maximum load methods also increase testosterone level, which further explains improved maximum strength. The level of testosterone in the blood appears to depend on the frequency (per day and per week) of sessions using the maximum load method. Testosterone increases when the number of these sessions per week is low, and it decreases when maximum load training is performed twice a day. A correct training frequency with maximum loads can lead to higher testosterone levels, while a too-high frequency may lead to depressed levels of testosterone. Such findings substantiate and further justify the suggestions made earlier (chapters 8 and 9) regarding the frequency of high-intensity training sessions per microcycle as well as the reduced duration of high-intensity macrocycles (2+1 weeks).

The maximum load method II can be used only after a minimum of one year (two years for junior athletes) of general strength training (using anatomical adaptation and the submaximum load method). Strength gains can be expected even during long-term use of the submaximum method, mainly because of the motor learning that occurs as athletes learn to better use and coordinate the muscles involved in training—that is, as they develop better intermuscular coordination.

However, highly trained athletes with four to five years of maximum strength training are so well adapted to such training that further increases in maximum strength may be difficult to achieve. Therefore, if further maximum strength development is necessary, alternate methods enable continued improvement. Options include the following:

- If an athlete has used periodization of training for three to four years and cannot see a further positive transfer of strength to his or her specific performance, he or she can alternate various stimulations of the neuromuscular system. Following anatomical adaptation and the first phase of maximum strength training, the athlete should alternate three weeks of maximum strength training with three weeks of power training. Power training, with its explosiveness and fast application of force, stimulates the CNS.

- For power sports, another option can be used for stimulation: Alternate three weeks of hypertrophy training with three weeks of maximum strength training. The additional hypertrophy phases result in slight enlargement in muscle size or an increase in lean muscle mass. This additional gain in hypertrophy provides a new biological base for further improvement of maximum strength.

- Increase the ratio between eccentric and concentric types of contraction, as explained later in this chapter. The additional eccentric training produces higher stimulation for maximum strength improvement because eccentric contraction creates higher tension in the muscle.

Important elements of success for training with the maximum load method include load, buffer, rest interval, exercise order, the speed performing the contraction, and the loading pattern. These factors are discussed in the following sections.

Load Maximum strength is developed only by creating the highest possible tension in the muscle. Although lower loads engage slow-twitch muscle fibers, loads of greater than 70 percent of 1RM, moved explosively, are necessary if most muscle fibers, especially fast-twitch fibers, are to be recruited in contraction. In fact, in terms of recruitment, loads of 80 percent or higher are even better. Using high loads with few reps results in significant CNS adaptation: better coordination of the muscles involved in a kinetic chain, and increased capacity to recruit fast-twitch fibers.

These changes are the reasons that maximum strength and explosive power training are also called nervous system training (Schmidtbleicher 1984). If, as Goldberg and colleagues (1975) suggested, the stimulus for protein synthesis is the tension developed in the myofilaments, it is further proof that maximum strength training should be carried out mainly with high loads (70 percent or higher).

To produce the most maximum strength improvement that transfer to the sport-specific activity, the prime movers must do the greatest amount of work. Coaches should plan training sessions with the highest number of sets per prime mover that the athlete can tolerate (3 to 8). Because this approach is possible only with a low number of fundamental exercises that work the prime movers (no more than 5), coaches should resist the temptation to use higher numbers of exercises.

In addition, exercises can be differentiated as either fundamental or accessory. Fundamental exercises lie at the core of the strength program, and their loading parameters are those of the maximum strength phase. Accessory exercises are isolation exercises aimed at addressing individual weaknesses or supporting the strength increase in a fundamental exercise—for example, using an adductor machine for an athlete deficient in adductor strength or the French press to increase an athlete's bench-press strength. Given the nature of accessory exercises, their loads are lower, and their rep counts higher, than those of the fundamental exercises.

Table 13.1 and table 13.2 provide the training parameters for the submaximum load method (MxS-I) and maximum load method (MxS-II).

Table 13.1 Training Parameters for the Submaximum Load Method (MxS-I)

Load	70%–80% (up to 100% for 1RM testing every 3 or 4 weeks)
No. of exercises	2-5 fundamental 1 to 3 accessory
No. of reps per set	2-6 fundamental 8-12 fundamental accessory
No. of sets per exercise	3-8 fundamental* 2 or 3 accessory
Rest interval	2-3 minutes fundamental 1-2 minutes accessory
Total sets per session	16-24
Frequency per week	2-4

*Lower figure for the higher number of fundamental exercises; higher figure for the lower number of fundamental exercises.

Table 13.2 Training Parameters for the Maximum Load Method (MxS-II)

Load	80%–90% of 1RM (up to 100% for 1RM testing every 3 or 4 weeks)
No. of exercises	2-5 fundamental 1 to 3 accessory
No. of reps per set	1-3 fundamental 8-10 accessory
No. of sets per exercise	3-8 fundamental 2 or 3 accessory
Rest interval	3-5 minutes fundamental 1 to 2 minutes accessory
Total sets per session	16-24
Frequency per week	2-4

When using a high load, the number of reps per set is kept low (1 to 5), and the suggested total number of reps per exercise for a training session is between 6 and 25. The number of reps per exercise varies depending on the athlete's classification, training background, and training phase. To stimulate the necessary physiological and morphological CNS changes, a higher number of sets should always take precedence over a higher number of reps. See table 13.3 for the number of reps per exercise proposed per training session.

The number of fundamental exercises dictates whether to use the lower or higher number of total reps (see table 13.3). Athletes performing five fundamental exercises should use the lower number, whereas those performing two fundamental exercises should use the higher number. If the number of total reps is much lower than recommended, maximum strength benefits decline seriously. These suggestions should reinforce the wisdom of selecting a low number of exercises—the fewer the exercises, the more sets and reps the athlete can perform, and the greater the maximum strength improvement will be for the prime movers.

Table 13.3   Proposed Number of Reps per Exercise per Training Session in the Maximum Strength Phase (MxS)

Percent of 1RM	Reps per set	Suggested range of reps and sets per session	Range of total reps per session
70–75	3–5	4×3 to 5×5	12–25
75–80	2–4	4×2 to 5×4	8–20
80–85	2–3	4×2 to 5×3	8–15
85–90	1 or 2	6×1 to 5×2	6–10
90–95	1	3×1 to 6×1	3–6

Buffer   Field experience tells us that taking sets to failure in maximum strength training soon creates a strength plateau. For this reason, we strongly suggest never taking a strength set to failure unless the goal is absolute strength (strength and hypertrophy). We can control how close a strength set comes to failure by using a purposeful buffer— the difference between the number of reps performed in a set and the number of reps that the athlete could perform to failure at that intensity.

For example, if we are doing sets of three reps with a load of 85 percent of 1RM, we are using a buffer of two reps or 5 percentage points. This buffer is calculated as follows: Using a load that is 85 percent of 1RM normally allows five reps to failure (5RM); therefore, performing only three reps gives a buffer of two reps. To calculate buffer more precisely, we can consider what intensity would make a set go to failure at a certain number of reps. In our case, a 3RM load is usually 90 percent of a 1RM load; therefore, by doing sets of three reps at 85 percent, we have a buffer of 5 percentage points.

Figure 13.1 shows sample progressions over the course of a six-week maximum strength phase (two 2+1 macrocycles) using a constant buffer (despite the load going up, the sets will be felt by the athlete more or less at the same level of effort) or a progressively lower buffer (the effort felt by the athlete will increase as the load increases). Figure 13.2 shows a sample nine-week progression, passing from the submaximum load method (the first two 2+1 macrocycles) to the maximum load method (the last 2+1 macrocycle). Notation

Phase 3: Maximum Strength

	CONSTANT BUFFER (5%)						PROGRESSIVE BUFFER (10% DOWN TO 5%)					
Relative strength	Week 1	Week 2	Week 3	Week 4	Week 5	Week 6	Week 1	Week 2	Week 3	Week 4	Week 5	Week 6
	$\frac{80}{5}$ 3	$\frac{85}{3}$ 4	$\frac{80}{2}$ 2	$\frac{85}{3}$ 3	$\frac{90}{2}$ 4	$\frac{80}{2}$ 2	$\frac{80}{3}$ 3	$\frac{82.5}{3}$ 4	$\frac{80}{2}$ 2	$\frac{82.5}{3}$ 3	$\frac{85}{3}$ 4	$\frac{80}{2}$ 2

	CONSTANT BUFFER (0%, I.E., TO FAILURE)						PROGRESSIVE BUFFER (5% DOWN TO FAILURE)					
Absolute strength	Week 1	Week 2	Week 3	Week 4	Week 5	Week 6	Week 1	Week 2	Week 3	Week 4	Week 5	Week 6
	$\frac{85}{5}$ 3	$\frac{87.5}{4}$ 4	$\frac{80}{2}$ 2	$\frac{87.5}{4}$ 3	$\frac{90}{3}$ 4	$\frac{80}{2}$ 2	$\frac{80}{5}$ 3	$\frac{82.5}{5}$ 4	$\frac{80}{2}$ 2	$\frac{82.5}{5}$ 3	$\frac{85}{5}$ 4	$\frac{80}{2}$ 2

Figure 13.1 Sample Progressions Over a Six-Week Maximum Strength Phase Using Either a Constant Buffer or a Progressively Lower Buffer for Relative or Absolute Strength

MXS-I (SUBMAXIMUM LOAD METHOD)						MXS-II (MAXIMUM LOAD METHOD)		
Week 1	Week 2	Week 3	Week 4	Week 5	Week 6	Week 7	Week 8	Week 9
$\frac{72.5}{5}$ 4	$\frac{75}{5}$ 4	$\frac{70}{5}$ 2	$\frac{77.5}{4}$ 3	$\frac{80}{3}$ 4	$\frac{75}{4}$ 2	$\frac{85}{3}$ 3	$\frac{90}{2}$ 4	$\frac{80}{2}$ 2
LOADING PATTERN								
Medium	High			Medium	High	Medium	High	
		Low						Low

Figure 13.2 Sample Nine-Week Progression Passing From the Submaximum Load Method to the Maximum Load Method

of load, number of reps, and number of sets is expressed as follows: The numerator (e.g., 80) refers to the load as a percentage of 1RM, the denomiter (e.g., 5) represents the number of reps, and the multiplier (e.g., 3) indicates the number of sets.

During each of the low steps, a 1RM testing session is planned for the latter part of the week, when the athlete has better recovered from the strain of the preceding high step. For the low step, the load is always decreased (by 5 percent to 10 percent), and the number of total reps per exercise is reduced (50 percent).

Rest Interval The rest interval between sets is a function of the athlete's fitness level and should be calculated to ensure adequate recovery of his or her neuromuscular system. For the submaximum load method, a rest of two to three minutes between sets is sufficient both for CNS and ATP-CP recovery. For the maximum load method, a three- to five-minute rest interval is necessary because maximum loads heavily tax the CNS, which therefore takes longer to recover. If the rest interval is much shorter, CNS participation could plummet in terms of maximum concentration, motivation, and the power of nerve impulses sent to the contracting muscles (Robinson et al. 1995; Pincivero, Lephart, and Karunakara 1997; Pincivero and Campy 2004; de Salles et al. 2010). Insufficient rest may also jeopardize complete restoration of the required fuel for contraction (ATP-CP).

Exercise Order   Ordering exercises to ensure better alternation of muscle groups facilitates local muscle recovery between sets. Four approaches have been developed for sequencing exercises in order to maximize muscle group involvement. Some people prefer to perform one set of each exercise from the top to the bottom of the exercise list and then repeat until all the prescribed sets are performed (vertical sequences—also known as a strength circuit). Others choose to perform all sets for the first exercise before moving on to the next exercise (horizontal sequence).

Still others prefer using the jump set, which is a mix between the vertical and horizontal approaches. In this sequence, the athlete alternates one set each of a pair of antagonist muscle exercises until the planned number of sets per exercise has been reached, then proceeds to another couple of antagonist muscles. For example:

- *A1*: squat
- *A2*: Stiff-leg deadlift
- *B1*: Bench press
- *B2*: Barbell row

Finally, some use the mini-circuit approach, which is especially suitable for team sports in which the strength session must be efficiently organized due to the high number of athletes training simultaneously. In this approach, the exercises are divided into groups—such as upper body, lower body, core, and plyometrics—and performed in a circuit fashion by rotating groups of athletes, who pass from one set of stations to the next.

Compared to all the other methods, the vertical approach provides better recovery between sets, less local and central fatigue, and less hypertrophic response. The vertical approach is particularly suited for macrocycles using the maximum load method (high load and low buffer), in which athletes train in the gym of their club or college (not in a commercial gym, where a customer could occupy a station or load or deload the athlete's barbell). The horizontal approach, on the other hand, is well suited to the submaximum load method (moderate to high loads with high buffer).

Speed of Contraction   Speed of contraction plays an important role in submaximum and maximum load training. Athletic movements are often performed fast and explosively, and for this reason athletes should perform explosive concentric actions almost all year long when performing strength training (the anatomical adaptation phase could be an exception). To maximize speed, the entire neuromuscular system must adapt to quickly recruiting fast-twitch fibers—a key factor in all sports dominated by speed and power. Therefore, even with the maximum loads typical of the maximum load method, the athlete's force application against resistance must be exerted as quickly as possible, even explosively.

To achieve explosive force, the athlete must maximize concentration and motivation before each set. The athlete must concentrate on activating the muscles quickly. Only a high speed of contraction performed against a submaximum or maximum load will quickly recruit fast-twitch fibers, resulting in the highest increase in maximum strength and power (Gonzalez-Badillo et al. 2014). For maximum training benefits, athletes must mobilize all strength potentials in the shortest time possible and from the early part of the lift.

Phase 3: Maximum Strength

Loading Pattern Considering the high demand placed on the neuromuscular system, most athletes should perform submaximum and maximum load training no more than two or three times per week. Only elite athletes, particularly shot-putters and American football linemen, should do this training four times a week. During the competitive phase, the frequency can be reduced to one or two maximum load sessions per week, often performed in combination with other strength components, such as power.

Figure 13.3 shows the maximum strength phase of a strength training program for Olympic-class sprinters. To better exemplify the step method for load increment, the step loading pattern is illustrated graphically at the bottom of the chart. This nine-week program is repeated twice a year because sprinters usually follow a bi-cycle annual plan. A testing session is planned in each of the low steps and is performed in the latter part of the week when the athlete has better recovered from the strain of a high step. For the low step, the load is always decreased (by 10 percent to 20 percent), and the number of sets is reduced (by 30 percent to 50 percent). The goal of the test, of course, is to determine the new 100 percent (1RM) so that it can be used to calculate the load for the following three-week cycle. The discrepancy in the number of sets results from the fact that fundamental exercises are given high priority, whereas accessory exercises are given lower priority. In this way, most of the athlete's energy and attention are focused on the high-priority exercises.

Exercise	Tempo	Rest interval (min.)	WEEK								
			1	2	3	4	5	6	7	8	9
1. Half squat	3.0.X	3	75 4 / 3	80 3 / 3	70 4 / 1	82.5 3 / 3	85 3 / 3	70 4 / 1	87.5 3 / 2	90 3 / 2	70 4 / 1
2. Bench press	3.0.X	3	75 4 / 3	80 3 / 3	70 4 / 1	82.5 3 / 3	85 3 / 3	70 4 / 1	87.5 3 / 2	90 3 / 2	70 4 / 1
3. Hip thrust	3.0.X	3	75 4 / 3	80 3 / 3	70 4 / 1	82.5 3 / 3	85 3 / 3	70 4 / 1	87.5 3 / 2	90 3 / 2	70 4 / 1
4. Chin-up	3.0.X	2	3×10	3×10	1×10	3×8	3×8	1×8	3×6	3×6	1×6
5. Back hyperextension	3.0.X	2	3×8	3×8	1×8	3×6	3×6	1×6	3×5	3×5	1×5
6. Military press	3.0.X	2	3×10	3×10	1×10	3×8	3×8	1×8	3×6	3×6	1×6
7. Standing calf raise	3.0.X	2	3×10	3×10	1×10	3×8	3×8	1×8	3×6	3×6	1×6
8. Crunch	3.0.3	1	3×10	3×10	1×10	3×8	3×8	1×8	3×6	3×6	1×6

LOADING PATTERN

Week	1	2	3	4	5	6	7	8	9
	Medium	High	Low	Medium	High	Low	Medium	High	Low

Figure 13.3 Sample Maximum Strength Phase of an Olympic-Class Sprinter

Figure 13.4 shows a sample six-week maximum strength program for a college-level women's volleyball team. In the program, force was applied aggressively without jerking or snapping. During the rest interval, the limbs used were shaken to relax the muscles. Dumbbells were used for deadlifts. The program was repeated three times a week.

Exercise	WEEK					
	1	2	3	4	5	6
1. Half squat	$\frac{70\ 3}{5}$	$\frac{75\ 3}{4}$	$\frac{80\ 3}{3}$	$\frac{75\ 2}{2}$	$\frac{85\ 3}{3}$	$\frac{90\ 3}{2}$
2. Lat pull-down	$\frac{70\ 3}{5}$	$\frac{75\ 3}{4}$	$\frac{80\ 3}{3}$	$\frac{75\ 2}{2}$	$\frac{85\ 3}{3}$	$\frac{90\ 3}{2}$
3. Romanian deadlift	$\frac{70\ 3}{5}$	$\frac{75\ 3}{4}$	$\frac{80\ 3}{3}$	$\frac{75\ 2}{2}$	$\frac{85\ 3}{3}$	$\frac{90\ 3}{2}$
4. Incline dumbbell press	$\frac{70\ 3}{5}$	$\frac{75\ 3}{4}$	$\frac{80\ 3}{3}$	$\frac{75\ 2}{2}$	$\frac{85\ 3}{3}$	$\frac{90\ 3}{2}$
5. Calf raise	2×12	2×10	1×10	2×8	2×6	1×6
6. Dumbbell French press	2×12	2×10	1×10	2×8	2×6	1×6
7. External rotator (sagittal)	2×15	2×12	1×12	2×10	2×8	1×8
8. Crunch with weight	2×12	2×10	1×10	2×8	2×6	1×6

LOADING PATTERN

Week 1: Low · Week 2: Medium · Week 3: High · Week 4: Low · Week 5: Medium · Week 6: High

Figure 13.4 Sample Six-Week Maximum Strength Phase for a College-Level Women's Volleyball Team

Isometric Method

The isometric training method was known and used for some time before Hettinger and Müler (1953) and again Hettinger (1966) scientifically justified the merits of static contractions in the development of maximum strength. This method's popularity peaked in the 1960s, then faded. Although static contraction has little functional effect overall, it is still useful for the development of maximum strength and can be used in strength training by fighters in grappling, Brazilian jiu-jitsu, mixed martial arts, sailboat racing, windsurfing, or any other sport where the activity requires repeated or prolonged isometric contractions. Static conditions can be realized through two techniques: (1) attempting to lift a weight heavier than one's potential and (2) applying force (by pushing or pulling) against an immobile object.

An isometric contraction produces high tension in the muscle, which makes this method most useful during the maximum strength phase, although it can be used for specific muscular endurance, too, if required. However, even if, as some enthusiasts claim, isometric training can increase maximum strength by 10 to 15 percent more than other methods, it has clear limitations in the development of power. in fact, maximum strength gains obtained through the isometric method cannot be applied readily to dynamic contractions because they do not shift the force–time curve to the left, a disadvantage that must not be ignored.

As isometric force is applied against a given resistance, the tension in the muscle builds progressively, reaching maximum in about two or three seconds and, toward the end, decreasing in a much shorter time (one or two seconds). Because training benefits are angle specific, each interested muscle group must be trained at sport-specific angles. For instance, if the range of motion of a joint is 180 degrees, and the isometric actions usually encountered during the sport-specific activity are at 180 and 45 degrees, then those are the angles at which the isometric contractions must be performed in training, either in isolation or interspersed in the eccentric–concentric motion of an exercise (this approach is referred to as functional isometrics).

The isometric method can also be used to rehabilitate injured muscles. Because no joint motion occurs, "the athlete may continue training even with a joint or bone injury" (Hartmann and Tünnemann 1988). This approach can certainly reduce the risk of muscular atrophy.

As stated previously, strength development is angle specific. In fact, to be more precise, strength increases in a range of 15 degrees—7.5 degrees above and below the angle at which the isometric contraction is performed. Athletes with heart, blood pressure, or circulation problems are strongly discouraged from engaging in isometric training, as blood flow is temporarily stopped in the isometrically contracted muscle, which increases blood pressure and might have severe consequences for people with such health conditions.

Achieving maximum transferable gains with isometric training requires the athlete to perform exercises that are as similar as possible to the sport-specific angle of force application. The isometric method should be used primarily by advanced athletes in combination with other maximum strength methods. See table 13.4 for training parameters.

Table 13.4   Training Parameters for the Isometric Method

Load	80–100 percent of 1RM or against an immobile resistance
No. of exercises	2–4
No. of sets per session	6–8
Duration of contraction per set	6–8 seconds for maximum strength, longer for specific muscle endurance
Total duration of isometric contractions per session	30–50 seconds for maximum strength, longer for specific muscle endurance
Rest interval	60–90 seconds
Frequency per week	2 or 3

Isometric contraction can be performed with all limbs using angles ranging from completely open to fully bent. The following issues should be considered.

- Isometric training is most effective when contraction is near maximum (80 percent to 100 percent).
- For maximum strength at sport-specific angles, a single contraction can range from 6 to 8 seconds, for a total of 30 to 50 seconds per muscle per training session.
- The training load is intensified by increasing either the load or the number of sets—not the duration of contraction.

- During the 60- to 90-second rest interval, relaxation and breathing exercises are recommended. Performance of breathing exercises is a compensatory necessity because static contraction is performed in a state of apnea (holding the breath). In addition, this training increases intrathoracic pressure, which restricts circulation and thus oxygen supply.

- For a more effective program, static contractions should be alternated with isotonic contractions, especially in sports that require speed and power.

- A more effective variant of the isometric method is the functional isometric contraction, which involves free weights. This variant combines isometric with isotonic exercises. The athlete executes the lift to a certain angle, then holds for 3 to 6 seconds. While working through the entire range of motion, the athlete may stop two to four times at sport-specific angles and for sport-specific durations, thus combining the isotonic and isometric methods. This variant provides better physiological benefit (hence the term *functional*), especially for sports that have repeated isometric actions.

Eccentric Method

Any strength exercise performed with free weights, or most isotonic equipment, employs both concentric and eccentric actions. During the concentric phase, force is produced while the muscle shortens; during the eccentric phase, force is produced as the muscle lengthens.

Practice has demonstrated that the eccentric phase always seems to be easier than the concentric phase. For example, when performing a bench press, the return of the barbell to the chest (the eccentric part of the lift) always seems easier than the lift itself. Thus, one could logically conclude that because an athlete can work with heavier loads during the eccentric action, strength is certainly improved to higher levels by using the eccentric method alone. Researchers have indeed concluded that eccentric training creates higher tension in the muscles than isometric or isotonic contractions do. In turn, because higher muscle tension normally means higher strength development (Goldberg et al. 1975), eccentric training could logically be considered a superior training method.

Other researchers have found that gains in maximum strength appear to result mostly from changes in neural activation rather than from hypertrophic response (Dudley and Fleck 1987). This finding means that maximum strength improvements do not result mainly from gains in muscle mass, but rather from specific neural adaptations, such as an increase in fast-twitch muscle fiber recruitment (intramuscular coordination), increased strength with little or no hypertrophy, and modifications in the neural commands used to control the movement (intermuscular coordination), resulting in increased strength with little or no hypertrophy.

The CNS commands the eccentric contraction differently than the concentric one. This process occurs mostly as grading, or ranking, the amount of muscle activation necessary to complete a task (Enoka 1996). Specifically, the amount of muscle activation and the number of fibers involved are proportional to the training load. The neural command for eccentric contraction is unique in that it decides (1) which motor units should be activated, (2) how much they need to be activated, (3) when they should be activated, and (4) how the activity should be distributed within a group of muscles (Abbruzzese et al. 1994).

Because muscles resist fatigue during eccentric action, such activity can be maintained longer than concentric (Tesch et al. 1978), possibly because of the altered recruitment order of motor units. In addition, the load in eccentric training can be much higher than the load in the maximum concentric contraction (up to 140 percent of the concentric 1RM).

When using supermaximum loads (for very advanced athletes, and only for one or two exercises, for a limited amount of time), one or two spotters (depending on the exercise and the athlete's strength level) are needed to help the athlete lift the barbell for the concentric phase because the load for eccentric training is higher than 1RM. The spotters should also ensure that as the bar is lowered, the athlete does not let it drop, which can cause injury. The need for careful assistance as the bar is slowly lowered makes it impossible to perform the exercise quickly. Another option for supermaximum training comes from unilateral exercises. in fact, when working one limb at a time, such as on a leg extension or leg curl machine, the other limb can help in the concentric phase, whereas the trained limb does the eccentric phase by itself (this is also referred to as the 2/1 method).

During the first few days of eccentric training, athletes may experience muscle soreness. This is to be expected because higher tension provokes more muscle damage. As athletes adapt, the muscle soreness disappears (in 5 to 7 days). Short-term discomfort can be avoided by increasing the load in steps.

As expected, the eccentric method shifts the force–time curve to the left. Heavy loads that generate high tension in the muscles improve strength because they result in high recruitment of the powerful fast-twitch motor units. The eccentric method is particularly useful for strengthening muscle groups whose peak of activation is encountered during an eccentric phase, such as the biceps femoris in the sprinting cycle.

The supramaximum eccentric training method should be used only by athletes with at least five years of strength training because it employs the heaviest loads (110 percent to 140 percent of 1RM). The eccentric method should always be limited to one or two muscle groups and should be combined with other methods, especially the maximum load method. Eccentric contractions should not be used excessively. Every time an athlete uses maximum or supramaximum loads, maximal mental concentration is required, which can be psychologically wearing. Therefore, athletes should use the eccentric method carefully—no more than twice a week—in combination with maximum strength training. In addition, the use of active recovery techniques eliminates discomfort, reduces soreness, and encourages faster regeneration (for additional information, see chapter 4).

Training parameters for the eccentric method are presented in table 13.5. The range of the load is presented as the percentage of maximum strength capacity for the concentric contraction and suggests a resistance between 110 and 140 percent. Athletes at all levels should be progressed from lower loads up to the highest load allowed by their capabilities. Because the load is supramaximum, the speed of execution is slow. Such loads should be used only after at least four seasons of maximum strength training.

Table 13.5 Training Parameters for the Eccentric Method

Load	110%–140% of 1RM
No. of exercises per session	1 to 2
No. of reps per set	1–5
No. of sets per exercise	2–4
Rest interval	2–8 minutes, depending on the size of the muscle group
Speed of execution	Slow (3 to 6 seconds, depending on the range of motion of the exercise)
Frequency per week	1 to 2

The rest interval is also an important element in the athlete's capacity to perform highly demanding work. If an athlete does not recover well enough between sets to complete the next set at the same level—insufficient recovery is indicated by inability to perform the eccentric phase in the time allowed—the rest interval must be increased accordingly. Other important factors include the athlete's motivation and concentration capacity. Because eccentric actions involve such heavy loads, athletes must be highly motivated and able to concentrate in order to perform them effectively.

The eccentric method should never be performed in isolation from the other maximum strength methods. Even during the maximum strength phase, the eccentric method is used with the maximum load method; therefore, only one eccentric training session per muscle group is suggested per week.

Figure 13.5 shows the last three weeks of a nine-week program developed for an international-class shot-putter. A three-week conversion-to-power phase followed, then two weeks of unloading prior to an important competition.

Exercise	WEEK		
	7	8	9
1. Squat (eccentric)	$\frac{110\ 3}{5}$	$\frac{120\ 3}{4}$	$\frac{130\ 3}{3}$
2. Incline bench press (eccentric)	$\frac{110\ 3}{5}$	$\frac{120\ 3}{4}$	$\frac{130\ 3}{3}$
3. Back hyperextension	$\frac{80\ 3}{3}$	$\frac{85\ 3}{2}$	$\frac{90\ 3}{1}$
4. Calf raise	$\frac{80\ 3}{5}$	$\frac{85\ 3}{3}$	$\frac{90\ 3}{3}$
5. Jump squat	$\frac{70\ 3}{5}$	$\frac{70\ 3}{5}$	$\frac{70\ 3}{5}$

Figure 13.5 Last Three Weeks of a Nine-Week Program for an International-Class Shot-Putter

Maxex Training

Maximum tension exercises can be combined with exercises requiring explosiveness. This method, which combines maximum strength exercises with high loads with exercises for explosiveness, is called *maxex training*.

Motor unit force is determined by the rate at which the CNS sends firing signals, called action potentials, from the motor neuron to the muscle fibers. A higher rate means a greater magnitude of motor unit force. As the frequency of the action potentials increases, tetanus changes from an irregular force profile to a "fused tetanus," or plateau profile (Enoka 2002). The peak force of a fused tetanus represents the maximum force that a motor unit can exert.

The goal of maximum strength exercises with very high loads performed before explosive exercises, then, is to create a period in which the motor units of the prime movers are maximally activated to produce the greatest possible force. This is really the only way to physiologically produce maximum force output. To this end, the maxex training discussed here, at its best, can be used to combine maximum force with exercises for explosiveness. More specifically, it can elicit a high level of motor unit recruitment and force production before the athlete performs a high-discharge-rate power exercise such as plyometrics. Maximum strength methods can be combined with plyometrics for all team sports; for sprinting, jumping, and throwing events in track and field; for the martial arts, boxing, and wrestling; for alpine skiing and ski jumping; for fencing; for diving; for figure skating; and for sprint events in swimming.

The variations of training proposed here need not be performed year-round. They can be planned at the end of the preparatory phase or, in the case of a long maximum strength phase, during the last macrocycle, as well as during the maintenance phase. A maximum strength phase is still necessary before any power training because power is a function of maximum strength. The incorporation of power training during the maximum strength phase enhances speed and explosiveness to ready athletes for the competitive phase.

However, combining maximum strength with power must be done carefully and conservatively. Although many combinations are possible, training must be simple so that athletes can focus on the main task of the workout or training phase. The more variations coaches use, the more they may confuse their athletes and disrupt the way their athletes' bodies adapt.

The concept of maxex training relies on science—specifically, manipulating two physiological concepts to produce speed and explosiveness and thereby improve athletic performance. The first part of the maxex routine is performed against a heavy (85 to 95 percent of 1RM) load, which stimulates high recruitment of fast-twitch muscle fibers. The follow-up explosive or quickness movements increase the firing rate of the fast-twitch muscle fibers, thus preparing the athlete for the quick, explosive actions required for all speed and power sports during the competitive phase.

Maxex training is suggested for the prime movers only. Because this training method can be quite stressful mentally and physically, only athletes with a good background in strength training should use it. The duration of Maxex training should be approximately three to six weeks, depending on the athlete's background. Maxex training should follow a maximum strength phase in which eccentric-concentric contraction has been used. One or two training sessions per week with at least 48 hours of rest between bouts are suggested.

Maxex training applies to the upper body as well as the lower body. Strong arms and shoulders are essential in various sports, including basketball, baseball, ice hockey, football, lacrosse, the martial arts, boxing, wrestling, kayaking, squash, European handball, water polo, wrestling, and throwing events in track and field. Without exhausting all options, exercises that can be applied in these sports for maxex training include drop jumps, jump squats, drop push-ups, short sprints, hurdle jumps, and medicine ball throws.

During the maximum strength phase, athletes can combine maximum strength methods with some of the following variations or with plyometrics (either low or medium impact). Coaches should consider the following methods:

- Isometric-dynamic—This is a near maximal or maximal isometric contraction immediately followed by a plyometric contraction for the same kinetic chain. Perform one or two sets of three or four reps of four to six seconds per isometric contraction. Each set is followed by a very short sprint or by three to five plyometric reps (reactive jumps). Take at least three minutes of rest between reps and five minutes between sets.

- Complex drill—For better exemplification, we use the squat exercise (for sprinters, jumpers, throwers, volleyball spikers, and martial artists). Perform one or two sets using a load of 80 percent to 85 percent of 1RM in the following sequence: (1) slow eccentric contraction, (2) isometric contraction for one or two seconds in the deepest part of the squat, and (3) concentric contraction with maximum acceleration. Immediately afterward, the athlete does a very short sprint or three to five plyometrics (reactive jumps). Alternatively, the athlete uses the quarter squat for two sets of two dymamic reps with 150 percent of the full-squat 1RM, followed immediately by a very short sprint or three to five plyometrics (reactive jumps).

All of these techniques increase speed, reactivity, explosive strength, and especially the discharge rate of fast-twitch muscle fibers.

Phase 4: Conversion to Specific Strength

14

Today almost every athlete uses some sort of strength training program to improve performance. However, most strength programs fail to transform the strength gains made during the maximum strength training phase into sport- or event-specific strength, such as power or muscular endurance. This failure prevents athletes from maximizing their athletic potential in order to increase their sport performance in tasks requiring speed, agility, or prolonged effort. Periodization of strength, on the other hand, is designed precisely to produce such transformations during the conversion phase so that the athlete achieves peak performance during his or her main competitions.

The loading parameters used in the conversion stage should reflect the characteristics of the sport, particularly the relationship between strength and the dominant energy system. Table 14.1 shows how an event's duration and intensity of effort determine the energy systems, and therefore the specific strength, that must be trained.

Table 14.1 Event Duration and Specific Strength Conversion

Event duration	Event intensity	Main energy system	Specific strength
<10 sec.	Maximum	ATP-CP	Power
10 to 30 sec.	Maximum to very high	Anaerobic glycolysis (power)	Power endurance
30 sec. to 2 min.	High	Anaerobic glycolysis (capacity)/aerobic glycolysis (power)	Muscular endurance short
2 to 8 min.	Moderately high	Aerobic glycolysis (power)	Muscular endurance medium
>8 min.	Moderately high to low	Aerobic glycolysis (power to capacity)/fat oxidation (capacity)	Muscular endurance long

During the year, the goals of strength training and their consistent methods vary depending on the characteristics of the sport, the characteristics of the athlete, and the competition calendar. The ultimate goal, however, is the maximization of specific strength. In relation to this final objective of strength training periodization, we can distinguish two main types of sport:

1. Sports that require power (a synonym for what is sometimes called "speed-strength," or starting strength and explosive strength in the force–time curve)—that is, the ability to apply force as quickly as possible, as in the jumps, throws, and sprints in athletics, most team sports, and all sports in which power strongly influences performance

2. Sports that require muscular endurance—that is, the ability to apply less force for a longer time, as in most events in swimming, rowing, kayaking, triathlon, cross-country skiing, and middle- and long-distance running

The human body can adapt to any environment and therefore any type of training. If an athlete is trained with bodybuilding methods, which is often the case in North America, the neuromuscular system adapts to those methods. More specifically, because bodybuilding methods focus on a slow rate of contraction, they increase muscle size (hypertrophy) but do not increase power, speed, agility, or quickness. Therefore, an athlete who trains in this way should not be expected to display fast, explosive power because his or her neuromuscular system has not been not trained for it.

To develop sport-specific power, a training program must be specifically designed to achieve that objective. Such a program must be specific to the sport or event and must use exercises that simulate the physiological and biomechanical characteristics of the sport's skills as closely as possible. Because power training addresses muscles at a high degree of specificity, the athlete's inter- and intramuscular coordination become more efficient and his or her skill performance becomes smoother, quicker, and more precise.

During the conversion phase, athletes should use more energy for technical and tactical training than they do for specific strength training. Coaches must plan training with the lowest possible number of exercises that closely relate to the skill. For maximum return, such programs must be efficient, with two or three exercises performed dynamically over several sets. Time and energy should not be wasted on anything else.

Power Training

Power is the main ingredient for all sports that require a high rate of force, speed, and agility. Sports that are speed and power dominant include sprinting, jumping, and throwing events in track and field; team sports; racket sports; gymnastics; diving; and the martial arts. For an athlete's performance to improve, his or her level of power must improve; indeed, power is the main ingredient necessary to produce a fast, quick, and agile athlete.

People use different terms for power, including *dynamic strength* and the aberrant and confusing terms *strength-speed* (which is, in fact, power training with high loads) and *speed-strength* (which is power training with low loads). If we are committed to employing science in sport training, the correct term should be borrowed from physics and physiology, both of which use the term *power*, which is defined as

- the rate of producing force,
- the product of force and velocity ($P = F \times V$, or force times velocity),
- the amount of work done per time unit, or
- the rate at which muscles can produce work (Enoka 2002).

For athletic purposes, any increase in power must be the result of improvements in either strength, speed, or a combination of the two. An athlete can be very strong, with a large muscle mass, yet be unable to display power because of an inability to contract already-strong muscles in a very short time. To overcome this deficiency, the athlete must undergo power training to improve his or her rate of force development.

The advantage of explosive, high-velocity power training is that it trains the central nervous system (CNS). Improvements in performance can be based on neural changes that help individual muscles achieve greater performance capability (Sale 1986). This gain is accomplished by shortening the time required for motor unit recruitment, especially of fast-twitch fibers (Häkkinen 1986; Häkkinen and Komi 1983).

Power training exercises activate and increase the discharge rate of fast-twitch muscle fibers leading to specific CNS adaptations. Adaptation, especially in well-trained athletes, shows itself in the form of discharging a greater number of muscle fibers in a very short time. Both training practice and research have shown that such adaptations require considerable time and that they progress from year to year.

Adaptation to power training is further evidenced by better intermuscular coordination, or the ability of agonist and antagonist muscles to cooperate in order to perform a movement. This coordination is achieved through better linkage between the excitatory and inhibitory reactions of a muscle in a complex motor pattern. As a result of such adaptation, the CNS learns when and when not to send a nerve impulse that signals the muscle to contract and perform a movement. In practical terms, improved intermuscular coordination enhances the athlete's ability to contract some muscles and relax others (i.e., to relax the antagonist muscles), which improves the speed of contraction of the prime movers—the agonist muscles.

During the conversion phase—except for the conversion to muscular endurance long—exercises must be performed quickly and explosively in order to recruit the highest number of motor units at the highest rate of contraction (in other words, at an increased discharge rate). Especially for the conversion to power, the entire program should be geared to achieving only one goal: moving the force–time curve as far to the left as possible (refer to figure 10.66) so that the neuromuscular system is trained to display force explosively. Coaches should select only training methods that fulfill the requirements of power development—that is, that enhance quickness, facilitate explosive application of force, and increase the reactivity of the relevant muscles.

The methods presented in this chapter can be used separately or in combination. When they are combined, the total work per session must be distributed among them.

Physiological Strategy to Increase Power

Some sport practitioners and authors maintain the philosophy that athletes who want to increase power should do only power drills all year long, that athletes who want to be fast should do only short reps with high speed, and that athletes who want to be quick and agile should do only agility drills. This training philosophy takes to the extreme the fundamental physiological principle that a given type of work results in a specific adaptation, but contradicts the methodological principle that specific adaptations are maximized on the base of general adaptations, especially for low-trainability biomotor abilities such as speed.

In addition, athletes who maintain the same type of work for longer periods of time experience a plateau, a stagnation of improvement, or even a slight detraining, which results in performance deterioration. To prevent this outcome, and to ensure that athletes consistently improve their power in order to benefit their performance during the competitive phase, they must constantly stimulate their neuromuscular system to produce the highest voluntary recruitment of fast-twitch muscle fibers and display higher levels of muscular strength more quickly. This stimulation can be achieved by applying the training methods of the periodization of strength.

Research shows that using lighter loads exclusively produces a more modest increase in peak power than is produced by using heavier loads. In fact, the greatest increases in power are obtained not from higher-velocity training but from a combination of high force and high velocity training (Verkhoshansky 1997; Aagaard et al. 1994; Enoka 2002). Indeed, the peak power that a muscle can produce depends directly on gains in maximum strength (Fitts and Widrick 1996).

The same is true for speed. As trainers have known since the 1950s, maximum velocity does not increase unless power is increased first. These findings validate and add more substance to the theory of periodization of strength, allowing us to draw the conclusion that speed, agility, and quickness never increase unless maximum strength is trained first and then converted to power.

With these realities in mind, we propose two training phases to maximize power, speed, agility, and quickness (see figure 14.1).

During the first phase, the scope of training is to train the CNS to recruit the highest number of fast-twitch fibers. This training usually occurs during the maximum strength phase, in which athletes use loads of more than 70 percent of 1-repetition maximum (1RM) moved explosively. These training loads result in high stimulation of the neuromuscular system, which then recruits high numbers of fast-twitch muscle fibers. To avoid detraining and a loss in strength, maximum strength training sessions should also be planned during the conversion and maintenance phases of the annual plan.

The power exerted during athletic actions depends on the number of active motor units, the number of fast-twitch fibers recruited into the action, and the rate at which those fibers are discharged, producing a high force-to-frequency ratio (Enoka 2002). The increase in the discharge rate of fast-twitch fibers is achieved by training with lighter loads, either by using less than 50 percent of 1RM for novice athletes and between 50 and 60 percent of 1RM for advanced athletes (Buzzichelli 2015; Enoka 2002; Moritani 1992; Van Cutsem, Duchateau, and Hainaut 1998) or by using any type of lighter implement (e.g., shots from track and field, power balls, medicine balls) or by performing plyometrics or specific drills for speed, agility, and quickness. Such exercises—performed with maximum power, speed, and quick application of force against the resistance provided by the implement, the pull of gravity, or both—facilitate activation of high-threshold motor units and high frequency of discharge. Such high-velocity exercises are necessary during the second phase when a higher discharge rate of the fast-twitch fibers is sought.

Clearly, then, the main scope of strength training for sports is to continually increase maximum strength so that 50 percent of 1RM is always higher. This gain, in turn, produces the maximum benefit of increasing peak performance.

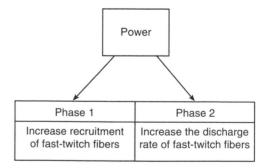

Figure 14.1 The physiological strategy used to increase power, speed, and agility.

Heavy Loads Versus Light Loads in Power Enhancement

Trainers and athletes often debate the merits of using heavy loads or light loads to improve power performance. The fact is that both play a role but at different points in training. Indeed, this is the beauty of periodization: All training methods have a place in the various phases of training.

The speed at which an athlete can perform concentric (shortening) movements—such as pushing a barbell up from the chest during a bench press—depends, of course, on the load that the athlete is using. As the load is increased, the velocity of the shortening activity decreases. However, the opposite is true for eccentric or lengthening movements. When performing an eccentric contraction, the force production is greater when the movement is performed at a high velocity. This relationship explains the positive transfer from plyometric exercises to power performance. The intrinsic elastic properties of muscles favor the absorption and reuse of stored elastic energy, which is optimized when a muscle is lengthened as quickly as possible. Therefore, to improve force expression of the full spectrum of velocity and increase the rate of force development, both heavy loads and light loads are necessary in training.

Moderate-velocity strength training (characteristic of the maximum strength phase) enhances intramuscular coordination as a result of both motor unit recruitment and the firing rate of motor units. In essence, moderate-velocity training using high resistance leads primarily to improvement in muscular strength. In contrast, high-velocity training (characteristic of power training) involves training with lighter resistances at higher velocities. This type of training increases the rate of force development, which obviously includes a speed component. The exact nature of that component may be a question in itself. One study, for instance, concluded that the *intent* to produce ballistic contractions—not the speed of movement per se—was responsible for a high-velocity training effect (Behm and Sale 1993).

However, because heavy loads cause a very slow angular speed—much lower than the sport-specific one—the transition from maximum strength training to sport-specific speed is vital in sports that require explosive movement. For example, a long jumper who spends hours squatting will develop a high level of strength, but that strength will not automatically transfer into jump-specific movements that synchronize the use of all prime movers. Such a transfer can be achieved only by performing plyometric and sport-specific drills.

The degree of emphasis placed on heavy loads versus light loads ultimately depends on the type of sport. The periodization of strength program is characterized by a maximum strength phase (using high loads) followed by a conversion phase (using low loads). The most effective approach is a combination of both, as presented in the periodization model. To explore this issue, one study compared the training of three groups. Group 1 performed heavy squat training, group 2 performed plyometric training with a light load, and group 3 combined squat and plyometric training. Because the largest gain in indexes of power occurred in group 3, the authors concluded that optimal training benefits are acquired by combining heavy-load training with explosive movements (Adams, Worlay, and Throgmartin 1987).

An even more intriguing study, conducted by Verkhoshansky in the 1970s, also compared three groups. Group 1 performed a macrocycle of heavy squat training followed by a macrocycle of plyometrics, group 2 performed a macrocycle of plyometrics followed by a macrocycle of heavy squat training, and group 3 combined both squat and plyometrics for the two macrocycles (that is, engaged in complex training). The third method (complex training) delivered the quickest improvement, but the first sequential method resulted in the highest improvement at the end of the two macrocycles (Verkhoshansky 1997). This is the same approach that we use in the periodization of strength.

Agility and Periodization of Power Training

Agility training is one of the most misunderstood elements of sport training. Agility refers to the athletic ability to swiftly accelerate and decelerate, to quickly change direction, and to rapidly vary movement patterns. Intrinsic elements of agility include high-frequency footwork or quick feet, speed of reaction and movement, dynamic flexibility, and effective rhythm and timing of movements.

Agility as an ability does not exist independently. Rather, it relies on the development of a host of other abilities, such as those just listed, in which the determinant factors are relative strength and power. Indeed, without high levels of relative strength and power, no one would ever be agile or quick. The higher an athlete's maximum strength is relative to body weight—that is, the higher his or her relative strength is, the easier it is for the athlete to decelerate and accelerate his or her own body weight. Similarly, the higher the athlete's level of power is, the more quickly he or she can do it. Agility, then, is the ability to accelerate quickly by using concentric strength; to decelerate by using eccentric strength, as in stop-and-go movements; and to change direction or perform the cuts that are so important in many sports, especially team and racket sports.

Agility does not improve as expected without consistent activation and increased recruitment of fast-twitch fibers. Therefore, athletes who repeatedly perform agility drills ultimately reach a plateau and stagnate in their performance of any skills in which agility is a determinant factor. For these reasons, the periodization of agility is based on the physiological strategy suggested earlier in figure 14.1.

More specifically, the periodization model illustrated in figure 14.2 results in the greatest improvement in agility (Bompa 2005). The top of the chart lists traditional training phases of the annual plan and specific phases of the periodization of strength, which are explained in other chapters. During the anatomical adaptation phase, which focuses on building a foundation of strength and general conditioning, repeating agility drills will not produce visible improvement because the neuromuscular system is not yet trained to recruit fast-twitch fibers.

Training phase	Preparation			Competitive	Transition
Periodization of strength	Anatomical adaptation	Maximum strength	Conversion to power	Maintenance: maximum strength, power	Compensation training
Periodization of agility	No agility drills	Learning phase: repeating known agility drills, learning new ones	Increasing velocity of agility drills	Increasing velocity of agility drills	No agility drills (not in scope of training for this phase)
Benefits to agility	Low	Good to high	Maximum		Low

Figure 14.2 Periodization of Agility

270

Phase 4: Conversion to Specific Strength

During the maximum strength phase, however, the recruitment of fast-twitch fibers becomes the scope of training, and therefore agility training can be initiated in the form of repeating known drills and learning new ones. As the neuromuscular system improves its ability to recruit more motor units, and in particular a higher numbers of fast-twitch fibers, especially toward the end of the maximum strength phase, the athlete improves in his or her velocity or quickness of performing agility drills. This ability is then maximized toward the end of the conversion phase and during the competitive phase, when the discharge rate of fast-twitch fibers increases as a result of increasing the velocity of agility drills and applying force against lighter implements or against the force of gravity. From this phase of training onward, and throughout the maintenance phase, agility is maximized and contributes to improvement in the athlete's performance.

Finally, many trainers still consider agility and quickness (quick feet) to be separate physical qualities. This view is apparent in many seminars and books published on these topics. In reality, however, when the neuromuscular system is trained according to the physiological strategy suggested in figure 14.1, the final physiological product is an increased discharge rate of the fast-twitch fibers. As a result of high adaptation to the periodization of strength, athletes possess more power, run faster, and can perform any type of drill with quickness. The human body doesn't care whether we use two different terms to describe the same neuromuscular quality. No matter what we call these movements, the properly trained body is capable of performing powerful actions, moving limbs fast, and changing direction quickly.

Some agility instructors or coaches have their athletes perform similar agility drills and quickness exercises throughout the year of training—thus disregarding the concept of periodization—and with pretty much the same duration, intensity, and number of repetitions. In addition, some instructors take no account of an athlete's age or training background. In these conditions, one should not be surprised that some athletes, especially those with a shallow training background, experience anatomical discomfort or even injury. The best method for avoiding injury is to apply the concept of periodization.

During the preparatory phase of the annual plan, athletes can improve their agility and quickness by using implements or types of training that include power balls, medicine balls, and plyometric exercises. For the best training organization and periodization, plyometric exercises are organized into five categories of intensity. These intensities can also be periodized, as can the weight of power and medicine balls (see figure 14.3).

Figure 14.3 shows particular activities and intensities used in the preparatory phase. During the anatomical adaptation portion, which emphasizes the foundation of strength,

Training phase	Preparatory						Competitive		
Periodization of strength	Anatomical adaptation	Maximum strength	Conversion to power, maximum strength				Maintenance: maximum strength, power		
Periodization of power ball or medicine ball (weight)*	Light	Medium to heavy		Medium		Light	Light		
Periodization of plyometrics (intensity)	5	4	4	3	2	2 or 1	2 or 1	1 and 3	3

*Power balls weigh between 2 and 35 pounds (about 1 and 16 kilograms). Light weight ranges from 2 to 10 pounds (about 1 to 4.5 kilograms); medium weight ranges from 12 to 20 pounds (about 5.5 to 9 kilograms), and heavy weight ranges from 22 to 35 pounds (about 9 to 16 kilograms). Medicine balls weigh between 2 and 20 pounds (about 1 and 9 kilograms). For plyometric intensity level descriptions, please refer to table 14.5 later in this chapter.

Figure 14.3 Periodization of Plyometrics and Power and Medicine Balls

low loads are used for the implements and low intensity (level 5) is used for plyometrics. During the maximum strength portion, the athlete uses high loads for power ball and medicine ball training in order to activate a higher number of motor units. At the same time, the intensity of plyometric exercises is increased in order to heighten the reactivity of the athlete's neuromuscular system. Finally, during the conversion portion, the loads are decreased for power ball and medicine ball training in order to maximize the benefits of quickness of force application. The intensity of plyometrics, however, is at its highest, pushing the eccentric contractions to their maximum, which results in higher force production. Under these conditions, the discharge rate of fast-twitch muscle fibers increases to ensure that the athlete reaches peak performance at the time of a major competition.

During the competitive phase, the first period features high-intensity plyometrics and is followed by alternating microcycles in which high- and medium-intensity plyometrics are used according to the macrocycle structure and the competitive calendar. In the week preceding the major competition of the year (for individual sports), medium-intensity plyometrics are used, and they are then suspended during the final, competitive microcycle.

Throughout this book, illustrations of the planning of periodization and training methods use a vertical bar to separate training phases. This approach may imply that a certain type of training ends on the last day of one phase and that a completely different type begins on the first day of the next phase. In reality, the transition between phases is not quite so abrupt. There is always an overlap, and a training method to be used in a given phase is introduced progressively in the previous phases. For instance, as depicted in figure 14.3, this approach is used for power training that starts from the beginning of the annual plan and gets its moment of emphasis after the maximum strength phase. Similarly, the method used in a previous phase is usually maintained in the next phase with a progressive reduction in emphasis. Thus each training phase focuses on a dominant method (or methods) but also involves another that is progressively introduced. This training approach allows for a more effective transition from one method to the next and finally higher levels of adaptation by the athlete.

A transition of emphasis between two training methods or phases can take place over the span of a few microcycles. Figure 14.4 shows that as the isotonic method for power development is progressively introduced, maximum strength work is progressively reduced. This transition can be accomplished by controlling the number of training sessions dedicated to each ability. An example is provided in figure 14.5, where, in the third maximum strength microcycle, all three training sessions are dedicated to maximum strength. In the following microcycles, however, maximum strength is decreased, whereas power is

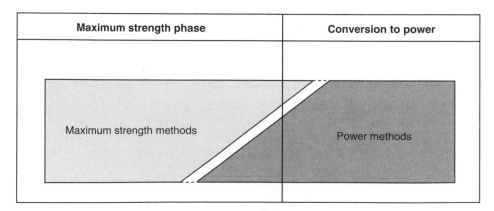

Figure 14.4 Switch of training emphasis in the preparation phase.

Phase 4: Conversion to Specific Strength

Macrocycle		Maximum strength		Power	
Microcycle		3	4	1	2
Training days	Maximum strength	3	2**	1***	1***
	Power	0	1	2	2

*Maximum strength is maintained via a dedicated session.

**Including one day for the 1RM test.

***Maximum strength maintenance session.

Figure 14.5 Progressive Transition From a Maximum Strength Macrocycle to a Power Macrocycle*

increased. As a result, during the power macrocycle, two of the three training days are dedicated to power, and one maximum strength session is planned to retain gains in maximum strength.

Another method of transitioning from the maximum strength phase to the conversion (power) phase is to create different combinations of sets of maximum strength and power, as illustrated in figure 14.6. This figure also depicts a different way to retain maximum strength during a power macrocycle. For easier presentation, it is assumed that each microcycle includes three strength training sessions of five sets per fundamental exercise. In this option, during the power phase, a lower number of maximum strength sets is performed in each training session in order to retain maximum strength levels.

Macrocycle		Maximum strength			Power					
		Microcycle 4			Microcycle 1			Microcycle 2		
Training day		1	2	3	1	2	3	1	2	3
Sets	Maximum strength	5	2	1RM test	3	2	1**	1**	1**	1**
	Power	0	1		2	3	4	4	4	4

*Maximum strength is maintained via maximum strength sets in each session.

**Maximum strength maintenance sets.

Figure 14.6 Progressive Transition From a Maximum Strength Macrocycle to a Power Macrocycle*

The transition from one type of training to another can also be planned more elaborately, as illustrated in figure 14.7. This chart shows the periodization of strength, the number of workouts per week, the duration of each phase in weeks, and the transition from one type of strength to another. In this case, the core strength for synchronized swimming—which is the strength of the hips, abdominal muscles, and low back—was emphasized or maintained throughout the annual plan. A well-organized coach also structures a plan that shows how to use a certain type of training method and for how long. In doing so, the coach plans the most appropriate methods for each training phase, showing the duration of each as well as which method is dominant.

Figure 14.8 illustrates how training methods can be planned. The example refers to hypothetical sports in which power is the dominant ability. As usual, the top of the chart shows the training phases of a monocycle, and the row below that shows the periodization of strength. The bottom part of the chart lists several methods. Three types of symbols are used because in a given training phase, a certain method can have a higher priority than the others. The solid line indicates the method with the highest priority, the dashed line shows second priority, and the dotted line shows the third priority. For instance, during

	Dates	Sept.	Oct.	Nov.	Dec.	Jan.	Feb.		Mar.	Apr.	May
PERIODIZATION	Competition	—			Provincial		Divisional			National	
	Training phase	Preparatory		Competitive							
	Periodization of strength	AA; core strength	MxS; maint. of core strength	Conversion to P; ME; maint. of core strength						Maint.	Cessation
	Duration in weeks	5	9	4		4	4		4	4	1
	No. of workouts per week	3	3 or 4	3						2	0
	No. of workouts per type of strength	2 AA, 1 core	2 or 3 MxS, 1 core	2 ME, 1 P, 1/2 MxS, 1/2 core		2 ME, 1 P, 1/2 MxS, 1/2 core		3 ME, 1 P	2 ME, 1 P	1 ME, 1 P	

Key: AA = anatomical adaptation, maint. = maintenance, ME = muscular endurance, MxS = maximum strength, and P = power.

Figure 14.7 Transition to Different Types of Strength for Synchronized Swimming

the anatomical adaptation phase, circuit training is the dominant training method. When the maximum strength phase begins, the submaximum load method prevails, and during the latter part of the maximum strength program, the maximum load method dominates.

In power training, the figure presents the ballistic method and plyometrics (explained a bit later in this chapter). The dotted line shows that these methods are a third priority in some phases. Please bear in mind that figure 14.8 is a hypothetical example and does not show all available methods or all possibilities for using those that are presented.

	Sept.	Oct.	Nov.	Dec.	Jan.	Feb.	Mar.	Apr.
Training phase	Preparatory						Precompetitive	Competitive
Periodization of strength	Anatomical adaptation		Maximum strength (MxS)			Conversion to power (P)	Maintenance: P 70%, MxS 30%	
			MxS | P | MxS | P | MxS					
Microcycles	1 2 3 4	5 6 7 8	9 10 11	12 13 14 15 16	17 18 19 20 21	22 23 24 25	26 27 28	29 30 31 32
Circuit training	<------------------>							
MAXIMUM STRENGTH								
Submaximum load			<--------------------->				<··························>	
Maximum load					<-->			
POWER TRAINING								
Plyometrics		<··························>	<>	<·····>	<>	<·····>	<------------------>	<······>
Ballistic			<-->	<··>	<-->	<··>	<-->	<··············> | <---->

Figure 14.8 Hypothetical Example of Planning the Training Methods for a Power-Dominated Sport

DECELERATION–ACCELERATION: THE KEY TO AGILITY

To change direction quickly, an athlete must first slow down before moving quickly in another direction. In other words, the action is performed in two phases: deceleration followed by acceleration, or deceleration–acceleration. Deceleration, or slowing down almost to a stop, results from the eccentric loading (lengthening) of the knee and hip extensors (quadriceps, hamstrings, glutes) and the plantar flexors (gastrocnemii). Elastic energy stored in the muscle–tendon unit during deceleration is then used to start the acceleration.

A high level of quickness and agility can be developed by improving the strength and power of the major lower-leg muscles (particularly the gastrocnemius) and major upper-leg muscles (the quadriceps, semimembranosus, semitendinosus, long head of the biceps femoris, and gluteui). The ability to decelerate and accelerate quickly relies heavily on the ability of these muscles to contract powerfully, both eccentrically and concentrically. In particular, deceleration (related to eccentric strength) appears to be the determinant and limiting factor for performance. Furthermore, deceleration–acceleration coupling is slow if power is not trained adequately.

An athlete should learn to perform deceleration and acceleration using a specific technique that involves not only the legs but also the arms. In the case of deceleration, the arms move in coordination with the legs but with a reduced amplitude and force. In other words the arms make a very slight action that influences deceleration. Quick deceleration, however, invariably depends on the strength of the legs. Do you want to decelerate fast? If so, then improve the strength (especially the eccentric strength) of the knee and hip extensors and the plantar flexors!

Acceleration, on the other hand, is greatly influenced by arm action. In particular, for an athlete to initiate the acceleration part of a sprint, an agility movement, or one requiring quick feet, the arms must move first! If one's legs are to move fast, the arms' back-and-forth drive must be very active, even powerfully performed. In addition, the stronger the push-off is against the ground (which is related to concentric strength), the more powerful the ground reaction force is that works in the opposite direction. Remember Newton's third law of motion: Every action has an equal and opposite reaction. Therefore, during the propulsion phase, an athlete exerts force onto the ground, and the ground simultaneously exerts a force back onto the athlete. As a result, maximizing an athlete's sprinting ability requires a high level of maximum strength and the ability to display it in the shortest possible time.

Methods for Power Training

A number of training methods can be used during the power phase; normally, this phase uses a combination of the isotonic, ballistic, power-resisting, and plyometric. The following sections describe these methods and how to implement them in a periodized training plan.

Isotonic Method

One classic method of power training is to attempt to move a weight as rapidly and forcefully as possible through the entire range of motion. Therefore, good means for developing power include free weights and other equipment that can be moved quickly. The weight of the equipment used in the isotonic method provides the external resistance. The force necessary to defeat the inertia of a barbell, or move it, is referred to as applied force—and the more the applied force exceeds the external resistance, the faster the acceleration of the weight.

If a novice athlete applies force equal to 95 percent of 1RM to lift a barbell loaded with the 1RM load, then he or she is incapable of generating any acceleration. However, if the same athlete works on maximum strength for one or two years, his or her strength increases so much that lifting the same weight equals only 40 percent to 50 percent of 1RM. The athlete is then capable of moving the barbell explosively and generating the acceleration that is necessary in order to increase power. This difference explains why the periodization of strength requires a maximum strength phase prior to power training. No visible increments of power are possible without clear gains in maximum strength.

A high level of maximum strength is also necessary for the early part of a lift or throw. Any barbell or implement (such as a ball) has a certain inertia, which is its mass or weight. The most difficult part of lifting a barbell or throwing an implement explosively is the early part. To overcome the inertia, the athlete must build a high level of tension in the relevant muscles. Consequently, the higher an athlete's maximum strength is, the easier it is for him or her to overcome the inertia, and the more explosive the start of the movement can be. As an athlete continues to apply force against the barbell or implement, he or she increases its velocity. As more velocity is developed, less force is necessary to maintain it.

Increasing velocity continuously means that the limb speed is also increasing. This increase is possible only if the athlete can contract the muscle quickly, which is why athletes involved in speed- and power-dominant sports need to power-train during the conversion phase. Without power training, an athlete will never be able to jump higher, run faster, throw farther, or deliver a quicker punch. In order to improve, the athlete needs more than just maximum strength. He or she must also be able to express maximum strength at a very high rate—a capacity that can be achieved only through power training methods.

During the maximum strength phase, the athlete gets accustomed to heavy loads. Therefore, using loads between 30 percent and 80 percent of 1RM helps the athlete develop sport-specific power and at the same time meet the challenge of creating the high acceleration needed for power performance.

For most sports involving cyclic motions (such as sprinting, team sports, and the martial arts), the load for the isotonic method can be 30 percent or higher (up to 50 percent). For sports involving acyclic motions (such as throwing, weightlifting, and line play in American football), the load can be higher—50 percent to 80 percent—because these athletes have much higher mass and maximum strength to start with and must defeat a higher external resistance. In fact, power improvements are very specific in terms of angular speed and load; as a result, we must choose the load according to the external resistance to be defeated. See table 14.2 for a summary of training parameters.

As a joint approaches its full extension, the nervous system would naturally activate the antagonist muscles to slow down the movement. At the same time, the exercise usually becomes biomechanically more advantageous as a joint "opens" (requiring less application of force). For these reasons, it is advisable to use accommodating resistance, such as bands or chains, when using lower loads (30 percent to 50 percent). In fact, research has proven that accommodating resistance leads to higher increase of power when light loads are used (Rhea et al. 2009).

Please remember, however, that the use of bands in particular heavily taxes the CNS, which means that one must appropriately adjust the rest between sets and the frequency of exposure to this type of training. In addition, because the key element for power training is not how many reps one performs but the ability to activate the highest number of fast-twitch fibers, we suggest a low number of reps (one to eight).

Table 14.2 Training Parameters for the Isotonic Method

Phase duration	3–6 weeks
Load	Cyclic: 30%–50% of 1RM Acyclic: 50%–80% of 1RM
No. of exercises	3–6
No. of reps per set	Cyclic: 5–8 reps at 30%–40% of 1RM, 3–6 reps at 40%–50% Acyclic: 5 or 6 reps at 50%–70%, 1–5 reps at 70%–80%
No. of sets per exercise	3–6*
Rest interval	Cyclic: 1–2 min. at 30%–40% of 1RM, 2–3 min. at 40%–50% Acyclic: 2–4 min.
Speed of execution	Explosive
Frequency per week	2 or 3

*Lower figure for the higher number of exercises; higher figure for the lower number of exercises.

Athletes should also attend to safety. When a limb is extended, it should not be snapped. In other words, exercises should be performed explosively but without jerking the barbell or implement. Again, perfect technique is paramount.

For sport actions that require power to be performed in an explosive, acyclic manner—for example, throwing, jumping, diving, cricket actions, batting, pitching, and line play in American football—reps must be performed with some rest between them so that the athlete can concentrate maximally in order to achieve the most dynamic move. This strategy also improves fast-twitch motor unit recruitment and power output (Gorostiaga et al. 2012). The athlete can perform one rep at a time, as long as it is performed explosively in order to achieve maximum recruitment of fast-twitch muscle fibers and increased discharge rate.

When the athlete can no longer perform a repetition explosively, he or she should stop, even if the set has not been completed. Continuing the reps without explosiveness trains power endurance (discussed at the end of this chapter) rather than power. Only the combination of maximum concentration and explosive action produces the greatest fast-twitch fiber recruitment and discharge rate, and these crucial elements are attainable only when the athlete is relatively fresh.

During the rest interval, regardless of whether the athlete is working on power or power endurance, he or she should try to relax the muscles previously involved. Relaxing during the rest interval enhances the resynthesis of ATP, thus helping resupply the working muscles with necessary fuel. This recommendation does not mean that the athlete must stretch the muscles involved, which in fact would lower the power output in the following set; therefore, stretching of agonist muscles should be avoided between sets.

Exercises for power training must be very sport specific in order to replicate the kinetic chain used in the sporting activity. From this perspective, we can see that bench presses and power cleans, despite being traditional power-training exercises, offer no built-in magic! Power cleans are useful for throwers and American football linebackers but not necessarily for, say, athletes in soccer or racket sports. These athletes can better use jumping squats and heavy kettlebell swings.

Selecting the lowest number of exercises (three to six) allows the athlete to perform the highest number of sets realistically possible (three to six per exercise for a maximum of eighteen sets per session) for maximum benefit of the prime movers. When deciding the number of sets and exercises, coaches should remember that power training is performed in conjunction with technical and tactical training. Therefore, it can be given only a certain amount of energy.

A key element in developing power through the isotonic method is the speed of exertion. For maximum power improvement, exertion speed must be as high as possible. Fast application of force against an implement or weight throughout the range of motion is essential and must start from the early part of the movement. To be able to displace the barbell or implement immediately and dynamically, the athlete must be maximally concentrated on the task.

Figure 14.9 shows a sample power training program for a college-level female basketball player with four years of strength training. Maximum mechanical power output is usually achieved at 50 percent of 1RM (plus or minus 5 percent) in strength exercise (Baker, Nance, and Moore 2001) and around 85 percent for Olympic lifts (Garhammer 1989). A power loss occurs at about the sixth rep of a given set (Baker and Newton 2007).

Exercise	WEEK		
	1	2	3
1. Power clean	$\frac{80\ 4}{2}$	$\frac{82.5\ 4}{2}$	$\frac{85\ 4}{2}$
2. Jump squat	$\frac{40\ 3}{5}$	$\frac{45\ 3}{5}$	$\frac{50\ 3}{5}$
3. Military press	$\frac{50\ 4}{3}$	$\frac{55\ 4}{3}$	$\frac{60\ 4}{3}$
4. Lat pull-down	$\frac{50\ 4}{3}$	$\frac{55\ 4}{3}$	$\frac{60\ 4}{3}$
5. Weighted crunch	2×12	2×10	2×8

Figure 14.9 Sample Power Training Program for a College-Level Female Basketball Player With Four Years of Strength Training

Ballistic Method

Muscle energy can be applied in different forms and against different resistances. When the resistance is equal to the force applied by the athlete, no motion occurs; this is isometric exercise. If the resistance is less than the force applied by the athlete, the barbell or strength training equipment moves either slow or fast; this is isotonic exercise. And if the athlete's applied force clearly exceeds the external resistance (e.g., with a medicine ball), a dynamic motion occurs, in which either the athlete's body or the implement is projected; this is ballistic exercise.

For power training purposes, an athlete's muscle power can be applied forcefully against implements such as the track-and-field shots, medicine balls, barbells, kettlebells, and rubber cords (surgical tubing). The resulting motion occurs explosively because the force of the athlete far exceeds the resistance of the implement. Therefore, employing such instruments to enhance power is referred to as the ballistic method.

During a ballistic action, the athlete's energy is exerted dynamically against resistance from the beginning to the end of the motion. As a result, the implement is projected for a distance proportional to the power applied against it. Throughout the motion, the athlete must apply considerable force in order to accelerate the equipment or implement continuously, culminating in the release. To project the implement for the maximum possible distance, the athlete must achieve the highest velocity at the instant of release.

Phase 4: Conversion to Specific Strength

The fast ballistic application of force is possible as a result of quick recruitment of fast-twitch muscle fibers, high discharge rate, and effective intermuscular coordination of the agonist and antagonist muscles. After years of practice, an athlete can contract the agonist muscles forcefully while the antagonist muscles reach a high level of relaxation. This superior intermuscular coordination maximizes the force capabilities of the agonist muscles because the antagonist muscles exert no opposition to the agonists' quick contraction.

Depending on training objectives, ballistic exercises can be planned to occur either after the warm-up or at the end of the training session. For example, if technical and tactical work has been planned for a given day, then the development and improvement of power is a secondary goal. However, for events in which speed and power are dominant—such as sprinting, field events in track and field, and the martial arts—power work can often be planned to occur immediately after the warm-up, especially in the late preparatory phase, thanks to the stimulatory effects on the nervous system, typical of power training. Training parameters for a ballistic program are summarized in table 14.3.

Table 14.3 Training Parameters for the Ballistic Method

Load	Load that allows projection of the body or implement
No. of exercises	2–6
No. of reps per set	5 or 6
No. of sets per session	2–6*
Rest interval	2–3 min.
Speed of execution	Explosive
Frequency of training	2–4

*Lower figure for the higher number of exercises; higher figure for the lower number of exercises.

Power training of an explosive nature is enhanced when the athlete is physiologically fresh. A well-rested CNS can send more powerful nerve impulses to the working muscles for quick contractions. The opposite is true, however, when the CNS and muscles are exhausted and inhibition is dominant; these conditions prevent the effective involvement of fast-twitch muscle fibers. Thus we see the problem of having an athlete perform intensive work prior to explosive power training: His or her energy supplies (ATP-CP) are exhausted, sufficient energy is not available, and high-quality work is impossible because fast-twitch fibers fatigue easily and are hardly activated. As a result, the athlete performs movements without vigor.

When using the ballistic method, speed of performance is paramount. Each rep should start dynamically, and the athlete should try to increase the speed constantly as the release or end of the motion approaches. This effort enables the involvement of a higher number of fast-twitch motor units. The critical element here is not the number of reps. Again, the athlete does not have to perform many reps in order to increase power. Instead, the determining factor is speed of performance, which is dictated by the speed of muscle contraction. Therefore, exercises should be performed only as long as quickness is possible. *Repetitions must be discontinued the moment that speed declines.*

The speed and explosiveness of an exercise are guaranteed only as long as a high number of fast-twitch fibers are involved. When they fatigue, speed decreases. Continuing an activity after speed declines is futile because at this point there is no full activation of fast-twitch motor units, and those that are activated adapt to become slower—an unwanted result for athletes seeking power development. Thus the plasticity of the CNS can work either for or against the objective of training. To be effective, adaptation must lead to the improvement of the athlete's sport performance.

Ballistic training load is dictated by the standard weight of the implements. Medicine balls weigh from 2 to 9 kilograms (about 4.5 to 20 pounds), whereas power balls weigh between 1 and 16 kilograms (about 2 to 35 pounds).

As in other power-related methods, the number of ballistic exercises must be as low as possible so that the athlete can perform a high number of sets in order to achieve maximum power benefits. Again, exercises should closely mimic technical skills. If such mimicry is not possible, then the coach should select exercises that involve the sport's prime movers.

For any explosive power method, the rest interval should be as long as necessary to reach full recovery so that the athlete can repeat the same quality of work in each set. In fact, because most ballistic exercises require a partner, a short interval between repetitions is often dictated by necessity. For instance, a shot must be fetched, a position taken, and a few preparatory swings made before the shot is heaved back to the first athlete. By that time, some 15 to 20 seconds have elapsed in which the first athlete can rest. For this reason, the number of reps can be higher in ballistic training than in other power training methods.

The frequency per week of using the ballistic method depends on the training phase. In the late preparatory phase, the frequency should be low (one or two sessions); during the conversion phase, it should be higher (two to four sessions). One must also consider the sport or event. The frequency is higher for speed- and power-dominant sports than for sports in which power is of secondary importance. Figure 14.10 shows a sample program combining ballistic and maximum acceleration exercises. This program has been used successfully by players in American football, baseball, lacrosse, soccer, and hockey.

Exercise	WEEK		
	Week 1	Week 2	Week 3*
1. Jump squat and medicine ball chest throw	2 × 5	3 × 5	3 × 5*
2. Medicine ball overhead backward throw	2 × 5	3 × 5	3 × 5*
3. Medicine ball chest throw	2 × 5	3 × 5	3 × 5*
4. Medicine ball overhead forward throw	2 × 5	3 × 5	3 × 5*
5. Medicine ball side throw (each side)	1 × 5	3 × 5	3 × 5*
6. Two-handed shot throw from chest followed by 15-yard (-meter) sprint	3 ×	4 ×	5 ×
7. Push-up followed by 15- yard (-meter) sprint	3 ×	4 ×	5 ×

*With a load heavier than the previous week.

Figure 14.10 Sample Program Combining Ballistic and Maximum Acceleration Exercises

Power-Resisting Method

This method represents a three-way combination of the isotonic, isometric, and ballistic methods. To help explain this method, here is a description of an exercise. An athlete lies down with knees bent to perform a sit-up. His or her toes are held against the ground by a partner, and the coach stands behind the athlete. The athlete begins the sit-up. When he or she reaches approximately a quarter of hip flexion (135 to 140 degrees), the coach places his or her palms on the athlete's chest or shoulders, thus stopping the movement. At this point, the athlete is in a maximum static contraction, trying to defeat the resisting power of the coach by recruiting most or all of the possible motor units. After three or four seconds, the coach removes his or her hands, and the maximum static contraction is converted into a dynamic ballistic motion for the rest of the sit-up. The athlete slowly then returns to the starting position and rests for 10 to 20 seconds before performing another rep.

The most important parts of this method are the maximum isometric contraction and the ensuing ballistic action. The ballistic-type motion, with its quick muscle contraction, results in power development. The actions used in this method are similar to those of a catapult machine. The initial isotonic action must be performed slowly. Following the stop, the maximum isometric contraction represents a high pretension (loading phase) of the muscles involved. In the case of the sit-up, as the chest or shoulders are released, the trunk is catapulted forward (the ballistic phase). Any other movements that duplicate the previous phases of action can be categorized under the ballistic method with similar effects on power development. In fact, similar power-resisting exercises can be performed for a variety of other movements, such as the following:

- *Pull-up*—The athlete performs an early elbow flexion, at which point the coach or partner stops the action for a few seconds; a dynamic action then follows.

- *Dip*—The athlete performs an early elbow extension, at which point the coach or partner stops the action for a few seconds; a dynamic action then follows.

- *Jump squat with no weights*—The athlete bends the knees, at which point the coach or partner stops the action for a few seconds; a dynamic action then follows.

- *Squat with weights*—Place a first set of safety pins at the height that results in the knee or hip angles at which you want the isometric action to happen (usually a half-squat angle). Place a second set of pins two or three holes below. The athlete pushes against the pins for two to four seconds, then one or two spotters remove the pins for the dynamic action to follow.

- *Bench press*—Place a bench inside a power rack; place a first set of safety pins in a way that the bar barely touches the chest and a second set one or two holes higher. The athlete pushes against the pins for two to four seconds, then one or two spotters remove the pins for the dynamic action to follow.

- *Trunk rotation with medicine ball held sideways in the hands*—The athlete performs a backward rotation, and as the rotation comes forward the athlete is stopped for two to four seconds; the ballistic action that follows culminates with the release of the ball. The same concept can be applied to most any medicine ball throw.

Another type of power stimulation can be achieved through isotonic weight training by alternating loads (this is also known as the contrast method). The athlete first performs one to three reps with a load of 80 percent to 90 percent of 1RM, then immediately performs five or six reps with a low-resistance load of 30 percent to 50 percent. The heavy-load reps produce neuromuscular stimulation, thus allowing the athlete to perform the low-resistance reps more dynamically. This method can be used with a large variety of exercises, from bench pulls to bench presses. However, here is one note of caution regarding motions that involve knee and arm extensions: Snapping or jerking actions (forced, snapped extensions) should be avoided because they can cause joint damage.

The load for the power-resisting method is related to the exercise performed. For the isometric phase, the contraction should last three or four seconds, or the duration necessary to reach maximum tension. For exercises in which the resistance is provided by a barbell, the load should be 80 percent to 90 percent of 1RM for the stimulating phase and 30 percent to 50 percent of 1RM for the explosive phase. Exercises should also match the direction of the prime movers' contraction during the sport-specific skills. For maximum power benefit, the number of exercises should be low (two to four) so that the athlete can perform a large number of sets (three to five).

Power-resisting training can be performed separately or combined with other power training methods. Training parameters for the power-resisting method are summarized in table 14.4.

Table 14.4 Training Parameters for the Power-Resisting Method

Load	Exercise dependent
No. of exercises	2–4
No. of reps per set	3–6
No. of sets per exercise	3–5*
Rest interval	2–4 min.
Speed of execution	Explosive
Frequency per week	1 or 2

*Lower figure for the higher number of exercises; higher figure for the lower number of exercises.

Plyometric Method

Since ancient times, athletes have explored a multitude of methods designed to enable them to run faster, jump higher, and throw farther. To achieve such goals, power is essential. Strength gains can be transformed into power only by applying specific power training. Perhaps one of the most successful power training methods is the plyometric method.

Plyometrics employs exercises that elicit the stretch–shortening cycle, or myotatic stretch reflex. These exercises load the muscle in a fast eccentric (lengthening) contraction, which is followed immediately by a concentric (shortening) contraction. Research has demonstrated that if a muscle is quickly stretched before a contraction, it contracts more forcefully and rapidly (Bosco and Komi 1980; Schmidtbleicher 1984; Verkhoshansky 1997). For example, by lowering the center of gravity to perform a takeoff or to swing a golf club, the athlete stretches the muscle rapidly, which results in a more forceful contraction.

Plyometric action relies on the stretch reflex originating in the spinal cord. The main purpose of the stretch reflex is to limit the degree of muscle stretch in order to prevent overstretching. Plyometric movement is based on the reflex contraction of the muscle fibers resulting from the rapid stretching of these same fibers. In fact, when excessive stretching and tearing become a possibility, the stretch receptors send proprioceptive nerve impulses to the spinal cord. The impulses then rebound to the stretch receptors, which produces a braking effect that prevents the muscle fiber from stretching farther, thereby initiating a powerful muscle contraction.

Thus, plyometric exercises work within complex neural mechanisms. Neural adaptations take place in the body's nervous system to enhance both strength and power in athletic training (Sale 1986; Schmidtbleicher 1992). In fact, as already stated, neural adaptations can increase the force of a muscle without increasing its size (Dons et al. 1979; Komi and Bosco 1978; Sale 1986; Tesch et al. 1990).

Phase 4: Conversion to Specific Strength

Plyometric training causes muscular and neural changes that facilitate and enhance the performance of more rapid and more powerful movements. The CNS controls muscle force by changing the activity of the muscle's motor units; if greater force generation is required, more motor units are recruited and fired at a higher rate. In this context, an increase in electromyographic recording output following a training program indicates one of three things: More motor units have been recruited, motor units are firing at higher rates, or some combination of these reactions has occurred (Sale 1992). The benefits of plyometric training include increased activation of fast-twitch motor units and, more important, a higher rate of firing.

The contractile elements of a muscle are the muscle fibers; however, certain noncontractile parts constitute what is known as the series elastic component. Stretching the series elastic component during eccentric muscle contraction produces elastic potential energy similar to that of a loaded spring. This energy augments the energy generated by muscle fibers. This synergy is visible in plyometric movements. When a muscle is stretched rapidly, the series elastic component is also stretched, and it stores a portion of the load force in the form of elastic potential energy. The recovery of the stored elastic energy occurs during the concentric, or overcoming, phase of muscle contraction triggered by the myotatic reflex.

In plyometric training a muscle contracts more forcefully and quickly from a prestretched position—and the faster the prestretch, the more forceful the concentric contraction. Correct technique is essential. The athlete must land with the legs slightly bent in order to prevent injury to the knee joints. The shortening contraction should occur immediately after completion of the prestretch phase. The transition from the prestretch phase should be smooth, continuous, and as swift as possible. Increased contact time indicates fatigue induced by repeated reactive training (Gollhofer et al. 1987).

Plyometric training produces the following results:

- Quick mobilization of greater innervation activity
- Recruitment of most, if not all, motor units and their corresponding muscle fibers
- Increased firing rate of motor neurons
- Transformation of muscle strength into explosive power
- Development of the nervous system so that it reacts with maximum speed to the lengthening of a muscle, which develops the athlete's ability to shorten (contract) rapidly with maximum force
- Improvement in explosive force with only slight increase in muscle girth due to increase in mean cross-sectional area of fast-twitch fibers (Häkkinen and Komi 1983), which indicates performance enhancement at the neuromuscular level
- Golgi tendon organ inhibition, which could lead to higher muscle tension and activation at landing, thus producing more powerful muscle contraction—all of which contributes to enhanced power output (Schmidtbleicher 1992)

An athlete can progress faster through the various intensity levels of plyometric training if he or she possesses a good strength training background of several years. Such a background also helps prevent injury. In addition, in the interest of establishing a good base of strength and developing shock-absorbing qualities, one should not dismiss the benefits of introducing children to plyometric exercises. However, these exercises must be performed over several years and conducted in a manner that respects the principle of progression. Indeed, patience and well-planned progression are the key elements of this approach.

MECHANICAL CHARACTERISTICS OF PLYOMETRICS

When an athlete jumps off the ground, much force is required to propel the body mass upward. The athlete must flex and extend the limbs very quickly. Plyometric exercise relies on this quick body action to muster the required power. More specifically, as we have seen, plyometric action relies on the stretch reflex, a protective mechanism that originates in the spinal cord and can be co-opted to increase the power of concentric contraction after a muscle is stretched through eccentric contraction.

When the takeoff leg is planted, the athlete must lower his or her center of gravity, thus creating downward velocity. During this amortization (or shock-absorbing) phase, the athlete must produce force to counter the downward motion and prepare for the upward thrusting phase that enables him or her to take off in a different direction. However, a long amortization phase results in loss of power. For example, a long jumper who plants the takeoff leg improperly loses the upward and horizontal velocity required to propel the body forward.

Therefore, the athlete must work toward a shorter and quicker amortization phase, which enables more powerful concentric contraction of the muscle that was stretched during the preceding eccentric contraction (Bosco and Komi 1980). Since force equals mass times acceleration, shortening the amortization phase requires the athlete to exert greater force in order to decelerate the body more quickly. This understanding points out the importance of keeping one's body fat low and one's power-to-weight ratio high. More body mass, and greater downward velocity at impact, require higher average force during the amortization phase.

To maximize jumping ability, one must use the entire body efficiently. For example, when a long jumper or high jumper lowers the center of gravity before takeoff, he or she reduces the impact of the forces. In addition, upward acceleration of the free limbs (the arms) after the amortization phase increases the vertical forces placed on the takeoff leg. Triple jumpers, for instance, must apply peak force as much as six times their body weight to compensate for the inability to lower their center of gravity during the more upward hopping phase. Long jumpers, on the other hand, can manipulate their bodies more easily just before takeoff. Again, jumpers achieve effective takeoff only if they apply large forces on impact and produce a shorter amortization phase.

The athlete can achieve this quick turnaround only when his or her neuromuscular system is trained to organize both the relevant kinetic chain and the agonist–antagonist activation and deactivation through a periodized power program. The program should start with lower-impact plyometrics and progress to higher-impact plyometrics aimed at achieving the highest possible jump, regardless of ground contact time and degree of knee and hip flexion (characteristics of the depth jump). After this progression is completed (possibly several times during the career of an athlete), the neuromuscular system is ready to perform shorter ground contact times even when the force to be opposed is higher. However, aiming for short contact time with an ill-prepared athlete results only in a small uncoordinated jump.

Training for the takeoff phase is difficult because few conventional exercises apply. Many jumpers use traditional weight training (e.g., squats), and this work puts a large load on the knee extensors, which over time does provide an adequate strength training base. However, relying only on weight training is problematic because a heavy squat lift is unlikely to be fast enough to use and enhance the elastic qualities of the muscles.

Bounding exercises, on the other hand, can simulate an effective takeoff and improve the athlete's overall jumping ability. Bounding has force–time characteristics similar to those of the takeoff. It also allows athletes to practice resisting heavy loads on the takeoff leg and to exert force in a short time. In addition, bounding exercises involve multijoint movement and facilitate development of the required muscle elasticity.

Phase 4: Conversion to Specific Strength

A healthy training progression for children first exposes them to low-intensity plyometrics (level 5 and 4) over several years, say, between the ages of 14 and 16. After this initial period, they can be introduced to more demanding reactive jumps (level 3). Throughout these years of long-term progression, teachers and coaches should teach young athletes the correct plyometric techniques by using the hop and step from the triple jump as the basics of plyometric training.

Plyometric exercises are the subject of some controversy. One area of consideration involves the amount of strength that should be developed before doing plyometrics. Some authors define the safe level as the ability to perform one half squat with a load that is twice one's body weight, but that standard applies only to level 1 plyometrics.

Others address the type of training surface, what equipment to use, and whether additional weights (such as heavy vests and ankle and waist belts) should be worn when performing these exercises. When injury is a concern, and at the start of general preparation, exercises should be performed on a soft surface—either on grass or soft ground or on a padded floor. However, though this precaution may be appropriate for beginners or athletes just starting their preparation, using a soft surface can dampen the stretch reflex; only a hard surface enhances the reactivity of the neuromuscular system. Therefore, athletes with an extensive background in sport, strength training, or both should use a hard surface, especially from the specific preparation phase onward.

Plyometric drills should not be performed with barbells, dumbbells, or weighted ankle or waist belts. These weights tend to decrease the reactive ability of the neuromuscular system by slowing down the coupling time (the passage from the eccentric action to the concentric action) and, more important, the concentric action itself. Therefore, although such overloading may result in increased strength, it slows the speed of contraction and the rebounding effect. If more eccentric loading is necessary, that can be accomplished by using depth jumps from a high box.

To design a plyometric program properly, coaches and trainers must be aware that the exercises vary in level of intensity and are classified into different groups for better progression. The level of intensity is directly proportional to the height or length of an exercise. High-intensity plyometric exercises, such as depth or drop jumps, result in higher tension in the muscle, which recruits more motor units to perform the action or to resist the pull of gravitational force.

Plyometric exercises can be categorized into two major groups that reflect their degree of impact on the neuromuscular system: low intensity and high intensity. From a more practical viewpoint, plyometric exercises can be divided into five levels of intensity (see table 14.5). This classification can be used to plan effective alternation of training demand throughout the week.

Any plan to incorporate plyometric exercises into a training program should account for the following factors:

- Age and physical development of the athlete
- Skills and techniques involved in plyometric exercises
- Principal performance factors of the sport
- Energy requirements of the sport
- Training phase of the annual plan
- Need, for younger athletes, to respect methodical progression over a long period (two to four years), progressing from low intensity (levels 5 and 4), to medium intensity (level 3) and then to high intensity (levels 2 and 1)

Table 14.5 Five Intensity Levels of Plyometric Exercise

Intensity	Classification	Exercise	Reps × sets	Reps (or ground contacts) per session	Rest interval (min.)
1	High intensity	Depth landing: 30–43 in. (75–110 cm)	1–5 × 3–6	3–20	5–8
		Depth jump: >28 in. (70 cm)	1–10 × 2–6	3–40	4–8
		Bounding on one leg (or alternating)	40–100 m (or yd.) × 2–4	30–150	3–5
2		Drop jump: 16–24 in. (40–60 cm)	3–10 × 2–6	6–40	3–6
		Hurdles: >24 in. (60 cm)	3–12 × 2–6	6–72	3–5
		Bounding on one leg or alternating	5–30 m (or yd.) × 2–6	20–60	3–5
		Speed squat (accentuated eccentric)– Jump squat – American or power Kettlebell swing	3–6 × 2–6	12–24	3–4
3		Hurdles: 12–24 in. (30–60 cm)	6–20 × 2–6	18–80	3–5
4	Low intensity	Jump-up: 24–43 in. (60–110 cm)	3–15 × 2–6	12–60	3–5
		Kettlebell swing	10–30 × 2–6	30–180	2–5
5		Low hurdles: <12 in. (30 cm)	6–20 × 3–6	18–80	2–3
		Skipping	10–30 m (or yd.) × 7–15	70–250	1–2
		Medicine ball	5–12 × 4–6	20–72	1–3
		Rope	15–50 × 2–6	30–300	1–3

Although plyometric exercises are fun, they demand a high level of concentration and are deceptively vigorous and taxing. The lack of discipline to wait for the right moment for each exercise can result in athletes performing high-impact exercises before they are ready. In such cases, the resulting injuries or physiological discomforts are not the fault of the plyometric exercises. Rather, they are the result of the coach's or instructor's lack of knowledge and improper application. The five levels of intensity help coaches design a plan including appropriate exercises that follow a consistent, steady, and orderly progression with appropriate rest intervals.

Progression through the five levels of intensity is achieved over the long term. The two to four years spent incorporating low-impact exercises into the training program of a young athlete are necessary for the progressive adaptation of his or her ligaments, tendons, and bones. They also allow for the gradual preparation of the shock-absorbing sections of the athlete's body, such as the hips and spine.

Table 14.6 illustrates a long-term comprehensive progression of strength and power training that includes plyometric training. Coaches should observe the age suggested for the introduction of plyometrics, as well as the precept that high-impact plyometrics should

Table 14.6   Long-Term Strength Development and the Progression of Strength Training

Age group (yr.)	Forms of training	Method	Volume	Intensity	Means of training
Prepuberty (12 or 13)	General exercises only Games	Muscular endurance Low-intensity plyometrics (level 5)	Low	Very low	Light resistance exercises Light implements Power or medicine ball
Beginner (13–15)	General strength Event-oriented exercises	Muscular endurance Low-intensity plyometrics (5, 4)	Low	Low	Light dumbbells and barbells Tubing Power ball or medicine ball Selected machines
Intermediate (15–17)	General strength Event-oriented exercises	Bodybuilding Maximum strength (high buffer) Power Plyometrics (4, 3)	Medium	Medium	All means from preceding levels Free weights
Advanced (>17)	Event-oriented exercises Specific strength	Power Maximum strength Plyometrics (3, 2)	High	Medium High	Free weights Special strength equipment
High-performance	Specific strength	All methods from preceding levels Eccentric method Plyometrics (3, 2, 1)	High	Medium High Supermaximum	As above

be introduced only after four years of training. This is the amount of time required to learn and stabilize proper technique and to allow for progressive anatomical adaptation. From this point on, high-impact plyometrics can be part of an athlete's normal training regimen.

The intensity of plyometric exercises—the amount of tension created in the muscle—depends on the eccentric load of the exercise, which is normally determined by the height from which the exercise is performed. (Therefore, jumps *onto* boxes have a low intensity even when 43-inch [109-centimeter] boxes are used, because their eccentric load is minimal.) Although the height used should be determined strictly by the individual qualities of the athlete, the following general principle applies: The stronger the muscular system is, the more energy is required to stretch it in order to obtain an elastic effect in the shortening phase. Thus, what is optimal height for one athlete may not generate enough stimulation for another.

Ideally, in fact, a force mat (such as the Just Jump System or the SmartJump) should be used to determine the optimal height for the desired power training effect. For instance, the optimal height for a depth jump is the box height that allows the highest rebounding jump, whereas the optimal height for a drop jump is the box height that allows the highest rebounding jump with a ground contact time below 250 milliseconds. This distinction means that depth jumps and drop jumps—despite their similar appearance to the untrained eye—not only serve different training objectives but also should be employed at different times during the annual plan. Therefore, the following information and height information in table 14.14 should be treated only as guidelines.

According to Verkhoshanski (1969), in order to facilitate an athlete's gains in dynamic strength (power), the optimal height for depth jumps for speed training should be between 30 and 43 inches (75 and 110 centimeters). Similar findings were reported by Bosco and Komi (1980), who also concluded that above 43 inches (110 centimeters) the mechanics of the action are changed; in fact, at such heights, the time and energy required to cushion the force of the drop to the ground defeat the purpose of plyometric training. More generally, remember to start your athletes from a lower box and have them progress to a higher box. Most athletes maximize their rebounding jump with a 15- to 20-inch (about 40- to 50-centimeter) box, and only the strongest athletes need a 30-inch (75-centimeter) or more box.

In terms of reps, plyometric drills fall into two categories: single-response and multiple-response. Drills in the first category consist of a single action—such as a high-reactive jump, or a drop jump (level 2)—in which the main purpose is to induce the highest level of tension in the muscles. The objective of such exercises is to develop maximum strength and power.

Multiple-response exercises—such as jumping over multiple medium- (level 3) or low-height (level 4) hurdles, and jump squats (level 2) can result in the development of power as well as power endurance.

Often, especially for multiple-response exercises, it is more convenient and practical to equate the number of reps with a distance—for example, 5 sets of 50 meters rather than 5 sets of 25 reps. This approach helps gauge the athlete's neuromuscular readiness as well as his or her progress.

High-quality training requires adequate physiological recuperation between exercises. Often, however, athletes and coaches either pay too little attention to the duration of the rest interval or simply get caught up in the traditions of a given sport, which often dictate that the only rest interval required is the time needed to move from one station to another. In reality, this amount of time is inadequate, especially considering the physiological characteristics of plyometric training.

Fatigue consists of local fatigue and CNS fatigue. Local fatigue results from depletion of the energy stored in the muscle (ATP-CP, the fuel necessary to perform explosive movements) and the accumulation of lactic acid from reps lasting longer than 10 seconds. During training, athletes also fatigue the CNS, the system that signals the working muscle to perform a given amount of high-quality work. Plyometric training is performed as a result of these nerve impulses, which are characterized by a certain power and frequency. Any high-quality training requires the highest possible levels of contraction power and frequency.

When the rest interval is short (one to two minutes), the athlete experiences both local and CNS fatigue. The working muscle is unable to remove lactic acid or replenish energy sufficiently to perform the next reps at the same intensity. Similarly, a fatigued CNS is unable to send the powerful nerve impulses necessary to ensure that the prescribed load is performed for the same number of reps and sets before exhaustion sets in. In addition, an exhausted athlete is often just a short step away from injury; therefore, coaches and athletes should pay utmost attention to rest intervals.

As suggested in table 14.5, the appropriate rest interval is a function of the load and type of plyometric training performed—the higher the exercise intensity, the longer the required rest interval. Consequently, for maximum-intensity exercises (high-reactive jumps), the rest interval between sets should be three to eight minutes, depending on the athlete's body mass and gender: longer rest intervals for heavier male athletes, and shorter rest intervals for lighter female athletes. The suggested rest interval for intensity level 2 is three to six minutes; for levels 3 and 4, it should be two to five minutes; and for low-impact activities (level 5), it should be one to three minutes.

The type of plyometric training performed by an athlete must be specific to his or her sport. For example, athletes who require a greater degree of horizontal power should engage in more bounding and hopping drills, whereas those whose sports require vertical power should perform vertical jumping exercises. Coaches should also consider the training environment. Many studies have demonstrated that reflexes can be altered or modified using specific training modes (Enoka 1994; Schmidtbleicher 1992), and plyometrics is one form of training that induces particular adaptations in various reflexive actions. However, for the reflexive learning process to be reproduced in the competitive realm, the athlete must be in the same psychological and physiological state as when the reflex adaptation was induced. Thus, the training environment should be a near-perfect replica of the competitive environment.

Sport-Specific Application of Power Training

To reiterate a key point: Power must be developed to meet the needs of a given sport, event, or team position. To further illustrate the need for *specific* application of power, definitive examples are presented in this section. Many elements of the previously described power training methods are also applicable.

Power Endurance

In some sports, athletes must apply a high degree of power repetitively. Examples include sprints in track and field, sprints in swimming, wrestling, and certain team-sport positions, such as American football running back and baseball pitcher.

Sprinting is often misjudged, including the sprinting performed in all team sports that require explosive running (such American football, basketball, baseball, ice hockey, rugby, soccer, and Australian football). When sprinters cover the classic 100 meters in 10 to 12 seconds, they have trained to perform powerful leg actions throughout the entire race, not just during the start and the following six to eight strides. In a 100-meter race, an athlete takes 48 to 54 strides, depending on stride length; thus each leg makes 24 to 27 contacts with the ground. In each ground contact, the force applied can be more than twice the athlete's body weight!

In certain sports—American football, rugby, soccer, and Australian football—athletes are often required to repeat a strenuous activity after only a few seconds of game interruption. Similar athletic performances are required in the martial arts, boxing, wrestling, and racket sports. Athletes who compete in such sports need to perform powerful actions over and over. To do so successfully, they need high power output and the ability to repeat it 20 to 30 (or even up to 60) times dynamically and as explosively as possible.

The formula for training power endurance is

$$HV \times HI$$

or high volume (HV) of reps performed explosively, fast, and quickly (at high intensity, or HI) using exercises as close as possible to the motor pattern of sport-specific skills. Athletes with a high level of power endurance possess the capacity to avoid a decrease in stride frequency and velocity at the end of a race or have a consistent level of power output throughout a game, depending on what type of power endurance they worked on according to their sporting activity.

Is there a difference between a football player repeating many sprints over the duration of a game and a sprinter maintaining high power output for 50 strides? Yes. Physiologically speaking, the football player is repeating an alactic power activity, often without enough recovery time to refill the ATP-CP stores. As a result, the player enters what we call the "lactic power short" realm. The sprinter, on the other hand, uses anaerobic alactic power during the first part of the race (the first six to eight seconds), then increasingly uses "lactic power long" as he or she approaches the finish line. For this reason, we say that both the football player and the sprinter need power endurance, yet, both physiologically and methodologically, their types of power endurance differ from each other.

Power endurance is the determinant abilities in several sports, and maximum strength is a determinant factor in both of these abilities. This section describes the training methodology for developing power endurance in an explosive manner.

Power endurance requires the athlete to apply 30 percent to 50 percent of maximum strength both rhythmically and explosively. To train appropriately in order to develop power endurance, an athlete is required to perform 12 to 30 dynamic reps explosively and nonstop. The needed training can be achieved progressively: for sports requiring power endurance short (most team sports), use a low number of reps (5 or 6) and progress to a high number of sets; for sports requiring power endurance long, start with a low number of reps (10 to 12) and progress to the sport-specific number of reps—for example, 15 for a 100-meter sprinter or 30 for a 200-meter sprinter.

Early in the conversion phase, the fast-twitch muscle fibers are trained to instantaneously display the highest possible level of power. Parallel with that work, athletes should also increase their quickness of performance for the purpose of increasing the discharge rate of the fast-twitch muscles as much as possible. Now, for power endurance purposes, the fast-twitch fibers are trained to cope with the fatigue and the buildup of lactic acid induced by performing many reps dynamically.

Training is now aimed at developing the endurance component of speed, or specific power moves, typical of the relevant sports. This goal is accomplished by progressively increasing the number of reps or sets. The progression requires the athlete to exert maximum willpower in order to overcome fatigue and reach optimal mental concentration before performing each set. The recommended length of this phase is six weeks, but sometimes it can be reduced to four weeks; however, a program any shorter than that is insufficient for achieving the physiological goal of power endurance.

To perform a high number of sets for each prime mover, the number of exercises must be as low as possible (two to four, or rarely five). Each rep of a set must be performed explosively. The rest interval between sets or series must be three to eight minutes to allow for CNS recovery. During this type of work, athletes experience a high level of lactic acid buildup. This is, in fact, why the number of explosive reps must be high—so that the athlete learns to tolerate the lactic acid buildup and perform successfully in this condition. Without such training, the athlete will not perform successfully during competition. This method also trains the CNS to keep a high frequency of discharge for an extended time despite the resulting muscle fatigue.

Speed of performance must be dynamic and explosive. Unless this rule is strictly observed, power training and power endurance training build muscle mass rather than power; as a result, the outcome is hypertrophy rather than power endurance! Athletes often require a few weeks of power endurance before they can perform 20 to 30 reps explosively and nonstop. In the meantime, they should stop when they become incapable of performing a rep dynamically because at that point power endurance is no longer being trained. Training parameters for power endurance are summarized in table 14.7. Figure 14.11 shows a sample four-week training program for a 100-meter sprinter. Figure 14.12 depicts a sample four-week training program for a team-sport athlete, using the series of sets method.

Table 14.7 Training Parameters for the Power Endurance Method

	POWER ENDURANCE SHORT	POWER ENDURANCE LONG
Phase duration	4–6 weeks	
Load	30%–60% of 1RM	
No. of exercises	2–5	
No. of reps per set	5 or 6	12–30
No. of sets per exercise	2–4 series of 3–6 sets (Series and sets must be progressed to sport-specific volume.)	2 or 3
Rest interval	5–20 seconds between sets; 3–5 minutes between series (Rest intervals between sets must be sport-specific.)	3–8 minutes
Speed of execution	Explosive	
Frequency per week	2	2 or 3

Exercise	WEEK 1	WEEK 2	WEEK 3	WEEK 4	Rest interval
1. Jumping half squat	$\frac{45\ 2}{15}$	$\frac{45\ 3}{15}$	$\frac{50\ 2}{15}$	$\frac{50\ 3}{15}$	5–6 min.
2. Heavy kettlebell swing	2 × 20	3 × 20	2 × 20 (heavier kettlebell than weeks 1 and 2)	3 × 20 (same kettlebell as week 3)	3–4 min.
3. Bench throw	$\frac{45\ 2}{15}$	$\frac{45\ 3}{15}$	$\frac{50\ 2}{15}$	$\frac{50\ 3}{15}$	3 min.
4. Lat pull-down (narrow supinated grip)	$\frac{45\ 2}{15}$	$\frac{45\ 3}{15}$	$\frac{50\ 2}{15}$	$\frac{50\ 3}{15}$	3 min.

LOADING PATTERN

		High		High
	Medium		Medium	

Figure 14.11 Sample Four-Week Training Program for a 100-Meter Sprinter

Exercise	Week 1	Rest intervals between sets and series	Week 2	Rest intervals between sets and series	Week 3	Rest intervals between sets and series	Week 4	Rest intervals between sets and series
1. Jumping half squat	$(\frac{45\ 3}{6}) \times 3$	15 sec. (sets), 3 min. (series)	$(\frac{45\ 3}{6}) \times 4$	10 sec. (sets), 3 min. (series)	$(\frac{50\ 3}{6}) \times 3$	10 sec. (sets), 3 min. (series)	$(\frac{50\ 3}{6}) \times 4$	5 sec. (sets), 3 min. (series)
2. Jumping lunge	$(\frac{45\ 3}{6}) \times 3$	15 sec. (sets), 3 min. (series)	$(\frac{45\ 3}{6}) \times 4$	10 sec. (sets), 3 min. (series)	$(\frac{50\ 3}{6}) \times 3$	10 sec. (sets), 3 min. (series)	$(\frac{50\ 3}{6}) \times 4$	5 sec. (sets), 3 min. (series)
3. Bench press with accommodating resistance (bands or chains)	$(\frac{45\ 3}{6}) \times 3$	15 sec. (sets), 3 min. (series)	$(\frac{45\ 3}{6}) \times 4$	10 sec. (sets), 3 min. (series)	$(\frac{50\ 3}{6}) \times 3$	10 sec. (sets), 3 min. (series)	$(\frac{50\ 3}{6}) \times 4$	5 sec. (sets), 3 min. (series)
4. Lat pull-down (narrow supinated grip)	$(\frac{45\ 3}{6}) \times 3$	15 sec. (sets), 3 min. (series)	$(\frac{45\ 3}{6}) \times 4$	10 sec. (sets), 3 min. (series)	$(\frac{50\ 3}{6}) \times 3$	10 sec. (sets), 3 min. (series)	$(\frac{50\ 3}{6}) \times 4$	5 sec. (sets), 3 min. (series)

LOADING PATTERN

		High				Medium		High
	Medium				Medium			

Figure 14.12 Sample Four-Week Training Program for a Team-Sport Athlete Using the Series-of-Sets Method

Landing and Reactive Power

In several sports, landing is not only an important skill but also one that is followed by the performance of another skill—for example, another jump in figure skating or a quick move in another direction in tennis and in many team sports. Therefore, the athlete must possess both the necessary power to control the landing and the reactive power to quickly perform the next move.

The power required for controlling and absorbing the shock of a landing is related to the height of the jump. For example, a landing after a drop or depth jump from 32 to 40 inches (about 80 to 100 centimeters) often loads the ankle joints with six to eight times the athlete's body weight. Similarly, absorbing the shock from a figure skating jump requires the power to handle five to eight times the athlete's body weight. To control such impact forces at the instant of landing, the athlete's muscles must be trained for shock-absorbing power.

Landing involves an eccentric contraction. Without proper training, the athlete lands incorrectly, which produces higher tension with the same amount of muscle fiber activity, thereby placing greater stress on the elastic tissue of the tendons and increasing the risk of injury. To avoid this pitfall, the athlete's training should include eccentric contractions and plyometrics.

Schmidtbleicher (1992) specified that at the instant of ground contact, athletes experience an inhibitory effect. At the same time, he noted that well-trained athletes cope with impact forces much better than poorly trained athletes do and that the inhibitory effect can be eliminated by drop-jump training. He concluded that the inhibitory mechanisms represent a protective system, especially for novice athletes, meant to shield them from injury.

To enhance landing and reactive power, both concentric and eccentric contractions should be part of an athlete's training. Eccentric strength training and plyometrics, primarily in the form of drop or depth jumps, should mimic the desired landing skill. Drop or depth jumps (also known as reactive jumps) are performed from a raised platform (a box, bench, or chair). The athlete lands in a flexed position (with the knees slightly bent) to absorb the shock. The athlete also lands on the balls of the feet without touching the heels to the ground. This technique is a requirement for most plyometric activities, because touching the ground with the heels indicates that the load is too high for the athlete's extensor muscles.

During the dropping phase, the athlete adopts a ready-to-work position, which enhances the muscles' tension and elastic properties. Upon landing, especially if the athlete is quickly preparing for another action, energy is stored in the elastic elements of the muscle. Upon the ensuing takeoff or quick move in another direction, this readily available energy releases summates to the stretching reflex, which recruits more fast-twitch fibers than normal strength training does. This process enables the athlete to perform another quick and explosive action immediately. Reflexes (including the muscle spindle reflex) are trainable, and well-periodized training can improve an athlete's reactive jumps.

Throwing Power

For a pitcher in baseball, a quarterback in American football, or a thrower in track and field, throwing power is generated mostly by fast-twitch muscle fibers. The larger an individual fiber's diameter is, the faster it contracts. Similarly, the more fibers a simultaneous contraction involves, the greater the athlete's power to deliver an implement.

Throwers and athletes in sports such as fencing and boxing must develop considerable power in order to accelerate the implement or equipment. These athletes must often overcome the inertia of an implement or piece of equipment with the greatest possible speed from the beginning of the movement and then increase velocity throughout the movement, especially before the release. To do so, they must apply force that greatly exceeds the resistance of the implement—the more the force exceeds the weight of the implement, the higher the acceleration. Higher acceleration, then, requires a greater difference between the resistance of the implement and the athlete's maximum strength. As a result, athletes whose sport uses throwing power must implement a well-planned maximum strength and power training phase.

Specific power training for throwing events and movements must focus on the maximum application of force and use the isotonic and ballistic methods. For the isotonic method, the reps (three to eight) need not be performed nonstop or at a high rate. In fact, for maximum benefit of explosive contraction in acyclic movements, in which the most fast-twitch fibers are recruited voluntarily at once, athletes should perform one rep at a time while achieving the highest mental concentration before each rep, possibly with an accommodating resistance (barbell plus bands or chains).

Takeoff Power

In many sports, good performance is possible only if the athlete is capable of an explosive takeoff. Examples include jumping events in track and field, ski jumping, volleyball, basketball, soccer, gymnastics, figure skating, and diving. In many cases, takeoff occurs following a short-distance, high-velocity run, during which the muscles prestretch and store energy. At takeoff, this energy is used as an acceleration thrust, thus producing a powerful jump.

The depth of the crouch needed at the instant of joint flexion depends on muscle fiber makeup as well as leg power. A deeper crouch requires greater force from the leg extensors. The crouch is a mechanical necessity, though, because it puts the muscles in a state of stretch, giving them a greater distance over which to accelerate for takeoff. The depth of the crouch is proportional to the power of the legs, and it is usually determined by the muscle fibers make-up of the athlete's lower-body extensor muscles. If the flexion is too great, the extension (or shortening phase) is performed slowly, and as a result the jump is low.

Starting Power

Starting power is an essential and often determinant ability in sports in which the initial speed of action dictates the final outcome. Relevant sports include boxing, karate, fencing, sprinting (the start), and teams sports that call for aggressive acceleration from standing. The fundamental physiological characteristic for successful performance in these situations is the athlete's ability to start the motion explosively by recruiting the highest possible number of fast-twitch fibers.

In sprinting, starting is performed with the muscles in the prestretched position (both knees and hips bent), from which they can generate greater power than when relaxed or shortened. In this position, the elastic elements of the muscles store kinetic energy that acts like a spring at the sound of the gun. The power used by national-class athletes is very high at the start: 290 pounds (132 kilograms) for the front leg and 225 pounds

(102 kilograms) for the back leg. Higher starting power enables a more explosive and faster start.

In boxing and the martial arts, a quick and powerful start in implementing an offensive skill prevents an opponent from using an effective defensive action. Quick action and powerful starts hinge on the elastic, reactive components of the neuromuscular system. These qualities can be maximized through more specific power training during the conversion phase, which better improves a muscle's stretch reflex and increases the power of the fast-twitch fibers.

Such aspects, which are key to starting a motion quickly and powerfully, can be trained through isotonic, ballistic, and especially maxex (chapter 13) and plyometric exercises. They can be performed in a set of repetitive motions or separately. In the latter case, exercises in a set are performed onc at a time so that the athlete has enough time to reach maximum mental concentration in order to perform them as explosively as possible. These conditions make it possible to recruit a high number of fast-twitch fibers; consequently, the athlete can perform the action with the greatest power available.

Acceleration Power

In sprinting, swimming, cycling, rowing, and most team sports, performance improvement requires the athlete to develop his or her ability to accelerate in order to develop high speed. Doing so requires power. Without power, an athlete cannot perform the required powerful push against the ground in running or overcome water resistance in aquatic sports. Therefore, power is an essential attribute in every sport that requires high acceleration.

In sprinting, for instance, the force applied against the ground is two to three times that of the athlete's body weight. In rowing, the oarsperson must use a constant blade pressure of 88 to 132 pounds (40 to 60 kilograms) per stroke in order to maintain high acceleration. And in all sports requiring acceleration power, the relevant forceful action must be performed repetitively and very rapidly. In these situations, more force applied against the ground—or a greater difference between the athlete's maximum strength and the water resistance—enables higher acceleration.

To achieve high acceleration, then, it essential to develop one's maximum strength. Because this goal is achieved during the maximum strength phase, the gains must be both maintained and converted to power through specific power training methods. More specifically, the isotonic, ballistic, power-resisting, and plyometric methods can help an athlete apply the series of muscle impulses that activate a great number of fast-twitch fibers at a high rate. Such activation enables the athlete to apply acceleration power at the desired high level.

These methods can either be implemented with a low number of reps (one to six) performed explosively and with high frequency or be implemented individually—one rep at a time. In the first case, the goal is repeated displays of cyclic power. In the second case, the goal is to apply the highest amount of power in a single, acyclic attempt in which the elastic–reactive component of strength is less used. Both methods must be used because athletes in sports requiring acceleration power must perform instantaneous powerful actions and do so with high frequency. By applying periodization of strength, athletes increase the likelihood of achieving these effects, as well as reaching peak acceleration power at the right time for major competitions.

Deceleration Power

In several sports, especially racket and team sports, deceleration is as important as acceleration. Team-sport players must be able to accelerate and run as quickly as possible in order to accomplish various goals, such as overtaking an opponent or making oneself available to receive a pass. In some sports—for example, soccer, basketball, lacrosse, and ice hockey—they also need the ability to decelerate quickly, then quickly change their running direction or jump to perform a sport-specific action, such as rebounding an incoming ball. Often, an athlete who can decelerate fast can create a tactical advantage.

Deceleration requires strong legs and good biomechanics; indeed, performing a quick deceleration can require leg force over twice one's body weight. Deceleration is performed through eccentric contraction of the leg muscles. This contraction is facilitated by placing the feet ahead of the center of gravity and leaving the upper body behind it. Muscles developed to decelerate quickly from a fast sprint rely on their elastic properties to amortize and reduce impact forces. The ability to amortize these forces requires power and degrees of knee and hip flexion similar to those needed for absorbing shock while landing.

To train the muscles to decelerate quickly, athletes must employ several methods, such as eccentric contraction and plyometrics. For eccentric contraction, the maximum strength method must be applied with progression from medium to supermaximum loads. For plyometrics, after a few years of normal progression from low- to high-impact exercises, the athlete can use drop or depth jumps.

Conversion to Muscular Endurance

No matter how intensive or comprehensive it is, strength training cannot produce adequate adaptation—or the resulting positive training effect—unless it addresses the specific physiological needs of the chosen sport. Even though most training specialists might agree with this statement, strength-training programs are often inadequate for sports and events in which endurance is a dominant or important component. These programs are still unduly influenced by Olympic weightlifting and bodybuilding training methods. However, though doing 20 reps may result in what bodybuilders consider muscular endurance, such a training regimen is grossly inadequate for sports such as mid- and long-distance swimming, rowing, canoeing, boxing, wrestling, cross-country skiing, speedskating, and triathlon—all of which are aerobic endurance dominant.

On the other hand, if an athlete uses only a low-rep strength training program with loads that are submaximal (70 percent of 1RM) or maximal (well over 80 percent), the athlete experiences adaptations to such loading in his or her energy supply, recovery, and physiological functioning of the organs and neuromuscular system. As a result, the athlete will achieve increased strength and movement efficiency but not muscular endurance. Such a program, therefore, does not enable optimal performance in endurance-dominant sports.

As we have seen, high-load strength training activates fast-twitch muscle fibers. This fact is well known, accepted, and applied in strength training for sports in which speed and power are the dominant abilities. However, athletic activities of long duration require a different type of training.

During longer-duration sports or events, the pace is often submaximal, and therefore the tension in the muscles is lower. As a result, the CNS first recruits muscle fibers that are specialized and adapted to cope with long-lasting physiological functioning: the slow-twitch (Type I) and the fast-twitch (Type IIa) muscle fibers. As a result of endurance training, the body is better able to use fat as fuel, thus sparing glycogen stores and disposing of and reusing lactic acid more efficiently.

However, these physiological adaptations cannot be accomplished solely by performing the sport. Because the sport-specific training represents a monotonous stimulus, the body is not forced to adapt to a higher level. In other words, for example, continuous rowing might be a sufficient stimulus for improving muscular endurance, but it is not sufficient for increasing sport performance. Instead, athletes should perform strength training with high reps using loads that are low to moderate but higher than what they encounter in their sport-specific activity. This kind of work trains the slow-twitch and fast-twitch muscle fibers to better respond to the dynamics of endurance sports.

Because fatigue seems to occur in stages (Wilmore and Costill 1993), when slow-twitch (Type I) and fast-twitch (Type IIa) fibers become exhausted the fast and powerful fast-twitch (Type IIx) fibers are recruited to work as well. Therefore, organizing a training program that recruits and maximizes the involvement of all three types of muscle fiber is the best method of enhancing muscular endurance. As a result, athletes in aerobic-dominant sports should do the following:

- Use training methods for muscular endurance of long duration that specifically address the adaptation of the muscle fibers, which are needed during long-duration sporting activities. The better they are trained, the longer they can produce the specific force in long-lasting events.

- Alternate strength training methods for muscular endurance of long duration with methods for power endurance of short duration so that fast-twitch (Type IIa) and fast-twitch (Type IIx) fibers are also recruited and, therefore, adapt to the specifics of long-duration activities.

- Use specific endurance training methods—such as long intervals (several reps of 10 to 30 minutes nonstop) and long-distance training—to adapt the body to effectively use free fatty acid as a fuel and improve cardiovascular efficiency.

Endurance training also enhances the oxidative capacity of fast-twitch fibers, which increases mitochondria and oxidative enzymes. As a result, the athlete relies more heavily on fat (free fatty acid) for ATP production, the most lasting energy reserve of the body (Wilmore and Costill 1993).

As we have discussed, a strength training program for endurance-dominant sports requires loads that are slightly higher than those encountered in competition. It also requires a high number of reps that approach the duration of the event. Implementing these parameters trains both the nervous system and the metabolic systems of the athlete to cope with the fatigue that is specific to his or her sport. The physiological requirements of training structured in this way closely resemble those of competition. Fortunately, the neuromuscular system is capable of adapting to any type of training.

The importance of maximum strength for endurance-dominant sports increases in proportion to external resistance. For instance, 400-meter swimmers move at a higher velocity than 1,500-meter swimmers. To create the higher velocity, 400-meter swimmers must pull against the water resistance with greater force than 1,500-meter swimmers do. Consequently, maximum strength is more important for 400-meter swimmers than for 1,500-meter swimmers.

In both cases, however, maximum strength must be improved from year to year if athletes expect to cover their distance faster. Such improvement is possible only if swimmers improve their specific metabolic endurance and increase the force used to pull against the water resistance. Only this increased force pushes the body through the water faster. The belief that maximum strength training makes swimmers slower because of the low velocity of training is a myth. In reality, maximum strength training is the only way to adapt the athlete's neuromuscular system to recruit more motor units for any sport task, thus providing a strong foundation on which to enhance muscular endurance.

Muscular endurance is best increased through a strength training program that emphasizes a high number of reps performed either explosively or at a steady pace, depending on the specifics of the sport. Both the selected exercises and the number of reps must be geared to produce the desired adaptation to the physiological requirements of the chosen sport or event. Athletes who do not apply adequate training methods during the conversion of maximum strength to muscular endurance cannot expect a positive transfer from training to the competitive environment. For example, a methodology borrowed from bodybuilding or Olympic weightlifting, in which 20 reps are considered optimal, will not help an athlete in a sport that requires 200 or more nonstop strokes (such as swimming, rowing, and canoeing) or in marathon running with its 50,000 strides.

However, as in all sport-specific periodization models, the number of reps performed in the sport cannot suddenly appear in the athlete's training schedule. To the contrary, the plan must gradually implement the needed increase in reps (at a specific load). The optimal progression is dictated by the time available for the muscle endurance phase and the target time under tension per set. Similarly, load increases, when necessary, must be between 2.5 percent and 5 percent from microcycle to microcycle, because a larger increase can affect the number of reps that the athlete is able to perform.

For endurance sports, aerobic endurance and muscular endurance must be trained at the same time. This requirement can be met either by training the two capabilities on separate days or, sometimes, by combining them in the same training session. In the latter case, muscular endurance should be performed at the end of the session because the specific endurance work often includes technical training. Combined workouts can be limited by fatigue, and if the total work per day must be decreased, the reduction is normally made in the muscular endurance work.

Here are the types of muscular endurance training for various sports:

- Muscular endurance dynamic (concentric–eccentric)—cyclic sports (e.g., rowing, swimming, cycling, cross-country skiing, canoeing, kayaking) and certain other sports (e.g., racket sports and boxing)
- Muscular endurance isometric—sports (e.g., sailing and driving) in which the athlete may stay in a specific position (i.e., in isometric contraction) for many minutes
- Muscular endurance mixed (combining dynamic with isometric)—grappling, Brazilian jiu-jitsu, shooting, and archery

Because sports can require anywhere from a few seconds to several hours of continuous physical activity, muscular endurance training must address these differences. For best training efficiency, muscular endurance is divided into three types according to the physiological characteristics of endurance sports: muscular endurance of short duration, muscular endurance of medium duration, and muscular endurance of long duration. After studying the following suggested training programs, coaches should feel free to adapt them to their athletes' specific needs and training backgrounds and to the physical environment of their sport.

Muscular Endurance of Short Duration

Sports with a duration between 30 seconds and two minutes include certain events in track and field, swimming, canoeing, speedskating, and skiing. In addition, some other sports require intense activity of this duration regularly during a game or match, such as ice hockey, basketball, boxing, and wrestling. During such intense activity, athletes build up a high level of lactic acid—often 12 to 20 millimoles or even more per liter—which shows that the lactic acid energy system is a dominant or at least important component in the overall performance of that sport or event. Most of these sports require very strong anaerobic capacity as well as very good aerobic power.

One key objective of training for endurance sports is to train athletes to tolerate fatigue; specific strength training should pursue the same goal. As the competitive phase approaches, strength training for muscular endurance short must be designed so that it challenges athletes' ability to tolerate a high buildup of lactic acid, as the energy sources of muscular endurance of short duration are blood glucose and, in particular, the glycogen stored in the muscles whose anaerobic metabolism determines an accumulation of lactic acid. Through training, the body adapts to tolerate the buildup of lactic acid by an increased expression of proteins responsible for removing lactate through its utilization as an energy substrate source (Billat et al. 2003). This adaptation better prepares the athlete for the vigor of competition and the fatigue that ultimately affects performance.

Training for muscular endurance of short duration, the athlete develops an oxygen debt. This condition is typical of activities in which the anaerobic energy system prevails. After 60 to 90 seconds of such activity, the heart rate can be as high as 200 beats per minute, and blood lactic acid concentration can be between 12 and 20 millimoles per liter or even higher.

Training for muscular endurance of short duration (MES) involves performing reps explosively at a very fast pace. The load is not very high (40 percent to 60 percent of 1RM) but reps are performed at high intensity—at or close to the rate in competition. For this reason, athletes should use the fewest possible exercises (two to six) to engage the prime movers.

The number of reps can be set precisely, but as in interval training it is more practical to decide the duration of each set—15 to 120 seconds—and the speed of performance: fast but steady. If the number of exercises is low, the athlete can perform three to six straight sets or two series of two or three sets. The duration and number of sets must be increased progressively.

To elicit the fastest and highest accumulation of lactic acid, the speed of performance must be explosive. In addition, in order to train an athlete to tolerate lactic acid buildup, the rest interval must be such that it enables a high power output in a very acidic environment (5 to 20 seconds between sets and 3 to 5 minutes between series, or 3 to 8 minutes between regular sets).

Training parameters for muscular endurance of short duration are given in table 14.8. The series-of-sets approach trains the athlete to maintain a very high power output despite lactic acid accumulation, whereas the straight-sets approach mimics the event-specific dynamics of lactate accumulation. A general example of MES periodization (e.g., for an 800-meter run, 200-meter freestyle, or 1,500-meter skate) is shown in figure 14.13; it goes from series of sets, which allows a higher mean power output, to straight sets performed up to event-specific duration. Figure 14.14 presents a sample six-week program for a national-class 100-meter fly swimmer (going from series of sets to straight sets).

Table 14.8 Training Parameters for Muscular Endurance of Short Duration

	SERIES OF SETS	STRAIGHT SETS
Phase duration	4–6 weeks	
Load	30%–50% of 1RM (according to sport-specific external resistance)	
No. of exercises	2–6	
Set duration	15–60 sec. (time split of specific event duration)	30–120 sec. (per specific event duration)
No. of sets per exercise	2–4 series of 2–6 sets (Series and sets must be progressed to and over sport-specific volume.)	3 or 4
Rest interval	5–20 sec. between sets, 3–5 min. between series	3–8 min.
Speed of execution	Explosive	
Frequency per week	2	

SERIES OF SETS			STRAIGHT SETS		
Week 1	Week 2	Week 3	Week 4	Week 5	Week 6
2 × (4 × 30 sec.)	3 × (3 × 40 sec.)	3 × (2 × 60 sec.)	3 × 100 sec.	3 × 110 sec.	3 × 120 sec.

Figure 14.13 General Example of MES Periodization for a Two-Minute Event

Exercise	WEEK					
	1	2	3	4	5	6
1. Cable pull while lying on belly (load=50% of 1RM)	2 × (4 × 15 sec.)	3 × (3 × 20 sec.)	4 × (2 × 30 sec.)	3 × 50 sec.	3 × 55 sec.	3 × 60 sec.
2. Medicine ball hold and forward throw while lying on back with arms above head	2 × (4 × 15 sec.)	3 × (3 × 20 sec.)	4 × (2 × 30 sec.)	3 × 50 sec.	3 × 55 sec.	3 × 60 sec.
3. Leg extension (load=50% of 1RM)	2 × (4 × 15 sec.)	3 × (3 × 20 sec.)	4 × (2 × 30 sec.)	3 × 50 sec.	3 × 55 sec.	3 × 60 sec.
4. Cable elbow extension (load=50% of 1RM)	2 × (4 × 15 sec.)	3 × (3 × 20 sec.)	4 × (2 × 30 sec.)	3 × 50 sec.	3 × 55 sec.	3 × 60 sec.
5. Abdominal V-sit	2 × 20	2 × 25	3 × 25	2 × 30	2 × 35	3 × 35
LOADING PATTERN						
			High			High
		Medium			Medium	
	Low			Low		

Figure 14.14 Sample Six-Week Program for a National-Class 100-Meter Fly Swimmer

Muscular Endurance of Medium and Long Duration

Muscular endurance of medium or long duration is a key factor in improving performance in all sports in which performance time lasts longer than two minutes. Examples include boxing, wrestling, rowing, swimming (400 to 1,500 meters), kayaking, canoeing (1,000 to 10,000 meters), road cycling, cross-country skiing, and biathlon and triathlon running. Training for muscular endurance of medium or long duration can be performed following the principles of interval training of long duration. This training method can also be referred to as extensive interval training because *extensive* implies a high-volume, long-duration type of activity.

The main objective of training for muscular endurance is to increase the athlete's ability to cope with fatigue. Such training improves the athlete's anaerobic and aerobic endurance because it employs a high number of reps—often more than 100. In the early part of a nonstop set with many reps, energy is provided by the anaerobic system. This process produces a buildup of lactic acid that creates physiological and psychological problems for the athlete as he or she attempts to continue the activity. As the athlete overcomes the challenge and continues to work, energy is supplied by the aerobic system. Therefore, repetitive muscular endurance training results in a specific adaptation that improves the necessary local aerobic metabolism.

Physiological adaptations promote better oxygen and energy supply and increase the removal of metabolic wastes. For example, repetitive muscular endurance training increases the amount of available glycogen stored both in the muscles and in the liver. Overall, then, muscular endurance training increases physiological efficiency.

Because muscular endurance training employs a relatively low load (around 30 percent to 50 percent of 1RM), muscles improve their long-term contracting capability without any evident increase in muscle fiber diameter. Only a certain number of motor units are active at one time; the others are at rest and are activated only when and where the contracting fibers become fatigued.

For sports in which muscular endurance represents an important training method, it is also beneficial to improve maximum strength. If the diameter of an individual muscle fiber increases as a result of maximum strength training, a lower number of motor units is required in order to perform a muscular endurance training task. In addition, maximum strength training and plyometric training have been proven to improve movement efficiency. This type of strength reserve created by using fewer units is critical and increases a muscle's capacity to produce work more effectively.

Therefore, maximum strength training should not be minimized. To the contrary, within limits, it should be used for all of the sports mentioned in this discussion. However, further once general preparation is over, doing more than simple maximum strength maintenance provide only negligible benefits for sports of long duration, such as a marathon, and for sports that require less than 30 percent of maximum strength (Hartmann and Tünnemann 1988).

Training for muscular endurance of medium duration (MEM) is suggested for sports in which the duration of competition is between 2 and 8 minutes (events dominated by aerobic power), whereas MEL training is suggested for sports in which the duration is 8 minutes or longer (events dominated by aerobic capacity). This distinction is necessary because muscular endurance of medium duration has a stronger anaerobic component, whereas muscular endurance of long duration is clearly aerobic. The program designs for each type of muscular endurance are described separately in the following sections because the load, set duration, and speed of execution are also clearly different.

Program Design for Muscular Endurance of Medium Duration

This program is recommended for events that last between two and eight minutes or otherwise require a high level of aerobic power. It can be designed in the form of circuit training, series of sets, or straight sets. The circuit training option is suggested for situations in which it is not possible to practice the sport-specific training with an adequate weekly frequency and therefore the cardiorespiratory adaptations must be stimulated also during the time devoted to training in the gym. The series approach is suggested especially for the first part of an MEM phase for events with a strong anaerobic component and for which the system must be trained to produce a steady output of high power (e.g., 1,500-meter run, 400-meter swim, 3,000-meter skate, 1,000-meter kayaking). It can also be used at the end of the MEM phase for intermittent sports. The straight-sets approach is suggested for the development of local muscular endurance in longer events; for the second part of an MEM phase, when sets must reach the sport-specific duration; for sports that require steady power output; and for the first part of an MEM phase for intermittent sports. Examples are presented for each of the three options.

The load in training for muscular endurance of medium duration ranges from 30 percent to 50 percent of 1RM (see table 14.9). Throughout the MEM phase, certain parameters are held constant: load, speed of execution, and number of exercises (more for sports in which several muscle groups must be trained, such as wrestling and boxing, and fewer for sports in which either the upper- or lower-body muscle groups prevail, such as speedskating and canoeing). Set duration, however, increases every week or every second week. The program is designed precisely to constantly expose athletes to high levels of fatigue so that they learn to cope with the pain and exhaustion of competition. Therefore, the rest interval between sets is short so that the athlete has insufficient time to recover adequately.

Figure 14.15 shows a general example of periodization of MEM (e.g., for 1,500-meter run, 400-meter freestyle swim, 3,000-meter skate, or 1,000-meter kayaking) and figure 14.16 a sample MEM program for a wrestler. Both these programs go from series of sets,

Table 14.9 Training Parameters for Muscular Endurance Medium

	SERIES OF SETS	STRAIGHT SETS
Phase duration	8–10 weeks	
Load	30%–50% of 1RM (according to sport-specific external resistance)	
No. of exercises	4–8	
Set duration	1–4 min. (time split of the specific event duration)	2–8 min. (according to specific event duration)
No. of sets per exercise	2–4 series of 2–4 sets (Series and sets must be progressed to and over sport-specific volume.)	3 or 4
Rest interval	5–10 sec. between sets, 2–4 min. between series	2–3 min.
Speed of execution	Fast	Fast to moderate
Frequency per week	2	

Phase 4: Conversion to Specific Strength

	SERIES OF SETS			STRAIGHT SETS	
Week 1	Week 2	Week 3	Week 4	Week 5	Week 6
2 × (4 × 60 sec.)	3 × (3 × 80 sec.)	3 × (2 × 120 sec.)	3 × 200 sec.	3 × 220 sec.	3 × 240 sec.

Figure 14.15 General Example of MEM Periodization for Events Lasting About Four Minutes and Requiring Steadily High Power Output

Exercises	WEEK							
	1	2	3	4	5	6	7	8
Zercher squat	2 × 120 sec.	2 × 120 sec.	3 × 120 sec.	3 × 120 sec.	2 × (2 × 60 sec.)	2 × (2 × 60 sec.)	3 × (3 × 40 sec.)	3 × (3 × 40 sec.)
Floor press	2 × 120 sec.	2 × 120 sec.	3 × 120 sec.	3 × 120 sec.	2 × (2 × 60 sec.)	2 × (2 × 60 sec.)	3 × (3 × 40 sec.)	3 × (3 × 40 sec.)
Hip bridge	2 × 120 sec.	2 × 120 sec.	3 × 120 sec.	3 × 120 sec.	2 × (2 × 60 sec.)	2 × (2 × 60 sec.)	3 × (3 × 40 sec.)	3 × (3 × 40 sec.)
Lat machine (neutral narrow grip)	2 × 120 sec.	2 × 120 sec.	3 × 120 sec.	3 × 120 sec.	2 × (2 × 60 sec.)	2 × (2 × 60 sec.)	3 × (3 × 40 sec.)	3 × (3 × 40 sec.)
Barbell curl	2 × 120 sec.	2 × 120 sec.	3 × 120 sec.	3 × 120 sec.	2 × (2 × 60 sec.)	2 × (2 × 60 sec.)	3 × (3 × 40 sec.)	3 × (3 × 40 sec.)
Farmer's walk	2 × 100 sec.	2 × 100 sec.	3 × 80 sec.	3 × 80 sec.	2 × (2 × 60 sec.)	2 × (2 × 60 sec.)	3 × (2 × 40 sec.)	3 × (2 × 40 sec.)

Figure 14.16 Program Moving From Straight Sets to Series of Sets for a Wrestler

which allow higher mean power output, to straight sets performed up to event-specific duration. As shown, the duration and number of reps are increased progressively over a long period. To achieve physiological adaptation in response to such high training, the duration of the conversion phase must be 8 to 10 weeks.

Circuit training designed for muscular endurance of medium (and long duration also) can use a barbell or any other piece of equipment. The advantage of using a barbell is that different limbs can be exercised without stopping to rest, as required in the circuit shown in figure 14.17.

The circuit in figure 14.17 includes eight exercises that, after 9 or 10 weeks, are performed as follows. The athlete places a barbell of 40 percent of maximum strength on the ground and performs 50 deadlifts. After completing the last rep, the athlete deloads the barbell, lies on the bench, and does 50 bench presses. The athlete then quickly reloads the bar, places the barbell back on the shoulders, and performs 50 half squats. After completing the last squat, the athlete sits on a bench and performs 50 arm curls, then grabs a kettlebell from the ground and performs 50 kettlebell swings. The athlete moves immediately to 50 rowing actions, then once again quickly places the barbell on the shoulders and performs 50 toe raises, which are followed by 50 V-sits performed on the ground. The total number of reps performed in our hypothetical circuit is 400!

The advantage of this method is that the cardiorespiratory system is involved throughout the circuit because training alternates between different muscle groups. This work develops muscular endurance and aerobic endurance—the two crucial abilities for any of the sports discussed in this chapter—which is particularly good when, for instance, the athlete cannot do much specific metabolic training during the macrocycle.

Exercise	NUMBER OF WEEKS			
	3 or 4	3	3	2
Pulley Row	Progressively aim to perform 50–60 reps nonstop per exercise with a load of 30%–50% of 1RM.	Perform 2 exercises nonstop, or 100 reps together (e.g., 50 half squats followed by 50 arm curls); pair the remaining 6 exercises.	Perform 4 exercises nonstop, or 200 reps together. After a rest interval, perform the other 4 exercises in the same manner.	Perform all exercises nonstop (8 exercises × 50 reps = 400 reps nonstop).
Bench press				
Half squat				
Arm curl				
Deadlift				
Bent-over row				
Toe raise				
V-sit				
Rest interval	1 minute between exercises	1–2 minutes between pairs	2 minutes between the groups	1 minute

A similar program can be developed for other sports, such as 400- to 1,500-meter swimming, middle-distance speedskating events, kayaking, and canoeing.

Figure 14.17 Sample MEM Circuit for a Rower

To further clarify the information presented in figure 14.17, coaches should consider the following guidelines:

- The number of reps increases progressively to reach 40 to 60 (or even higher); doing so may take two to four weeks.
- The number of exercises may vary depending on the needs of the sport.
- The number of reps may differ between the first exercises and the last exercises when the latter ones are given lower priority.
- The same exercise can be repeated twice in the same circuit to emphasize the importance of that group of muscles in a given sport.
- The number of exercises may not be the same for upper and lower body. This decision should be based on the athlete's strengths and weaknesses and the sport's demands.
- With beginners, the load for a deadlift must be lower (30 percent to 40 percent of 1RM) and used carefully (employing long-term progression).
- Athletes should maintain a steady speed throughout the circuit, even though they may have the urge to move faster and get the exercise over with.
- Coaches and trainers should set up all needed equipment before training so that the athlete needs as little time as possible to move from one exercise to another, especially in a gym setting. Good choices in such settings include barbell and dumbbell exercises that can be performed in a close space.
- Athletes should perform two exercises nonstop in the second phase, four nonstop in the third phase, and all eight nonstop in the last phase.

Phase 4: Conversion to Specific Strength

- The athlete may need eight to ten minutes or longer to perform an eight-exercise circuit nonstop, depending on his or her classification. An even longer circuit can be designed for better improvement of muscular endurance of long duration.

- Because both MEM and MEL involve severe physiological demands, this method should be used only by athletes with a strong background in both strength and endurance training (national-class athletes and higher). For a less demanding circuit (for juniors), include only four to six exercises.

- It is best to perform an even number of exercises because of the recommended progression—two exercises performed nonstop, then four, then all eight.

- As an athlete adapts to performing the total number of exercises nonstop during the last phase, the coach can use a stopwatch to monitor improvement. The time required to complete the circuit should decrease as a result of adaptation.

Figure 14.18 depicts a suggested MEM program for boxing. This program has to be performed nonstop, from the first to the last exercise, with a steady rhythm, but as fast as possible. The only exception is the jump squat, in which the eccentric phase has to be performed in a fast but controlled fashion to avoid deep knee compression.

For the one-arm standing medicine ball throw, the athlete needs to throw the ball against a solid rebounding wall. The throw must imitate a boxing punch, performed horizontally forward with the other arm being used just as a support, to hold the ball in front of the chest. The weight of the ball can start (depending on the boxer's conditioning) at 6 to 8 pounds (2.7 to 3.6 kilograms). The weight should decrease every one or two weeks by

Exercise	Week 1	Week 2	Week 3	Week 4
One-arm standing medicine ball chest throw	4 × 10 reps, 10 sec. rest interval	5 × 10 reps, 10 sec. rest interval	6 × 10 reps, 10 sec. rest interval	6 × 10 reps, 10 sec. rest interval
Jump squat (50% of 1RM)	30 reps	30 reps	30 reps	30 reps
Kettlebell swing (power swing or American swing style)	1 min.	1 min.	1.5 min. (lighter kettlebell than in weeks 1 and 2)	1.5 minutes (same kettlebell as in week 3)
Within a circuit rest interval	1 min.	1 min.	1 min.	1 min.
One-arm standing medicine ball chest throw	4 × 10 reps, 10 sec. rest interval	5 × 10 reps, 10 sec. rest interval	6 × 10 reps, 10 sec. rest interval	6 × 10 reps, 10 sec. rest interval
Two-arm standing medicine ball smash-down	4 × 10 sec., 10 sec. rest interval	5 × 10 sec., 10 sec. rest interval	6 × 10 sec., 10 sec. rest interval	6 × 10 sec., 10 sec. rest interval
Rest interval between circuits	1 min.	1 min.	1 min.	1 min.
Number of circuits	3	3	3 or 4	4 or 5
Total duration of single circuit	8 min.	9 min.	10 min.	10 min.

To prolong the duration of a circuit, add another exercise, such as the abdomen crunch. Professional boxers must progressively use a higher number of circuits to meet the muscular endurance requirements of going 10 or 12 rounds in the ring (e.g., repeat the circuit 5 to 7 times).

Figure 14.18 Sample Program for Muscular Endurance Medium for Boxing

one or two pounds. During the last week or two, the ball should weigh 2 to 4 pounds (0.9 to 1.8 kilograms).

Because the upper body musculature of a boxer must endure a more anaerobic kind of activity, the duration of the upper-body exercise sets is split. The rest intervals are planned after roughly the duration of a round, then after a progressively longer time, to ensure both a high power output and the development of specific muscular endurance.

Program Design for Muscular Endurance of Long Duration

Sports of longer duration require a different kind of physiological training. In most of these sports, the athlete applies force against a given resistance—for example, water in swimming, rowing, and canoeing; pedals in cycling (with body weight applied as strength, especially uphill); ice in speedskating; and snow and various terrains in cross-country skiing and biathlon. The dominant energy system in such sports is aerobic capacity, and improved performance is expected to come from increments in both central and peripheral aerobic endurance. Central (cardiovascular) adaptations are addressed mainly by sport-specific training; therefore, strength training must be designed to enhance local muscular endurance.

To increase muscular endurance of long duration, the key training ingredient is a high number of reps performed nonstop. The other training parameters remain constant, as indicated in table 14.10.

Because one training goal of muscular endurance long is to enable the athlete to cope with fatigue, the rest interval does not allow full recovery. In fact, only a very short rest (usually five to ten seconds) is afforded as the athlete changes stations. Similarly, for straight-sets training, only a short rest interval is programmed—again, to prevent a complete muscular recovery—thus further challenging local muscular endurance.

Figure 14.19 shows a typical training program for sports such as triathlon, marathon, kayaking and canoeing (10,000-meter and marathon), long-distance swimming, road cycling, and cross-country skiing. To facilitate monitoring the many minutes of steady work, duration is expressed in minutes rather than number of reps.

The first two exercises can be performed with any combination machine available in a fitness center or school gymnasium. The last two exercises must be performed using rubber cords, often called elastic cords, which are available in many sporting goods stores. To train long-distance kayakers and canoeists, the elastic cords must be anchored before training so that arm pulls or elbow extensions—typical motions for these two sports—can be performed in a seated position.

The set duration per exercise must be based on the work tolerance and performance level of each athlete. It must also take into consideration the resulting total workout

Table 14.10 Training Parameters for Muscular Endurance Long

Phase duration	8–12 weeks
Load	30%–40% of 1RM
No. of exercises	4–6
No. of sets per session	2–4
Rest interval	2 minutes between circuits, 1 minute between sets
Speed of execution	Moderate
Frequency per week	2 or 3

Phase 4: Conversion to Specific Strength

Exercise	NUMBER OF WEEKS					
	2	**2**	**2**	**2**	**2**	**2 or 3**
Leg press	With a load of 30% of 1RM, do 4 minutes of nonstop work for each exercise.	Do the same work for 7 minutes nonstop per exercise. To maintain proper workout duration, perform only one between leg presses and arm pulls per circuit(thus do 5 exercises per circuit).	Do 10 minutes of nonstop work of an exercise. To maintain proper workout duration, eliminate the leg presses and arm pulls (thus do 4 exercises per circuit).	Do 6 minutes of nonstop work of an exercise. Take a 1-minute rest, repeat the set, then proceed to the next exercise.	Do 8 minutes of nonstop work of an exercise. Take a 1-minute rest, repeat the set, then proceed to the next exercise. To maintain proper workout duration, only perform one set of leg presses and arm pulls.	Do 10 minutes of nonstop work of an exercise. Take a 1-minute rest, repeat the set, then proceed to the next exercise. To maintain proper workout duration, eliminate the leg press and arm pulls (thus do 4 total exercises).
Arm pull (cords)						
Bench press						
Leg press						
Arm pull (cords)						
Elbow extension (cords)						
Number of circuits completed	3	2	2	—	—	—
Number of sets per exercise	—	—	—	2	2	2
Rest interval between circuits	2 minutes	2 minutes	2 minutes	—	—	—
Rest interval between exercises	—	—	—	1 minute	1 minute	1 minute
Workout duration	76 minutes	72 minutes	82 minutes	84 minutes	84 minutes	84 minutes

A similar concept of training can be applied to other sports, such as long-distance cross-country skiing, kayaking, marathon swimming, and triathlon.

Figure 14.19 Sample MEL Training Program for an Experienced Marathon Canoeist

duration. To train muscular endurance of long duration, some have suggested progressing from straight sets to circuits; instead, we suggest progressing from circuits to straight sets in order to further increase local muscular endurance. Here is the reasoning: Circuit training has a greater cardiorespiratory impact than straight sets do. However, long-endurance athletes already have a high level of cardiorespiratory endurance because they devote, on average, 90 percent of their total annual training time to sport-specific activity. Therefore, their specific strength training must focus on local muscular endurance of the prime movers.

Muscular Endurance Isometric

A limited number of sports require athletes to use isometric contraction of long duration during competition. Examples include sailing and motor sports (driving). During training and competition in sailing, the athlete takes a specific position (static in most cases) in which parts of the body perform long-duration isometric contraction. For instance, a sailor may be seated on a side of the board while holding a rope in order to maintain the mast in the most wind-effective position. To do so, the athlete contracts certain parts of the body, such as the abdomen, legs, low back, and arms.

Unlike driving (motor sports), in which specific strength training is performed in the gym, the muscular endurance isometric training for sailing can be performed on the boat and off the boat, as illustrated in the following example. During training, the athlete can use a heavy vest to overload the upper body, thus creating an additional physiological challenge against the pull of gravity and the centrifugal force during turns. Heavy vests can carry different weights, often as high as 35 pounds (about 16 kilograms). The scope of training can involve progressively increasing either the weight of the vest or the duration of using it.

Figure 14.20 suggests a progression for using a weighted vest for training in the boat. This progression is only a guideline, applicable as appropriate for the athlete's individual physical capabilities, needs, and training environment. Training for sailing should include a preparatory phase regardless of whether the sailor lives in a climate that favors year-round training. Figure 14.21 illustrates a suggested strength training program for sailing, in which isometric training is dominant. The angle at which the athlete holds the isometric contraction must be sport-specific. Again, this is only a progression guideline; coaches should adapt it to fit the needs of their athletes, for both sailing and driving.

Weight of vest	10 kg (about 22 lb.)	12 kg (about 26.5 lb.)	15 kg (about 33 lb.)
Duration	2 × 15 min.	3 × 15 min.	4 × 20 min.

Figure 14.20 Sample Progression for In-Boat Use of Heavy Vests in Sailing

| Exercise | WEEK | | | | | | Rest interval |
	1	2	3	4	5	6	
1. Arm pull	5 × 60 sec.	4 × 90 sec.	3 × 120 sec.	2 × 180 sec.	2 × 240 sec.	2 × 240 sec.	1 min.
2. Leg press	5 × 60 sec.	4 × 90 sec.	3 × 120 sec.	2 × 180 sec.	2 × 240 sec.	2 × 240 sec.	2 min.
3. Leg curl	4 × 30 sec.	4 × 45 sec.	2 × 60 sec.	2 × 90 sec.	2 × 120 sec.	2 × 120 sec.	2 min.
4. Back extension	5 × 60 sec.	4 × 90 sec.	3 × 120 sec.	2 × 180 sec.	2 × 240 sec.	2 × 240 sec.	2 min.
5. Bench press	5 × 60 sec.	4 × 90 sec.	3 × 120 sec.	2 × 180 sec.	2 × 240 sec.	2 × 240 sec.	1 min.
6. Roman chair iso crunch	5 × 60 sec.	4 × 90 sec.	3 × 120 sec.	2 × 180 sec.	2 × 240 sec.	2 × 240 sec.	1 min.

Figure 14.21 Sample Strength Training Program for Sailing

Muscular Endurance Using Mixed Contractions Method

Muscular endurance using mixed contractions is very specific to certain sports, such as grappling, Brazilian jiu-jitsu, shooting, and archery. The main scope of training for such sports is to expose athletes to mixed-contraction training, such as concentric–isometric–eccentric, in order to ready them for major competition.

Consider pistol shooting, in which the pistol weighs 3 pounds (about 1.4 kilograms). During competition, the shooter lifts the pistol 20 times, each time holding an isometric contraction of 10 to 15 seconds, with limited rest intervals. Poorly trained athletes have a shaky arm, mostly toward the end of a competition, which is of course far from conducive to high shooting accuracy. Therefore, the scope of training in this sport (see figure 14.22) is to prepare the athlete to lift the pistol at least as many times as needed during competition, using weights higher than the weight of the pistol, for a sport-specific duration of isometric contraction and with sport-specific rest intervals between sets (50 seconds during a final).

Weeks	2	2	2
Weight of dumbbell	1.5 kg (about 3.3 lb.)	2 kg (about 4.4 lb.)	2.5 kg (about 5.5 lb.)
45-degree raise	18 sets × 1 rep	16 sets × 1 rep	14 sets × 1 rep
Isometric contraction duration at specific joint angle	15 sec.	15 sec.	12 sec.
Rest interval between sets	50 sec.	50 sec.	50 sec.

Figure 14.22 Sample Progression for Mixed Concentric–Isometric–Eccentric Training for Shooting

The technical action in pistol shooting is as follows: Lift the pistol from the hip to shoulder level, hold it still for 10 to 15 seconds, shoot, and then lower the pistol to the starting position. The longest shooting round lasts 14 shots. A similar type of action is required in archery, in which the archer performs concentric–isometric contraction against resistance while stretching the bowstring and holding it for a few seconds (5 to 10). The archer then releases the arrow and lowers the bow to prepare for a new attempt.

Mixed martial arts (MMA) also features a mix of eccentric–concentric and isometric contractions during the ground portion of a fight. Such contractions are also needed in grappling and Brazilian jiu-jitsu. As always, these sport-specific strength requirements must be reflected in the athletes' strength training. This need can be met by targeting the prime movers that undergo the isometric contractions either through functional isometrics interspersed with eccentric–concentric exercises or through straight isometric exercises; see figure 14.23.

WORKOUTS 1-3-5**				
Exercise	**Sets**	**Reps**	**Tempo**	**Rest interval**
Deadlift	3	1 (75% of 1RM)	3.0.X	2 min.
Bench press	3	2 (75%)	3.0.X	2 min.
Good morning	3	5 (2 reps short to failure)	3.0.X	2 min.
Pull-up with functional isometrics	3	3 (70% 1RM)	2.0.1+1+1iso.X	2 min.
Hip bridge	3	3 (70% 1RM)	3.0.X	2 min.
Radial deviation	2	8	3.0.1	1 min.
Sit-up with weight	2	6	3.0.1	1 min.

WORKOUTS 2-4-6***				
Exercise	**Sets**	**Reps**	**Tempo**	**Rest interval**
Isometric kneeling good morning	3	60 sec.	—	2 min.
Isometric floor press	3	60 sec.	3.0.X	3 min.
One-arm dumbbell row	3	5 (2 reps short to failure)	3.0.1	90 sec.
Front raise	3	8	3.0.1	90 sec.
Standing calf raise	3	8	3.0.X	90 sec.
Iso neck extension on Swiss ball	3	60 sec.	—	1 min.
Turkish get-up	3	3+3 (L/R)	—	90 sec.
Farmer walk	3	60 sec. + 60 sec. (L/R)	—	90 sec.

*Two-week block before a two-week precompetition taper.

**Workouts 1 and 3 performed in the first week; workout 5 performed in the second week.

***Workout 2 performed in the first week; workouts 4 and 6 performed in the second week.

Figure 14.23 Sample Program Using Mixed Concentric–Eccentric and Isometric Training for MMA, Grappling, or Brazilian Jiu-Jitsu Fighter During the Competitive Phase*

15

Phases 5, 6, and 7: Maintenance, Cessation, and Compensation

Strength training is an important physiological contributor to overall athletic performance. In particular, more explosive skills require more maximum strength and power, and longer activities require more muscular endurance. In all cases, superior performance requires the vital contribution of strength.

The benefits of strength to athletic performance are experienced as long as the neuromuscular system maintains the cellular adaptations induced by training. When strength training is ceased, the benefits soon decrease as the contractile properties of the muscles diminish. The consequence is the process of detraining—a visible decrease in the contribution of strength to athletic performance. To avoid detraining, athletes must implement sport-specific strength programs during the competitive phase.

Strength training also affects peaking, or performing at peak level during the year's main competition(s). In several sports, especially power sports, peak performance is often achieved in the early part of the competitive phase. During this time, coaches tend to overlook strength training because specific technical and tactical training become dominant. Unfortunately, this lack of strength training causes decreased performance as the season progresses. In the early part of the season, while strength training remains in effect, the athlete can perform as expected. However, when the athlete's ability to powerfully contract the muscles diminishes, so does his or her performance.

According to the theory of periodization of strength, gains in maximum strength during the maximum strength phase should be transformed into either muscular endurance or power during the conversion phase while maintaining maximum strength levels. Doing so enables the athlete to develop the best possible sport-specific strength and equips him or her with the physiological capabilities necessary for strong performance during the competitive phase. This physiological base must be maintained if the athlete is to maintain his or her performance level throughout the competitive phase.

This reality means that the coach must plan a sport-specific strength maintenance program throughout the competitive phase. Maximum strength is a crucial ingredient for sport-specific strength programs. Many sports require maintenance of some maximum strength during the competitive season, mostly using the low-volume-of-maximum-load method (usually 40 percent to 50 percent of the volume used for the highest-load microcycle of the maximum strength phase). Gains in maximum strength decline faster if they resulted from a too-short maximum strength phase.

In addition, in many sports, the only type of strength training performed is event-specific power training. Maximum strength training is often overlooked, and gains are therefore short lived. Another methodological error occurs when strength training is done mostly during the preparatory phase; in this case, strength gains deteriorate as the competitive phase progresses and approaches its peak.

With all of this in mind, coaches should not question *whether* to prescribe strength maintenance training during the competitive phase, but rather *how* to do so. They must keep in mind the dominant ability of the sport and carefully consider what types of strength the athlete needs to maintain. Most sports require some elements of maximum strength, power, and muscular endurance. The most important decision, therefore, is not which of the three to maintain but in what proportion—and how best to integrate them into training.

Athletes in power sports must maintain both maximum strength and power. Because these abilities cannot be substituted for each other—rather, they are complementary—one should not be maintained at the expense of the other. For instance, throwers in track and field and linemen in American football must maintain maximum strength during the competitive phase with a roughly equal proportion between maximum strength and power. Most athletes in team sports should maintain maximum strength, power, and either power endurance or muscular endurance, depending on the position they play. For endurance sports, however, the proportion between maximum strength and muscular endurance depends both on the duration of the event and on which energy system is dominant. For the majority of endurance sports, muscular endurance is the dominant component of strength.

The proportion of different types of strength to maintain also depends on the duration of the competitive phase. The longer this phase is, the more important it is to maintain some elements of maximum strength, because this type of strength is an important component of both power and muscular endurance. Overlooking this fact results in the detraining of maximum strength, which affects both power and muscular endurance. Table 15.1 shows the proportions of different types of strength to be maintained during the competitive phase for various sports and positions.

Table 15.1 Strength Proportions for the Competitive Phase

Sport or event	Maximum strength %	Power %	Power endurance %	Muscular endurance %
Athletics				
Sprinting	40	40	20	—
Jumping	30	70	—	—
Throwing	50	50	—	—
Baseball				
Pitcher	40	40	20	—
Field player	20	70	10	—

Sport or event	Maximum strength %	Power %	Power endurance %	Muscular endurance %
Basketball	20	60	20	—
Biathlon	—	—	20	80
Boxing	20	20	30	30
Canoeing/Kayaking				
500 m	40	30	20	10
1,000 m	20	20	20	40
10,000 m	—	—	20	80
Cycling				
Track 200 m	40	40	20	—
4,000 m pursuit	10	30	20	40
Diving	30	70	—	—
Fencing	20	50	30	—
Field hockey	—	40	20	40
Figure skating	40	40	20	—
Football (American)				
Linemen	50	50	—	—
Linebackers	30	50	20	—
Running backs	30	50	20	—
Wide receivers	30	50	20	—
Defensive backs	30	50	20	—
Tailbacks	30	40	20	10
Football (Australian)	30	40	20	10
Ice hockey	20	40	30	10
Martial arts	—	60	30	10
Rowing	20	—	20	60
Rugby	30	40	30	—
Skiing				
Alpine	40	30	30	—
Nordic	—	—	20	80
Soccer				
Goalie	40	60	—	—
Field positions	30	50	20	—
Speedskating				
Sprinting	30	50	20	—
Distance	—	10	20	70
Swimming				
Sprinting	40	40	20	—
Middle distance	10	10	20	60
Long distance	—	—	20	80
Tennis	10	50	30	10
Volleyball	40	50	10	—
Water polo	10	20	20	50
Wrestling	20	20	20	40

The same training methods suggested in earlier chapters should be applied during the maintenance phase. What differs during this phase is not the methodology but the volume of strength training as compared with the volume of technical, tactical, and other training. During this phase, the strength maintenance program should be subordinate to other types of training. Therefore, the athlete should use the lowest number of exercises (two to four, or six for some multiplanar sports) to address the prime movers. With this approach, the athlete expends the least possible energy for maintenance of strength, leaving the majority of energy for technical and tactical training.

The one to three strength training sessions per week during the competitive phase should be as short as possible. Indeed, a good maintenance program can often be accomplished in 20 to 30 minutes. Of course, the frequency of strength training sessions also depends on the competition schedule. If no competitions are scheduled on the weekend, then a microcycle may include two (or perhaps three) strength training sessions. If a game or competition is planned on the weekend, then one (or perhaps two) short strength training sessions can be planned.

The number of sets is also usually low (one to four), depending on whether the athlete is training for power endurance or muscular endurance. For power and maximum strength, a range of two to four sets is possible because the number of reps is usually low. The rest interval should be longer than usual so that the athlete can recover almost entirely during the break. The intent of the maintenance phase is not to create fatigue but to stabilize performance and maintain high power output. For muscular endurance training, only one or two sets should be performed because the number of reps is higher. For muscular endurance medium training during the competitive phase, the set duration should not exceed one minute; for muscular endurance long, it should not exceed six minutes.

The planning for each microcycle of a maintenance program depends on the type of strength being sought. For power training, athletes should perform exercises that enhance explosiveness by using resistance close to that encountered in competition. Two types of resistance are suggested: increased load and decreased load. Increased-load training involves using a resistance slightly higher than that of competition, and it enhances both maximum strength and power. Exercises of this type should be specific to the prevailing skills of the particular sport. This type of exercise is suggested mostly for the early part of the competitive phase as a transition from maximum strength to power. Decreased-load training, on the other hand, involves using a resistance below that encountered in competition. It enhances explosiveness and should prevail in the phase prior to major competition.

Both types of load increase the ability to recruit a high number of fast-twitch muscle fibers and improve coordination of the muscles involved. More generally, if the competitive phase is longer than five months, athletes should dedicate at least 25 percent of the total work to the maintenance of maximum strength because the detraining of maximum strength negatively affects sport-specific strength.

Variations of Loading Pattern for the Competitive Phase

Strength training is not a rigid process. To the contrary, programs should be flexible and adapted to the athlete's well-being and training progress, to the requirements of the sport, and to the competition schedule. The content of a training session must be planned to match the overall intensity or demand of sport-specific elements in that session, and take into account the proximity of the competition or game. The examples suggested in this section assume that strength training is performed following specific work on technique and tactics and drills for speed and specific endurance. Consequently, the athlete is little time or energy to spare, and strength training must be short and sport specific.

The following guidelines explain in some detail the loading parameter of strength and power maintenance sessions throughout the competitive microcycle. Description is provided for heavy, medium, and low loads sessions and for certain other general considerations.

- A heavy-load or heavy-demand strength training session lasts 20 to 30 minutes. It trains maximum strength or a combination of maximum strength and power. Athletes perform four or five total exercises specifically for the prime movers. Strength is trained with a load of 70 percent to 80 percent of 1-repetition maximum (1RM) as fast and dynamically as possible while maintaining good technique. Athletes perform one to three reps (with a buffer of 15 percent to 20 percent) in two to four sets with a rest interval of two to three minutes between sets.

- A medium-load strength training session lasts 20 to 30 minutes. It trains maximum strength, power, or a combination of the two. Athletes perform three or four total exercises. For strength, they use a load of 70 percent of 1RM. They perform three to five explosive reps (with a buffer of 15 percent to 20 percent) in two or three sets with a rest interval of two to three minutes between sets.

- A low-load strength training session lasts 15 to 30 minutes. It trains maximum strength, power, or a combination of the two. Athletes perform two or three total exercises and explosively move a load of 60 percent to 70 percent of 1RM. They perform one to six reps (with a buffer of 20 percent to 30 percent) over two or three sets with a rest interval of two to three minutes between sets.

- Rest intervals should be adjusted according to the number of exercises and the volume of the set to fit within the allotted training time.

- Strength and power exercises that work the same muscle groups can be paired in jump-set fashion to save training time yet allow sufficient time for recovery between two sets of the same exercise.

The following sections present several practical examples of loading pattern dynamics for both individual and team sports during competitive-phase microcycles.

Individual Sports

Figure 15.1 shows a suggested strength training plan for athletes in the competitive phase of speed and power sports (e.g., sprinting, jumping, and throwing events in track and field; 50-meter swimming; martial arts; fencing). For the first two or three days following competition, the objective of training is regeneration. Only two strength training sessions are planned, both later in the week, and the first is of low intensity.

The only time strength training is challenging is during week 2. The third week involves peaking for competition again, so only two strength training sessions are planned, and the second one is of low intensity. To ensure that the Wednesday session is of low demand, the rest interval(s) between two or three sets of strength and power training should be long (three to four minutes) for full regeneration. In addition, the load should have a buffer of no less than 20 percent (e.g., three to six reps at 60 percent of 1RM, two to five reps at 65 percent, or one or two reps at 70 percent). This approach prevents residual fatigue that could affect the athlete's performance in the upcoming competition.

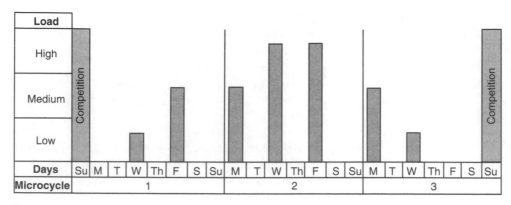

Figure 15.1 Suggested plan for strength training (and loading magnitude) for a speed-and-power-dominant sport in which competitions occur three weeks apart.

Figure 15.2 addresses similar concerns for an athlete whose competitions occur two weeks apart. When designing such a plan, coaches should allow two or three days of regenerative, low-intensity training following the first competition. Training must then involve low intensity again on the last two or three days before the next competition in order to facilitate peaking.

Weekly competition in individual sports is far from ideal simply because the more athletes compete, the less time they have for training. During periods marked by weekly competition, especially when fatigue is high, most coaches look for training elements to cut, and unfortunately strength training is often the first to go. Instead, coaches should lower the volume of specific training and keep general training higher in order to compensate for specific physiological systems fatigue.

For sports in which weekly competition is the norm, figure 15.3 illustrates a strength training plan that can be altered to accommodate high levels of fatigue. Coaches should keep in mind, however, that planning too many training cycles amid weekly competition produces a predictable outcome: overtraining, with its ensuing loss of speed and power.

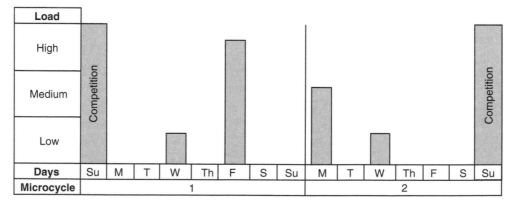

Figure 15.2 Proposed strength training schedule for an athlete whose competitions occur two weeks apart.

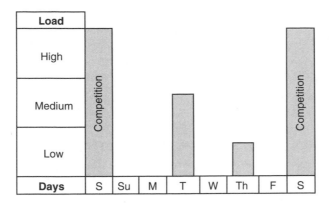

Figure 15.3 Possible strength training schedule for sports in which weekly competition is the norm.

Team Sports

Without negating the importance of specific endurance, power is the dominant ability for most team sports. To avoid detraining of power, a maintenance program must be planned throughout the competitive phase. The examples presented in this section address two competitive schedules: one game per week and two games per week. These examples are valid for college baseball, college basketball, volleyball, American football, ice hockey, field hockey, Australian football, soccer, rugby, lacrosse, and water polo.

Despite the various pressures faced by a team—such as the need for more technical or tactical training and the team's rank in league standings—the coach must find the time, and athletes must find the energy, to work on maintaining strength and power. In fact, the longer the competitive phase is, the more important it is to maintain power. Figure 15.4 suggests a plan for a cycle with a game scheduled every Saturday, but it can be adjusted for any other day of the week. A strength training session of medium demand is proposed for Tuesday. If an athlete's level of fatigue is higher than expected, the overall demand can be reduced by using a low load.

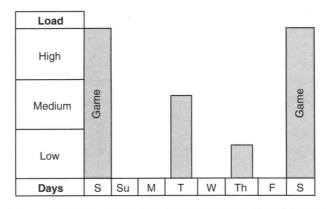

Figure 15.4 Suggested strength training schedule for a team sport involving a game every weekend.

Even for team sports with two games per week, it is possible to implement a maintenance program for strength training. However, the program should be limited to one or two sets of three exercises at 70 percent of 1RM, or a maximum of 20 minutes (see figure 15.5).

Strength training programs look quite different for athletes in some sports, such as linemen in American football, throwers in track and field, and heavyweight boxers and wrestlers. The suggested program for such athletes lasts 60 to 75 minutes. The strength sought is made up of 40 percent to 50 percent maximum strength and 50 percent to 60 percent power. Athletes perform four to six exercises as explosively as possible using a load of 70 percent to 80 percent of 1RM. They perform three to six reps (with a buffer of 10 percent) over three to six sets with a rest interval of three to four minutes between sets.

For team-sport athletes who perform many jumps during training and games (e.g., in basketball or volleyball), plyometric training should be reduced to a minimum as compared with the end of the preparatory phase. This reduction alleviates strain on the athlete's legs throughout the season.

The strength maintenance program should end 3 to 14 days before the most important competition of the year so that athletes can use all of their energy to achieve their best possible performance.

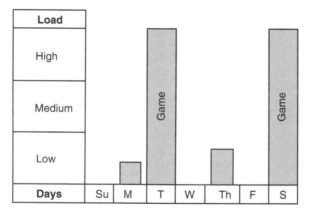

Figure 15.5 Suggested maintenance program for strength training for a team sport involving two games per week.

Peaking for Maximum Performance

Many coaches and athletes consider peaking to be something akin to a heavenly favor. In reality, however, the ability to peak for competition represents nothing more than a strategy that you design by manipulating load variables to reach physical and psychological supercompensation before an important event. The performance inconsistencies we often witness may depend on the training that the athlete does during the preparatory period; on the ratio between volume, intensity, and recovery during preparation; or on the number of competitions in which the athlete takes part.

The following sequencing is essential for an athlete's ability to peak for competition.

1. Train to compete.
2. Recover and regenerate before starting to train again.
3. Train for the next competition.
4. Manipulate load variables to supercompensate and reach peak performance during the next competition.

Phases 5, 6, and 7: Maintenance, Cessation, and Compensation

We can define peak status as a temporary athletic shape status—maintainable for two or three weeks at most—that is marked by maximal psychological and physiological efficiency and an optimal level of technical and tactical preparedness. This superior biological status is characterized by perfect health and expressed by very fast adaptation to training stimuli and quick recovery after training sessions and competition.

From a psychological point of view, peaking is a status of readiness for action with intense emotional arousal. The objective aspects of peaking from a psychological point of view manifest themselves as a capacity for quicker and more efficient adaptation to the stress of competition. Subjectively, the athlete experiences greater self-confidence and great motivation and perceives the state of high physical readiness to perform. When peaking, the athlete possesses greater capacity than usual to withstand frustration before, during, and after competition. The athlete's achievement of this status is facilitated by the coach's use of model planning (i.e., the adjustment of the competitive microcycles to match the weekly and daily schedules of the most important competitions of the year) and preparatory competitions beginning with the precompetitive phase.

The biological characteristics of peaking status vary according to the specific characteristics of the sport.

- For anaerobic-dominant sports, peaking is the capacity for maximal activation in a short time with fast recovery.
- For aerobic-dominant sports, peaking is high working capacity based on high physiological efficiency.
- For mixed sports, such as team sports, it is the capacity to repeat high-intensity efforts on the basis of high physiological efficiency.

As depicted in figure 15.6, the athlete's degree of training represents the basis on which he or she can build various states of athletic shape (some authors refer to degree of training as "preparedness"). It includes a general and a specific training component. Since the peak of athletic shape results from progressing through other levels of athletic shape, a status of optimal athletic shape (referred to by some authors as "readiness") is

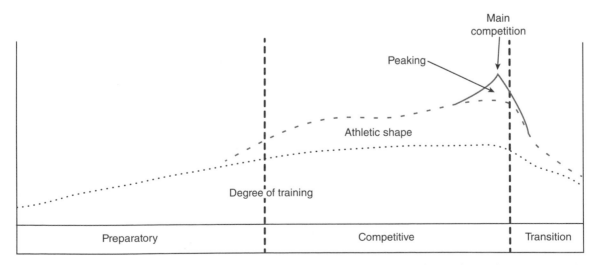

Figure 15.6 Accumulation and elevation of training states throughout training phases in a monocycle.
Reprinted, by permission, from T.O. Bompa, 1999, *Periodization: Theory and methodology of training*, 4th ed. (Champaign, IL: Human Kinetics), 294.

the basis for peaking. The peak of athletic shape can be reached for the most important competition of the year by implementing a planned decrease of training load referred to as the taper.

Tapering for Peak Performance

Tapering, or unloading, consists of the strategies that the coach uses to facilitate the athlete's supercompensation and, as a direct benefit, to help him or her reach peak performance. As shown in a recent review by Pyne and colleagues (2009), most of the scientific literature addressing the taper deals with individual sports rather than team sports. According to Bosquet et al. (2007), this imbalance derives mostly from two factors:

a. Higher correlation in individual sports between shape level, training input (modification of volume, intensity, and frequency), and performance output

b. The greater ease in individual sports than in team sports of quantifying and isolating training load factors and performance components, due to the multifactorial nature of team sports (e.g., different types of activity, variable environmental conditions, interindividual variability of response and adaptation to training)

Tapering Methodology

The dynamics of the peaking microcycles allow the athlete to face the most important competition of the year at the top of his or her psychophysical energy. Together, these microcycles represent an unloading macrocycle referred to as the taper macrocycle. They are used in most sports—in particular, individual sports—regardless of the annual plan structure (mono, bi-cycle, or tri-cycle) in order to reach peak performance. During the taper, the training load is gradually reduced both to eliminate the fatigue induced by the preceding training period and to maintain or enhance the positive adaptations elicited by that training.

The taper macrocycle has a maximum duration of three weeks in order to avoid detraining of physiological systems that are key to performance, unlike the tradition in some sports, such as swimming, which uses a 5- to 6-week taper with a reduction of training volume and its simultaneous intensification that might elicit subpar performance when performance counts the most.

The scientific literature includes at least 35 studies indicating the positive effects of taper on sport performance. In one study, conducted with 99 swimmers three weeks before the 2000 Sidney Olympics, researchers determined that performance improved for 91 of the athletes (Mujika et al. 2002) by an average of 2.18 percent (+/−1.5 percent). At first glance, this improvement might seem insignificant. However, the same study found that the improvement induced by tapering was greater than the difference between a gold medal and fourth place and greater than the difference between the bronze medal and last place in the final (1.6 percent). These results shows that the taper can exert a decisive influence on the final result in the most important event of the year.

Other studies of the taper have observed an improvement of the ratio between endogenous testosterone and cortisol (Adlercreutz et al. 1986; Kuoppasalmi and Adlercreutz 1985), which suggests better recovery, elimination of previous fatigue, and greater readiness of the athlete's system to face competition demands, especially neural demands. Improvements found during the taper are not limited to the hormonal profile (increase of testosterone, increase of IGF-1, and decrease of cortisol). They also include hematologic factors (increase of cell volume, hematocrit, hemoglobin, haptoglobin, and reticulocytes), biochemical factors (decrease of CPK, increase of muscle glycogen), and psychological factors (reduced effort perception, fewer mood swings, less fatigue perception, greater vigor, and better sleep quality) (Mujika 2009).

The taper, which usually lasts two weeks, entails a planned, progressive reduction of training load, as well as a reduction of stress-inducing factors of all types, especially in the psychological sphere. The taper is a key factor in the success of the training program and of the entire season because of its proximity to the most important competition. It eliminates fatigue, restores working capacity suppressed by the previous training volume, facilitates adaptations induced by training (to which are added adaptations induced by taper training itself), and enables supercompensation of all physiological systems, including the CNS, whose recovery is fundamental to generating a positive emotional state during competition.

According to Krestovnikov (1938), a nervous system cell recovers seven times more slowly than a musculoskeletal cell. This difference suggests the importance of CNS recovery before, during, and after competition (Bompa 1965b).

During the taper, new protocols or exercises should *never* be introduced. To the contrary, during the competitive season you must create a precompetition training routine to be followed for the most important event of the year.

The trainer, then, must manipulate the following parameters:

a. Type of load reduction

b. Taper duration

c. Load reduction components (volume, intensity, frequency)

Types of Load Reduction

The scientific literature recognizes four types of taper depending on the modality by which training load is decreased in the precompetition weeks:

1. Linear

2. Exponential (slow decay)

3. Exponential (fast decay)

4. Step

The percentage variation of the training load is represented graphically in figure 15.7. As indicated, the total training load is higher in a linear taper, the final training load is lower in an exponential (fast-decay) taper, and the lowest mean load is used in the step taper. Two studies have found that the fast-decay exponential taper usually produces better results than either the step taper or the slow-decay exponential taper (Banister and Zarkadas 1995, 1999). This result is probably due to the fact that the step taper leads only to maintenance of (if not a decrease in) previous positive adaptations, and the slow-decay taper (like the linear type) uses a mean load in the first microcycle that does not maximize the elimination of fatigue.

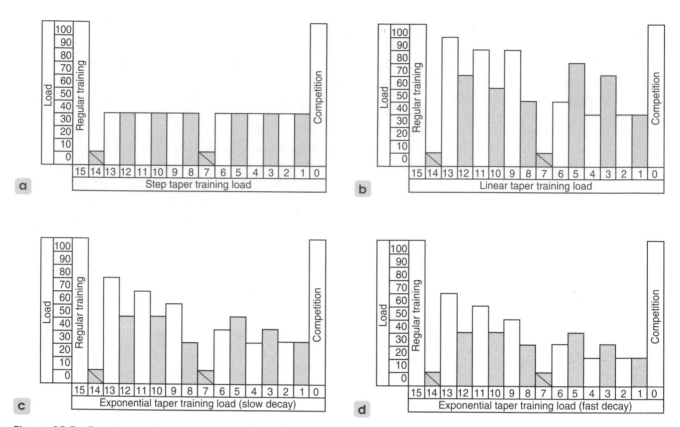

Figure 15.7 Four taper strategies according to the dynamics of load reduction.

Adapted from I. Mujika and S. Padilla, 2003, "Scientific bases for precompetition tapering strategies," *Medicine & Science in Sports & Exercise* 35: 1182-1187.

Taper Duration

Both research and experience have proven that athletes do not all respond in the same way to the same type of tapering. As a result, the type of unloading must be individualized according to the adaptive profile of each athlete (Mujika 2009). Even the timing of response to the taper varies by the individual, and on this basis we can distinguish three types of athlete:

a. Slow responder

b. Fast responder

c. Biphasic responder

Given the same internal load, a slow responder needs three unloading weeks to maximize performance, and his or her improvement becomes evident almost completely during the third week. In contrast, a fast responder needs only two weeks. For a biphasic responder, the final improvement is distributed over the course of the three weeks in the following proportion: 50 percent in the first week, 5 percent in the second, and 45 percent in the third (Trinity et al. 2006).

Most athletes who are not in an overreaching status respond quickly to the unloading period and begin to become detrained by the third week. Because an overreaching status is exactly a status of high internal load, we can therefore claim that the fundamental factor in determining taper duration is the athlete's internal load status three weeks before the most important competition of the year. Other factors, such as body weight, sex, weekly training hours, and load-reduction strategy of choice, influence the way the taper is planned. Some general rules about the taper are summarized in the following tables.

The shortest taper is one made by a female athlete in an alactic discipline (e.g., 60-meter indoor sprint in track and field) who trained at high intensity but low volume, and with a low internal load, three weeks out from the main competition. For her, the taper lasts last just five days.

Of course, even the type of load reduction strategy used during the taper relates to the total load of the pre-taper macrocycle (and thus to the internal load). A high-load pre-taper macrocycle that led to an overreaching status calls for a quicker load reduction, such as the fast-decay exponential taper in the case of a three-week duration or the step taper in the case of a two-week duration. On the other hand, a pre-taper macrocycle with a lower load may call for a slower reduction of the load (slow-decay exponential taper or linear taper) or a reduction of the taper length to 7 to 10 days rather than 14. Faced with these options, the coach must use his or her experience, along with the information provided in this chapter, to decide whether the unloading period will be longer or shorter and whether the load reduction will slower or quicker.

Table 15.2 Factors Affecting Duration of the Precompetition Unloading Period

CHARACTERISTICS		EFFECT OVER THE DURATION OF THE TAPER
Body weight	High	More lasting
	Low	Less lasting
Gender	Male	More lasting with less time dedicated to strength maintenance
	Female	Less lasting with more time dedicated to strength maintenance
Load of pre-taper macrocycle	High	More lasting
	Low	Less lasting
Load reduction strategy during taper	Linear	More lasting
	Step	Less lasting
Weekly training hours	High	More lasting (>15 hours)
	Low	Less lasting (<10 hours)

Taper Guidelines

As a starting point for establishing the ideal taper for each athlete, we suggest using a fast-decay exponential taper of two weeks with a volume reduction of 60 percent, preceded by a three-week macrocycle of high-intensity training. Again, the training factors that can be manipulated during the taper to reduce the athlete's internal load are intensity, volume, and frequency of training.

Intensity Manipulation

Several studies have demonstrated that the intensity used during the taper is fundamentally important both to maintaining the adaptations induced by the athlete's previous training and to stimulating additional adaptations (Hickson et al. 1985; Shepley et al. 1992; Convertino et al. 1981; Mujika 1998; Bosquet et al. 2007; McNeely and Sandler 2007). More specifically, intensity is reduced by an average of 5 percent to 10 percent for power sports and 10 percent to 30 percent for endurance sports.

The highest reduction percentage should be reached only in the last days of the taper. In addition, recent computer simulations suggest that the most reduced level intensity reduction should be reached four days before the event and that intensity should be increased again by using medium and medium-high intensities during the last three days in order to stimulate further adaptations without affecting the elimination of fatigue (Thomas, Mujika, and Busso 2009).

Volume Manipulation

One study has shown that training adaptations obtained in 10 weeks can be maintained for an additional 28 weeks with a reduction of volume ranging from 30 percent to 60 percent (Graves et al. 1988). In addition, several studies of elite athletes have reported positive effects on performance with a reduction of maximum volume during the taper ranging from 40 percent to 85 percent; the most important improvements came with a reduction in the range of 40 percent to 60 percent (Houmard et al. 1989; McConell et al. 1993; Martin et al. 1994; Rietjens et al. 2001; Mujika et al. 1995; Shepley et al. 1992; Bosquet et al. 2007). As shown in table 15.3, the percentage of volume reduction throughout the taper is determined by several factors, including taper duration, residual internal fatigue, and type of load reduction.

Table 15.3 Factors Affecting Training Volume in the Precompetition Unloading Period

	CHARACTERISTIC	EFFECT ON TAPER VOLUME
Load of pre-taper macrocycle	High	Greater reduction
	Low	Smaller reduction
Taper duration	Short	Greater reduction
	Long	Smaller reduction
Type of load reduction	Linear	Higher mean volume Lower final volume
	Step	Lower mean volume Higher final volume

Frequency Manipulation

Part of the reduction in volume that is needed in order to reach peaking form can be obtained by reducing the number of weekly training sessions. However, this practice is not recommended. Instead, we suggest reducing the volume of each session, especially in sports with an elevated technical aspect (e.g., swimming, rowing, cross-country skiing, kayaking, gymnastics) and for high-level athletes in general.

It is a common practice in high-level team sports to plan two or three days off from training either during the first week of the taper or between the first and second weeks.

This approach is taken because team-sport athletes usually enter the taper period before tournaments or cup finals in an overreaching state due to the long competitive season. For this reason, for professional and national teams, sports medicine practitioners are strongly advised to check athletes' testosterone-to-cortisol ratio and level of free testosterone (possibly checking them throughout the season for comparative purposes). The results give strength and conditioning coaches more information to use in establishing training load during the taper for each player.

As shown in table 15.4, the progressive decrease in volume and intensity of all training activities during the competitive phase—as well as the increased use of recovery

Table 15.4 Training and Recovery Strategies and Benefits During the Taper

	STRATEGIES	BENEFITS
Dynamics of volume	• Decrease total distance or duration by 40% to 60%. • Decrease number of reps. • Increase rest interval to full recovery. • Don't introduce new exercises.	• Achieve supercompen-sation of all physiological systems. • Increase readiness of the neuromuscular system. • Facilitate replenishment of energy stores.
Dynamics of intensity	• Reduce intensity by 5% to 10% for power sports and 20% to 30% for endurance sports, especially in the first week. • Raise intensity a few days before competition.	
Neuromuscular stimulation	Use the neuromuscular system potentiation methods described in this chapter.	• Induce prepeaking neuromuscular state. • Increase recruitment of fast-twitch (FT) muscle fibers. • Increase discharge rate of FT fibers. • Maximize arousal of the neuromuscular system. • Increase reactivity of the neuromuscular system.
Recovery methods	• Use soft tissue management techniques (e.g., deep massage, myofascial release). • Control heart rate variability (HRV) values to ensure proper recovery dynamics. • Control sleep quality (e.g., with the Sleep as Android app). • Use psychological relaxation, motivation, and visualization techniques (e.g., hypnosis, which can induce a deep state of relaxation and faster nervous system recovery). • Ensure proper nutrition and sport-specific food supplementation.	• Improve soft tissue compliance and joint mobility. • Increase readiness of the neuromuscular system. • Relax mentally. • Increase confidence. • Increase arousal. • Replenish energy stores. • Sustain maximal power output throughout competition.

techniques—helps the athlete replenish energy stores, achieve supercompensation, relax mentally, and build motivation to attain his or her best possible results in the competition targeted for peak performance. The strategy presented in the table must be applied for the duration of the tapering period to ensure maximum neuromuscular benefits prior to major competition. During this time, the focus shifts to recovery and regeneration through proper rest, nutrition, supplementation, and soft tissue therapies (e.g., deep massage, myofascial release). In terms of training, this is a time to reap the benefits of your well-planned preparation and competitive periods.

Peaking Microcycles for Power or Speed Sports, Endurance Sports, and Team Sports

The obvious overarching training goal of every athlete is to achieve maximum performance during the year's major competition(s). This is the reason that athletes put forth such great effort for many months during the training year. As a major competition approaches, an athlete looking to achieve maximum performance must use the right option among the various peaking strategies, which differ significantly for individual power and speed sports, individual endurance sports, and team sports. Peaking strategies for each of these categories are presented in the following subsections.

Tapering for Power and Speed Sports

For power- and speed-dominant sports, maximum intensities (especially with specific exercises) are used for the last time about 14 or 15 days before competition, preceded by 5 to 7 days of unloading. During the first week of the taper that follows, the volume is reduced significantly, since it is the main stressor for the intense exercises used in these sports. In fact, volume is usually reduced by 50 percent to 60 percent while maintaining two high-intensity sessions; intensity peaks again in the first part of the second week. The other sessions use low intensity, and the microcycles largely mirror the undulatory approach of previous training phases. In the second week, total volume is further reduced, by 10 percent to 20 percent, and weight training can be eliminated—according to the coach's informed opinion based on the athlete's response to various unloading strategies used throughout the year—to preserve energy for specific exercises. Throughout the two tapering weeks, high-intensity exercises are done every three days at a volume that is 50 percent to 60 percent lower than usual. Also, longer rest intervals are employed to avoid fatigue accumulation before the most important competition of the year.

For power and speed athletes, moods correlates strongly with internal load. Therefore, higher-intensity sessions can be displaced if need be, depending on how the athlete feels (if HRV monitoring devices are not used). The day before the main competition begins can either be a rest day or include a neuromuscular potentiation session with either strength exercises or specific exercises—for instance, short acceleration from the blocks for a sprinter. See figure 15.8.

Tapering for Endurance Sports

The latest research analyzing successful unloading models suggests that, like power and speed athletes, athletes in endurance sports must maintain some high-intensity sessions during the taper (intensity is reduced by only 10 percent to 15 percent for each session during the two weeks). Therefore, a short high-intensity specific session should be

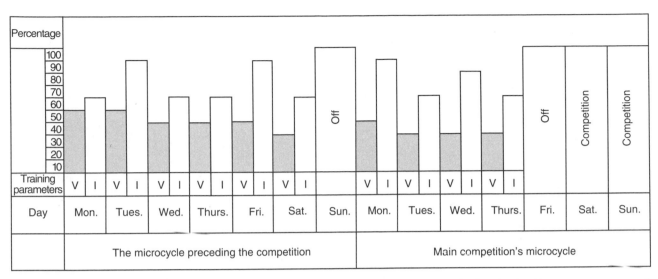

Figure 15.8 Dynamics of volume and intensity for the unloading phase in sports dominated by power or speed.

planned during both unloading weeks. Strength training is generally reduced to two short sessions in the first week and eliminated in the second week. The exceptions are female athletes, athletes with light body weight, and those who tend to lose strength quickly; these individuals must maintain strength training even during the last week of the taper if the event duration is less than 10 minutes.

Volume should be progressively reduced by 40 percent to 60 percent over the course of two weeks, and the majority of training sessions should be of medium or low intensity. Athletes should use intensities higher than race pace at a very low volume during the taper in order to avoid inducing further fatigue or losing the feeling of race pace. See figure 15.9.

In addition, low-intensity sessions with continuous methods must not be voluminous, in order to avoid negatively affecting the athlete's hormone profile and muscle recovery (Mujika 2009). This approach enables the athlete to maintain shape without inducing stress.

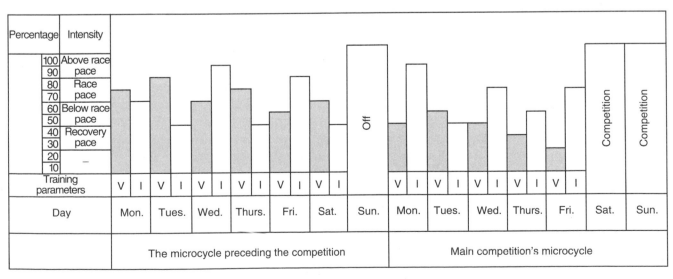

Figure 15.9 Dynamics of volume and intensity for the unloading phase in endurance sports.

According to tapering expert, researcher, and coach Inigo Mujika, athletes in endurance sports usually report negative sensations at the beginning of the taper: tiredness, muscle weakness, and greater fatigue for a given training load. However, these feelings need not worry the coach; rather, they are symptomatic of the recovery process taking place and probably result from a parasympathetic system hypertonia.

In the case of a short taper (one week), the athlete should use a strategy similar to the one used for power sports. Volume is progressively but rapidly reduced by 60 percent to 70 percent; the intensity of each session is reduced by only 10 percent to 15 percent.

Finally, the greater erythropoiesis, red blood cells production process, during the taper may cause an endurance athlete to require iron supplementation. This possibility must be monitored by the medical staff.

Tapering for Team Sports

For team sports, there are two moments when it is possible to adopt a peaking strategy: the end of the preparatory phase (short taper) and the period preceding a playoff, finals match, tournament, or the like (long taper).

Short taper before the regular season

Both research and practice have proven that the extensive training used during the preparatory phase for team sports significantly reduces players' strength, power, and speed (Sirotic and Coutts 2007; Edge et al. 2005; Coutts et al. 2007). As a result, in practical terms, they enter the competitive phase in an overreaching status. The same studies show that 7 to 10 days of taper lead to improvement in the same parameters. This approach does not ensure complete elimination of accumulated fatigue, which necessitates two or three more weeks, due to the presence of weekly competition. We suggest taking two or three days off and performing low volume of training for four or five days before the start of the regular season.

Long taper

The taper after the regular season (before playoffs or the like) should last more than the seven days of the short taper before the regular season because of the greater fatigue experienced by players at this late point in the season. If this taper is skipped or is too short, the athlete is at greater risk of suboptimal performance (Ekstrand et al. 2004; Bangsbo et al. 1999; Ferret and Cotte 2003).

Ferret and Cotte's study on how the different preparation approaches taken by the French national soccer team for the 1998 and 2002 World Cup affected the final outcome is quite interesting. In 1998, the French team that won the tournament used two short loading macrocycles followed by a two-week taper. In 2002, however, all players joined the national team only eight days before the tournament, and biochemical markers demonstrated clear fatigue due to the just-finished French national championships. The lack of time for implementing a well-done, and much-needed, taper produced a very bad result.

The importance of removing fatigue after the national championships is further illustrated by the case of the Danish national soccer team that won the European Championship in 1992. In this case, in fact, the national team was asked to take part in the tournament only 10 days before the event, but all of the players had finished their championships three to five weeks earlier. Thus the Danish team's victory was partly attributed to the fact that its players were not exhausted, either physically or psychologically (Bangsbo 1999).

In team sports, training volume and training intensity carry almost the same importance. During the taper, however, volume is reduced more than intensity, training is highly specific, and the duration of training sessions is reduced even as the use of recovery techniques is increased. During the first week, volume is reduced, and the athlete performs only one high-intensity specific session. If more high-intensity sessions (game simulation) are planned during the whole period, they must be performed three to five days apart from each other (depending on the amount of time necessary for the team to completely dissipate the fatigue induced by such sessions).

During the second week, volume is further reduced by means of a reduction in the training sessions' duration. Intensity is maintained at the beginning of the week, and then the two days immediately before competition include short low-intensity sessions focused on confidence, optimism, and team spirit.

During these two weeks, players' psychophysical recovery is paramount. Furthermore, the practice of successful teams in various sports (e.g., soccer, rugby, water polo, hockey) suggests devoting two or three days to complete rest either before the taper or between its first and second weeks. See figure 15.10.

Nutrition is also particularly relevant when an athlete faces an important competition soon after the end of the championships. Research shows that the repetitive twice-weekly competition schedule of a team that reaches a Cup final makes it very difficult for athletes to restore muscle glycogen; this situation is exacerbated by the concentration of games in a few days of tournament action, whether in playoffs or international tournaments with the national team (Zehnder et al. 2001; Reilly and Ekblom 2005; Mohr, Krustrup, and Bangsbo 2005; 1994; Bangsbo, Iaia, and Krustrup 2007). As a result, athletes may see a great decline in performance quality, especially in the second half of a game.

It is obvious that such a decline derives not from a lack of physical conditioning, since the athletes' degree of specific training at that time is very high. Instead, the main factor is a considerable reduction in glycogen stores that have not been replenished through a proper nutrition strategy, which would provide great quantities of carbohydrate (both simple and complex). Glycogen restoration can be further stimulated by planning short, aerobic, tactical sessions before main meals. Double daily sessions of this type have been used in a microcycle developed by the Argentinean soccer federation for international tournaments (Bompa and Claro 2008; see figure 15.11).

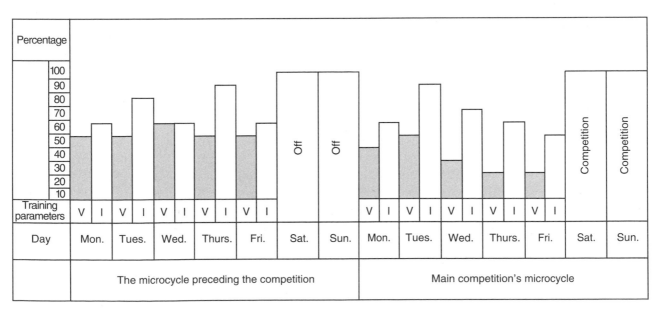

Figure 15.10 Dynamics of volume and intensity for the unloading phase in team sports in which the aerobic and anaerobic energy systems make almost equal contributions.

Day	1	2	3	4	5	6	7
Morning	Pregame arousal	• Recovery • Regeneration • Physiotherapy	TA aerobic	Pregame arousal	• Recovery • Regeneration • Physiotherapy	A aerobic	Pregame arousal
Afternoon	Game	• TA aerobic • Relaxing techniques	• TA aerobic • Psychological game strategy	Game	• TA aerobic • Relaxing techniques	• TA aerobic • Psychological game strategy	Game

Key: TA = tactical.

Figure 15.11 International Tournament Microcycle Developed by the Argentinean National Soccer Team

Peaking and Arousal

To peak for competition, the athlete must be in a state of arousal—that is, a state of alertness mediated by the neuroendocrine system. Measured markers of elevated arousal include (to name a few) elevated levels of catecholamines, cortisol, and growth hormone (Enoka 2002).

Prior to major competition, athletes are often in a state of anxiety, restlessness, and excitement. A theory known as the inverted U hypothesis (Raglin 1992) states that a moderate amount of arousal can maximize performance. Along these lines, Enoka (2002) speculated that strength production might be increased by arousal-induced changes in the contractility of muscle and in the coordination of involved limbs. Arousal now appears more likely to contribute to increases in strength because some of the previously listed neuroendocrine factors positively affect the central nervous system.

From a sport perspective, the athlete's physical and mental preparation should be optimal during major competition; the neuromuscular system is stimulated and ready for optimal performance. However, though training adaptations are no longer the focus, athletes can use certain methods to gain a neuromuscular edge on the day of competition. That edge is the essence of what are referred to as methods of neuromuscular system potentiation. In fact, because arousal is influenced by the performance of the central nervous system, an athlete's performance may well be enhanced by short and intense exercises performed on the day before competition, the morning of competition, or even immediately before competition, depending on what method and training parameters are employed.

Peaking and Neuromuscular Potentiation

Many successful coaches use periodization of training, tapering, and methods of neuromuscular system potentiation to help their athletes achieve peak performance. This section discusses how coaches can induce peak performance by using special training techniques: post-activation potentiation and post-contraction sensory discharge. These methods are geared to develop maximum tension in the muscle; however, maximum tension is difficult to achieve in a practical setting. Effective techniques for stimulating the neuromuscular system and promoting maximum motor unit recruitment include training with heavy loads, performing high-impact plyometrics, and implementing isometric contractions. Increased motor unit recruitment heightens an athlete's force development, which can then be applied to power activities.

Considering their specific physiological benefits, these techniques are suggested mostly for speed and power sports—for example, sprinting, jumping, and throwing in track and field; the martial arts; short events in water sports (e.g., diving, swimming sprints); track cycling; and speedskating. On the other hand, neuromuscular system potentiation methods are *not* suggested for long-lasting events (e.g., soccer) and even more emphatically not for sports in which the aerobic system is dominant, as the benefits to the sport-specific performance would be negligible if present at all.

The greatest challenge faced by coaches and trainers lies in applying systematic laboratory research to athletic training. Following intense isometric contractions or electrical stimulation causing a summation of twitches up to a tetanus state, any further stimulation would elicit a maximal twitch force (Enoka 2002), yet even strong concentric actions can elicit a potentiation (Gullich and Schmidtbleicher 1996; Chiu et al. 2003; Rixon, Lamont, and Bemben 2007).

Maximal twitch force, or post- activation potentiation, can be maintained for about 8 to 12 minutes before returning to control levels (Enoka 2002). When heavy eccentric–concentric exercises (over 80 percent of 1RM) are used, such as those presented in figure 15.12, a further potentiation—post-activation potentiation—appears after 6 to 7 hours and can last up to 24 hours. For this reason, such exercises can be used either on the morning of competition or on the day before.

Post-contraction sensory discharge, on the other hand, is a physiological mechanism that can be applied right before competition. Brief and intense episodes of activity 5 to 20 minutes prior to the competition can be used to heighten the athlete's neural contribution to subsequent movements that occur in sport (Enoka 2002). For instance, highly trained sprinters often perform one or two sets of two to four reps of explosive plyometric (level 2 or 3) exercises 5 to 10 minutes prior to a race. This activity increases the muscle spindle discharge (Enoka 2002) and the subsequent neural drive to the prime movers. Thus short and intense activities lasting seconds harness greater power output for the movement that follows.

Post-activation potentiation is smaller in the slow-twitch muscle fibers than in the fast-twitch fibers (O'Leary, Hope, and Sale 1998; Hamada et al. 2000), which explains the important application of post-activation potentiation to speed and power sports, for which the activation of fast-twitch fibers is paramount. Furthermore, warm muscle elicits higher post-activation potentiations than cold muscle does (Gossen, Allingham, and Sale 2001). Therefore, proper warm-up not only prevents injury but also should increase the force-generating capability of muscle. In addition, through a process of adaptation, as the force-generating capacity of a muscle increases, so does the post-activation potentiation. See figure 15.12.

Exercise	Tempo	Load (% of 1RM)	Reps	RI (min.)	Load (% of 1RM)	Reps	RI (min.)	Load (% of 1RM)	Reps	RI (min.)
Quarter squat	1.0.X	100*	3	4	110*	3	6	120*	3	4
Walking lunge	3.0.X	80	2+2 (R+L)	4	80	2+2 (R+L)	4	—	—	—
Bench press	2.0.X	75	3	3	82.5	3	—	—	—	—

RI = rest interval; R+L = right plus left
*Of full squat 1RM

Figure 15.12 Neuromuscular Potentiation Session for Use on the Morning off a Race by a 60-Meter, 100-Meter, or 200-Meter Sprinter

PERIODIZATION GUIDELINES FOR DIFFERENT SPORTS

The periodization of training and its component, the periodization of strength, are applied differently in individual sports, team sports, racket sports, the martial arts, and artistic sports. Peak performance is directly influenced and facilitated by a well-organized periodization of training, in which the length of the preparatory phase is critical. Equally important, especially for speed and power sports, is the way in which periodization of strength is used to increase an athlete's physical potential. The following list of selected periodization issues—and how they affect peak performance—prompts coaches to reflect on their own techniques for planning periodization.

- Certain individual sports (e.g., running, cycling, triathlon) tend to use a much longer preparatory phase than other sports because of specific issues such as planning competitions around climatic conditions.

- Because team sports, the martial arts, and racket sports use either longer or more numerous competitive phases than individual sports, they follow a bi-, tri-, or multicycle periodization. Therefore, the preparatory phase in these sports is comparatively shorter than in other sports.

- Team sports with shorter preparatory phases tend to have a more superficial foundation of physical training. Coaches in these sports should try to lengthen the preparatory phase within the competitive phase (reaching at least 12 weeks of preparatory phase) by keeping on progressing the physical training parameters despite a decrease of time devoted to physical training. This approach is particularly indicated for teams and athletes whose technical level is higher than the average level possessed by opponents.

- Athletes in individual sports have more days for general training than do their counterparts in other sports.

- Coaches in individual sports tend to pay more attention to the benefits of physical training than do coaches in team sports.

- The more important technical and tactical training are in a given sport, the more they are emphasized by coaches. The end result can be quite predictable: neglecting the physical support necessary to achieve best performance.

- Reaching higher levels of performance in the competitive phase depends on the effectiveness of training performed during the preparatory phase.

- Periodization of strength is not well known or applied in many sports, especially some team sports. This lack may negatively affect peak performance.

- Maximum strength training is either missing during the preparatory phase or is treated as a mere formality in some sports (e.g., team sports, racket sports, the martial arts). However, employing only a very short or superficial maximum strength phase negatively affects the athlete's ability to maximize power, speed, and agility or quickness.

- Athletes in individual sports, especially endurance-dominant sports, may need to reach peak performance only two or three times per year. Athletes in team sports, however, must play at a high level throughout the competitive season. Therefore, coaches in team sports may consider a pre-preparation program for their players. This approach offers athletes more time for physical training, including strength training.

Strength Training During the Transition Phase

Following a lengthy period of hard work and stressful competition—during which an athlete's determination, motivation, and will are tested—the athlete experiences a high degree of physiological and psychological fatigue. Although muscular fatigue may disappear in a few days, fatigue of the central nervous system and the psyche (as observed in an athlete's behavior) can last much longer.

The more intensive the training is and the more competitions the athlete is exposed to, the greater his or her fatigue will be. In such conditions, any athlete would have difficulty beginning a new yearly training cycle; therefore, before starting another season of training, the athlete must rest, both physically and psychologically. When the new preparatory phase does begin, he or she should be completely regenerated and ready to participate in training. In fact, following a successful transition phase, the athlete should feel a strong desire to train again.

The transition phase, often inappropriately referred to as the "off-season," serves as a link between two annual plans. Its major objectives are psychological rest, relaxation, and biological regeneration, as well as maintenance of an acceptable level of general physical preparation. This phase should last no longer than six weeks; otherwise, the athlete will detrain, visibly losing most of his or her fitness.

To maintain a decent level of fitness, athletes should train two or three times a week during the transition phase, and at least one workout should be used for strength training. Less effort is required to maintain at least 50 percent of the previous fitness level than to redevelop it from zero. In fact, an athlete who starts from zero after the transition phase has experienced a great deal of detraining. The phenomenon of detraining of strength has been documented since the 1960s. Hettinger (1966) found that muscles can lose up to 30 percent of their strength capacity in one week of immobilization! Although that is an extreme case, a wealth of similar findings is contained in exercise physiology and strength training books, and coaches can expect a great loss of muscle strength after just two weeks of complete inactivity.

During transition, athletes should also perform compensation work to involve muscle groups that receive little attention throughout the preparatory and competitive phases. This means paying attention to the antagonist muscles and stabilizers. For example, these two muscle groups can be activated in a dedicated 20- to 30-minute session after any informal physical training (e.g., a pickup game or recreational play). The program can be relaxed, and athletes can work at their own pace for as long as they desire. The program need not be stressful. In fact, stress is undesirable during transition. Forget the formal program with its specific load, tempo, specific numbers of reps and sets, and rest intervals. For once, athletes should do as they please.

References

Aagaard, P., et al. 2011. Effects of resistance training on endurance capacity and muscle fiber composition in young top-level cyclists. *Scandinavian Journal of Medicine and Science in Sports* 21 (6): e298–307. doi:10.1111/j.1600-0838.2010.01283.x.

Aagaard, P., Simonsen, E.B., Anderson, J.L., Magnusson, S.P., and Halkaer-Kristensen, K. 1994. Moment and power generation during maximal knee extensions performed at low and high speeds. *European Journal of Applied Physiology* 89:2249–57.

Abbruzzese, G., Morena, M., Spadavecchia, L., and Schieppati, M. 1994. Response of arm flexor muscles to magnetic and electrical brain stimulation during shortening and lengthening tasks in man. *Journal of Physiology—London* 481:499–507.

Adams, T.M., Worlay, D., and Throgmartin, D. 1987. The effects of selected plyometric and weight training on muscular leg power. *Track and Field Quarterly Review* 87: 45–47.

Adlercreutz, H. et al. 1986. Effect of training on plasma anabolic and catabolic steroid hormones and their response during physical exercise. *International Journal of Sports Medicine.* 7(1):27–8.

Ahtiainen, J.P., et al. 2011. Recovery after heavy resistance exercise and skeletal muscle androgen receptor and insulin-like growth factor-I isoform expression in strength trained men. *Journal of Strength and Conditioning Research* 25 (3): 767–77. doi:10.1519/JSC.0b013e318202e449.

American College of Sports Medicine. 2000. Joint position statement of the American College of Sports Medicine, American Dietetic Association, and Dietitians of Canada on nutrition and athletic performance. *Medicine and Science in Sports and Exercise* 32 (12): 2130–45.Andersen, J.L., and Aagaard, P. 2000. Myosin heavy chain IIX overshoot in human skeletal muscle. *Muscle Nerve* 23 (7): 1095–1104.

Andersen, J.L., et al. 1994. *Myosin* heavy chain isoforms in single fibres from m. vastus lateralis of sprinters: Influence of training. *Acta Physiologica Scandinavica* 151 (2): 135–42.

Andersen JL, Aagaard P. 2000. Myosin heavy chain IIX overshoot in human skeletal muscle. *Muscle Nerve.* 23 (7): 1095-104.

Andersen, L.L., et al. 2005. Changes in the human muscle force-velocity relationship in response to resistance training and subsequent detraining. *Journal of Applied Physiology* 99 (1): 87–94.

Andersen, L.L., et al. 2010. Early and late rate of force development: Differential adaptive responses to resistance training? *Scandinavian Journal of Medicine and Science in Sports* 20 (1): e162-69. doi:10.1111/j.1600-0838.2009.00933.x.

Anderson, K., and Behm, D.G. 2004. Maintenance of EMG activity and loss of force output with instability. *Journal of Strength and Conditioning Research* 18:637–40.

Anderson, K., Behm, D.G., and Curnew R.S. 2002. Muscle force and neuromuscular activation under stable and unstable conditions. *Journal of Strength and Conditioning Research* 16:416–22.

Appell, H.J. 1990. Muscular atrophy following immobilization: A review. *Sports Medicine* 10 (1): 42–58.

Armstrong, R.B. 1986. Muscle damage and endurance events. *Sports Medicine* 3:370–81.

Armstrong, R.B., Warren, G.L., and Warren, J.A. 1991. Mechanics of exercise-induced muscle fiber injury. *Sports Medicine* 12 (3): 184–207.

Ashton-Miller, J.A., Wojtys, E.M., Huston, L.J., and Fry-Welch, D. 2001. Can proprioception be improved by exercise? *Knee Surgery Sports Traumatology Arthroscopy* 9 (3): 128–36.

Asmussen, E., and Mazin, B. 1978. A central nervous system component in local muscular fatigue. *European Journal of Applied Physiology* 38:9–15.

Åstrand, P.O., and Rodahl, K. 1985. *Textbook of work physiology.* New York: McGraw-Hill.

Atha, J. 1984. Strengthening muscle. *Exercise and Sport Sciences Reviews* 9:1–73.

References

Ahtiainen JP et al. 2011. Recovery after heavy resistance exercise and skeletal muscle androgen receptor and insulin-like growth factor-I isoform expression in strength trained men. *J Strength Cond Res.* 25 (3): 767–77. doi: 10.1519/JSC.0b013e318202e449.

Augustsson, J., Thomee, R., Hornstedt, P., Lindblom, J., Karlsson, J., and Grimby, G. 2003. Effect of pre-exhaustion exercise on lower extremity muscle activation during a leg press exercise. *Journal of Strength and Conditioning Research* 17 (2): 411–16.

Babraj, J.A., et al. 2005. Collagen synthesis in human musculoskeletal tissues and skin. *American Journal of Physiology—Endocrinology and Metabolism* 289 (5): E864–69.

Baker, D.G., Nance, S., and Moore, M. 1989. The load that maximizes the average mechanical power output during jump squats in power-trained athletes. J Strength Cond Res. 15(1):20–4.

———.The load that maximizes the average mechanical power output during explosive bench press throws in highly trained athletes. *Journal of Strength and Conditioning Research* 15 (1): 20–24.

Baker, D.G., and Newton, R.U. 2007. Change in power output across a high-repetition set of bench throws and jump squats in highly trained athletes. *Journal of Strength and Conditioning Research* 21 (4): 1007–11.

Balsom, P.D., et al. 1999. Carbohydrate intake and multiple sprint sports: With special reference to football. *International Journal of Sport Medicine* 20:48–52.

Bangsbo, J. 1994. Energy demands in competitive soccer. *Journal of Sports Sciences.* 12 Spec. No.: S5–12.

———. 1999. Science and football, J Sports Sci. 17(10):755–6.

Bangsbo, J., Iaia, F.M., and Krustrup, P. 2007. Metabolic response and fatigue in soccer. *International Journal of Sports Physiology and Performance* 2 (2): 111–27.

Baroga, L. 1978. Contemporary tendencies in the methodology of strength development. *Educatie Fizica si Sport* 6:22–36.

Banister E.W., Carter J.B., and Zarkadas, P.C. 1999. Training theory and taper: Validation in triathlon athletes, *Eur J Appl Physiol Occup Physiol.* 79(2):179–86.

———. 1995. Modelling the effect of taper on performance, maximal oxygen uptake, and the anaerobic threshold in endurance triathletes, *Adv Exp Med Biol.* 393:179–86.

Bazyler, et al. 2014. The efficacy of incorporating partial squats in maximal strength training, *J Strength Cond Res.*

Behm, D., and Sale, D.G. 1993. Intended rather than actual movement velocity determines velocity-specific training response. *Journal of Applied Physiology* 74:359–68.

Belli, A., et al. 2002. Moment and power of lower limb joints in running. *International Journal of Sports Medicine* 23 (2): 136–41.

Bennet, W.M., and Rennie, M.J. 1991. Protein anabolic actions of insulin in the human body. *Diabetic Medicine* 8:199–207.

Berardi, J., and Andrews, R. 2009. *Nutrition: The complete guide.* California: Carpintiria. International Sport Science Association.

Bergeron, G. 1982. Therapeutic massage. *Canadian Athletic Therapist Association Journal* Summer:15–17.

Bergstrom, J., Hermansen, L., Hultman, E., and Saltin, B. 1967. Diet, muscle glycogen and physical performance. *Acta Physiologica Scandinavica* 71:140–50.

Bigland-Ritchie, B., Johansson, R., Lippold, O.C.J., and Woods, J.J. 1983. Contractile speed and EMG changes during fatigue of sustained maximal voluntary contractions. *Journal of Neurophysiology* 50 (1): 313–24.

Billat, V.L., et al. 1999. Interval training at $\dot{V}O_2$max: Effects on aerobic performance and overtraining markers. *Medicine and Science in Sports and Exercise* 31 (1): 156–63.

Billat, V.L., et al. 2013. The sustainability of $\dot{V}O_2$max: Effect of decreasing the workload. *European Journal of Applied Physiology* 113 (2): 385–94.

Billat, V.L., Sirvent, P., Py, G., Koralsztein, J.P., and Mercier, J. 2003. The concept of maximal lactate steady state: A bridge between biochemistry, physiology and sport science. *Sports Medicine* 33 (6): 407–26.Biolo, G., Fleming, R.Y.D., and Wolfe, R.R. 1995. Physiologic hyperinsulinemia stimulates protein synthesis and enhances transport of selected amino acids in human skeletal muscle. *Journal of Clinical Investigation* 95:811–19.

Biolo, G., Tipton, K.D., et al. 1997. An abundant supply of amino acids enhances the metabolic effect of exercise on muscle protein. *American Journal of Physiology* 273:E119–E122.

References

Biolo, G., Williams, B.D., Fleming, R.Y.D., and Wolfe, R.R. 1999. Insulin action on muscle protein kinetics and amino acid transport during recovery after resistance exercise. *Diabetes* 48:949–57.

Bishop, N.C., Blannin, A.K., Rand, L., et al. 1999. Effect of carbohydrate and fluid intake on the blood leukocyte responses to prolonged cycling. *International Journal of Sports Medicine* 17:26–27.

Bishop, N.C., Blannin, A.K., Walsh, N.P., et al. 2001. Carbohydrate beverage ingestion and neutrophil degranulation responses following cycling to fatigue at 75% of $\dot{V}O_2$max. *International Journal of Sports Medicine* 22:226–31.

Bloomquist, K., et al. 2013. Effect of range of motion in heavy load squatting on muscle and tendon adaptations, *Eur J Appl Physiol* 8: 2133–61.

Bogdanis, G.C., et al. 1996. Contribution of phosphocreatine and aerobic metabolism to energy supply during repeated sprint exercise. *Journal of Applied Physiology* 80:876–84.

Bompa, T. 1965a. Periodization of strength. *Sports Review* 1:26–31.

———. 1965b. Periodization of strength for power sports. International Conference on Advancements in Sports Training, Moscow.

———. 1977. Characteristics of strength training for rowing. International Seminar on Training in Rowing, Stockholm.

———. 1993. *Periodization of strength: The new wave in strength training.* Toronto: Veritas.

———. 1999. *Periodization: Theory and methodology of training.* 4th ed. Champaign, IL: Human Kinetics.

Bompa, T., and Frederick, C. 2008. *Periodization in Rugby.* Aachen, Germany: Meyer & Meyer Sport.

Bompa T., Hebbelinck, M., and Van Gheluwe, B. 1978. A biomechanical analysis of the rowing stroke employing two different oar grips. The XXI World Congress in Sports Medicine, Brasilia, Brazil.

Bompa, T.O. 2005. *Treinando atletas de deporto colectivo.* San Paulo, Brazil: Phorte Editora.

Bompa, T.O., and Haff, G.G. 2009. *Periodization: Theory and methodology of training.* 5th ed. Champaign, IL: Human Kinetics.

Bonen, A. 2001. The expression of lactate transporters (MCT1 and MCT4) in heart and muscle. *European Journal of Applied Physiology* 86 (1): 6–11.

Bonen, A., and Belcastro, A. 1977. A physiological rationale for active recovery exercise. *Canadian Journal of Applied Sports Sciences* 2:63–64.

Borsheim, E., Cree, M.G., Tipton, K.D., Elliott, T.A., Aarsland, A., and Wolfe, R.R. 2004. Effect of carbohydrate intake on net muscle protein synthesis during recovery from resistance exercise. *Journal of Applied Physiology* 96 (2): 674–78.

Bosco, C., and Komi, P.V. 1980. Influence of countermovement amplitude in potentiation of muscular performance. In *Biomechanics VII proceedings*, 129–35. Baltimore: University Park Press.

Bosquet, L., Montpetit, J., Arvisais, D., and Mujika, I. 2007. Effects of tapering on performance: A meta-analysis. *Medicine and Science in Sports and Exercise* 39 (8): 1358–65.

Brooks, G.A., Brauner, K.T., and Cassens, R.G. 1973. Glycogen synthesis and metabolism of lactic acid after exercise. *American Journal of Physiology* 224:1162–66.

Brooks, G.A., and Fahey, T. 1985. *Exercise physiology: Human bioenergetics and its application.* New York: Wiley.

Brooks, G.A., Fahey, T.D., and White, T.P. 1996. *Exercise physiology: Human bioenergetics and its applications.* 2nd ed. Mountainview, CA: Mayfield.

Broughton, A. 2001. *Neural mechanisms are the most important determinants of strength adaptations.* Proposition for debate. School of Physiotherapy, Curtin University.

Brughelli, M., et al. 2011. Effects of running velocity on running kinetics and kinematics. *Journal of Strength and Conditioning Research* 25 (4): 933-39. doi:10.1519/JSC.0b013e3181c64308.

Bührle, M. 1985. *Grundlagen des maximal-und schnellkraft trainings.* Schorndorf: Hofmann Verlag.

Bührle, M., and Schmidtbleicher, D. 1981. Komponenten der maximal-und schnellkraft-versuch einer neus-trukturierung auf der basis empirischer ergenbnisse. *Sportwissenschaft* 11:11–27.

Burd, N.A., et al. 2010. Low-load high-volume resistance exercise stimulates muscle protein synthesis more than high-load low-volume resistance exercise in young men. *PLOS ONE* 5 (8): e12033. doi:10.1371/journal.pone.0012033.

References

Burkes, L.M., Collier, G.R., and Hargreaves, M. 1998. Glycemic index—A new tool in sport nutrition? *International Journal of Sport Nutrition* 8 (4): 401–15.

Caraffa, A., Cerulli, G., Projetti, M., Aisa, G., and Rizzo, A. 1996. Prevention of anterior cruciate ligament injuries in soccer. A prospective controlled study of proprioceptive training. *Knee Surgery, Sports Traumatology, Arthroscopy* 4 (1): 19–21.

Chen, J.L., et al. 2011. Parasympathetic nervous activity mirrors recovery status in weightlifting performance after training. *Journal of Strength and Conditioning Research.* 25(6):1546–52. doi: 10.1519/JSO.0b013e3181da7858.

Chiu, L.Z., et al. 2003. Postactivation potentiation response in athletic and recreationally trained individuals. *Journal of Strength and Conditioning Research* 17 (4): 671–77.

Cinique, C. 1989. Massage for cyclists: The winning touch? *The Physician and Sportsmedicine* 17 (10): 167–70.

Clark, N. 1985. Recovering from exhaustive workouts. *National Strength and Conditioning Journal* January:36–37.

Colado, J.C., et al. 2011. The progression of paraspinal muscle recruitment intensity in localized and global strength training exercises is not based on instability alone. *Archives of Physical Medicine And Rehabilitation* 92 (11): 1875–83. doi:10.1016/j.apmr.2011.05.015.

Compton, D., Hill, P.M., and Sinclair, J.D. 1973. Weight-lifters' blackout. *Lancet* 302 (7840): 1234–1237.

Conlee, R.K. 1987. Muscle glycogen and exercise endurance: A twenty-year perspective. *Exercise and Sport Sciences Reviews* 15:1–28.

Convertino, V.A., Keil, L.C., Bernauer, E.M., and Greenleaf, J.E. 1981. Plasma volume, osmolality, vasopressin, and renin activity during graded exercise in man. *Journal of Applied Physiology* 50 (1): 123–28.

Conwit, R.A. et al. 2000. Fatigue effects on motor unit activity during submaximal contractions, *Archives of Physical Medicine and Rehabilitation,* 81(9): 1211–1216.

Coombes, J.S., and Hamilton, K.L. 2000. The effectiveness of commercially available sports drinks. *Sports Medicine* 29 (3): 181–209.

Councilman, J.E. 1968. *The science of swimming.* Englewood Cliffs, NJ: Prentice Hall.

Coutts, A., Reaburn, P., Piva, T.J., and Murphy, A. 2007. Changes in selected biochemical, muscular strength, power, and endurance measures during deliberate overreaching and tapering in rugby league players. *International Journal of Sports Medicine* 28 (2): 116–24.

Coyle, E.F. 1999. Physiological determinants of endurance exercise performance. *Journal of Science and Medicine in Sport* 2 (3): 181–89.

Coyle, E.F., Feiring, D.C., Rotkis, T.C., Cote, R.W., Roby, F.B., Lee, W., and Wilmore, J.H. 1991. Specificity of power improvements through slow and fast isokinetic training. *Journal of Applied Physiology: Respiratory Environment Exercise Physiology* 51 (6): 1437–42.

Cramer, J.T., et al. 2005. The acute effects of static stretching on peak torque, mean power output, electromyography, and mechanomyography. *European Journal of Applied Physiology* 93 (5–6): 530–39.

Crameri, R.M., et al. 2004. Enhanced procollagen processing in skeletal muscle after a single bout of eccentric loading in humans. *Matrix Biology* 23 (4): 259–64.

D'Amico, A., and Morin, C. 2012. Effects of Myofascial Release on Human Performance: A Review of the Literature.

Davis, J., Jackson, D.A., Broadwell, M.S., Queary, J.L., and Lambert, C.L. 1997. Carbohydrate drinks delay fatigue during intermittent, high-intensity cycling in active men and women. *International Journal of Sports Nutrition* 7 (4): 261–73.

Davis, R.M., Welsh, R.S., De Volve, K.L., and Alderson, N.A. 1999. Effects of branched-chain amino acids and carbohydrate on fatigue during intermittent, high-intensity running, *International Journal of Sports Medicine* 20 (5): 309–14.

De Luca, C.J. and Erim, Z. 1994. Common drive of motor units in regulation of muscle force, *Trends in Neuroscience,* 17: 299–305.

De Luca, C.J., LeFever, R.S., McCue, M.P., and Xenakis, A.P. 1982. Behaviour of human motor units in different muscles during linearly varying contractions. *Journal of Physiology—London* 329:113–28.

de Salles, B.F., et al. 2010. Strength increases in upper and lower body are larger with longer inter-set rest intervals in trained men. *Journal of Science and Medicine in Sport* 13 (4): 429–33.

References

Devine, K.L., LeVeau, B.F., and Yack, H.J. 1981. Electromyographic activity recorded from an unexercised muscle during maximal isometric exercise of the contralateral agonists and antagonists. *Physical Therapy* 6 (6): 898–903.

Doessing S. and Kjaer. 2005. Growth hormone and connective tissue in exercise. *Scandinavian Journal of Medicine and Science in Sports,* 15(4): 202–210.

Dons, B., Bollerup, K., Bonde-Petersen, F., and Hancke, S. 1979. The effects of weight lifting exercise related to muscle fibre composition and muscle cross-sectional area in humans. *European Journal of Applied Physiology* 40:95–106.

Dorado, C., Sanchis-Moysi, J., and Calbet, J.A., 2004. Effects of recovery mode on performance, O_2 uptake, and O_2 deficit during high-intensity intermittent exercise. *Canadian Journal of Applied Physiology* 29 (3): 227–44.

Dudley, G.A., and Fleck, S.J. 1987. Strength and endurance training: Are they mutually exclusive? *Sports Medicine* 4:79–85.

Ebbing, C., and Clarkson, P. 1989. Exercise-induced muscle damage and adaptation. *Sports Medicine* 7:207–34.

Edge, J., Bishop, D., Goodman, C., and Dawson, B. 2005. Effects of high- and moderate-intensity training on metabolism and repeated sprints. *Medicine and Science in Sports and Exercise* 37 (11): 1975–82.

Edgerton, R.V. 1976. Neuromuscular adaptation to power and endurance work. *Canadian Journal of Applied Sports Sciences* 1: 49–58.

Ekstrand, J., Waldén, M., and Hägglund, M. 2004. Risk for injury when playing in a national football team, *Scand J Med Sci Sports.* 14(1):34–8.

Enoka, R. 1996. Eccentric contractions require unique activation strategies by the nervous system. *Journal of Applied Physiology* 81 (6): 2339–46.

Enoka, R.M. 1994. *Neuromechanical basis of kinesiology.* 2nd ed. Champaign, IL: Human Kinetics.

———. 2002. *Neuromechanics of human movement.* 3rd ed. Champaign, IL: Human Kinetics.

Enoka, R.M., and Stuart, D.G. 1992. Neurobiology of muscle fatigue. *Journal of Applied Physiology* 72 (5): 1631–38.

Evangelista, P. 2010. Principles of Strength Training, a presentation for the Tudor Bompa Institute - Italia. Ciccarelli Editore.

Evertsen, F., Medbo, J.I., Jebens, E.P., and Gjovaag, T.F. 1999. Effect of training on the activity of five muscle enzymes studied in elite cross-country skiers. *Acta Physiologica Scandinavica* 167 (3): 247–57.

Fabiato, A., and Fabiato, F. 1978. The effect of pH on myofilaments and the sarcoplasmic reticulum of skinned cells from cardiac and skeletal muscle. *Journal of Physiology* 276:233–55.

Fahey, T.D. 1992. How to cope with muscle soreness, *Powerlifting USA.* 15(7):10–11.

Fama, B.J., and Bueti, D.R. 2011. The acute effect of self-myofascial release on lower extremity plyometric performance. Theses and Dissertations. Paper 2. Sacred Heart University.

Febbraio, M.A., and Pedersen, B.K. 2005. Contraction-induced myokine production and release: Is skeletal muscle an endocrine organ? *Exercise and Sport Sciences Reviews* 33 (3): 114–19.

Ferret, J.M. and Cotte, T. 2003. Analyse des difference de preparation médicosportive de l'Equipe de France de football pour le coupes du monde 1998 et 2002, Lutter contre le Dopage en géran la recuperation physique, Publications de l'Université de Saint-Etienne. 23–26.

Fitts, R.H., and Widrick, J.J. 1996. Muscle mechanics: Adaptations with exercise-training. *Exercise and Sport Sciences Reviews* 24: 427–73.

Fleck, S.J., and Kraemer, W.J. 1996. *Periodization breakthrough.* New York: Advanced Research Press.

Forslund, A.H., et al. 2000. The 24-h whole body leucine and urea kinetics at normal and high protein intake with exercise in healthy adults. *American Journal of Physiology* 278:E857–67.

Fox, E.L. 1984. *Sports physiology.* New York: CBS College.

Fox, E.L., Bowes, R.W., and Foss, M.L. 1989. *The physiological basis of physical education and athletics.* Dubuque, IA: Brown.

Frank, C.B. 1996. Ligament injuries: Pathophysiology and healing. In *Athletic injuries and rehabilitation,* ed. J.E. Zachazewski, D.J. Magee, and W.S. Wilson, 9–26. Philadelphia: Saunders.

Friden, J., and Lieber, R.L. 1992. Structural and mechanical basis of exercise-induced muscle injury. *Medicine in Science and Sports Exercise* 24:521–30.

References

Fritzsche, R.G., et al. 2000. Water and carbohydrate ingestion during prolonged exercise increase maximal neuromuscular power. *Journal of Applied Physiology*. 88 (2): 730–37.

Fry, R.W., Morton, R., and Keast, D. 1991. Overtraining in athletics. *Sports Medicine* 2 (1): 32–65.

Garhammer, J. 1989. Weightlifting and training. In *Biomechanics of sport*, ed. C.L. Vaughn, 169–211. Boca Raton, FL: CRC Press.

Gauron, E.F. 1984. *Mental training for peak performance*. New York: Sports Science Associates.

Gibala, M.J., MacDougall, J.D., Tarnopolsky, M.A., Stauber, W.T., and Elorriaga, A. 1995. Changes in human skeletal muscle ultrastructure and force production after acute resistance exercise. *Journal of Applied Physiology* 78 (2): 702–8.

Godfrey, R.J., et al. 2003. The exercise-induced growth hormone response in athletes. *Sports Medicine* 33:599–613.

Goldberg, A.L., Etlinger, J.D., Goldspink, D.F., and Jablecki, C. 1975. Mechanism of work-induced hypertrophy of skeletal muscle. *Medicine and Science in Sports and Exercise* 7:185–98.

Goldspink, G. 2005. Mechanical signals, IGF-I gene splicing, and muscle adaptation. *Physiology* 20:232–38.

———. 2012. Age-related loss of muscle mass and strength. *J Aging Res* 2012:158279 doi: 10.1155/2012/158279.

Gollhofer, A., Fujitsuka, P.A., Miyashita, N., and Yashita, M. 1987. Fatigue during stretch–shortening cycle exercises: Changes in neuro-muscular activation patterns of human skeletal muscle. *Journal of Sports Medicine* 8:30–47.

Gollnick, P., Armstrong, R., Saubert, C., Piehl, K., and Saltin, B. 1972. Enzyme activity and fibre composition in skeletal muscle of untrained and trained men. *Journal of Applied Physiology* 33 (3): 312–19.

González-Badillo, J.J., et al. 2014. Maximal intended velocity training induces greater gains in bench press performance than deliberately slower half-velocity training, *Eur J Sport Sci*. 15:1–10.

Gorostiaga, E.M., Navarro-Amézqueta, I., Calbet, J.A., Hellsten, Y., Cusso, R., Guerrero, M., Granados, C., González-Izal, M., Ibañez, J., and Izquierdo, M. 2012. Energy metabolism during repeated sets of leg press exercise leading to failure or not. *PLOS One* 7 (7): e40621. doi: 10.1371/journal.pone.0040621.

Gossen, R.E., Allingham, K., and Sale, D.G. 2001. Effect of temperature on post-tetanic potentiation in human dorsiflexor muscles. *Canadian Journal of Physiology and Pharmacology* 79: 49–58.

Goto, K., et al. 2004. Muscular adaptations to combinations of high- and low-intensity resistance exercises. *Journal of Strength and Conditioning Research* 18 (4): 730–37.

Goto, K., et al. 2007. Effects of resistance exercise on lipolysis during subsequent submaximal exercise. *Med Sci Sports Exerc*. 39(2):308–15.

Graves, et al. 1988. Effect of reduced training frequency on muscular strength, *Int J Sports Med*. 9(5):316–9.

Gregg, R.A., and Mastellone, A.F. 1957. Cross exercise: A review of the literature and study utilizing electromyographic techniques. *American Journal of Physical Medicine* 38:269–80.

Grizard, J., et al. 1999. Insulin action on skeletal muscle protein metabolism during catabolic states. *Reproduction Nutrition Development* 39 (1): 61–74.

Gullich, A., and Schmidtbleicher, D. 1996. MVC-induced short-term potentiation of explosive force. *New Studies in Athletics* 11 (4): 67–81.Haff, G.G, et al. 2000. Carbohydrate supplementation attenuates muscle glycogen loss during acute bouts of resistance exercise. *International Journal of Sport Nutrition and Exercise Metabolism* 10:326–39.

Hagberg, et al. 1979. Effect of training on hormonal responses to exercise in competitive swimmers. Eur J Appl Physiol Occup Physiol. 41(3):211–9.

Hainaut, K., and Duchatteau, J. 1989. Muscle fatigue: Effects of training and disuse. Muscle & Nerve 12:660–69.

Haiyan, L., et al. 2011. Macrophages recruited via CCR2 produce insulin-like growth factor-1 to repair acute skeletal muscle injury. *FASEB Journal* 25 (1): 358–69.

Häkkinen, K. 1986. Training and detraining adaptations in electromyography. Muscle fibre and force production characteristics of human leg extensor muscle with special reference to prolonged heavy resistance and explosive-type strength training. *Studies in Sport, Physical Education and Health* 20. Jyväskylä, Finland: University of Jyväskylä.

———. 1989. Neuromuscular and hormonal adaptations during strength and power training. *Journal of Sports Medicine and Physical Fitness* 29 (1): 9–26.

References

Häkkinen, K., and Komi, P. 1983. Electromyographic changes during strength training and detraining. *Medicine and Science in Sports and Exercise, 15*: 455–460.

Häkkinen, K., & Pakarinen, A. 1993. Acute hormonal responses to two different fatiguing heavy-resistance protocols in male athletes. *Journal of Applied Physiology* 74 (2):882–7.

Hamada, T., et al. 2000. Post activation potentiation, fiber type, and twitch contraction time in human knee extensor muscles. *Journal of Applied Physiology.* 88 (6): 2131–37.

Hameed, M., et al. 2008. Effects of eccentric cycling exercise on IGF-I splice variant expression in the muscles of young and elderly people. *Scandinavian Journal of Medicine and Science in Sports* 18 (4): 447–52.

Hamlyn, N., et al. 2007. Trunk muscle activation during dynamic weight-training exercises and isometric instability activities. *Journal of Strength and Conditioning Research* 21 (4): 1108–12.

Harre, D., ed. 1982. *Trainingslehre*. Berlin: Sportverlag.

———. 2005. *Teoria dell' allenamento*. Roma, Società Stampa Sportiva.Harrison, B.C., et al. 2011. IIb or not IIb? Regulation of myosin heavy chain gene expression in mice and men. *Skeletal Muscle* 1 (1):1–5. doi:10.1186/2044-5040-1-5.

Harrison BC. et al. 2011. IIb or not IIb? Regulation of myosin heavy chain gene expression in mice and men. *Skeletal Muscle.* 1 (1): 5. doi: 10.1186/2044-5040-1-5.

Hartmann, J., and Tünnemann, H. 1988. *Fitness and strength training*. Berlin: Sportverlag.

Hartmann, H. et al. 2012. Influence of squatting depth on jumping performance, *J Strength Cond Res* 26(12): 3243–61.

Hawley, J.A., Tipton, K.D., and Millard-Stafford, M.L. 2006. Promoting training adaptations through nutritional interventions. *Journal of Sports Sciences* 24 (7): 709–21.

Hay, J.G. 1993. *The biomechanics of sports techniques*. Englewood Cliffs, NJ: Prentice Hall.

Healey, K.C., et al. 2014 The effects of myofascial release with foam rolling on performance. *Journal of Strength and Conditioning Research.* 28(1): 61–68.

———. 2014. The effects of myofascial release with foam rolling on performance. *Journal of Strength and Conditioning Research* 28 (1): 61–68.

Kyröläinen, H., Avela, J., and Komi, P.V. 2005. Changes in muscle activity with increasing running speed, *J Sports Sci.* 23(1):1101–9.

Hellebrand, F., and Houtz, S. 1956. Mechanism of muscle training in man: Experimental demonstration of the overload principle. *Physical Therapy Review* 36:371–83.

Hellebrandt, F.A., Parrish, A.M., and Houtz, S.J. 1947. Cross education: The influence of unilateral exercise on the contralateral limb. *Archive of Physical Medicine* 28:78–84.

Helms, Eric. 2010. *Effects of Training-Induced Hormonal Changes on Muscular Hypertrophy*. http:www.3dmusclejourney.com/resources/Effects_of_Training-Induced_Hormonal_Changes_on_Muscular_Hypertrophy_by_Eric_Helms.pdf.

Henneman, E., Somjen, G., and Carpenter, D.O. 1965. Functional significance of cell size in spinal motoneurons. *J. Neurophysiol.* 28:560–580.

Hennig, R., and Lomo, T. 1987. Gradation of force output in normal fast and slow muscle of the rat. *Acta Physiologica Scandinavica* 130:133–42.

Hermansen, L., and Vaage, O. 1977. Lactate disappearance and glycogen synthesis in human muscle after maximal exercise. *American Journal of Physiology* 233 (5): E422–29.

Hettinger, T. 1966. *Isometric muscle training*. Stuttgart: Georg Thieme Verlag.

Hettinger, T., and Müler, E. 1953. Muskelleistung and muskel training. *Arbeitsphysiologie*, 15:111–26.

Hickson, R., et al. 1985. Reduced training intensities and loss of aerobic power, endurance, and cardiac growth. *Journal of Applied Physiology* 58:492–99.

Hickson, R.C., Dvorak, B.A., Corostiaga, T.T., and Foster, C. 1988. Strength training and performance in endurance-trained subjects. *Medicine and Science in Sports and Exercise* 20 (2) (Suppl.): 586.

Hoff, J., Gran, A., and Helgerud, J. 2002. Maximal strength training improves aerobic endurance performance. *Scandinavian Journal of Medicine and Science in Sports* 12 (5): 288–95.

Hoffman, J.R., Ratamess, N.A., Tranchina, C.P., Rashti, S.L., Kang, J., and Faigenbaum A.D. 2010. Effect of a proprietary protein supplement on recovery indices following resistance exercise in strength/power athletes. *Amino Acids* 38 (3): 771–78.

References

Hornberger, T.A., et al. 2006. The role of phospholipase D and phosphatidic acid in the mechanical activation of mTOR signaling in skeletal muscle. *Proceedings of the National Academy of Science of the United States of America* 103 (12): 4741-46.

Hortobagyi, T., Hill, J., Houmard, A., Fraser, D., Lambert, J., and Israel, G. 1996. Adaptive responses to muscle lengthening and shortening in humans. *Journal of Applied Physiology* 80 (3): 765-72.

Houmard, J.A., Kirwan, J.P., Flynn, M.G., and Mitchell, J.B. 1989. Effects of reduced training on submaximal and maximal running responses. *International Journal of Sports Medicine* 10:30-33.

Houmard, J.A. 1991. Impact of reduced training on performance in endurance athletes. *Sports Medicine* 12 (6): 380-93.

Howard, J.D., Ritchie, M.R., Gater, D.A., Gater, D.R., and Enoka, R.M. 1985. Determining factors of strength: Physiological foundations. *National Strength and Conditioning Journal* 7 (6): 16-21.

Hubbard, T.J., et al. 2004. Does cryotherapy hasten return to participation? A systematic literature review. *Journal of Athletic Training* 39 (1): 88-94.

Hultman, E., and Sjoholm, H. 1983. Energy metabolism and contraction force of skeletal muscle in-situ during electrical stimulation. *Journal of Physiology* 345:525-32.

International Olympic Committee. 2010. *Consensus Statement on Sport Nutrition.* www.olympic.org/Documents/Reports/EN/CONSENSUS-FINAL-v8-en.pdf

Israel, S. 1972. *The acute syndrome of detraining.* Berlin: GDR National Olympic Committee. 2: 30-35.

Ivy, J., and Portman, R. 2004. *Nutrient timing.* Laguna Beach, California: Basic Health Publications.

Ivy, J.L, et al. 2003. Effect of carbohydrate-protein supplement on endurance performance during exercise of varying intensity. *International Journal of Sport Nutrition and Exercise Metabolism* 13:42-49, 52-56, 338-401.

Izquierdo, M., et al. 2006. Differential effects of strength training leading to failure versus not to failure on hormonal responses, strength and muscle power increases. *Journal of Applied Physiology* 100:1647-56.

Jacobs, I., Esbornsson, M., Sylven, C., Holm, I., and Jansson, E. 1987. Sprint training effects on muscle myoglobin, enzymes, fibre types, and blood lactate. *Medicine and Science in Sports and Exercise* 19 (4): 368-74.

Janssen, P. 2001. *Lactate threshold training.* Champaign, IL: Human Kinetics.

Jezova, D. et al. 1985. Plasma testosterone and catecholamine responses to physical exercise of different intensities in men. *European Journal of Applied Physiology and Occupational Physiology,* 54(1):62-66.

Johns, R.J., and Wright, V. 1962. Relative importance of various tissues in joint stiffness. *Journal of Applied Physiology* 17:824.

Jorgensen, J.O. et al. 2003. Exercise, hormones and body temperature: Regulation and action of Gh during exercise. *Journal of Endocrinological Investigation,* 26 (9): 838-42.

Kandarian, S.C., and Jackman, R.W. 2006. Intracellular signaling during skeletal muscle atrophy. *Muscle and Nerve* 33 (2): 155-65.

Kanehisa, J., and Miyashita, M. 1983. Effect of isometric and isokinetic muscle training on static strength and dynamic power. *European Journal of Applied Physiology* 50: 365-71.

Kannus, P., Alosa, D., Cook, L., Johnson, R.J., Renstrom, P., Pope, M., Beynnon, B., Yasuda, K., Nichols, C., and Kaplan, M. 1992. Effect of one-legged exercise on the strength, power and endurance of the contralateral leg: A randomized, controlled study using isometric and concentric isokinetic training. *European Journal of Applied Physiology* 64 (2): 117-26.Karlsson, J., and Saltin, B. 1971. Diet, muscle glycogen and endurance performance. *Journal of Applied Physiology* 31 (2): 203-6.

Kawamori, N., et al. 2013. Relationships between ground reaction impulse and sprint acceleration performance in team sport athletes. *Journal of Strength and Conditioning Research* 27 (3): 568-73. doi:10.1519/JSC.0b013e318257805a.

Kerksick, C., et al. 2008. International society of sport nutrition position stand: Nutrient timing. *Journal of the International Society of Sport Nutrition* 5:17.

King, I., 1998. *How to Write Strength Training Programs.* Toowong (AUS): Kings Sport Publishing.

Kjaer, M., et al. 2005. Metabolic activity and collagen turnover in human tendon in response to physical activity. *Journal of Musculoskeletal and Neuronal Interactions* 5 (1): 41-52.

Kjaer, M., et al. 2006. Extracellular matrix adaptation of tendon and skeletal muscle to exercise. *Journal of Anatomy* 208 (4): 445-50.

References

Komi, P.V., and Bosco, C. 1978. Utilization of stored elastic energy in leg extensor muscles by men and women. *Medicine and Science in Sports and Exercise* 10 (4): 261–65.

Komi, P.V., and Buskirk, E.R. 1972. Effect of eccentric and concentric muscle conditioning on tension and electrical activity of human muscle. *Ergonomics* 15 (4): 417–34.

Kraemer, W.J., and Ratamess, N.A. 2005. Hormonal responses and adaptations to resistance exercise and training. *Sports Medicine* 35:339–61.

Kraemer, W.J., Ratamess, N.A., Volek, J.S., Häkkinen, K., Rubin, M.R., French, D.N., Gómez, et al. 2006. The effects of amino acid supplementation on hormonal responses to resistance training overreaching. *Metabolism* 55 (3): 282–91.

Kugler, A., Kruger-Franke, M., Reininger, S., Trouillier, H.H., and Rosemeyer, B. 1996. Muscular imbalance and shoulder pain in volleyball attackers. *British Journal of Sports Medicine* 30 (3): 256–59.

Kuipers, H., and Keizer, H.A. 1988. Overtraining in elite athletes: Review and directions for the future. *Sports Medicine* 6:79–92.

Kuoppasalmi and Adlercreutz. 1985. Interaction between anabolic and catabolic steroid hormones in muscular exercise. *Exercise Endocrinology*. Berlin: deGuyter: 65–98.

Kyröläinen, H., et al. 2001. Biomechanical factors affecting running economy. *Medicine and Science in Sports and Exercise* 33 (8): 1330–37.

Lamb, D.R. 1984. *Physiology of Exercise: Responses and Adaptations*, 2nd ed. New York: MacMillan Publishing Company.

Langberg, H., et al. 2007. Eccentric rehabilitation exercise increases peritendinous type I collagen synthesis in humans with Achilles tendinosis. *Scandinavian Journal of Medicine and Science in Sports*. 17:61–66.

Lange, L. 1919. *Über functionelle anpassung*. Berlin: Springer Verlag.

Latash, M.L. 1998. *Neurophysiological basis of movement*. Champaign, IL: Human Kinetics.

La Torre, A., et al. 2010. Acute effects of static stretching on squat jump performance at different knee starting angles. *Journal of Strength and Conditioning Research* 24 (3): 687–94. doi:10.1519/JSC.0b013e3181c7b443.

Laubach, L.L. 1976. Comparative muscle strength of men and women: A review of the literature. *Aviation, Space, and Environmental Medicine* 47:534–42.

Lee, M., and Carroll, T. 2007. Cross-education: Possible mechanisms for the contralateral effects of unilateral resistance training. *Sports Medicine* 37 (1): 1–14.

Lemon, P.W. et al. 1997. Moderate physical activity can increase dietary protein needs. *Canadian Journal of Applied Physiology* 22:494–503.

Lephart, S.M., Ferris, C.M., Riemann, B.L., Myers, J.B., and Fu, F.H. 2002. Gender differences in strength and lower extremity kinematics during landing. *Clinical Orthopaedics and Related Research* 402:162–69.

Liu, Y., et al. 2008. Response of growth and myogenic factors in human skeletal muscle to strength training. *British Journal of Sports Medicine* 42 (12): 989–93. doi:10.1136/bjsm.2007.045518.

MacDonald, G., et al. 2013. An acute bout of self myofascial release increases range of motion without a subsequent decrease in neuromuscular performance. *Journal of Strength and Conditioning Research*. 27(3):812–21. doi: 10.1519/JSC.0bb013e31825c2bc1.

MacDougall, J.D., Tuxen, D., Sale, D.G., Moroz, J.R., and Sutton, J.R. 1985. Arterial blood pressure response to heavy resistance exercise. *Journal of Applied Physiology* 58 (3): 785–90.

Marsden, C., Meadows, J.F., and Merton, P.A. 1971. Isolated single motor units in human muscle and their rate of discharge during maximal voluntary effort. *Journal of Physiology—London* 217:12P–13P.

Martin, D.T, Scifres, J.C, Zimmerman, S.D, and Wilkinson, J.G. 1994. Effects of interval training and a taper on cycling performance and isokinetic leg strength. *International Journal of Sports Medicine* 15:485–91.

Martuscello, J., et al. 2012. Systematic review of core muscle electromyographic activity during physical fitness exercises. *J Strength Cond Res*. 27(6):1684–98. doi: 10.1519/JSC.0b013e318291b8da..

Mathews, D.K., and Fox, E.L. 1976. *The physiological basis of physical education and athletics*. Philadelphia: Saunders.

Maughan, R.J., Goodburn, R., Griffin, J., Irani, M., Kirwan, J.P., Leiper, J.B., MacLaren, D.P., McLatchie, G., Tsintsas, K., and Williams, C. 1993. Fluid replacement in sport and exercise—A consensus statement. *British Journal of Sports Medicine* 27 (1): 34–35.

References

McConell, G.K., Costill, D.L., Widrick, J.J., Hickey, M.S., Tanaka, H., and Gastin, P.B. 1993. Reduced training volume and intensity maintain capacity but not performance in distance runners. *International Journal of Sports Medicine* 14:33–37.

McDonagh, M.J.N., and Davies, C.T.M. 1984. Adaptive response of mammalian skeletal muscle to exercise with high loads. *European Journal of Applied Physiology* 52:139–55.

McDonald, G.Z., et al. 2013. An acute bout of self-myofascial release increases range of motion without subsequent decrease in muscle activation force. *Journal of Strength and Conditioning Research* 27 (3): 812–21.

McNeely, E., and Sandler, D. 2007. Tapering for endurance athletes. *Strength and Conditioning Journal* 29 (5): 18–24.

Micheli, L.J. 1988. Strength training in the young athlete. In *Competitive sports for children and youth*, ed. E.W. Brown and C.E. Branta, 99–105. Champaign, IL: Human Kinetics.

Miller, B.F., et al. 2005. Coordinated collagen and muscle protein synthesis in human patella tendon and quadriceps muscle after exercise. *Journal of Physiology* 567 (Pt 3): 1021–33.

Moeller, F. et al. 1985. Duration of stretching effect on range of motion in lower extremities. *Archives of Physical Medicine and Rehabilitation* 66:171–73.

Mohr, M., Krustrup, P., and Bangsbo, J. 2005. Fatigue in soccer: A brief review. *Journal of Sports Sciences* 23 (6): 593–99.

Morgan, R.E., and Adamson, G.T. 1959. *Circuit weight training*. London: Bell.

Morin, J.B. 2011. Technical ability of force application as a determinant factor of sprint performance. *Medicine and Science in Sports and Exercise* 43 (9): 1680–88. doi:10.1249/MSS.0b013e318216ea37.

Morin, J.B., et al. 2012. Mechanical determinants of 100-m sprint running performance. *European Journal of Applied Physiology* 112 (11): 3921–30. doi:10.1007/s00421-012-2379-8.

Moritani, T. 1992. Time course of adaptations during strength and power training. In *Strength and power in sport*, ed. P.V. Komi, 266–78. Champaign, IL: Human Kinetics.

Moritani, T., and deVries, H.A. 1979. Neural factors versus hypertrophy in the time course of muscle strength gain. *American Journal of Physical Medicine* 58 (3): 115–30.

Mujika, I. 1998. The influence of training characteristics and tapering on adaptation in highly trained individuals: A review. *International Journal of Sports Medicine* 19:439–46.

———. 2009. *Tapering and peaking for optimal performance*. Champaign, IL: Human Kinetics.

Mujika, I., Chatard, J.C., Busso, T., Geyssant, A., Barale, F., and Lacoste, L. 1995. Effects of training on performance in competitive swimming. *Canadian Journal of Applied Physiology* 20 (4): 395–406.

Mujika, I.I., Padilla, S., and Pyne, D. 2002. Swimming performance changes during the final 3 weeks of training leading to the Sydney 2000 Olympic Games, *Int J Sports Med.* 23(8):582–7.

Nardone, A., Romanò, C., and Schieppati, M. 1989. Selective recruitment of high-threshold human motor units during voluntary isotonic lengthening of active muscles. *Journal of Physiology* 409:451–71.

Nelson, A.G., Arnall, D.A., Loy, S.F., Silvester, L.J., and Conlee, R.K. 1990. Consequences of combining strength and endurance training regimens. *Physical Therapy* 70 (5): 287–94.

Nelson, A.G., et al. 2005. Acute effects of passive muscle stretching on sprint performance. *Journal of Sports Sciences* 23 (5): 449–54.

Newsholme, E. 2005. Keep on running: The science of training and performance. Hoboken, NJ: Wiley.

Noakes, T.D., et al. 2005. From catastrophe to complexity: A novel model of integrative central neural regulation of effort and fatigue during exercise in humans: Summary and conclusions. *British Journal of Sports Medicine* 39:120–24. doi:10.1136/bjsm.2003.010330.

Nummela, A., et al. 2007. Factors related to top running speed and economy. *International Journal of Sports Medicine* 28 (8): 655–61.

Nuzzo, J.L. 2008. Trunk muscle activity during stability ball and free weight exercises. *Journal of Strength and Conditioning Research* 22 (1): 95–102. doi:10.1519/JSC.0b013e31815ef8cd.

Okamura, K., et al. 1997. Effect of amino acid and glucose administration during post-exercise recovery on protein kinetics in dogs. *American Journal of Physiology* 272:E1023–30.

O'Leary, D.D., Hope, K., and Sale, D.G. 1998. Influence of gender on post-tetanic potentiation in human dorsiflexors. *Canadian Journal of Physiology and Pharmacology* 76:772–79.

References

Owino, V., et al. 2001 Age-related loss of skeletal muscle function and the inability to express the autocrine form of insulin-like growth factor-1 (MGF) in response to mechanical overload *FEBS Letters* 505 (2): 259–63.

Ozolin, N.G. 1971. *Athlete's training system for competition.* Moscow: Phyzkultura i sports.

Piehl, K. 1974. Time course for refilling of glycogen stores in human muscle fibres following exercise-induced glycogen depletion. *Acta Physiologica Scandinavica* 90: 297–302.

Pincivero, D.M., and Campy, R.M. 2004. The effects of rest interval length and training on quadriceps femoris muscle. Part I: Knee extensor torque and muscle fatigue. *Journal of Sports Medicine and Physical Fitness* 44 (2): 111–18.

Pincivero, D.M., Lephart, S.M., and Karunakara, R.G. 1997. Effects of rest interval on isokinetic strength and functional performance after short-term high intensity training. *British Journal of Sports Medicine* 31 (3): 229–34.

Ploutz, L., et al. 1994. Effect of resistance training on muscle use during exercise, *Journal of Applied Physiology*, 76: 1675–1681.

Power, K., et al. 2004. An acute bout of static stretching: Effects on force and jumping performance. *Medicine and Science in Sports and Exercise* 36 (8): 1389–96.

Powers, S.K., Lawler, J., Dodd, S., Tulley, R., Landry, G., and Wheeler, K. 1990. Fluid replacement drinks during high intensity exercise: Effects on minimizing exercise-induced disturbances in homeostasis. *European Journal of Applied Physiology and Occupational Physiology* 60 (1): 54–60.

Pyne, D.B., et al. 2009. *Peaking for optimal performance: Research limitations and future directions, Journal of Sports Sciences.* 27(3):195–202.

Raglin, J.S. 1992. Anxiety and sport performance. *Exercise Sports Science Review* 20:243–74.

Ranieri, F. and Di Lazzaro, V. 2012. The role of motor neuron drive in muscle fatigue, *Neurumuscul Disord* 22(3): S157–61.

Rasmussen, R.B., and Phillips, S.M. 2003. Contractile and nutritional regulation of human muscle growth. *Exercise and Sport Sciences Reviews* 31 (3): 127–31.

Ready, S.L., Seifert, J., Burke, E. 1999. Effect of two sport drinks on muscle tissue stress and performance. *Medicine and Science in Sports and Exercise* 31 (5): S119.

Reilly, T., and Ekblom, B. 2005. The use of recovery methods post-exercise. *Journal of Sports Sciences* 23 (6): 619–27.

Rennie, M.J., and Millward, D.J. 1983. 3-methylhistidine excretion and the urinary 3-methylhistidine/creatinine ratio are poor indicators of skeletal muscle protein breakdown. *Clinical Science* 65:217–25.

Rhea, M.R., et al. 2009. Alterations in speed of squat movement and the use of accommodated resistance among college athletes training for power. *Journal of Strength and Conditioning Research* 23 (9): 2645–50. doi:10.1519/JSC.0b013e3181b3e1b6.

Rietjens, G.J., Keizer, H.A., Kuipers, H., and Saris, W.H. 2001. A reduction in training volume and intensity for 21 days does not impair performance in cyclists. *British Journal of Sports Medicine* 35 (6): 431–34.

Rixon, K.P., Lamont, H.S., & Bemben, M.G. 2007. Influence of type of muscle contraction, gender, and lifting experience on postactivation potentiation performance. *Journal of Strength and Conditioning Research* 21 (2): 500–505.

Robinson, J.M., et al. 1995. Effects of different weight training exercise/rest intervals on strength, power, and high intensity exercise endurance. *Journal of Strength and Conditioning Research* 9 (4): 216–21.

Roemmich, J.N., and Rogol, A.D. 1997. Exercise and growth hormone: Does one affect the other? *Journal of Pediatrics* 131:S75–80.

Roman Suarez, I. 1986. *Levantamiento de pesas—Periodo competitivo.* La Habana, Cuba: Editorial Cientifico Tecnico.

Rønnestad, B.R., and Mujika, I. 2013. Optimizing strength training for running and cycling endurance performance: A review. *Scandinavian Journal of Medicine and Science in Sports.* 24(4):603–612.

Roschel, H., et al. 2011. Effect of eccentric exercise velocity on akt/mtor/p70(s6k) signaling in human skeletal muscle. *Applied Physiology Nutrition and Metabolism* 36 (2): 283–90. doi:10.1139/h10-111.

Sahlin, K. 1986. Metabolic changes limiting muscular performance. *Biochemistry of Exercise* 16:86–98.

Sale, D. 1986. Neural adaptation in strength and power training. In *Human muscle power*, ed. L. Jones, L.N. McCartney, and A. McConias, 289–304. Champaign, IL: Human Kinetics.

References

———. 1992. Neural adaptations to strength training. In *Strength and power in sport*, ed. P.V. Komi, 249–65. Oxford: Blackwell Scientific.

Sale, D.G., MacDougall, J.D., Jakobs, I., and Garner, S. 1990. Interaction between concurrent strength and endurance training. *Journal of Applied Physiology* 68 (1): 260–70.Saltin, B. 1973. Metabolic fundamentals in exercise. *Medicine and Science in Sports* 5:137–46.

Samuel, M.N., et al. 2008. Acute effects of static and ballistic stretching on measures of strength and power. *Journal of Strength and Conditioning Research* 22 (5): 1422–28. doi:10.1519/JSC.0b013e318181a314.

Sariyildiz, M., et al. 2011. Cross-education of muscle strength: Cross-training effects are not confined to untrained contralateral homologous muscle. *Scandinavian Journal of Medicine and Science in Sport.* 21(6):e359–64. doi: 10.1111/j.1600-0838.2011.01311.x. Epub 2011.

Schanzer, W. 2002. *Analysis of Non-Hormonal Nutritional Supplements for Anabolic-Androgenic Steroids.* www.olympic.org/Documents/Reports/EN/en_report_324.pdf

Schillings, M.L., et al. 2000. *Central and peripheral aspects of exercise-induced fatigue.* www.med.uni-jena.de/motorik/pdk/schillings.pdf.

Schmidtbleicher, D. 1984. *Sportliches krafttraining.* Berlin: Jung, Haltong, und Bewegung bei Menchen.

———. 1992. Training for power events. In *Strength and power in sport*, ed. P.V. Komi, 381–95. Oxford, UK: Blackwell Scientific.

Schmidtbleicher, D., et al. 2014. Long-term strength training effects on change-of-direction sprint performance. *Journal of Strength and Conditioning Research* 28 (1): 223–31.

Schoenfeld, B.J. 2012. Does exercise-induced muscle damage play a role in skeletal muscle hypertrophy? *Journal of Strength and Conditioning Research* 26 (5): 1441–53. doi:10.1519/JSC.0b013e31824f207e.

Shepley, B., MacDougall, J.D., Cipriano, N., Sutton, J.R., Tarnopolsky, M.A., and Coates, G. 1992. Physiological effects of tapering in highly trained athletes. *Journal of Applied Physiology* 72:706–11.

Sirotic, A.C., and Coutts, A.J. 2007. Physiological and performance test correlates of prolonged, high-intensity, intermittent running performance in moderately trained women team sport athletes. *Journal of Strength and Conditioning Research* 21 (1): 138–44.

Sjøgaard, G., et al. 1985. Water and ion shifts in skeletal muscle of humans with intense dynamic knee extension. *American Journal of Physiology* 248 (2 pt 2): R190–96.

Soderman, K., Wener, S., Pietila, T., Engstrom. B., and Alfredson, H. 2000. Balance board training: Prevention of traumatic injuries of the lower extremities in female soccer players? A perspective randomized intervention study. *Knee Surgery, Sports Traumatology, Arthroscopy* 8 (6): 356–63.

Staley, C. 2005. *Muscle logic,* Rodale Press.

Staron, R.S., Hagerman, F.C., and Hikida, R.S. 1981. The effects of detraining on an elite power lifter. *Journal of Neurological Sciences* 51:247–57.

Stone, M.H., and O'Bryant, H.S. 1984. *Weight training: A scientific approach.* Minneapolis, MN: Burgess.

Sullivan, K.M., et al. 2013. Roller-massager application to the hamstrings increases sit-and-reach range of motion within five to ten seconds without performance impairments. *Int J Sports Phys Therapy* 8 (3): 228–36.

Takagi, R., et al. 2011. Influence of icing on muscle regeneration after crush injury to skeletal muscles in rats. *Journal of Applied Physiology* 110 (2): 382–88.

Takarada, Y., et al. 2000. Rapid increase in plasma growth hormone after low-intensity resistance exercise with vascular occlusion, *J Appl Physiol.* 88(1):61–5.

Taylor, J.L., Todd, G., and Gandevia, S.C. 2006. Evidence for a supraspinal contribution to human muscle fatigue, *Clin Exp Pharmacol Physiol* 33(4): 400–5.

Terjung, R.L. and Hood, D.A. 1986. Biochemical adaptations in skeletal muscle induced by exercise training. In *Nutrition and aerobic exercise*, ed. D.K. Layman, 8–27. Washington, DC: American Chemical Society.

Tesch, P. 1980. Muscle fatigue in man. *Acta Physiologica Scandinavica Supplementum* 480:3–40.

Tesch, P., Sjšdon, B., Thorstensson, A., and Karlsson, J. 1978. Muscle fatigue and its relation to lactate accumulation and LDH activity in man. *Acta Physiologica Scandinavica* 103:413–20.

Tesch, P.A., and Larsson, L. 1982. Muscle hypertrophy in bodybuilders. *European Journal of Applied Physiology and Occupational Physiology* 49 (3): 301–6.

Tesch, P.A., Thorsson, A., and Kaiser, P. 1984. Muscle capillary supply and fiber type characteristics in weight and power lifters. *Journal of Applied Physiology* 56:35–38.

References

Thacker, S.B., Stroup, D.F., Branche, C.M., Gilchrist, J., Goodman, R.A., and Porter Kelling, E. 2003. Prevention of knee injuries in sports. A systematic review of literature. *Journal of Sports Medicine and Physical Fitness* 43 (2): 165–79.

Thomas, L., Mujika, I., and Busso, T. 2009. Computer simulations assessing the potential performance benefit of a final increase in training during pre-event taper, *J Strength Cond Res.* 23(6):1729–36.

Thorstensson, A. 1977. Observations on strength training and detraining. *Acta Physiologica Scandinavica* 100:491–93.

Tipton, K.D., Ferrando, A.A., Phillips, S.M., Doyle, D., Jr., and Wolfe, R.R. 1999. Postexercise net protein synthesis in human muscle from orally administered amino acids. *American Journal of Physiology* 276:E628–34.

Tipton, K.D., and Wolfe, R.R. 2001. Exercise, protein metabolism, and muscle growth. *International Journal of Sport Nutrition and Exercise Metabolism* 11 (1): 109–32.

———. 2004. Protein and amino acid for athletes. *Journal of Sports Science* 22 (1): 65–79.

Trinity, J.D., et al. 2006. Maximal mechanical power during taper in elite swimmer. *Medicine and Science in Sports & Exercise,* 38(9):1643–9.

Van Cutsem, M., Duchateau, J., and Hainaut, K. 1998. Changes in single motor unit behaviour contribute to the increase in contraction speed after dynamic training in humans. *Journal of Physiology* 513:295–305.

Van Someren, K.A. 2006. The physiology of anaerobic endurance training. In *The Physiology of Training,* ed. G. Whyte. London: Elsevier, 88.

Verkhoshansky, Y.L.V. 1969. Perspectives in the improvement of speed-strength preparation of jumpers. *Yessis Review of Soviet Physical Education and Sports* 4 (2): 28–29.

———. 1997. *Tutto sul metodo d'urto.* Società Stampa Sportiva.

Wade, A.J., Broadhead, M.W., Cady, E.B., Llewelyn, M.E., Tong, H.N., and Newham, D.J. 2000. Influence of muscle temperature during fatiguing work with the first dorsal interosseous muscle in man: A 31P-NMR spectroscopy study. *European Journal of Applied Physiology* 81 (3): 203–9.

Wathen, D. 1994. Agonist–antagonist ratios for slow concentric isokinetic movements. In *Essentials of strength training and conditioning,* ed. T.R. Baechle. Champaign, IL: Human Kinetics.

Wee, J., et al. 2005. GH secretion in acute exercise may result in post-exercise lipolysis. *Growth Hormone & IGF Research Journal.* 15 (6): 397–404.

Weir, J.P., et al. 2006. Is fatigue all in your head? A critical review of the central governor model. *British Journal of Sports Medicine* 40 (7): 573–86.

Welsh, R.S., Davis, J.M., Burke, J.R., and Williams, H.G. 2002. Carbohydrates and physical/mental performance during intermittent exercise to fatigue. *Medicine and Science in Sports and Exercise* 34 (4): 723–31.

Wester, J.U., Jespersen, S.M., Nielsen, K.D., and Neumann, L. 1996. Wobble board training after partial sprains of the lateral ligaments of the ankle: A prospective randomized study. *Journal of Orthopaedic & Sports Physical Therapy* 23 (5): 332–36.

Weyand, P.G., et al. 2000. Faster top running speeds are achieved with greater ground forces, not more rapid leg movements. *Journal of Applied Physiology* 89 (5): 1991–99.

White, J.P., et al. 2013. Testosterone regulation of Akt/mTORC1/FoxO3a signaling in skeletal muscle. *Molecular and Cellular Endocrinology* 365 (2): 174–86.

Wiemann, K., and Tidow, G. 1995. Relative activity of hip and knee extensors in sprinting—Implications for training. *New Studies in Athletics* 10 (1): 29–49.

Wigernaes, I., Hostmark, A.T., Stromme, S.B., Kierulf, P., and Birkeland, K. 2001. Active recovery and post-exercise white blood cell count, free fatty acids and hormones in endurance athletes. *European Journal of Applied Physiology* 84 (4): 358–66.

Willems, T., Witvrouw, E., Verstuyft, J., Vaes, P., and Clercq, D.D. 2002. Proprioception and muscle strength in subjects with a history of ankle sprains and chronic instability. *Journal of Athletic Training* 37 (4): 487–93.

Wilmore, J., and Costill, D. 2004. *Physiology of sport and exercise.* 3rd ed. Champaign, IL: Human Kinetics.

Wilmore, J.H., and Costill, D.L. 1993. *Training for sport and activity: The physiological basis of the conditioning process.* Champaign, IL: Human Kinetics.

Wilmore, J.H., Parr, R.B., Girandola, R.N., Ward, P., Vodak, P.A., Barstow, T.J., Pipes, T.V., Romero, G.T., and Leslie, P. 1978. Physiological alterations consequent to circuit weight training. *Medicine and Science in Sports and Exercise* 10:79–84.

References

Wojtys, E.M., Huston, L.J., Schock, H.J., Boylan, J.P., and Ashton-Miller, J.A. 2003. Gender differences in muscular protection of the knee in torsion in size-matched athletes. *Journal of Bone and Joint Surgery—American Volume* 85-A (5): 782–89.

Woo, S.L.-Y., An, K.-N., Arnoczky, S.P., Wayne, J.S., Fithian, D.C., and Myers, B.S. 1994. Anatomy, biology and biomechanics of tendon, ligament, and meniscus. In *Orthopaedic basic science*, ed. S.R. Simon, 45–87. Park Ridge, IL: American Academy of Orthopaedic Surgeons.

Wright, J.E. 1980. Anabolic steroids and athletics. *Exercise and sport sciences reviews*: 149–202.

Yamaguchi, T., et al. 2006. Acute effect of static stretching on power output during concentric dynamic constant external resistance leg extension. *Journal of Strength and Conditioning Research* 20 (4): 804–10.

Yarasheski, K.E., et al. 1992. Effect of growth hormone and resistance exercise on muscle growth in young men. *American Journal of Physiology*. 262(3 Pt.1):E261–7.

Yessis, M. 1990. *Soviet training methods*. New York: Barnes & Noble.

Zatsiorsky, V.M. 1995. *Science and Practice of Strength Training*. Champaign, IL: Human Kinetics.

Zawadzki, K.M., Yaspelkis, B.B., and Ivy, J.L. 1992. Carbohydrate-protein complex increases the rate of muscle glycogen storage after exercise. *Journal of Applied Physiology* 72:1854–59.

Zehnder, M., Rico-Sanz, J., Kühne, G., and Boutellier, U. 2001. Resynthesis of muscle glycogen after soccer-specific performance examined by 13C-magnetic resonance spectroscopy in elite players. *European Journal of Applied Physiology* 84 (5): 443–47.

Zeller, B.L., McCrory, J.L., Kibler, W.B., and Uhl, T.L. 2003. Differences in kinematics and electromyographical activity between men and women during the single-legged squat. *American Journal of Sports Medicine* 31 (3): 449–56.

Zhang, P., et al. 2007. Signaling mechanisms involved in disuse muscle atrophy. *Medical Hypotheses* 69 (2): 310–21.

Zhou, S. 2003. Cross-education and neuromuscular adaptations during early stage of strength training. *Journal of Exercise Science and Fitness* 1 (1): 54–60.

Zijdewind, I., and Kernell, D. 2001. Bilateral interactions during contractions of intrinsic hand muscles. *Journal of Neurophysiology* 85 (5): 1907–13.

Index

Note: The italicized *f* and *t* following page numbers refer to figures and tables, respectively.

Index

Index

About the Authors

Tudor O. Bompa, PhD, revolutionized Western training methods when he introduced his groundbreaking theory of periodization in Romania in 1963. After adopting his training system, the Eastern Bloc countries dominated international sports through the 1970s and 1980s. In 1988, Dr. Bompa applied his principle of periodization to the sport of bodybuilding. He has personally trained 11 Olympic medalists (including four gold medalists) and has served as a consultant to coaches and athletes worldwide.

Dr. Bompa's books on training methods, including *Theory and Methodology of Training: The Key to Athletic Performance* and *Periodization of Training for Sports,* have been translated into 17 languages and used in more than 130 countries for training athletes and educating and certifying coaches. Bompa has been invited to speak about training in more than 30 countries and has been awarded certificates of honor and appreciation from such prestigious organizations as the Argentinean Ministry of Culture, the Australian Sports Council, the Spanish Olympic Committee, and the International Olympic Committee.

A member of the Canadian Olympic Association and the Romanian National Council of Sports, Dr. Bompa is professor emeritus at York University, where he has taught training theories since 1987. He and his wife, Tamara, live in Sharon, Ontario.

Carlo Buzzichelli, AAS, is a professional strength and conditioning coach and the technical director of the Tudor Bompa Institute–International. Carlo was a pupil of Tudor Bompa and is considered one of the foremost experts on strength training. He has held seminars at various universities and sport institutes worldwide, including the Superior Institute of Physical Education and Sports of Camaguey in Cuba; the University of Makati in Manila, Philippines; the Superior Institute of Physical Education and Sports of Ciego de Avila in Cuba; the Universidade Paulista and the Olympic Center of Sao Paulo, Brazil; and the World Athletic Center in Arizona. In 2012 Carlo was a speaker at the International Workshop on Strength and Conditioning of Trivandrum in India. Carlo's teams have conquered

eight promotions and placed first and second place in league cups. Carlo was a team coach in the World Track and Field Championships and Commonwealth Games. He has coached athletes who have won 17 medals at national championships in track and field, swimming, Brazilian jiu-jitsu, and powerlifting. His athletes have won two international golds in track and field and three silvers and one bronze in track and field and Brazilian jiu-jitsu; they also have set five national records powerlifting.

You'll find other outstanding strength training resources at

www.HumanKinetics.com/strengthtraining

In the U.S. call 1-800-747-4457

Australia 08 8372 0999 • Canada 1-800-465-7301
Europe +44 (0) 113 255 5665 • New Zealand 0800 222 062

HUMAN KINETICS
The Premier Publisher for Sports & Fitness
P.O. Box 5076 • Champaign, IL 61825-5076 USA

available at
HumanKinetics.com